Contemporary
Austrian Politics

Contemporary Austrian Politics

EDITED BY
Volkmar Lauber

LONDON AND NEW YORK

First published 1996 by Westview Press, Inc.

Published 2018 by Routledge
52 Vanderbilt Avenue, New York, NY 10017
2 Park Square, Milton Park, Abingdon, Oxon OX14 4RN

Routledge is an imprint of the Taylor & Francis Group, an informa business

Copyright © 1996 Taylor & Francis

All rights reserved. No part of this book may be reprinted or reproduced or utilised in any form or by any electronic, mechanical, or other means, now known or hereafter invented, including photocopying and recording, or in any information storage or retrieval system, without permission in writing from the publishers.

Notice:
Product or corporate names may be trademarks or registered trademarks, and are used only for identification and explanation without intent to infringe.

Library of Congress Cataloging-in-Publication Data
Contemporary Austrian politics / edited by Volkmar Lauber.
   p.   cm.
Includes bibliographical references and index.
ISBN 0-8133-2890-X (hc)
  1. Austria—Politics and government—1945-   2. Political parties—Austria.   I. Lauber, Volkmar.
JN2012.3.C66   1996
320.9430—dc20   95-50931
                                                                              CIP

ISBN 13: 978-0-367-00963-2 (hbk)
ISBN 13: 978-0-367-15950-4 (pbk)

Contents

	Tables, Figures and Graphs	ix
	Acknowledgments	xi
	Map of Austria	xiii
1	History and International Context *Helmut Kramer*	1
	Introduction, 1	
	Habsburg Monarchy, 5	
	First Republic, 10	
	Second Republic, 16	
2	Political Institutions *Wolfgang C. Müller*	23
	Institutional Framework, 23	
	Direct Democracy, 25	
	Parliament, 26	
	Federal President, 29	
	Cabinet, 32	
	Administration, 36	
	Constitutional Court, 39	
	Judiciary, 42	
	Audit Office, 43	
	Federalism, 45	
	Conclusion, 50	
3	Political Parties *Wolfgang C. Müller*	59
	Introduction, 59	
	Origin and History, 60	

Challenge to Political Parties, 63
Legal and Financial Status, 64
Electoral System, 68
Parties in the Electorate, 71
Party Organizations, 76
Ideology, 87
Party System, 90
Conclusion, 93

4   Corporatism - The Austrian Model
    Emmerich Tálos   103
    Preconditions, 104
    Development and Structure, 109
    Political Role, 113
    Social Partnership Since the 1980s, 117

5   Economic Policy
    Volkmar Lauber   125
    Introduction, 125
    Establishment of Austro-Keynesianism, 127
    1975-1986: Full Employment by Public Debt, 132
    1987-1993: Consolidation and Restructuring, 137
    Austrian Economy Today, 141
    New Fiscal Crisis, 145

6   Foreign Policy
    Helmut Kramer   151
    Introduction, 151
    World War II to State Treaty (1945-1955), 153
    Foreign Policy and Neutrality (1955-1968/70), 156
    Globalization (1968/70-1983/84), 162
    "Realistic Foreign and Neutrality Policy"
    (1983/84-1989), 169
    Road to EU Membership (1989-1995), 175
    Conclusion, 192

7   Environmental Politics and Policy
    Volkmar Lauber   201

Contents   *vii*

      Career of the Environmental Issue, 201
      Ecological Modernization of the State, 203
      Environmental Situation Today, 206
      Summary, 209

8 Political Culture
   Peter Gerlich   213
      Patterns, 213
      Origins, 218
      Implications, 219

9 Agencies of Socialization
   Franz Horner   223
      Mass Media, 223
      Educational System, 226
      Catholic Church, 230

10 The Politics of Regional Subdivisions
   Herbert Dachs   235
      Defining the Problem, 235
      Historical Developments, 235
      Provincial (*Land*) Governments, 238
      Constitutional System of the *Länder*, 240
      "Cooperative Federal State", 242
      Cooperation Among the *Länder*, 243
      Parties and Politics, 244
      Changing Trends, 248

11 Conclusion and Outlook
   Volkmar Lauber   253
      SPÖ-ÖVP Duopoly, 253
      Changing Stage of Politics, 256

Basic Statistics   263
Chronology   265
List of Acronyms   267
Selected Bibliography   271

Postscript: The Elections of 1995 277
About the Contributors 279
About the Book 281
Index 283

Tables, Figures and Graphs

Tables

1.1	Direct Investment Compared Internationally (1985)	3
1.2	Per Capita Level of Industrialization 1750-1913	6
1.3	Industrial Production Index 1929	12
1.4	Unemployment in Austria in the Inter-War Years	13
2.1	Federal Presidential Elections Since 1945	31
2.2	Austrian Cabinets Since 1945	33
3.1	Austrian Parliamentary Elections, 1945-1994	74
3.2	Party Loyalty in Elections, 1979-1994	75
3.3	Popular Disenchantment with Parties and Politicians, 1979-1989	76
3.4	Party Members and Organizational Density, 1945-1994	81
3.5	Motives for Joining a Party, 1969-1985	83
3.6	The Austrian Party System, 1945-1994	91
5.1	Public Debt as Percentage of GDP 1974-1991: An International Comparison	133
6.1	Austrian Diplomatic Missions	155
6.2	Development Aid by Country in International Comparison	168
6.3	Interest in Foreign Policy Issues	175
6.4	Sense of Being Affected by Foreign Policy	175
6.5	Number of Persons Requesting and Number of Persons Granted Official Refugee Status, 1982-1994	187

9.1	Austrian Newspapers Distribution	224
10.1	Austrian *Länder* (Provinces)	236

Figures

2.1	The Creation of Austrian Governmental Institutions	24
3.1	Social Structure of Austrian Parties, 1983-1991	72
3.2	Party Identification, 1954-1992	73
3.3	Organizational Links Between the Major Parties and Interest Groups in Austria	77
3.4	The Mechanics of Party Competition, 1945-1995	92
4.1	The Structure of the Joint Commission on Wages and Prices	112
8.1	Cultural Patterns of the Political Subsystem	214
9.1	The Austrian Educational System	228

Graphs

5.1	Unemployment in Austria, Germany and OECD Europe Since 1974	135
6.1	Austrian Exports to the EU, EFTA and Eastern Europe	163
6.2	Attitudes Towards EU-Membership, 1987-1994	174
6.3	Neutrality or EU Membership: Preferences in Public Opinion Polls	181
6.4	Results of the National Referenda on EU-Membership in Austria, Finland, Sweden and Norway	183

Acknowledgments

The Austrian political system seems to experience the most fundamental change since the pattern of the Second Republic settled into place in the first post-war decade. The present book will attempt to describe this cumulative change. For that very reason it is not limited to the description of the current state of affairs but rather deals with the larger patterns which evolved during the Second Republic, i.e., since 1945. Obviously the more recent period will receive privileged treatment.

About ten years ago, the contributors to this volume started work on editing an encyclopaedic volume on Austrian politics which was first published in Vienna in 1991 and which is now undergoing a major revision.* The present book is based on the fifty-five contributions of that volume; at the same time, it is more concentrated, more clearly focused on a few essential topics, and--hopefully--geared to an Anglo-American audience. It was also brought up to date.

On this occasion, I would like to thank all those who have contributed to the completion of this book. The contributors showed great patience in dealing with my suggestions. Catherine Cardona--herself a political scientist who began her studies in the United States and finished them in Salzburg--translated almost half of the contributions and reworked those that were written in English. Aleksandra Thurman as language editor came up with many further improvements; after studying political science for a year at the University of Vienna, she returned to Berkeley this summer. Jacqueline Trendos, our secretary, typed a long succession of corrections. Barbara Blümel and Petra Grabner, both students of political science at Salzburg, did the layout and all the formatting, composed or reworked most of the tables, graphs and figures, and undertook a variety of other tasks.

My thanks also go to the *Stiftungs- und Förderungsgesellschaft* of the University of Salzburg and the Austrian Ministry of Foreign Affairs for funding the translation, the Evers-Marcic-Fund for supporting language editing, and the *Manz Verlag* and the many authors of the 1991 volume for granting free use of all materials.

Volkmar Lauber

* Herbert Dachs, Peter Gerlich, Herbert Gottweis, Franz Horner, Helmut Kramer, Volkmar Lauber, Wolfgang C. Müller, and Emmerich Tálos, eds., *Handbuch des politischen Systems Österreichs* (Vienna, 1991). A substantially revised edition is forthcoming.

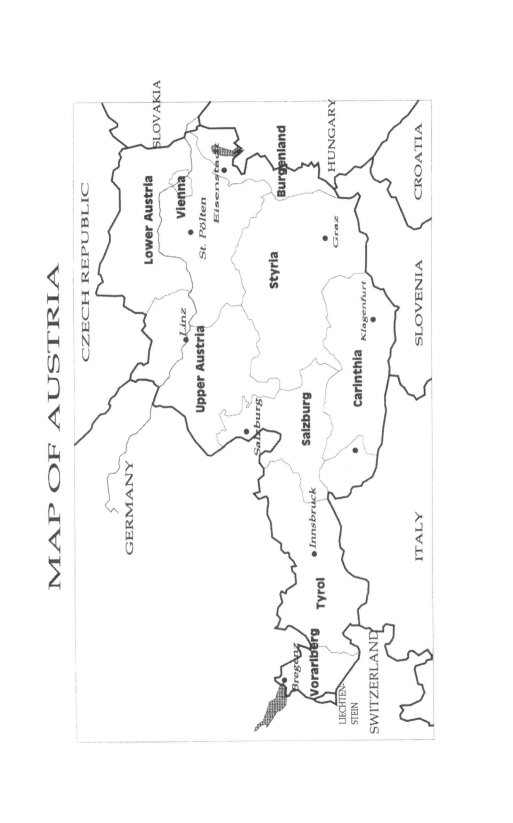

1

History and International Context

Helmut Kramer

Introduction

At the beginning of the 1990s, on the basis of the indicators most commonly used to rank countries economically, it is clear that Austria is one of the dozen or so of the world´s most prosperous countries. Austria is classified as a small state with respect to its total population, and it could be considered a middle power in the areas of art and culture (Austria has 0.14 percent of the world population, about 1 percent of world output and a 1.32 percent share of world trade).

This advantageous position, according to the dominant standards of development (Kramer 1983; Katzenstein 1984; Höll 1985), goes hand in hand with the extremely intensive interconnection between society and economic policy in the international system. As with other economically successful small states--nine of the fifteen richest countries in the world have a total population of less than 10 million--the Austrian economy is to a high degree open to world trade. More than a quarter (26 percent) of the goods produced in Austria are exported. If one adds services produced for the international market, particularly tourism, the export quota increases to 47 percent. The consequences of the rapidly increasing economic internationalization of the last decades--that is, the intensification and consolidation of international economic relations (and at the same time the increasing importance of economics in international relations) and the dependency that results from it--in many ways affect small countries more strongly and directly (Kramer 1983; Höll 1983; Jaeggi 1983). Therefore, measures to promote economic recovery, decisions on economic and social policy, foreign trade and monetary policy must be made while carefully considering international developments, the positions of the major powers and of the transnational corporations that have been pushing for economic internationalization. The costs of halting international transactions would be considerable. The latest developments in (transit) traffic, environmental policy and the question of refugees make it clear that the problems and crises in the international system at the end of the twentieth century can no longer be solved within the confines of national borders and with the policies and measures of a single state (Ziebura 1984; Zolberg 1985; Camilleri, and Falk 1992).

The foreign policy behavior of the neutral, small state Austria is significantly influenced by the high degree of sensitivity it must expect to encounter, being so intensely connected with the international system. Furthermore, the necessity of reacting to international developments and crises, but also of being aware of the different options available for taking action, considerably influence that behavior. By skillfully taking advantage of the temporary phase of reduced tension in East-West relations, Austria was able to gain its independence in 1955. As the globally-oriented active policy of neutrality unfolding in the early 1970s particularly showed, favorable conditions in world politics were the most important prerequisites for Austria's foreign policy activities. Austria attempted thereby to defend its own economic and political interests and at the same time to make, in conjunction with other small and neutral states, a (modest) contribution that would ease tensions, bring about more legal security and establish democratic norms in international relations (see chapter 6).

Until now we have spoken only in general terms of the "sensitivities" and structures of dependence that arise from the many levels of international transactions. The problem of combining external interconnection and dependence with the objectives of social self-determination and national independence is the "dilemma of small states" (*Kleinstaatendilemma*) (Vogel 1979; Höll 1985; Kramer 1993). Two specific features of dependence structures and constellations in Austria stand out:

1. Austria's economy shows, in comparison to most other wealthy industrial countries in the West, a much less active internationalization profile (Pichl 1989; Beirat für Wirtschafts- und Sozialfragen 1989). This is particularly true in the area of capital and technology integration. Austria is dependent to a large degree on capital imports and is permeated with foreign capital. Constitutive for the passive internationalization profile of the Austrian economy is above all, compared to other industrialized countries, the small amount of Austrian capital exports, in particular the small number of business enterprises owned by

Austrians abroad. As table 1.1 shows, in the mid-1980s Austria was in this regard far below the level of the other neutral small states, i.e. Switzerland, Sweden and even Finland. However, at the end of the 1980s, as a result of the liberalization of capital and the economic opening of Eastern Europe, Austrian investment abroad increased considerably. While the total flow of such investments was only Sch19.5 billion in 1985 (compared to Sch60 billion of foreign capital investment in Austria), the total sum rose in 1992 to Sch81 billion for investments abroad (compared with Sch120 billion of foreign capital investment in Austria).

TABLE 1.1 Direct Investment Compared Internationally (1985)

	Capital resources (incl. loans) in billions of the national currency		Direct Investment as percent of GDP (in %)	
	active	passive	active	passive
USA	232.7	183.0	5.80	4.56
Japan	83.6	6.2	6.31	0.47
Canada	41.7	81.8	8.97	17.59
United Kingdom	76.7	40.6	21.51	11.39
Switzerland	50.5	22.9	20.91	9.48
West Germany	147.8	119.1	8.01	6.45
France	192.2	147.2	4.10	3.71
Netherlands	143.7	58.3	34.38	13.95
Sweden	98.7	28.2	11.77	3.36
Italy	26,104.0	31,769.0	3.22	3.92
Belgium/ Luxembourg	160.7	591.7	3.17	11.69
Denmark	22.9	31.6	3.86	5.33
Spain	258.9	996.7	0.94	3.62
Austria	18.7	61.9	1.39	4.62

Source: Beirat für Wirtschafts- und Sozialfragen 1989, p. 9.

2. The second obvious feature of Austria's external interconnection is the heavy concentration of its economic dependence on Germany. In the area of direct foreign investment in Austria, Germany leads with about 40 percent. West German companies dominate the electrical, metal, automobile and chemical industries as well as trade, banking, finance and insurance. West German groups acquired decisive influence over the Austrian print media in the 1980s. Another dimension of the close integration of the two economies consists in the fact that the Austrian currency is tied to the German mark (about German influence see Kramer 1983; Scherb and Morawetz 1990; Riekhoff-Neuhold 1993).

Does this high level of economic dependence mean that the chances of achieving the basic goals and priorities of Austrian society (economic and social well-being, national self-determination) will be diminished? Does the high degree of economic and social dependency imply some kind of control from abroad? Will developments be started here that are not in the interests of or not in accordance with the moral values of the Austrian people and that will lead to the marginalization of socially and politically weaker groups? We are assuming that, in the case of Austria in the Second Republic, the negative consequences of dependent internationalization are more than compensated by a number of positive developments and social advantages. In the fifty years since the Second World War an overwhelmingly positive interaction of external and internal developments can be seen (Arndt 1982; Kramer 1983; Katzenstein 1984; Höll 1985). That structural dependence did not prevent Austria from achieving most of its basic goals will become clearer when the Second Republic is compared to the inter-war years and the last decades of the Danube Monarchy. The present chapter will attempt to make this comparison by historically analyzing Austria's incorporation into the international system and the division of labor since the middle of the nineteenth century.

An historical reconstruction in this respect, upgraded and systematized with the concepts and theorems of political science, should, however, not only include the main differences and discontinuities in Austria's development that are affected by external circumstances. The purpose of historical reflection and analysis is to "organize the past according to its function in the present" (Febvre 1988, 4). Therefore, in this description of the interaction between the external environment and the internal social development profile, an historical search for clues to the roots of the "internationalist disposition" characteristic of contemporary Austria, which includes its attitude towards the outside world, to the international system and to the values that are prevailing internationally, will also be included (on the historical foundations of "mentalities" in Austria see Lehmbruch 1967; Fürstenberg 1985).

The Habsburg Monarchy in the International Context

Economic Development and External Factors

The position of a society in the international system, its ability to secure a place in the international division of labor that guarantees or opens the way to the best possible chances for security and welfare to its population, is to a great degree determined by whether the economic and social structures, the behavioral patterns and the "mentality" of its population are in accord with the dominating tendencies of international development. A society's international position is determined by its ability to use the rules of the international (economic) system to its advantage, for its own puposes and goals. A review of the rise and fall of the great hegemonic powers in the history of Europe and the world, and above all of the structural problems of the "developing" countries in the past and the present, clearly shows how important, even how crucial a favorable international environment is for the chances of a nationally organized society to develop. An international environment that supports rather than hinders the internal development of a society is extremely important, if not decisive (for England and the USA, see Hobsbawm 1968; Kennedy 1987).

Of course, the development and structural profile within a society is not determined solely from the outside. The available capacities to solve problems, the chances or failure to develop depend to a large extent on internal factors. These include, above all, flexibility within a society and the ability of the state to effectively mobilize the productive energies of society and the leadership capacity of its governing elite (Burns 1978).

Industrialization in the Danube Monarchy was clearly slower and later than the other European powers England, France and Germany. Research on the process of industrialization during the Monarchy attributes a substantial role to external factors, the consequences of the international political constellation, in explaining this delay. The Habsburg Monarchy fell behind France and Germany during the nineteenth century, as table 1.2 shows, with respect to economic growth and integration in the international trade system (Koren 1961, 236; Gross 1973, 23) after having started at about the same position.

The Danube Monarchy's less successful economic development in comparison to its political rivals and the progressive deterioration of its great power status were mutually dependent processes:

The Monarchy was...the only state in which the transition to modern economic growth coincided with the gradual decline of its position as a great power and the constant costly attempts to stop the decline or at least to conceal it, which clearly slowed growth down. In the end its economic power was not strong enough to support its foreign policy, while foreign and domestic political setbacks contributed to the relative backwardness of its economy (Gross 1973, 14).

TABLE 1.2 Per Capita Level of Industrialization 1750-1913
(in relation to Great Britain 1900 = 100)

	1750	1800	1830	1869	1880	1900	1913
Europe	8	8	11	16	24	35	-
United Kingdom	10	16	25	64	87	(100)	-
Habsburg Monarchy	7	7	8	11	15	23	32
France	9	9	12	20	28	39	59
German States/ Germany	8	8	9	15	25	52	85
Italian States/Italy	8	8	8	10	12	17	26
Russia/Soviet Union	6	6	7	8	10	15	20
USA	4	8	14	21	38	69	126
Japan	7	7	7	7	9	12	20

Source: Kennedy 1987, pp. 148 and 200.

Particularly in the second half of the nineteenth century, a country's economic power and industrial organization became more and more decisive to its success in war. Without a doubt, the military defeats of the Habsburg Monarchy in Italy (1859) and then against Prussia in 1866 can be attributed to the fact that it could not keep up with the other great powers financially or technologically due to the lack of capital, the ruined currency and the outmoded economic structures (Kennedy 1987, 165f). The wars, conducted from this position of weakness, involved heavy losses and strained the economic resources of the Monarchy enormously. They also resulted in the loss of territory, which in turn further reduced and weakened the economic potential and the dynamism of industrialization.

With the loss of the Italian provinces of Lombardy and Venetia in the wars of 1859 and 1866, the Danube Monarchy lost important protected markets; also, this area produced about one third of the Monarchy's total economic output in the early 1840s (Katzenstein 1976, 43). The military defeat by the Prussians (1866) forced the retreat of the Habsburgs from the German *Zollverein*; this also had serious consequences. And, finally, in the last decades of the nineteenth century and the early twentieth century the Danube Monarchy was challenged in its last area of influence in Europe, the Balkans. The structurally superior and aggressive economic policy and power politics of Berlin forced the Danube Monarchy to become a mere "second" and a quasi-satellite of Germany (Bridge 1989, 197f, 234; Engel-Janosi 1964, 23f). The debacle of the Monarchy's Balkan policy, the basically untenable nature of the strategy of "drawing a clear dividing line to the West while opening up to the East" (Palotás 1989, 588) could no longer be overlooked and concealed. The internal problems of a "monarchy on notice" caused by the "dual rule" with Hungary and the conflict of nationalities had became even more hopeless. The Habsburg Monarchy, allied with undying loyalty (*Nibelungentreue*) to the expansionist German Reich, staggered into the First World War and its own downfall.

> The single-minded push of the Austrian-Hungarian diplomats and army leaders to go forward aggressively against Serbia was, considering the multinational character of the Habsburg Monarchy, politically blind and suicidal, but the real decision over war and peace was made by the stronger partner in the double alliance, by Germany (Koralka 1993, 137).

Emperor Franz Josef's "unlucky hand" in foreign policy, to which his contemporaries had unanimously attested--he considered foreign policy his inherent political domain and allowed the few experienced, far-sighted foreign policy experts only little room to maneuver (Engel-Janosi 1964, 9f; Rumpler 1989, 21, 44f)--was to a large degree caused by structural problems. The dynastically-orientated foreign policy, interested in preserving the status quo and insisting on traditional claims and rights (Bridge 1989, 221), allowed the Danube Monarchy steadily fewer opportunities to act as a great power during the mid-nineteenth century, a period when the international power constellation took on a shape that was increasingly unfavorable to it (Bridge 1989, 208, 219f; Kennedy 1987, 16, 215f).

The lack of strength as a great power, the inability of the Habsburg Monarchy's leadership to achieve commonly shared state concepts and a consensus on internal and external goals, was without a doubt due largely to the problem of the many nationalities in the Monarchy, which produced centrifugal tendencies within society. The Danube Monarchy stood against the tide of history--"for decades I have been aware of how much of an anomaly we are in today's world" (Franz Josef 1916)--against the politically dominating currents of time, against national unification, liberalism, and against the politically unifying strength of the industrialization process that is based on it. "The multinationality of the Danube Monarchy created problems that did not appear elsewhere. The growing national sentiment that was the fuel of the economic development elsewhere became the cause of the conflict here" (Rothschild 1961, 36).

As a result of the "geographical and statistical fact" that none of the largest eleven national groups of the Monarchy constituted a majority (German speaking Austrians made up 23.9 percent in 1900, Hungarians 20.2 percent), and that the majority of only five of the eleven largest national groups lived within the territory of the empire, insoluble problems for internal and external politics in the age of nationalism and imperialism were created (Kann 1980, 1312).

> Our whole Austrian economy lacks the powerful impulses that luckier wars, national unification, or enormous colonial expansion, have given other states enormous impetus, that happy, bold feature that is specific to those people, because they have the cheerful hope of belonging to a blossoming state

was the mournful proclamation of an Austrian politician on the eve of the First World War (quoted by Dinklage 1989, 460). This brings up another important dimension of the politics of large countries at the end of the nineteenth century where the Danube Monarchy could not keep up with the other European powers: vigorously forcing the violent partition and economic opening of colonial territories--especially by Great Britain and France.

Because it was largely landlocked, the economic development of the Habsburg Monarchy was stimulated much less than the other European great powers by the "formation of large movable capital in overseas trade" (Rothschild 1961, 31). Despite several attempts, the Habsburg Empire was never able to gain political and economic control over territories outside of Europe. Once again, the economic weakness of the Danube Monarchy was decisive. The Monarchy could not raise enough money, as many European countries did, to intervene with troops during the confusion of the Boxer Rebellion in China (followed by businessmen on the second front). Franz Ferdinand, the heir to the throne, spoke of a "scandal...since even pint-sized states (*Schnackerl-Staaten*) like Belgium and Portugal have troops there" (quoted by Allmayer-Beck 1987, 65). Lenin noted in the preliminary texts to his momentous work, *Imperialism, the Highest Phase of Capitalism*, on the position of the Danube Monarchy in the colonial race: "like Italy, an example of a second or third-rate power" (Lenin 1972, 89, 581). The Habsburg Monarchy lacked an effective structural basis, a firm ground to stand on, for its colonial policy. The Danube Monarchy's business community had neither the interest nor the capacity to export capital overseas. Austrian businessmen and banks limited their investments to the Balkan peninsula and the eastern regions of the Monarchy itself.

"Belated Industrialism" and Social Development

In an international environment that was so difficult and unfavorable, the Danube Monarchy was forced in the "Concert of the Great Powers" to play the role of a great power with the resources of a second-rate power. This brought about the formation of a strongly inward-looking and security-oriented social and economic structure. Austrian society developed a passive internationalization profile in nearly all areas as well as the tendency to cut itself off from the outside world (on the Habsburg Monarchy as the "China of Europe," see Hanisch 1978, 33f).

Research in the field of economic history has worked out the characteristics and the roots of the "traditional introversion of Austria's history" (März 1981, 30). Weak integration in the European and world economy (foreign trade intergration, capital exports) went hand in hand with a thoroughly protectionist economic outlook. The economy of the Danube Monarchy, in which a unified, dynamic internal market never developed, encouraged "economic pacification" by associative solutions and collective rules and sought to avoid competition (domestic or international) as far as possible.

Until its dissolution, the Danube Monarchy remained economically dependent on foreign capital as well as on the immigration of dynamic entrepreneurs, particularly from Germany (Mentschl 1989; for the import of foreign policy experts see Engel-Janosi 1964, 12). Another indicator of the weak dynamics of industrialization in the Monarchy is the fact that this process, dominated by the banks, was characterized by the tendency to make cartel-like agreements. This emphasis of both business and the state on minimizing international competition should be seen within the context of the weak development of liberalism and parliamentarism when compared to countries in Western and Northern Europe (Kurth 1979, 327f).

Until now, we have considered and assessed the economic development and the industrialization dynamics of the Danube Monarchy predominantly on the basis of the criteria of world market oriented, successful "capitalistic" development. When compared to England and France, but also to Switzerland and the Scandinavian countries, the Danube Monarchy with its feudalistic tradition had weaker and less dynamic economic and social structures, yet this also had important positive aspects and consequences. It was because of the structural weaknesses of capitalism and imperialism that the labor movement in the industrial areas of the Monarchy managed more successfully than in many other European countries (and particularly the USA) "within a relatively short amount of time to put socio-political reins on the growing industries" (Rothschild 1961, 45; Tálos 1981, 52, 83f).

Furthermore, the artistic and cultural upsurge in fin-de-siècle Vienna that brought Austria undisputed world prestige must also be seen in the context of late industrialization and the practical social barriers that prevented advanced (capitalistic) modernity. The artists and scholars in Vienna at the turn of the century, who could not find or push through their ideas on rationality and modernity in the practical spheres of social reality, created in art and in science a world without moral falsity (Sigmund Freud, Arthur Schnitzler), hypocritical ornamentation (Adolf Loos, Karl Kraus), without baroque metaphysics (Ludwig Wittgenstein, Arnold Schönberg) and without feudal irrationality (Joseph Schumpeter) (Janik and Toulmin 1973; Schorske 1981).

The First Republic in the International Context

The Structural Economic Problems of the Newly Founded Small State

The new state *Deutsch-Österreich* (German Austria) was viewed by many as an "unwanted, deformed small state" (Hornbostel 1958, 132). As a result of the First World War and the collapse of the Habsburg Monarchy it found exceptionally unfavorable internal and external conditions for its basic economic, social and political goals. The new Republic was the "torso of a wreck" (Rothschild 1961, 51), an economic area that contained a relatively large part of the industrial capacity, but was still fraught with major structural weaknesses.

The new Austrian Republic was part of the industrialized areas of the former monarchy, but its economic structure displayed huge disproportions. Some branches of industry--particularly those that were expanded during the war as, for example, the armaments industry, iron and metal industries as well as locomotive and railway car production--were too large for a small state. Others--like the sugar and textile industries--could not satisfy domestic needs. Altogether, manufacturing, processing and finishing, all of which depended on imported intermediate products and raw materials, predominated. Most industries were orientated towards cooperation with business enterprises that were no longer in the same country. The interrelation between the individual sectors was so loose, as a contemporary observer noted, that the "sum of (Austria's) economic sectors" could not even be called a "national economy" (Bayer 1929, 89).

As we have seen, Austrian industries were protectionist in their structure and traditions and showed little capability for competing in the (stagnating) international market. In order to reduce the balance of trade deficit, caused mainly by the importation of food, foreign markets for Austrian products had to be found (Koren 1961, 237). Restructuring the Austrian economy on the ruins of a large traditional economic area would have been difficult even if the new country, that "miserable and completely helpless object, German Austria" (Karl Renner quoted in Panzenböck 1985, 117; similarly, also Hans Kelsen quoted in Stourzh 1990, 33) had found more favorable economic conditions, a world economic climate that promoted economic reconstruction and modernization and more willingness on the part of the victors of the First World War to cooperate (Rothschild 1961; Kindleberger 1973; Weber 1985). That kind of "friendly" international environment did not exist by any means. In contrast to the years after 1945, the economy in Europe developed very unsatisfactorily. The USA rose to become the leading economic power in the world despite considerable structural problems, while the economies of the three largest industrial countries in Europe, England, France and Germany, which were also heavily in debt to the USA, only stagnated. The fixation of economic policy on stable currencies, fighting inflation and the thoughtless implementation of protectionist instruments in world trade prevented the world market and world trade, as was the case after 1945, from becoming the decisive factor for economic reconstruction and the continuous successful economic development of (Western) Europe after its destruction in the war (Ziebura 1984, 83f). In this extremely unfavorable economic context, Austria's economy started to stagnate seriously. The inter-war period was a difficult era for all of Europe, whose economy grew much slower than in the rest of the world. Central and Eastern Europe, with the exception of Czechoslovakia, were the most disadvantaged regions. In this context Austria came off particularly badly (table 1.3).

TABLE 1.3 Industrial Production Index 1929 (1913 = 100)

World	USA	Europe	Austria
153.3	181.8	127.8	98.0

Source: Weber 1991, p. 25.

Austria, like the other states that were formerly a part of the Danube Monarchy, suffered from a chronic lack of capital and was forced, as a result, to depend on foreign loans and investments. Unlike the development after 1945, economic aid and capital imports from abroad did not have beneficial effects and were in some way clearly dysfunctional in the sense of causing a "retrogressive adjustment" (Rothschild 1961, 88). Foreign capital, which flowed primarily from England and France into Central and Southern Europe, essentially had the effect in Austria of increasing the already existent disproportions in the economic structure and of hindering productive structural developments for the whole economy (März 1981; Müller 1983, 265, 358; Teichova 1988, 126).

Only a small part of the foreign loans were channelled to productive areas of the economy, and foreign investments did not effect sustained economic growth or improvements in the economic structures. Economic conditions in Austria were worsened further when high trade barriers cut off the markets of the other former parts of the Monarchy (Rothschild 1961, 89f; März 1981, 284f; Teichova 14f). While trade among the former parts of the Monarchy in the early 1920s made up half of their total foreign trade, by the end of the 1920s it shrank to one third as a result of discriminating tariffs and the absence of any attempt to form a common trade policy (Teichova 1988, 89f, 181).

In order to make or keep Austria economically "viable" (*lebensfähig* was the German word often cited at the time), it was essential to restructure the economy and society in many areas. The loss of the regions that formerly supplied agrarian products, as a result of the dissolution of the Austrian-Hungarian Monarchy and the protectionist trade policies of the neighboring countries, forced Austrian agriculture to significantly increase its market capacity. Furthermore, domestic energy resources, water-power in particular, had to be redeveloped, and to a considerable degree industry had to be converted to processing local raw materials. This restructuring and reorientation was carried out very slowly and sometimes in a very uncoordinated fashion. The adjustment and modernization process was by no means concluded when the world economic crisis broke out. The depression hit the country with extreme force because the decline in economic activity started from an already very low level. In 1929 the GNP was just barely more than what it had been in 1913. Industrial production was even 2 percent lower. Even foreign trade showed unfavorable figures: in 1929 Austria exported about 14 percent less than before the First World War (Weber 1991, 28f).

During the world economic crisis, trade broke down almost entirely. At current prices Austrian exports shrank by two-thirds (1928-1932). At real prices (1937 prices) imports declined by more than 50 percent from 1929 to 1932. The drop in the export of machinery was nearly 80 percent. Friedrich Hertz (1947, 83f) calculated that trade within the Danube area sank to 15 percent of the value it had had in 1914. It is easy to imagine what this means for a country whose industry has to sell a large part of its products (on the basis of contemporary export estimates, between 20 and 30 percent) in that market. In those years Austria experienced, according to the fitting words of Kurt W. Rothschild, a "retrogressive" structural change; "in the general shrinking process the superfluous and the poorly adjusted branches of the economy died out faster than the more efficient" (Rothschild 1961, 88f).

TABLE 1.4 Unemployment in Austria in the Inter-War Years
(Unemployed as percentage of the active population)

Time period	Unemployment rate
1919	18.4
1920-1922	2.1
1923-1927	9.6
1928-1929	8.6
1930-1931	13.3
1932-1937	23.9

Source: Stiefel 1979, p. 29.

The problems that the Austrian economy had in adapting were clearly expressed in its structural unemployment. In early 1925, unemployment in the chemical industry was 3 percent; in the iron and metal industry, however, it amounted to 30 percent (Rothschild 1961, 80). Only in the years of the extremely inflationary economy (1920-1922) was unemployment low. In 1923 the yearly average surpassed 8 percent. It did not fall below that mark until 1938, not even in the years of rising economic activity, 1928 and 1929. In the 1930s--according to optimistic estimates--about a quarter of the population was unemployed (see table 1.4).

In Austria, the GNP in 1937 was still below the level of 1913. It is hardly surprising, then, that many--businessmen, farmers as well as blue-collar workers--felt that with the German troops marching into Austria in March 1938, the era of economic stagnation had come to an end, and thus took new hope. The investment boom that seized Austria after the *Anschluss* should be seen from this point of view.

Austria was not poor--as those who thought Austria was not "viable" had believed. It had potential wealth at its disposal. The new rulers in Berlin were much more aware of this than the Austrian political and economic elites had been. Austrian raw materials (like oil or iron ore), untapped water power, underused industrial capacities, banking and trading expertise with the East and the army of the unemployed could all be incorporated into the armaments industry of the Third Reich, which was running at top speed.

Foreign Dependency and Authoritarian Policies

Massive pressure and diktats by foreign powers and actors restricted the Austrian First Republic's economic sovereignty to a minimum. The economic "aid" that was given within the framework of the deflationist Geneva Agreement (1922) led to total control over Austria's economy (Kernbauer et al. 1983, 354f). With broad powers, "with a sharp eye and a hard hand" (Goldinger 1954, 132), the commissioner appointed by the League of Nations controlled Austria's economic and financial policy from the end of 1922 until June 1926. Similarly drastic were the economic and political conditions that Austria had to accept in 1932 (Lausanne Protocol) in order to obtain international credits, which were only used to pay back foreign and state debts. Economic policy consisted of lowering production and especially labor costs. Hardly any government measures were taken to create jobs. This was carried out in the interests of the foreign creditors, of Western finance capital (German capital started to flow into the Austrian economy at the end of the 1920s, Weber and Haas 1980) and with the help of the aggressive conservative wing of the Austrian middle class. Reinforced by authoritarian political developments in Austria, these policies led to the erosion and, finally, to the destruction of democracy and a brief civil war in 1933/34.

The most likely reason for the strong and encompassing external determination of the Austrian economy and society in the First Republic was this direct "connection between foreign (capital) influence and the conservative *Lager* in Austria" (Müller 1983, 267). The common strategy of foreign capital and the Austrian middle class aimed at the repression and political elimination of the working class by insisting on a particular form of economic stabilization and an authoritarian and retrogressive accumulation model. Under strong pressure from abroad the authoritarian variation prevailed as a result of the disastrous conditions arising from the world economic crisis (Kurth 1979). The dominating role was played by fascist Italy. Mussolini's open strategy was to eliminate democracy and the party system in Austria and "to help the political right to come into power" (Haas 1984, 80; also Hornbostel 1958, 133f).

Powerless Foreign Policy

These conditions, when the "situation in the world worked against Austria" (Hornbostel 1958, 137), restricted the chances and the freedom to maneuver of Austrian foreign policy extremely. The "state (was) powerless and had little influence on its own destiny;" all it could do was to "make the best out of all the confusion and misery" (Goldinger 1954, 96). From the first days of the Republic, the Austrian government had to face this situation of external dependence, as it soon discovered when the victorous powers dictated the new borders and explicitly banned the *Anschluss* with Germany (Hornbostel 1958, 133; Staudinger 1984, 173). In the years after the war it attempted to at least limit the damage with regard to the Treaty of St. Germain and the territorial claims of the neighboring countries.

In the 1920s Austria attempted to normalize relations with its neighbors and the other former parts of the Monarchy. Furthermore, it tried to improve its international image in order to be granted foreign loans and economic aid. By joining the League of Nations and by cultivating diplomatic relations, Austria hoped to improve its status in Europe and the world. Under those circumstances, there was no question about having an active foreign policy (the dissolution of the Foreign Ministry as a separate government department in 1923 illustrates the situation perfectly). As a characterization of Chancellor Seipel's foreign policy course points out, the Austrian government had to maneuver constantly and avoid every conflict: "The path he took in foreign policy was basically that he had no foreign policy. Given Austria's position-- various 'force fields' clashed on its ground--that was much more difficult than it might seem at first glance" (Goldinger 1954, 167).

The only long-range foreign policy goal pursued by Austria, aside from day-to-day politics, was the *Anschluss* with Germany. It was supported above all by the leaders of the Social Democrats, but also by influential members of the Christian Social Party. This strategy, which was only abandoned in 1933 when the National Socialists seized power in Germany, was the expression of the political hopelessness and the lack of a plan with regard to an independent, active Austrian foreign policy (Kreissler 1984; Panzenböck 1985).

The development of a foreign policy course that could improve Austria's economic and political position and preserve its independence was critically handicapped by the domestic political situation, in which no consensus among the parties, or *Lager,* on the fundamental objectives and basic goals in foreign policy could be found (Verosta 1983, 122). After a short period of foreign policy and economic cooperation between the middle class and the working class (1919-1920), the Social Democrats increasingly questioned a foreign policy course that threatened their very political existence. Between 1934 and 1938, Chancellor Schuschnigg's attempts to stop Hitler from undermining the bastions of Austria's independence were doomed to failure, including his last-minute appeal to the League of Nations and the international community. This development was not only a consequence of the weak position of the League of Nations and the appeasement policy of Great Britain and France. It was also the result of the Austrofascists' authoritarian political course, which excluded the working class from the political process. Austria's international image was much too unfavorable to inspire an international show of solidarity (Stuhlpfarrer 1987; Stourzh 1990, 38).

In this extremely difficult international situation in which, as Bruno Kreisky wrote about the era of his youth, Austria and Vienna were degraded into becoming the "spineless material of world history," (Kreisky 1986, 20) the feeling of powerlessness in the Austrian population with respect to social and foreign policy hardened. The doubts about Austria's economic viability, which affected the self-confidence of the First Republic, had already existed in the nineteenth century as an "economic inferiority complex" (Hagspiel 1989, 710). After the economic and social model based on exports, currency stability and restrictive economic policy had failed, a strategy was pushed through by the authoritarian corporative state that aimed at a stronger role for the lower middle class and small businesses. This policy, which could not put an end to economic stagnation, led to the erosion and destruction of democracy and finally to the end of an independent Austrian state.

Austria's International Position During the Second Republic

The conditions for economic and political development in Austria after the Second World War were in many ways similar to those after the First World War. As in 1918, a large economic area that had supplied the needs of Austria's economic structures also broke apart in 1945. Left over was a small state in terms of territory, population and economic power. Both times a war economy had to be converted to civilian use. After both the First and the Second World Wars, the population had disastrously inadequate supplies of bare necessities. As a result of the direct effects of war and the dismantling of industrial plant by the occupying powers, the damage after 1945 was significantly greater than after 1918 (Weber 1985, 129). Austria's cultural, scientific and economic life was also impoverished by the near-total disappearance of the Jewish population (about 200,000 in 1938 - two thirds of them in Vienna) who had been murdered or driven into exile under National Socialist rule (Kreissler 1984, 162).

Nonetheless, the social, economic and political development in the two post war periods proceeded very differently. The First Republic (1918-1934) was characterized by hyperinflation, economic crisis, mass unemployment and political destabilization. The Second Republic in contrast experienced economic prosperity, a long phase of full employment and relatively broad social affluence, and it proved to be extremely stable politically (Kausel 1993; see chapter 5 in this volume).

Compared to the 1920s and 1930s, the Austrian population had a positive attitude towards economic and social developments, which in turn strengthened the national consensus. Increasingly, a national identity in the sense of an Austrian consciousness and patriotism developed (Kreissler 1984 and 1988; Stourzh 1990). This was accentuated by the State Treaty and neutrality as important pillars of Austria's foreign policy (see chapter 6 in this volume).

The "Austrian model" with its very positive economic development based on economic growth, a strong role of the state in economic policy, low unemployment and high social policy expenditures came into a crisis in the early 1980s (Höll and Kramer 1983). Beginning in the 1970s, the transformation process in the world economy (Wallerstein 1989) deepened the economic sensivity of small state economies in Europe. The anti-cyclical economic policies of the Kreisky era, which had been successful in the 1970s, turned out to be more and more ineffective and dysfunctional as they preserved obsolete industrial structures. The low level of active internationalization of Austrian industry was a serious shortcoming in the international economic competition. The crisis in the nationalized industries, the slowing down of the economy and the rise of unemployment, as well as a number of scandals which seriously damaged Austria's image abroad, constituted the background for a quite hectic discussion on the merits of an Austrian candidature for EC/EU membership. In the late 1980s the economic situation improved again and the recession of the early 1990s did not seriously upset the Austrian economy, which gained new strength particularly by intensifying economic relations with the new democracies in Eastern Europe. When Austria joined the European Union in January 1995, its economy and the state of its public finances did not compare unfavorably to those of most other members.

Conclusion

The history of Austria's integration into world politics and the world economy during the last decades of the Habsburg Monarchy has been characterized by increasing external dependence in economics and politics, and by growing domestic fragmentation along national and ideological cleavage lines. After the breakdown of the Danube Monarchy in 1918, the inherited economic problems and an international environment which was largely unfavorable made it very difficult to realize the basic economic, social and political goals of the newly founded small state. In the Second Republic Austria was able to use the existing economic dependencies in the international sphere productively in order to improve the welfare of its own citizens and to build a stable and prosperous community. Favorable international conditions, but also the conciliatory and consensus-building cooperation between the political, social and economic forces of the country, as well as its active foreign policy, contributed to the success. The new awareness of an independent Austrian identity has lessened the old problem of differentiating itself from its powerful neighbor, Germany. During the Second Republic, the question of closer cooperation with a large integration area was a central one. The radical processes that reshaped global and European economic and political structures from the mid-1980s have given this tendency new impulses. The tendency towards stronger internationalization of central social and economic dimensions and the increasing competitive pressure in the international system have shattered traditional ideas about sovereignty. Moreover, it has unsettled out-dated structures in the economy and bureaucracy, thereby also casting doubt on traditional values, to such a degree that radical changes seem unavoidable.

Note

More detailed bibliographical information can be found in the respective chapters of the *Handbuch des politischen Systems Österreichs* (Kramer and Höll 1991 and Weber 1991). My thanks go to Otmar Höll for his comments.

References

Allmayer-Beck, Johann C. 1987. "Die bewaffnete Macht in Staat und Gesellschaft," in Adam Wandruszka, and Peter Urbanitsch, eds., *Die Habsburgermonarchie 1848-1918. Vol. V. Die bewaffnete Macht.* Pp. 1-127. Vienna.

Arndt, Sven W., ed., 1982. *The Political Economy of Austria.* Washington.

Bayer, Hans. 1929. *Strukturwandlungen der österreichischen Volkswirtschaft nach dem Kriege.* Vienna.

Beirat für Wirtschafts- und Sozialfragen. 1989. *Internationalisierung.* Vienna.

Bridge, Francis R. 1989. "Österreich(-Ungarn) unter den Großmächten," in Adam Wandruszka, and Peter Urbanitsch, eds., *Die Habsburgermonarchie 1848-1918. Vol. VI/I. Die Habsburgermonarchie im System der Internationalen Beziehungen.* Pp. 196-373. Vienna.

Burns, James M. 1978. *Leadership.* New York.

Camilleri, Joseph A., and Jim Falk. 1992. *The End of Sovereignty? The Politics of a Shrinking and Fragmented World.* Aldershot.

Dinklage, Karl. 1973. "Die Landwirtschaftliche Entwicklung," in Alois Brusatti, ed., *Die Habsburgermonarchie 1849-1918. Vol. I. Die landwirtschaftliche Entwicklung.* Pp. 413-416. Vienna.

Engel-Janosi, Friedrich. 1964. *Geschichte auf dem Ballhausplatz. Essays zur österreichischen Außenpolitik 1830-1945.* Graz.

Febvre, Lucien. 1988. *Das Gewissen des Historikers.* Berlin.

Fukuyama, Francis. 1989. "The End of History." *The National Interest* 16: 3-18.

Fürstenberg, Friedrich. 1985. "Soziokulturelle Aspekte der Sozialpartnerschaft," in Peter Gerlich, Edgar Grande, and Wolfgang C. Müller, eds., *Sozialpartnerschaft in der Krise, Leistungen und Grenzen des Neokorporatismus in Österreich.* Pp. 29-39. Vienna.

Goldinger, Walter. 1954. "Der geschichtliche Ablauf der Ereignisse in Österreich von 1918 bis 1945," in Heinrich Benedikt, ed., *Geschichte der Republik Österreich.* Pp. 15-288. Munich.

Gross, Nachum T. 1973. "Die Stellung der Habsburgermonarchie in der Weltwirtschaft," in Alois Brusatti, ed., *Die Habsburgermonarchie 1848-1918.. Vol. I. Die wirtschaftliche Entwicklung.* Pp. 1-28. Vienna.

Haas, Karl. 1984. "Die Römische Allianz 1934," in Erich Fröschl, and Helge Zoitl, eds., *Der 4. März 1933. Vom Verfassungsbruch zur Diktatur.* Pp. 69-91. Vienna.

Hagspiel, Hermann. 1989. "Außenwirtschaftliche Beziehungen zu Frankreich," in Adam Wandruszka, and Peter Urbanitsch, eds., *Die Habsburgermonarchie 1848-1918. Vol. VI/I. Die Habsburgermonarchie im System der Internationalen Beziehungen.* Pp. 687-710. Vienna.

Hanisch, Ernst. 1978. *Der kranke Mann an der Donau. Marx und Engels über Österreich.* Vienna.

Hobsbawm, Eric. 1968. *Industrie und Empire. Britische Wirtschaftsgeschichte.* 2 vols. Frankfurt/Main.

Höll, Otmar. 1985. "Abhängigkeit oder Autonomie: Österreich im Internationalisierungsprozeß," in *Österreichisches Jahrbuch für internationale Politik 1984.* Pp. 26-63.

___ , and Helmut Kramer. 1983. "The Process of Internationalization and the Position of Austria. Problems and Current Development Trends of the 'Austrian Model'," in Otmar Höll, ed., *Small States and Dependence in Europe.* Pp. 184-219. Vienna.

Hornbostel, Theodor. 1958. "Fremde Einflüsse auf die Politik der Ersten Republik Österreich." *Österreich in Geschichte und Literatur* 2: 129-138.

Janik, Allan, and Stephan Toulmin. 1973. *Wittgenstein's Vienna.* New York.

Kann, Robert A. 1980. "Zur Problematik der Nationalitätenfrage in der Habsburgermonarchie 1848-1918," in Adam Wandruszka, and Peter Urbanitsch, eds., *Die Habsburgermonarchie 1848-1918. Vol. III. Die Nationalitäten.* Pp. 1304-1338. Vienna.

Katzenstein, Peter J. 1976. *Disjointed Partners. Austria and Germany Since 1815.* Berkeley.

___ . 1984. *Corporatism and Change: Austria, Switzerland, and the Politics of Industry.* Ithaca.

Kausel, Anton et al. 1965. *Österreichs Volkseinkommen 1913-1963.* (Monatsberichte des österreichischen Instituts für Wirtschaftsforschung, special issue no. 14). Vienna.

Kausel, Anton. 1993. *Four Decades of Success. Austria's Economic Rise within the OECD from 1950 to 1992.* Vienna.

Kennedy, Paul. 1987. *The Rise and Fall of the Great Powers. Economic Change and Military Conflict from 1500 to 2000.* New York.

Kernbauer, Hans, Eduard März, and Fritz Weber. 1983. "Die wirtschaftliche Entwicklung," in Erika Weinzierl, and Kurt Skalnik, eds., *Österreich 1918-1938. Geschichte der Ersten Republik.* Pp. 343-379. Graz.

Kindleberger, Charles P. 1973. *Die Weltwirtschaftskrise 1929-1939.* Munich.

Koralka, Jiri. 1993. "Deutschland und die Habsburgermonarchie 1848-1918," in Adam Wandruszka, and Peter Urbanitsch, eds., *Die Habsburgermonarchie 1948-1918. Vol. VI/2. Die Habsburgermonarchie im System der Internationalen Beziehungen.* Pp. 1-158. Vienna.

Koren, Stephan. 1961. "Die Industrialisierung Österreichs," in Wilhelm Weber, ed., *Österreichs Wirtschaftsstruktur gestern-heute-morgen. Vol. 1.* Pp. 223-550. Berlin.

Kramer, Helmut, ed., 1983. *Österreich im internationalen System.* Vienna.

___ , and Otmar Höll. 1991. "Österreich in der internationalen Entwicklung," in Herbert Dachs et al., eds., *Handbuch des politischen Systems Österreichs.* Pp. 50-69. Vienna.

Kreisky, Bruno. 1986. *Zwischen den Zeiten. Erinnerungen aus fünf Jahrzehnten.* Berlin.

Kreissler, Felix. 1984. *Der Österreicher und seine Nation. Ein Lernprozeß mit Hindernissen.* Vienna.

___. 1988. "The Making of an Austrian Nation," in Jim Sweeny, and Josef Weidenholzer, eds., *Austria: A Study in Modern Achievement.* Pp. 1-26. Aldershot et.al.
Kurth, James R. 1979. "Industrial Change and Political Change: A European Perspective," in David Collier, ed., *The New Authoritarianism in Latin America.* Pp. 319-362. Princeton.
Lehmbruch, Gerhard. 1967. *Proporzdemokratie. Politisches System und politische Kultur in der Schweiz und in Österreich.* Tübingen.
Lenin, Wladimir I. 1972. *Werke. Vol. 39. Hefte zum Imperialismus.* Berlin.
März, Eduard. 1981. *Österreichische Bankpolitik in der Zeit der Großen Wende 1913-1923.* Vienna.
Mentschl, Josef. 1973. "Das österreichische Unternehmertum," in Alois Brusatti, ed., *Die Habsburgermonarchie 1848-1918. Vol. I. Die wirtschaftliche Entwicklung.* Pp. 251-277. Vienna.
Müller, Wolfgang C. 1983. *Zur Entwicklung der politischen Ökonomie Österreichs. Industriepolitik von Staat und Banken vom Aufgeklärten Absolutismus bis zum Ende der Ersten Republik.* Doctoral dissertation. University of Vienna.
Palotas, Emil. 1989. "Die außenwirtschaftlichen Beziehungen zum Balkan und zu Rußland," in Adam Wandruszka, and Peter Urbanitsch, eds., *Die Habsburger Monarchie 1848-1918. Vol. VI/1. Die Habsburger Monarchie im System der Internationalen Beziehungen.* Pp. 584-629. Vienna.
Panzenböck, Ernst. 1985. *Ein deutscher Traum. Die Anschluß-Idee und Anschlußpolitik bei Karl Renner und Otto Bauer.* Vienna.
Pichl, Claudia. 1989. "Internationale Investitionen. Verflechtung der österreichischen Wirtschaft." *WIFO Monatsberichte* 62: 161-176.
Riekhoff, Harald, and Hanspeter Neuhold, eds., 1993. *Unequal Partners. A Comparative Analysis of Relations Between Austria and the Federal Republic of Germany and Between Canada and the United States.* Boulder.
Rothschild, Kurt W. 1961. "Wurzeln und Triebkräfte der Entwicklung der österreichischen Wirtschaftsstruktur," in Wilhelm Weber, ed., *Österreichs Wirtschaftsstruktur gestern-heute-morgen.* Pp. 1-157. Vienna.
Rumpler, Helmut. 1989. "Die rechtlich-organisatorischen und sozialen Rahmenbedingungen für die Außenpolitik der Habsburger Monarchie 1848-1918," in Adam Wandruszka, and Peter Urbanitsch, eds., *Die Habsburger Monarchie 1848-1918. Vol. VI/1. Die Habsburger Monarchie im System der Internationalen Beziehungen.* Pp. 1-121. Vienna.
Schausberger, Norbert. 1978. *Der Griff nach Österreich. Der Anschluß.* Vienna.
Scherb, Margit, and Inge Morawetz, eds., 1990. *In deutscher Hand? Österreich und sein großer Nachbar.* Vienna.
Schorske, Carl E. 1981. *Fin-de-Siècle Vienna. Politics and Culture.* New York.
Staudinger, Anton. 1984. "Die nationale Frage im Österreich der Ersten und Zweiten Republik," in Otto Zöllner, ed., *Volk, Land und Staat. Landesbewußtsein, Staatsidee und nationale Frage in der Geschichte Österreichs.* Pp. 168-179. Vienna.

Stiefel, Dieter. 1979. *Arbeitslosigkeit. Soziale, politische und wirtschaftliche Auswirkungen--Am Beispiel Österreichs 1918-1938.* Berlin.

Stourzh, Gerald. 1990. *Vom Reich zur Republik. Studien zum Österreichbewußtsein im 20. Jahrhundert.* Vienna.

Stuhlpfarrer, Karl. 1988. "Austrofaschistische Außenpolitik--ihre Rahmenbedingungen und ihre Auswirkungen," in Emmerich Talos, and Wolfgang Neugebauer, eds., *"Austrofaschismus". Beiträge über Politik, Ökonomie und Kultur 1934-38.* Pp. 267-285. Vienna.

Tálos, Emmerich. 1981. *Staatliche Sozialpolitik in Österreich. Rekonstruktion und Analyse.* Vienna.

Teichova, Alice. 1988. *Kleinstaaten im Spannungsfeld der Großmächte. Wirtschaft und Politik in Mittel- und Südeuropa in der Zwischenkriegszeit.* Vienna.

Verosta, Stephan. 1983. "Die österreichische Außenpolitik 1918-1938 im europäischen Staatensystem 1914-1955," in Erika Weinzierl, and Kurt Skalnik, eds., *Österreich 1918-1938. Geschichte der Ersten Republik.* Pp. 107-146. Graz.

Vogel, Hans. 1979. *Der Kleinstaat in der Weltpolitik. Aspekte der schweizerischen Außenbeziehungen.* Frauenfeld.

Wallerstein, Immanuel. 1989. "The Capitalist World Economy: Middle-run Prospects." *Alternatives* 14: 279-288.

Weber, Fritz. 1985. "Wirtschaft und Wirtschaftspolitik in der Ersten und Zweiten Republik," in Erich Zöllner, ed., *Österreichs Erste und Zweite Republik.* Pp. 121-152. Vienna.

___. 1991. "Die wirtschaftliche Entwicklung," in Herbert Dachs et al., eds., *Handbuch des politischen Systems Österreichs.* Pp. 20-36. Vienna

___, and Karl Haas. 1980. "Deutsches Kapital in Österreich. Zur Frage der deutschen Direktinvestitionen in der Zeit vom Ende des Ersten Weltkrieges bis zur Weltwirtschaftskrise." *Jahrbuch für Zeitgeschichte* 1979: 169-235.

Ziebura, Gilbert. 1984. *Weltwirtschaft und Weltpolitik 1922/24-1931.* Frankfurt.

Zolberg, Aristide R. 1985. "L'influence des facteurs ´externes´ pour l'ordre politique interne," in Madeleine Frawitz, and Jean Leca, eds., *Traité de science politique.* Pp. 567-598. Paris.

2

Political Institutions

Wolfgang C. Müller

This chapter examines the formal role that the constitution prescribes for governmental institutions, as well as their actual role in the political process. Its main focus is on the changes that have occurred during the Second Republic, i.e., since 1945. Of course, the emphasis will lie on the more recent period.

The Institutional Framework

Austria's governmental institutions were established by its constitution, the main body of which dates back to 1920. In 1929, a major amendment was made in the anti-parliamentary and anti-party spirit prevailing at that time. After 1945, both the US and the Soviet occupation powers as well as the Austrian Communists pressed for a new constitution; the Socialist Party in turn wanted to go back to that adopted in 1920. Nonetheless, the constitution as amended in 1929 was re-introduced in 1945 and thus brought to an end the short life of a provisional constitution. Since then, numerous amendments to the constitution and to constitutional laws and clauses[1] have somewhat modified, but not substantially changed, the formal framework in which politics take place.

Figure 2.1 provides an overview of the framework of governmental institutions in Austria. Popular sovereignty is one of the key principles of the Austrian constitution. The people are involved in the creation of governmental institutions through three kinds of elections: they directly elect the federal president, the *Nationalrat* (lower house of parliament) and the nine *Landtage* (the *Land* legislatures). The *Landtage* in turn elect the members of the second chamber of the Austrian parliament, the

Bundesrat (federal council), through a proportional formula. The federal parliament and the president then create the other governmental

FIGURE 2.1 The Creation of Austrian Governmental Institutions

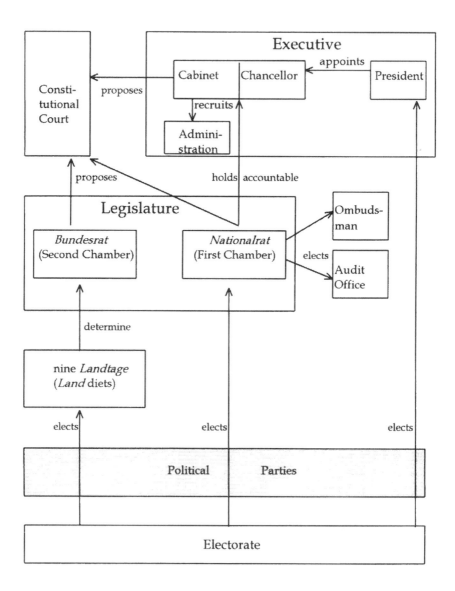

institutions, in particular the cabinet *(Bundesregierung)* and the Constitutional Court *(Verfassungsgerichtshof)*. The *Nationalrat* elects the president and the vice-president of the audit office *(Rechnungshof)* as well as the three ombudsmen *(Volksanwaltschaft)*. The cabinet and individual cabinet ministers recruit the civil servants and direct the administration.

Direct Democracy

In addition to the elections, there are also three instruments of direct democracy: the referendum, the people's initiative and the consultative referendum.

A referendum (*Volksabstimmung*) is required for a "total revision" of the constitution (Article 44) or to remove the federal president from office (Article 60). The second type of referendum has never been utilised. Austria's accession to the EU in 1995 implied a "total revision" of the constitution and thus required a referendum according to Article 44, which was held in 1994 (Pelinka 1995).[2] Other constitutional amendments are subject to a referendum if this is demanded by a third of the members of one of the two chambers of parliament, though a referendum has never yet been demanded in this way. This is due to the fact that until 1994 the two major parties, the Social Democratic Party of Austria (SPÖ) and the Austrian People's Party (ÖVP), have held between them more than two thirds of the *Nationalrat* seats; given their high levels of party discipline, there has never been any realistic prospect of a members' coalition being able to collect the requisite amount of support for such a motion. This applies even more to the *Bundesrat*, which has been even more clearly dominated by these two parties. A referendum can also be held on any law, provided that the *Nationalrat* demands it. This provision has been utilised only once: in 1978 the people were asked about the use of nuclear energy in Austria. This was done primarily in order to remove the issue from the political agenda for the 1979 parliamentary election rather than because of a commitment to direct popular sovereignty. The strategy proved to be successful in terms of managing the 1979 electoral agenda, though the political establishment was rather surprised and disappointed with the result of the referendum (which decided against nuclear energy) and consequently did not use this instrument again.

The people's initiative *(Volksbegehren)* has been a constitutional instrument since 1920, but the ordinary law which established the required details, and thus made this instrument available in practice, was not enacted until 1963. The people's initiative is one way of putting a bill before parliament. It must be framed in terms of an actual bill and has to be supported by at least 100,000 voters (200,000 before 1981), or by half of the voters of each of three *Länder*. These supporters have to sign the initiative in the presence of the authorities and all the signatures must be collected within one week. The *Nationalrat* is then obliged to deal with this proposal, although there is no *legal* requirement beyond this (thus, constitutional lawyers have argued that it is best regarded as a right for petition). *Politically*, however, a people's initiative clearly has more weight than other kinds of bills, though the chances for enactment are certainly higher for government proposals. From 1963 to 1994, fourteen people's initiatives were launched and succeeded in raising the requisite number of signatures.[3] Most of them were organized or supported by one of the opposition parties. The people's initiatives helped to lend weight to the opposition party's arguments, in particular when a high number of voters supported them. On the other hand, the party-political origin of most people's initiatives also made it easier for the parliamentary majority to reject them. Three of the people's initiatives were successful in leading to the enactment of a law which met their demands.

The consultative referendum *(Volksbefragung)* is the most recent addition to the instruments of direct democracy in Austria. It has existed since 1989, but has not been used as of 1995. In matters of principal importance which require regulation by law, the *Nationalrat* may decide to ask the people for their opinion. In contrast to the binding *Volksabstimmung*, the consultative referendum does not mean popular acceptance or rejection of a statute already enacted by parliament; however, that body certainly would be bound *politically*. This clause was introduced in order to maintain flexibility regarding the precise terms of legislation since the *Volksabstimmung* does not permit even an iota of the published text to be changed.

The Austrian constitution thus contains a variety of direct-democratic instruments, which gained considerably in importance since the 1960s. However, the primacy of representative democracy and its institutions was clearly preserved.

Parliament

Austria has a parliamentary system of government, with the cabinet obliged to resign after a parliamentary election. A new cabinet must face the *Nationalrat* within one week after its appointment (Article 70). The *Nationalrat* can issue a vote of no confidence against individual cabinet members or the whole cabinet at any point in time (Article 74). If it is supported by a majority of MPs (Members of Parliament), either the cabinet member concerned or the whole cabinet is automatically removed from office. This means that a government requires a majority in the *Nationalrat* to survive and to govern effectively. Since the MPs are accustomed to voting along party lines, this means that the parties represented in the government normally hold a majority of seats in the *Nationalrat*.[4] Since Austria is an extremely legalistic state, most relevant government decisions must have the form of a *law*, which implies that parliament must be involved. The formal powers of parliament are thus very important.

The traditional picture of Austrian politics, however, portrays parliament quite differently.[5] Despite its formal powers, it was argued, parliament merely played the role of a rubber-stamp for decisions previously made in the cabinet, the coalition committee, or within the institutions of social partnership. It acted only as a notary public. Indeed, coalition agreements between the ÖVP and SPÖ (until 1966) explicitly ruled out parliamentary amendments to government legislative proposals. Since the parties in parliament were highly disciplined and operated under the tight control of their leaders, the parliamentary treatment of government bills was irrelevant for the outcome of the legislative process. Only a few short plenary meetings were held and little public attention was given to parliamentary debates. The opposition was powerless; it had no influence on the decisions and could hardly attract public attention for its arguments.

This picture changed somewhat when the old grand coalition was replaced by the ÖVP single-party government in 1966. Parliamentary activity tripled and more attention was given to the confrontation between government and opposition (Gerlich 1973). The opposition's opportunities to attract public attention and to control the government effectively were improved by two reforms of parliamentary procedure in 1975 and 1988. Since the opposition acted as a watchdog of parliament's rights, formal parliamentary procedures became a greater constraint than hitherto. (From the government perspective, however, this was more than compensated for by the fact that the change to single-party government removed at a stroke the most severe problems of internal cabinet decision-making.) Despite increased confrontation in parliament, a basically consensual policy style prevailed and parliament became one of the arenas in which negotiations between government and the opposition took place. The various attempts at consensus-building between 1966 and 1986 resulted in about 80 percent of the legislation being passed unanimously by the *Nationalrat*. Parliamentary decision-making, however, remained very much a top-down process, with the MPs implementing party leaders' decisions (particularly for the MPs of the governing parties, whose *raison d'être* was to support their government). This pattern prevailed until 1987.[6] The introduction in that year of the new grand coalition reduced the willingness of the government to negotiate and compromise with the opposition. On the one hand, a government in control of more than three quarters of the MPs (as was the case until 1994) does not need the votes of opposition members to achieve either a qualified majority, or to exclude items from the political agenda. On the other hand, the fact that the government was now confronted with opposition both from its right (FPÖ) and from its left (Greens) made it nearly impossible for it to achieve unanimous acceptance of important bills. To compromise with just one of the opposition parties would have intensified the criticism of the other and could lead to a public perception that the government was moving too far left or right, as the case may be. Moreover, both opposition parties took more radical positions than used to be the case. Consequently, the proportion of legislation passed unanimously was reduced to 47 percent in the 1986-90 parliament. In the 1990-94 parliament, the share of unanimously accepted laws dropped further to 27 percent. This was partly caused by the emergence of a fifth party, the Liberal Forum, establishing itself as a breakaway from the FPÖ in 1993.

Even among the parliamentary groups of the governing parties, a substantial increase in activity and influence can be observed (Müller 1993). Many government proposals now only set out the main principles of proposed legislation and leave it to parliament to work out the details. Moreover, the MPs of the governing parties have started to re-open discussions on government bills which had been regarded as finalized by the cabinet members. In addition, more MPs from the governing parties have been incorporated as experts and party representatives in cabinet-level negotiations. Thus the influence of parliament has increased substantially (Müller 1988).

The iron discipline of the parliamentary parties is also eroding. In each of the 1986-90 and 1990-94 parliaments, there were more votes of dissent against, or abstentions from, the party line than had occurred in all other parliaments since 1945 put together. While violations of party discipline in previous parliaments were truly exceptional, in about 10 percent of the legislation of the 1986-90 and 1990-94 parliaments several MPs voted against their party. These are not merely parliamentary snipers who vote against their party in closed lobbies, but MPs or intra-party groups who take their case to the floor of the chamber. Nowadays, MPs also table partly critical parliamentary questions to ministers of their own party. In three investigative committees of the 1986-90 parliament, which for the first time were open to the public, the members tended to deemphasize their party affiliation. The most spectacular events, however, were a motion of no-confidence by a group of People's Party MPs against their own minister of defence and the rejection by a majority of MPs of the FPÖ candidate for the third president of parliament, on whose candidature the party leaders had previously agreed. This trend towards a loosening of the cohesion of the parliamentary groups is likely to continue, not least because of the 1992 reform of the electoral system which strengthens the MPs local ties.

According to the constitution, the electoral system is one of proportional representation. Between 1970 and 1992, nine electoral districts existed which were identical to the *Länder*. In each of them, a rather large number of MPs (from nine to thirty-six) was elected according to the relative strength of the parties which sponsor them. This is quite different from the single-member districts as they exist in Britain and the United States. A 1992 reform increased the number of electoral districts to forty-three and strenghtened the system of preference voting through which voters can express their preference for particular candidates rather than for parties (see chapter 3).

Membership in the EU, which became effective in 1995, has reduced the scope of legislation for the Austrian parliament. Nevertheless, it seems that EU membership may also strengthen parliament in some respects (Neisser 1994). The *Nationalrat*'s main committee (*Hauptausschuß*) has established a sub-committee to which the government has to report all decisions to be taken at the EU level. Government representatives in the EU bodies are fairly closely bound to instructions from the parliamentary sub-committee.

Thus parliament went through a number of substantial and important changes over the post-war period. From a rather irrelevant institution in the days of the old grand coalition it became a major political arena. Recent developments have even moved the Austrian parliament in a direction where it is a political actor in its own right.

The Federal President

The Austrian president has a strong institutional position (Berchtold 1967; Welan 1986 and 1992). He is directly elected and thus has a legitimacy which is independent of other institutions. At six years, with a maximum of two consecutive terms, his period of office is longer than that of any other elected official. The president appoints the cabinet members and can dismiss them (Article 70) without being subject to any *legal* restriction in this respect. The strongest weapon available to him, however, is his right to dissolve parliament (Article 29). In the use of this weapon, the president is restricted only inasmuch as he can dissolve parliament only once for any one particular reason. Though it is in principle possible to dismiss the president from office, this would require a complex and risky procedure that could backfire on the parliamentarians initiating it.[7] Moreover, despite his nominal party-political independence, the president has always been a party nominee and it is thus highly unlikely that his sponsoring party would be prepared to initiate dismissal procedures against him. Finally, the president's stong institutional position is combined with very little policy-making capacity, since in almost all cases he can act only on government proposals and also needs the government's approval for his decisions.

The federal president traditionally has little impact on Austrian politics. He does not intervene in day-to-day politics and has never used the strongest institutional instruments mentioned earlier. This is, to some degree, a heritage of the First Republic (the inter-war years) when presidents were powerless figureheads. This remained the case despite the constitutional reform of 1929, which considerably strengthened the legitimacy and formal powers of the presidency. However, an important element of this reform, the direct election of the president, did not become effective until 1951. Moreover, from 1945 until 1986, socialist candidates always held the presidency. During the 1918-20 state-building process, the Social Democrats preferred a constitution without a president and opposed the strengthening of the presidency in later years (Ucakar 1985). Despite their occupying the presidency for such a long time during the Second Republic, they maintained their general attitude that the authority and considerable powers of the president should not be used in day-to-day politics, but should rather be preserved for crisis situations. Such situations may have existed in 1953 and 1959, when presidents Körner and Schärf used their influence to maintain a grand coalition government. In 1962-63, Schärf also applied pressure on the parties to complete their exceptionally long coalition negotiations and, in 1960, did the same in order to force them to produce a definitive budget.[8]

The presidency is generally not regarded as a party-political office. The parties which fielded candidates in presidential elections normally did not nominate their most powerful leaders, but one of their "elder statesmen." The only exception was the candidacy of the Socialist Party's chairman Schärf in 1957. He was pushed and pulled by his younger party comrades, who wanted to take over his party and government positions; he stood for election in order to postpone his retirement from politics by gaining presidential office. Because of the system of direct election, and in view of their re-election ambitions, all presidents adopted a non-partisan image. The pattern of the passive, non-partisan president--or, to put it more positively, the authority-in-reserve president--soon became self-perpetuating, since presidential candidates used to make reference in their campaigns to the role-interpretation and style of the former presidents and promised to follow this pattern should they be elected.

Only the campaigns of the two most recent presidents constitute exceptions to this electoral strategy. Kurt Waldheim in 1986, and Thomas Klestil in 1992, promised to be "active" presidents and to intervene in domestic politics. Although Waldheim occasionally made public statements which constituted interventions in current domestic politics, he had, in effect, no more impact than his immediate predecessor and certainly less than the first three presidents of the Second Republic (Müller 1992, 107)[9]. In Klestil's case it is too early to judge whether he will manage to substantially redefine the role of the presidency in Austrian politics. Having won the presidential election of 1992 with an unprecedented lead (save Kirchschläger's reelection in 1980) and having done so on a platform of being an active president who controls the government, Klestil probably has a better chance and greater ambition than any of his predecessors to reshape his office.

TABLE 2.1 Federal Presidential Elections Since 1945

Presidents	Nominating Party	Date in	Date out	Number of ballots	Percentage of votes[1]
Karl Renner[2]	SPÖ	12.12.1945	31.12.1950[3]	(1)	(100)
Theodor Körner	SPÖ	21.06.1951	04.01.1957[3]	2	52.1
Adolf Schärf	SPÖ	22.05.1957	21.05.1963	2	51.1
Adolf Schärf	SPÖ	22.05.1963	28.02.1965[3]	1	55.4
Franz Jonas	SPÖ	09.06.1965	08.06.1971	1	50.7
Franz Jonas	SPÖ	09.06.1971	24.04.1974[3]	1	52.8
Rudolf Kirchschläger	SPÖ	08.07.1974	07.07.1980	1	51.7
Rudolf Kirchschläger	SPÖ	08.07.1980	08.07.1986	1	79.9
Kurt Waldheim	ÖVP	08.07.1986	08.07.1992	2	53.9
Thomas Klestil	ÖVP	08.07.1992		2	56.9

1. In the decisive ballot.
2. Dr. Karl Renner was not directly elected by the people but by the two houses of parliament.
3. Died in office. According to the constitution the Chancellor acted as president until the new president was elected and sworn in.

The Cabinet

The cabinet is the most important political institution and the main prize in the political game. This section will first discuss cabinet recruitment and then will move to cabinet decision-making.

The federal chancellor and, upon his proposal, the cabinet ministers are appointed by the federal president. These constitutional provisions tell us little, however, about the actual practice of government formation and cabinet recruitment. Government formation has always been the domain of party politics. The federal president has always given the leader (or "chancellor candidate") of the strongest party in parliament the task of forming a government. If his party is not in command of an absolute parliamentary majority, cabinet formation is a matter of negotiation between the parties. While some of the presidents exerted some influence on government formation, the supremacy of political parties is without doubt. This is even more apparent when it comes to the recruitment of cabinet members, with appointments discussed and decided in the national party executives. One of the iron rules of traditional coalition government was that once the cabinet positions were distributed amongst the parties, each party was free to nominate whomever it wished.[10] Within the SPÖ, a decisive influence in the recruitment process was exercised by the party leader. His influence was not unlimited, however, in particular when it came to the reshuffling of existing government teams. Within the ÖVP, the factionalised party structure caused a more fragmented recruitment process, with the leagues *(Bünde)* and the *Land* party organizations playing a major role.

During the period of the various single-party governments (1966-83), the process of recruitment to the cabinet became less party-centered. The victorious chancellor candidates (Klaus in 1966 and Kreisky thereafter) stressed their constitutional role. Though decisions on cabinet membership were formally still made in the party executives, both leaders had more leeway than their predecessors. Kreisky, in particular, managed in most cases to make the party's approval of his personnel decisions a pure formality. The return to coalition governments since 1983 has not reversed this trend towards leader-centered cabinet recruitment. The current chancellor and SPÖ leader Vranitzky constitutes the best example.[11] He stressed his constitutional role as chancellor vis-à-vis his party even more and, consequently, did not seek explicit approval from the SPÖ party executive for his personnel decisions. Despite their poor electoral performances in recent elections, ÖVP chairmen have also managed to exercise more influence on cabinet appointments than their electorally more successful predecessors in the old grand coalition. Moreover, in 1987, the cabinet post of the minster of justice was taken out of the realm of party politics altogether. This department has since been assigned to an independent expert who must be acceptable to both governing parties; however, such a person proved difficult to find.

TABLE 2.2 Austrian Cabinets Since 1945

Cabinet[1]	Date in	Date out	Duration (in years)	Party Composition[2]	Parliamentary support (in % of seats)
Renner	27.04.1945	20.12.1945	0.6	SPÖ-ÖVP-KPÖ	no parliament
Figl I	20.12.1945	20.11.1947	1.9	ÖVP-SPÖ-KPÖ	100
Figl II	20.11.1947	08.11.1949	2.0	ÖVP-SPÖ	97.6
Figl III	08.11.1949	02.04.1953	3.4	ÖVP-SPÖ	87.3
Raab I	02.04.1953	29.06.1956	3.2	ÖVP-SPÖ	89.1
Raab II	29.06.1956	16.07.1959	3.0	ÖVP-SPÖ	94.5
Raab III	16.07.1959	11.04.1961	1.7	ÖVP-SPÖ	95.1
Gorbach I	11.04.1961	27.03.1963	2.0	ÖVP-SPÖ	95.1
Gorbach II	27.03.1963	02.04.1964	1.0	ÖVP-SPÖ	95.2
Klaus I	02.04.1964	19.04.1966	2.0	ÖVP-SPÖ	95.2
Klaus II	19.04.1966	21.04.1970	4.0	ÖVP	51.5
Kreisky I	21.04.1970	04.11.1971	1.5	SPÖ	49.1
Kreisky II	04.11.1971	28.10.1975	4.0	SPÖ	50.8
Kreisky III	28.10.1975	05.06.1979	3.6	SPÖ	50.8
Kreisky IV	05.06.1979	24.05.1983	4.0	SPÖ	51.9
Sinowatz	24.05.1983	16.06.1986	3.0	SPÖ-FPÖ	55.8
Vranitzky I	16.06.1986	21.01.1987	0.6	SPÖ-FPÖ	55.8
Vranitzky II	21.01.1987	17.12.1990	4.0	SPÖ-ÖVP	85.8
Vranitzky III	17.12.1990	29.11.1994	4.0	SPÖ-ÖVP	76.5
Vranitzky IV	29.11.1994			SPÖ-ÖVP	63.9

1. To define a cabinet the criteria "same chancellor", "same party composition" and "between parliamentary elections" were used.
2. The first-listed party is the one of the Federal Chancellor.

According to the constitution (Article 69), cabinet members are entrusted with the highest administrative business of the federal government *(Bund)*, insofar as this is not assigned to the federal president. The cabinet holds a monopoly on all the resources required for initiating policy. Cabinet decision-making is not subject to detailed constitutional regulation (Berchtold 1974; Adamovich 1973). All government decisions rest with the individual ministers concerned. The only exceptions concern functions explicitly mentioned in the constitution. The most significant of these are the power formally to propose legislation to parliament, the power to propose persons for appointment by the federal president and the power to submit appeals to the Constitutional Court. Those tasks which are assigned to the cabinet as such have to be decided unanimously. Here, the constitutional role of the chancellor is that of chairman, not of hierarchical superior. He is entitled to co-ordinate cabinet work, but not to issue instructions to ministers.

Notwithstanding the constitutional importance of the cabinet, in the 1950s and early 1960s it was not the most powerful political body. That distinction was held by the coalition committee, which comprised the ten or so most powerful members of the political elite of both *Lager*, only a few of them had a seat in the cabinet. The coalition committee not only dealt with top-level policy issues, but also used to negotiate and decide upon rather specialised policy questions, where these had become the subject of inter-party dispute. As may be imagined, there was hardly a political issue over which the parties did not, at some stage, have contradicting proposals. Thus during that period of classic consociationalism, the cabinet ministers' role was to a large extent one of policy initiation and implementation, while the intermediate phase of the policy process, namely, substantive decision-making, was beyond their capacity (Rudzio 1971).

It is true that bodies outside the cabinet have also been relevant for cabinet decision-making since the end of the grand coalition in 1966, yet things have changed considerably (Müller 1988; 1991a; 1994). First, all bodies established in the cabinet system since 1966 have been much more cabinet-centered in terms of recruitment than the coalition committee of the old grand coalition. The coalition committee of the new grand coalition (since 1987) is closer to the cabinet than to the parties. Moreover, in contrast to the old grand coalition, the two most powerful cabinet members, namely the chancellor and the vice-chancellor, who are also the two party chairmen, are not permanent members of this committee, thus indicating its reduced importance. The involvement of the chancellor and the vice-chancellor is restricted to the most tricky problems, which are referred to them for decision. Though it is clear that they do so on the basis of their party rather than their cabinet positions, the fact remains that politicians from outside the cabinet do not participate in these decisions.

Second, the decision-making role of ministers has increased considerably since 1966. They enjoyed their greatest autonomy in the single-party governments from 1966 to 1983. Being the trusted policy specialists of their respective party and benefitting from the principle of mutual non-interference within the politically homogeneous cabinet, they had considerable leeway in determining the policy of their departments. Not much changed in the 1983-86 SPÖ-FPÖ government, which was based on mutual trust and the idea that each party should be permitted to use its government departments to appeal to its potential clientele. As we have seen, the incumbent new grand coalition has established a powerful coalition committee. However, its scope is much more limited than that of its predecessor. It does not normally decide matters over the heads of the responsible cabinet ministers. Though it is often necessary for the ministers to compromise in order to get the cabinet's approval, their role in cabinet decision-making has remained almost as central as during the last two decades.

The chancellor's role in cabinet decision-making never corresponded to the *primus inter pares* model outlined by the constitution. His power to determine the cabinet's composition and his role as party leader provide the chancellor with additional power and authority. However, both are effective only vis-à-vis his party colleagues. In coalition governments, the leader of the second party is usually appointed vice-chancellor and *de facto* also has these resources available with regard to his party's government team. He thus constitutes something of a second chancellor. Indeed, for most of the old grand coalition's duration, the vice-chancellor did not take over departmental responsibility, but was the co-ordinator of his party's government team. A kind of dual leadership of the chancellor and the vice-chancellor was thereby established in the eyes of the public.

From what has been said so far, it is clear that the powers of the chancellor were most extensive during the periods of single-party government. In this form of government, the chancellor's capacity to dominate cabinet decision-making increased substantially; he could play on his exclusive role of representing the government before the citizenry. This took place in particular through television, which in the late 1960s became the most important medium of mass communication. Internal and external chancellor dominance were mutually re-enforcing. It was during this period that academic observers noted the establishment of "chancellor government" or "chancellor democracy" (Welan and Neisser 1971; Welan 1976; Gerlich et al. 1988; Müller 1994).

In the coalition governments since 1983 and in particular in the grand coalition government which has been in power since 1987, the chancellor's "internal capacity," i.e., his influence on cabinet decision-making, diminished. While continuing to be the cabinet's chairman, he is the head only of his party's government team. However, the chancellor's "external capacity," i.e., his communication capability vis-à-vis the public, was not likewise reduced. It is still the chancellor who dominates the public's image of politics. Taking into account his limited "internal capacity" and the public's weariness with old-style party politics, however, Vranitzky changed the chancellor's public image from partisan actor towards reasonable, non-partisan commentator of cabinet work. This style, which of course requires a suitable personality, initially proved quite successful. The 1986 and in particular the 1990 general elections were, more than ever before, "chancellor elections," with considerable beneficial spillovers for Vranitzky's political position (Meth-Cohn and Müller 1991; Müller 1991).

Since 1995, when Austria joined the EU, cabinet members have the additional task of representing the country in the EU's Council of Ministers. The chancellor represents Austria in the European Council, i.e., the regular meeting of the heads of government, against the wishes of the the federal president who would like this position for himself; the question has not been settled definitively yet.

Taken together, the developments that the cabinet underwent since the mid-1960s indicate that it became less of a mirror of social forces. Though the cabinet retained of course its party-political underpinning, it increasingly became a political force in its own right, i.e., it assumed a political identity that is increasingly distinct from the parties. This development was fostered not only by the changed nature of coalition government in the post-1983 (as opposed to the pre-1966) period, but also by the personality of recent chancellors, as well as by the political requirement for a united external front placed upon the cabinet in recent years as it faced the need to introduce policies that are unpopular with the members of the two main political subcultures.

The Administration

According to the "father" of the Austrian constitution, Hans Kelsen, the administration[12] should be perfectly neutral, in the sense that all its activities should be governed by law, as stipulated in Article 18 of the constitution: "The entire public administration shall be based on law." It is to the law and not to the minister that civil servants' prime loyalty should be directed. A neutrality (or rather instrumentality) of the civil service is required only in *functional* terms; however; civil servants may still engage in political activities in their capacity as citizens and, to a large extent, actually do so.

As elsewhere, the Austrian bureaucracy is in reality much more influential than the constitution outlines (Kneucker 1973 and 1981; Neisser 1974 and 1991). Its role in the making and implementation of laws is generally viewed as very important, in particular in view of the fact that Austria is not accustomed to the practice of providing each government minister with a group of temporary civil servants appointed on the basis of political criteria for the duration of the government's term of office as a sort of buffer between ministers and their departments. Though the government departments have a monocratic structure and ministers can force through each particular policy decision, they generally depend on the co-operation of the bureaucracy. If it does not provide its expertise readily, if it overinforms or underinforms the minister, or if it follows a policy of deliberately limiting his alternatives in decision-making to the department's conventional wisdoms, the minister will have little policy impact and may run into political problems.

It is not necessarily the case, however, that the minister is faced with a single, monolithic bloc of bureaucrats. The common legal background of most civil servants and the socialization within the bureaucracy certainly have an unifying effect, but as elsewhere, personal rivalries and career interests constitute limiting factors. The most important division within the bureaucracy since 1945, however, has been the political one. Traditionally, the Austrian bureaucracy had been conservative, mainly Catholic-conservative but also German-national; social democrats were excluded. During the First Republic and in particular between 1934 and 1938, the civil service was further colonized and made more partisan by the Catholic-conservative *Lager*. In the subsequent period of Nazi rule (1938-45), the bureaucracy was purged of Jews, of the partisans of the previous regime and of those who had remained highly loyal to the notion of an independent Austrian state. The remaining bureaucrats were either genuine Nazis or were forced to join the Nazi party in order to keep their job (Steiner 1972, 375-383). In 1945, denazification removed some of them and brought some of the former civil servants back. However, the new government needed experts and the Socialists suspected that, if denazification was carried out properly, the civil service would consist entirely of supporters of the Austro-fascist regime (1934-38) and ÖVP partisans. Thus both governing parties decided to give some of the ex-Nazis among the civil servants a second chance and absorbed them.[13]

In order to recruit SPÖ members for the higher ranks of the civil service, the *Proporz* system was established. It granted each of the two governing parties a proportion of public sector jobs roughly equal to their share of the vote in the last general election. While this was made explicit for public sector firms in the coalition contracts, the *Proporz* was implicit regarding the civil service. Each party enjoyed personnel autonomy in the department under its control; the departments in turn were distributed according to electoral strength (Secher 1958, 796-808; Steiner 1972, 383-397). Due to the lack of qualified personnel in the socialist subculture and in view of the fact that the system of a tenured civil service does not permit large-scale adjustments of civil service personnel in the short term, *Proporz* was never fully established in the civil service (Engelmann 1966, 274). Nevertheless, during the period of grand coalition government, the bureaucracy became almost entirely party controlled. Both parties had their strongholds in those government departments which were under their respective permanent control but also had bridge-heads in the other ministries. Both parties could rely on a number of top civil servants with extremely strong *Lager* ties and who were inclined to instinctively think along the same lines as politicians from the same party. This of course had consequences for the minister/civil servant relationship and for the civil servants' role in general. Civil servants acted as *party* experts and (if a ministry was controlled by a party other than their own) even party spies. Though all this violated the classical concept of a "neutral" or "nonpartisan" bureaucracy, it led to a civil service and an army which for the first time in modern Austrian history incorporated both major political subcultures and were thus fully acceptable to both major *Lager* (Secher 1958, 809).

After the end of the old grand coalition in 1966, the picture became more complicated. The single-party governments (1966-83) felt obliged to announce a non-partisan approach to their civil service recruitment and promotion policy. Kreisky in particular was keen to appoint some "blood group zero" people (i.e., non party members) to top positions in the civil service and in the public sector more generally. On the other hand, the results of the elections of personnel representatives reveal that during the periods of their respective single-party governments, the ÖVP and SPÖ maintained their traditional strongholds and increased their respective support in the strongholds of the other party by roughly one percent in each year (Müller 1989, 337; Luther 1989, 16-18). However, it would be wrong to arrive, on the basis of this evidence, at the conclusion that nothing has changed in respect of the party loyalties of civil servants. This author's interviews with about fifty post-war cabinet ministers indicate a diminishing importance of civil servants' party affiliation. In many cases, the desire for party patronage replaced the conviction of earlier generations of partisan civil servants. As one long-serving minister put it: "In terms of predicting loyalty to the minister's policies, the party book is nowadays often not worth the paper it is written on." Indeed, many insiders assume that civil servants' party membership now primarily works the other way round, namely, to make it easier to convince the minister of the merits of their views.

If the loyalties of civil servants no longer can be taken for granted on the basis of their party affiliation, cabinet ministers recur to two strategies in order to get the required administrative support: the introduction of ministerial cabinets and the building up of civil servants' personal loyalties by means of motivational techniques. Some ministers succeeded with both strategies, even though these cannot easily be applied simultanously.

The bureaucracy of the immediate post-war decades was characterized in many respects by structures and behaviour patterns vis-à-vis the public which it had managed to maintain since the days of monarchy (i.e., prior to 1918). Among other things, this meant little public accountability and little responsiveness. Since the mid-1960s, attempts were made to improve civil servants' training, to change the incentive structure in which they operate and to modernise the administration. These include the creation of a civil service training academy in 1975, the introduction in the 1980s of fixed-term appointments to a few top positions in the bureaucracy and the plan of the new grand coalition to carry out a comprehensive administrative reform. These internal reforms were accompanied by external changes. In short, the administration is nowadays exposed to more public scrutiny and criticism than ever before. The mutually re-enforcing activities of the media, the audit office, the ombudsman's office and, more recently, of parliamentary investigative committees and independent administrative review bodies have made life much more troublesome for bureaucrats. Moreover, citizens are no longer the docile, subject-oriented clients that they had been until about the 1970s.

Though changes in the bureaucracy occur at a notoriously slow pace and are difficult to assess, it seems to be clear that significant changes have taken place since the 1960s. The power of *Lager* ties to determine bureaucratic structures and behaviour has been reduced, as has their general significance for Austrian society. Other principles, which for many decades guided the "servants of the state," have also been eroded, albeit as yet without having been replaced by new paradigms.

The Constitutional Court

The Austrian Constitutional Court *(Verfassungsgerichtshof)* is fairly powerful. It can settle disputes between the branches of the federal government, as well as between the federal level and the *Länder*, most importantly it decides on the constitutionality of legislation and of government decrees (Welan 1988). In addition, it has numerous other tasks.[14] The Constitutional Court can only become active when a relevant appeal has been filed with it. Until the 1970s, only other courts, the cabinet and the *Land* governments had the right to appeal to the

Constitutional Court. That right has subsequently been extended, however, as will be illustrated below.

The judges are appointed by the federal president upon a proposal from the cabinet (for the court's president, its vice-president and six judges) and the parliament (six judges, three by each of the two chambers). Once appointed, judges may remain in office until the age of seventy. Decisions are anounced as decisions of the court; there are no dissenting opinions, and normally the decision-making process remains well hidden from public view.

The recruitment of the judges was always party-controlled. In the intermediate post-war period, the two big parties agreed to apply *Proporz* rules, that is, to have fixed proportions of socialist and conservative judges and not to exploit situations when they were in control of one of the nominating institutions at a time when a vacancy arose. In the first two post-war decades, the conservatives had a slim majority of seven to six among the voting members (the president does not vote). In this period, the political impact of the court was limited. During the ten year period of allied occupation (1945-55), the court usually backed the government. It accepted ordinary legislation where constitutional laws were required by making reference to a clause of the constitution (Article 10) which grants the central state the right to undertake "whatever measures seem necessary by reason or in consequence of war to ensure the uniform conduct of economic affairs." Since the government was in command of a parliamentary majority of up to 97 percent, it would not have been a problem in terms of domestic politics to pass constitutional laws instead of ordinary legislation. This would, however, have allowed the occupation forces to intervene, since according to the Second Control Agreement of the allied forces, constitutional legislation needed unanimous approval by them, thus giving *each* of them an absolute veto power. Ordinary legislation, however, could only be influenced by the allied forces if they acted jointly, which seldom happened during this period. If the Constitutional Court did hold government legislation to be unconstitutional in the period up to 1966, the grand coalition government often decided to use its parliamentary majority (more than two thirds) to re-introduce the same bill as a constitutional law, which screened it from the scrutiny of the court. Sometimes the parties anticipated problems with the Constitutional Court and introduced their bills as constitutional legislation from the outset.

By 1973, the Socialists were in command of all the institutions empowered to nominate judges to the Constitutional Court. They used this to reverse the traditional power-distribution within the court in their favor. After initial protests this was accepted by the ÖVP (Welan 1974, 295-299).

In 1975, two constitutional amendments facilitated access to the Constitutional Court. Since then, a parliamentary minority (at least one third of the MPs) in each of the chambers of parliament may appeal to the court. The second amendment entitled all individuals to demand an examination of the constitutionality of laws and government decrees which personally affect them. As a result, the number of appeals increased from under 200 in 1973 to almost 2,000 in 1987 (Michalitsch 1990, 190f).

The various single-party governments of 1966 to 1983 lacked the possibility of bypassing the Constitutional Court. Nevertheless, the number of decisions holding federal laws unconstitutional remained moderate, though each rejection was uncomfortable for the governing party. In a few cases which caused ideological debate in the mid-1970s, in particular the legalization on abortion and the broadcasting and university reforms, the political background of the judges was important.[15] In general, however, the court practiced judicial self-restraint.

Since the 1980s, the Constitutional Court has assumed a more active role. It switched from a formal to a more substantive interpretation of the constitution and also became less predictable; in several cases it reversed its earlier decisions.

Some of the most important decisions concerned sex discrimination; the court took upholding the principle of non-discrimination more seriously than parliament. It often took action in subject matters that had been on the political agenda for years, but had not been tackled because they affected the vested interests of powerful groups and/or because they were extremely complex. Thus earlier political immobilism on the governmental and parliamentary levels left a series of important issues unsolved which a more self-confident Constitutional Court is now addressing.

What caused this new behavioural pattern in the Constitutional Court? One reason for this is the reduction of its workload. Constitutional amendments in 1981 and 1984 permitted the summary rejection of certain appeals, particularly in cases not involving questions of constitutional principle. This freed the Court's energies and increased its capacity to engage in more strategic judgments (Michalitsch 1990, 190). Most observers argue also that a generational change among the judges paved the way to the new interpretation of the constitution, with the younger members of the court interpreting constitutional law in a more substantive way and feeling less duty-bound to the political party which nominated them for appointment.[16]

Currently, the decisions of the Constitutional Court are increasingly incorporated into existing legislation. In the days of the old Grand coalition, it was common to enact the same bill again as a constitutional law and thus to amend the constitution; this has been rare since the reestablishment of grand coalition government in 1987. If one side of the coalition--and it is usually the ÖVP--is perfectly happy with a court decision, it has no incentive to circumvent the verdict by constitutional amendments. Also, public opinion would interpret the introduction of such a law as one more sign of party misbehaviour. In addition, since 1994, the grand coalition no longer commands the required two-thirds majority in parliament. Thus the Constitutional Court, reduces the scope of party policies. The same holds true for the EU Court of Justice since 1995. In contrast to the Austrian Constitutional Court, its yardstick is not the Austrian Constitution but the EU Treaty.

The Judiciary

All judges are guaranteed independence in the exercise of their juridical function and also enjoy constitutional guarantees against dismissal and transfer; yet there are some links between the judiciary and politics (Steiner 1972, 398-408). In their role as judicial administrators, judges are subordinate to the minister of justice. They are appointed by the federal president or the minister of justice on the basis of a cabinet proposal. In drawing up the proposal, the cabinet as a matter of practice restricts itself to considering the personnel proposed by the courts (Keller 1974, 328; Markel 1984). In effect, the judiciary is thus largely self-recruiting.

Public prosecutors *(Staatsanwälte)*, unlike judges, are subject to instructions from their superiors. At the top of the command chain is the minister of justice. Social Democrats and top bureaucrats argued that this right to give instructions is necessary to unify judicial decision-making, to take into account new academic findings and to ensure the equal treatment of all citizens (Leser 1963, 221-224). In any case, the justice minister's right to give instructions is potentially a highly effective means of influencing the mix of cases brought to the attention of the judiciary: without an effective prosecution, there is no real judge.

Traditionally, the judiciary has not played a great role in politics. Although for many socialists the judiciary still displayed a class bias, political controversy over court decisions seldom arose. There were a few politically relevant cases in the 1950s and 1960s which basically concerned politicians who had been involved in cases of corruption, but these cases mostly became juridical matters only *after* they had been decided politically. Politics was generally seen to be determined by politicians, not judges. A transfer of issues from the political arena to the arena of the courts by one of the two big parties against the other would have violated unwritten consociational rules. Though both parties tried to make political capital out of corruption cases in the realm of the other *Lager*, in particular before elections, only few politicians suffered from this.

In the late 1970s, and in particular in the 1980s, the picture began to change. The judiciary increasingly came to have a political impact by not only investigating cases involving politicians, but by also prosecuting them. Initially, the existing links between politics and the judiciary seems to have been used for delaying or preventing prosecution, which in turn led to a decline in the population's trust in the judiciary. More recently, however, there has been a relatively large number of important judicial cases with political implications, and the list of politicians who were either accused of crimes, or who were actually found guilty by the courts of serious offences--including, for example, tax evasion, acting as an accessory after the fact and perjury--reads like an extract from the Who's Who of Austrian politics. Verdicts against politicians increased the population's trust in the judiciary,[17] whilst simultaneously confirming its increasing cynicism about the character and activities of the political elites.

Those parties whose politicians are implicated in such cases tend to criticise the judicial decisions while the others usually present themselves as the defenders of an independent judiciary (until, of course, their turn comes to have one of their politicians under fire). For some observers, the increased political impact of the judiciary is not a sign of increased political corruption or rule-breaking, but of more independence on the part of the judiciary and greater professional ethics within it (Heinrich and Welan 1991, 148). Such a development does indeed seem to have taken place. The wording of some of the verdicts, however, clearly displayed an anti-party-politics bias, containing negative general statements about parties and politicians. While from a normative perspective this may be a step too far, from an analytical perspective it indicates that the judiciary has assumed the status of an actor in the political process.

Control of Government and Administration: the Audit Office

The audit office *(Rechnungshof)* is formally a parliamentary institution, since its president and vice-president are elected by the *Nationalrat* (formerly for an unlimited period, but since 1988 for a twelve year term only). Other audit office personnel is appointed by its president and governed by his instructions. Its tasks include the financial oversight of the federal and the *Land* administrations, public sector firms and large towns. In doing so, the audit office has to check the legality, economy and expediency of management and policy. Its findings are reported to the *Nationalrat* and the *Land* parliaments and are subsequently published. In cases of maladministration, the parliament may hold the respective member of the executive responsible (Hengstschläger 1982; Widder 1991).

During most of the old grand coalition, the presidency of the audit office was one of the many positions to be shared among the two governing parties according to *Proporz* rules. This office was considered to count almost as much as a ministerial post. The presidency was assigned to the junior partner in the coalition, the SPÖ. Consequently, the findings of the audit office were formerly seen within the context of coalition politics. While the media and the public did not normally pay much attention to the audit office's scrutiny, the ÖVP used to interpret criticism of the parts of the governmental and administrative system under the control of its own subculture as party-politically motivated. On the few occasions that the SPÖ's "realm" was criticised by the audit office, the SPÖ also expressed its dissatisfaction with the audit office and in particular with its president.

During a temporary flirtation with the FPÖ, the SPÖ in 1964 decided to nominate an FPÖ MP for the presidency of the audit office, the control of which the SPÖ increasingly regarded as providing no real pay-offs. After the retirement of this FPÖ president in the 1980s, another FPÖ MP was elected who held this position until 1992. The SPÖ and ÖVP had agreed by then on a de-politicization of the audit office and had nominated a politically independent, certified public accountant as their joint candidate. However, this de-politicization came to nothing since he withdrew his candidacy because of criticism from the opposition. Eventually, the FPÖ (which had its own candidate) unexpectedly moved to propose the original ÖVP candidate (who had been nominated before the government parties agreed on a joint candidate) and insured his election against Social Democratic opposition (Wögerbauer 1993).[18] This move was first and foremost an attempt to split the grand coalition, its consequences for the role of the audit office remain to be seen.

Since 1964, the impact of the audit office has changed considerably. Though with a prominent opposition politician occupying its presidency, it could still be argued that party politics influences audit office activities, yet the public has become more willing to accept it as a neutral institution. In 1975, new rules of procedure granted parliamentary minorities comprising at least one third of the MPs the right to instruct the audit office to scrutinize a particular branch of the executive. In 1988, the required number of MPs was reduced to twenty. Thus the opposition is no longer obliged to wait to see what the audit office will place under scrutiny of its own accord. This means that the opposition can now select a branch of the executive which it believes to constitute a weak point of the government and get the audit office to investigate further. The audit office's investigation normally not only provides the opposition with new facts and insights, but also makes its critique of the government more credible. Giving the opposition formal access to the audit office certainly has increased the latter's political relevance. Moreover, in the 1970s, investigative journalism established itself as a main branch of the Austrian media system. Popularizing the findings of the audit office became one of its principal activities (Müller and Bubendorfer 1989). It is common that the confidential draft versions of the audit office's reports, which normally are more critical than the final ones, are leaked to the media. The publication of a confidential version that has not yet been toned-down is more "newsworthy" than that of a final version, which includes the reaction of the criticized authorities and is usually worded more gently.

The increased role of the audit office in Austrian politics has provoked discussions about its reform. The governing parties' declared aim is to enable the office to provide suggestions for general administrative reform rather than limit itself to the detailed *post hoc* critique of administrative decisions.[19]

Federalism

Austria is formally a federal state. Its two main levels are the central state *(Bund)* and the regional subdivisions *(Länder)*. This article, however, does not intend to deal with the whole complex issue of relations between the *Bund* and the *Länder,* nor with the *Länder* themselves[20]. Instead, our intention is to elucidate the borderline between federal and provincial *(Länder)* institutions (Luther 1991). There are three main federal elements in the Austrian constitution:

- the distribution of powers between the central state and the *Länder,*
- the second chamber of parliament, the *Bundesrat,* and
- indirect federal administration by the *Länder* and, in particular, the governor *(Landeshauptmann)*.

The Distribution of Powers

In the first two decades of the Second Republic, a tendency to grant the central state more powers at the expense of the *Länder* prevailed (Werndl 1984). The old grand coalition, of course, constituted a rather comfortable framework for the reshuffling of powers, the more so since the more "federalist" party, the ÖVP, was for most of this time under the command of "centralists" from Lower Austria, the *Land* sourrounding Vienna. Since the end of the old grand coalition, the reshuffling of powers, which still required the consensus of both big parties, became a much more complicated matter. The party in opposition at the federal level tried to capitalize on its remaining positions at the *Land* level and thus was not willing to give up powers in favor of a federal government under the control of the other party. The early 1960s also saw the beginning of a more fundamental change (Luther 1986). Within the big parties, the *Land* party organizations gained power and thus reduced centralist tendencies within their national leaderships. At the same time, the *Länder* also started to show more self-confidence vis-à-vis the federal government. In 1964, they addressed a program of demands--mainly for an extension of powers--to the federal government, which in 1974 led to a constitutional amendment which brought some, albeit modest, reforms. Since then, the *Länder* have continued to push for more power. From the mid-1960s, changes in the distribution of powers between the two levels were increasingly the result of bargaining between the federal government and the *Länder,* rather than of a unilateral decision by the former. There is more of a balance between the gains and losses of both sides (Berchtold 1988). The return to a grand coalition government in 1987 initially resulted in a net gain in power for the federal government. However, in order to win the support of the *Länder* for EU membership, the federal government agreed to a substantial transfer of powers to the *Länder*, partly in compensation for the transfer of *Länder* powers to EU bodies (Pernthaler 1992). This reform was agreed to in detail between the federal government and the *Länder* in 1994. However it was not passed by parliament before the 1994 general election. In this election, the grand coalition lost the two-thirds parliamentary majority necessary to enact the reform. Subsequent parliamentary negotiations with the opposition parties led to a compromise which, however, was not acceptable to the *Länder* and therefore was not enacted. At present (mid-1995), the major reform of power distribution between the federal and *Land* levels has not yet been introduced (Öhlinger 1995; Pernthaler and Schernthanner 1995).

The Bundesrat

Traditionally, the prime role of a second chamber in a federal system is to permit the constituent units to participate in the decision-making process of the center and thus to ensure that their interests are represented. However, the institutional position of the Austrian *Bundesrat* has always been very weak both constitutionally and politically. With respect to most matters, it has only a suspensive veto, and some matters, in particular the budget, are not referred to it at all (Article 42). Only since 1984 has the *Bundesrat* been in a stronger position to prevent constitutional legislation which would reduce the powers of the *Länder*. In contrast to other constitutional legislation, such changes now require a two thirds majority in the *Bundesrat* (Article 44). Furthermore, there was in 1984 a reform of the *Bundesrat's* rules of procedure which included a question hour and also provided the governors, who are the most visible representatives of the *Länder* (see below), with the right to speak in the *Bundesrat*.

In practice, however, the *Bundesrat* has not defended *Länder* interests very effectively. Its party composition is similar to that of the *Nationalrat*; debates and voting strictly followed party lines and have mirrored those in the first chamber. During the old grand coalition, the most significant function of the *Bundesrat* was to provide by its veto the chance for a second treatment of a *Nationalrat* bill which contained legal or textual errors. These vetoes enjoyed the government's approval and were made in order to avoid the more time-consuming process of legislating an amendment to the defective law (Koja 1969; Walter 1969). The activities of the *Bundesrat* have increased since the mid-1960s as a consequence of increased party competition and growing conflict between the parties (Kathrein 1986, 377-385 and 391-396). Having argued and voted against government legislation in the *Nationalrat*, the opposition did not want to miss the opportunity of presenting its arguments again in the *Bundesrat* and, if possible, to delay a law by using the suspensive veto of the second chamber. However, little public attention was given to the parliamentary battles in the *Bundesrat* and the government soon anticipated possible delays by an "alien" majority in the second chamber. Only in exceptional cases did the *Bundesrat* have an impact on the conduct and outcome of the political process.[21] The new veto rights of the *Bundesrat* have not yet proved significant; the speaking rights of the governors have been used only rarely and thus have not added much to the *Bundesrat's* relevance as political arena for *Land* interests.

Summing up the developments, it can be said that the *Bundesrat* was transformed from an irrelevant addendum to the legislative process to an additional, though not significant, arena for inter-party duels. It has, however, not gained the status of an actor in its own right.

The Indirect Federal Administration

Neither the role of the *Bundesrat* nor the *Länder*'s formal powers are impressive when compared to the powers of the constituent units of other Western countries with federal systems (such as the United States, Germany and Switzerland). However, there is still one formal institution through which *Länder* may exert influence, i.e., through the system of indirect federal administration and, in particular, the governor *(Landeshauptmann)*. In a number of important matters such as citizenship, agricultural interest organizations and traffic policing, laws are made at the federal level, but the *Land* administrations are entrusted with their execution (Weber 1987).

The governor has a double function in this system. On the one hand, he is the chairman of the *Land* government and politically responsible to the *Land* parliament (the *Landtag*). On the other hand, however, he is the top representative of the federal government in the *Land*. According to the constitution (Article 103), the governor in his role as indirect federal administrator has to follow the directives of the federal ministers and must use all his resources, including those of the *Land* government, to implement the policies of the central state (Pesendorfer 1986). A governor who does not behave accordingly may be brought before the Constitutional Court, which may declare the behaviour of the governor unconstitutional, deprive him of his office, or deprive him temporarily of his political rights.

Their double role made the governors extremely powerful and visible within their respective *Länder*. Since the distribution of powers between the federal and the *Länder* levels tends to assign the more popular tasks to the *Länder* (in particular, they only spend, but do not tax), the governors are in a good position to become very popular. The local media, to which the governors have privileged access, contributed to this tendency. On this basis, many governors succeeded in gaining the image of a provincial patriarch (*Landesvater*). Just as the federal president, they were exposed to very little political criticism; however, they are the most powerful men in their respective *Länder*. All this led to a very substantial incumbency bonus for the governor's party in *Land* elections and to governors who stayed in office for decades, clearly outranking the duration of members of the national executive (Nick 1989; Dachs et al. 1995).

In the past, indirect federal administration did not lead to problems. Some governors may have implemented federal laws and directives from the Viennese ministries with more energy than others, but it seems that there were no attempts to reverse federal decisions and no governor openly violated the will of the central state. This did not necessarily indicate the supremacy of the constitution over conflicting political values the governors may have held. The smooth process of indirect federal administration rather resulted from the fact that federal policies were quite acceptable to the *Länder,* despite the weak representation of their interests in the constitutional structure. Indeed, the formal constitutional structures with which this article is concerned are not the main way in which *Länder* interests are articulated and brought to bear in the process of decision-making (Luther 1991). Most important are the political parties, which will not normally enact legislation at the federal level against the will of their *Land* party organizations. Moreover, a variety of extra-constitutional mechanisms exist in order to represent the *Länder* interests vis-à-vis the central state. The most significant of these are the governors' conference *(Landeshauptmännerkonferenz)* and the meetings of the *Länder's* finance "ministers" (Weber 1992).[22]

Since the 1980s, however, the problematic nature of the constitutional regulation of indirect federal administration has become apparent. Two governors, both from parties in opposition at the national level at that time, openly refused to follow instructions from the central government. Their political rationale was to take a position which was popular within the *Land* and then to define the conflict with the central state in terms of federalism, or rather anti-centralism (anti-Vienna), which substantially increased the support for the governor within his *Land.* Such a case may be brought before the Constitutional Court by the federal cabinet, as happened in the first case that occurred (1984). Yet whatever the verdict of the Constitutional Court may be, the governor is likely to benefit politically. If the court accepts his behaviour, then he is vindicated as a lawful defender of the rights of his *Land* (against Viennese interference). If he is punished, he can claim to be a martyr for his *Land.* If he is in command of a majority in the *Land* parliament, he is likely to dissolve the latter and hold elections. The governor's party would undoubtedly profit electorally and the party or parties which represented the government at the federal level would suffer. The *Land* parliament would then most likely re-elect the governor just deprived of his office by the Constitutional Court, which would be powerless to prevent this occurrence unless it had taken the highly unlikely step of suspending the governor's political rights. Whilst this is as yet only a scenario, it makes quite clear how the institutional framework can be abused for the purpose of conducting party fights. The difference between the constitutional and the de facto distribution of power between the federal government and the *Länder* in the system of indirect federal administration probably made it easier for the former to envisage a substantial shift of powers in favour of the *Länder*, with budgetary reasons as another major incentive to do so. According to a 1992 agreement between the central state and the *Länder*, the role of the latter was to be considerably strengthened in the implementation of national legislation once Austria had become a member of the EU. This implies making the governors free from central directives and strengthening their responsibility vis-à-vis the *Land* legislatures (Pernthaler 1992, 372f.).

In sum, the discussion above shows that since the 1970s the impact of political institutions of the *Länder* on Austrian national politics has increased. This resulted, first, from stepped-up party competition and, second, from the greater significance of the institutions themselves in shaping the roles of political actors.

Conclusion

Until the 1960s, the institutional framework of the Austrian government seemed to be almost irrelevant and played little role either in politics or in political science analyses; it was jointly controlled by the elites of the two major *Lager* who tended to override constitutional norms by political fiat. When in 1966 the elites of the major *Lager* opted for a more competitive approach to politics by putting an end to grand coalition government, the institutional framework gained in importance. A strong opposition acted as a watchdog of governments' compliance with institutional rules and tried to use the constitutional framework to contain governmental actions, thus making it highly relevant for the political process. This development was further fostered by the reduction of the duopoly of the two major *Lager*. First, the Third *Lager* became more acceptable as a potential or actual partner in government coalitions. From 1986 onwards, it subscribed to a vote-maximizing protest strategy and gained considerably in strength. Second, the Greens and the Liberal Forum established themselves as new and additional political forces in the 1980s and 1990s respectively.

There was another way in which formal institutions gained a new lease on life. The political core institutions, such as parliament and the cabinet, are now less dominated by the political subcultures than they used to be in the first two post-war decades. The behaviour of political office-holders is now shaped more by their respective institutions than used to be the case. Other institutions such as the Constitutional Court, the audit office and the judiciary, which in the period of classic consociationalism were under the control of the party elites or practiced self restraint, gained in importance in recent years. In short, many of the political institutions moved towards being political actors in their own right. Consequently, the current political system has many more relevant actors than in the immediate post-war period and the political process has become more complex and less predictable.

Both developments were facilitated by a number of institutional reforms, many of which were illustrated above, but even more importantly by the transformation of the political culture and the media system. These encouraged the traditional *Lager* elites to engage in more competitive behaviour, pressing office-holders to stress their formal roles and to exercise more fully the powers which their respective institutions had been granted by the constitution. Additional important changes follow from Austria's membership in the EU which became effective in 1995.

Notes

1. Besides the *Bundes-Verfassungsgesetz*, which is referred to as the constitution in this chapter, there are other constitutional laws and clauses with constitutional status within ordinary statute; legally all three are at the same level. They are all equally binding.

2. The constitution itself does not indicate what constitutes a "total revision". Constitutional lawyers and the Constitutional Court have interpreted this clause as referring to amendments which involve changes to one or more of the guiding principles of the 1920 constitution. These unquestionably include the principles of democracy, of federalism, of the rule of law, of the separation of powers and of liberalism. See Robert Walter, *Österreichisches Bundesverfassungsrecht* (Vienna: Manz, 1972). Pp. 101-113.

3. There was also one attempt at a people's initiative which failed to get the required support in 1980 and one in 1995.

4. In post-war history Austria experienced only one minority government (1970-71).

5. See Otto Kirchheimer, "The Waning of Opposition in Parliamentary Regimes," in *Social Research*, Vol. 24, No. 2, 1957. Pp. 127-156; Frederick C. Engelmann, "Austria: The Pooling of Opposition," in Robert A. Dahl, ed., *Political Opposition in Western Democracies* (New Haven: Yale University Press, 1966). Pp. 260-283; Karl-Heinz Nassmacher, *Das österreichische Regierungssystem* (Cologne: Westdeutscher Verlag, 1968); Kurt Steiner, *Politics in Austria* (Boston: Little, Brown and Co., 1972); Helmut Widder, *Parlamentarische Strukturen im politischen System* (Berlin: Duncker & Humblot, 1979).

6. Good descriptive accounts of the parliamentary activities are contained in Heinz Wittmann, "Regierung und Opposition um parlamentarischen Prozeß," in Andreas Khol et al., eds., *Österreichisches Jahrbuch für Politik 1977* (Vienna.

Verlag für Geschichte und Politik, 1978). Pp.21-90, and H. Wittmann, "Regierung und Opposition im parlamentarischen Prozeß - Struktur und Arbeit des Parlaments in der XIV. Gesetzgebungsperiode 1975-1979," in Andreas Khol et al., eds., *Österreichisches Jahrbuch für Politik 1979* (Vienna: Verlag für Geschichte und Politik, 1980). Pp. 39-68; Anton Nevlacsil, "Regierung und Opposition im parlamentarischen Prozeß," in Andreas Khol et al., eds., *Österreichisches Jahrbuch für Politik 1983* (Vienna: Verlag für Geschichte und Politik, 1984). Pp. 209-257; A. Nevlacsil, "Der Nationalrat in der XVI.GP," in Andreas Khol et al., eds., *Österreichisches Jahrbuch für Politik 1986* (Vienna: Verlag für Geschichte Und Politik, 1987). Pp. 465-494 and A. Nevlacsil, "Der Nationalrat in der XVII.GP," in Andreas Khol et al., eds., *Österreichisches Jahrbuch für Politik 1990* (Vienna: Verlag für Geschichte und Politik, 1991). Pp. 431-459; Helmut Wohnout, "Politische Bilanz der XVIII. Gesetzgebungsperiode des Nationalrates," in Andreas Khol et al., eds., *Österreichisches Jahrbuch für Politik 1994* (Vienna: Verlag für Geschichte und Politik). Pp. 737-768. For more general surveys of parliament see Helmut Widder, "Der Nationalrat," in Herbert Schambeck, ed., *Österreichs Parlamentarismus. Werden und System* (Berlin: Duncker & Humblot, 1986). Pp. 261-336 and Heinz Fischer, "Das Parlament," in Herbert Dachs et al., eds., *Handbuch des politischen Systems Österreichs* (Vienna: Manz, 1991). Pp. 88-109.

7. The dismissal procedure requires first a two thirds majority of the *Nationalrat* in order to summon the *Bundesversammlung*, the joint meeting of the two parliamentary chambers. Second, the *Bundesversammlung* must vote (by simple majority) for a referendum to dismiss the president. The third requirement is a majority in the referendum itself. If, however, the referendum results in a majority against the dismissal, it is counted as the re-election of the president for another six-year term. (This clause may not, however, extend the length of his total term over twelve consecutive years.) A referendum which approves the president is also considered as a vote of no-confidence against the *Nationalrat*: it is automatically dissolved and a new parliamentary election has to be called.

8. See Eric C. Kollmann, *Theodor Körner. Militär und Politik* (Vienna: Verlag für Geschichte und Politik, 1973); Frederick C. Engelmann, "Haggling for the Equilibrium: The Renegotiation of the Austrian Coalition," in *American Political Science Review*, Vol. 56, 1962, pp. 651-662; Karl R. Stadler, *Adolf Schärf. Mensch- -Politiker–Staatsmann* (Vienna: Europaverlag, 1982); Friedrich Weissensteiner, *Die österreichischen Bundespräsidenten* (Vienna: Österreichischer Bundesverlag, 1982); Herbert Dachs et al., eds., *Die Politiker* (Vienna: Manz, 1995).

9. However, taking also into account the fact that Waldheim was elected after an extremely acrimonious electoral campaign (Luther 1987) and henceforth remained internationally isolated and a matter of internal controversy, Waldheim's impact on Austrian politics was considerable and exceeded that of some of his predecessors.

10.This principle which once has been referred to as the "monkey principle" (if one party choses a monkey as minister this must be accepted by its coalition partner) was violated only once. In 1990, the SPÖ responded to the ÖVP's rejection of a candidate for the minister of justice (who already had been accepted in the negotiations) by rejecting its former general secretary as a state secretary.

11. It is worth mentioning that Vranitzky's political career did not progress via party positions, but started in government. He became chancellor without having been a member of the party executive and only then ascended to the party leadership.

12. This section is about bureaucratic, not governmental "administration."

13. Initially also the Communists participated in the government. They advocated a more rigorous denazification policy.

14. These include acting as an impeachment tribunal, i.e. to decide in cases where government members e.g. have been impeached, as well as as an electoral tribunal, i.e. to decide in cases in which elections are challenged.

15. It was reported that in these cases the decisions were made along party lines, with a seven to six majority, upholding the legislation of the Socialist parliamentary majority. Cf. Felix Ermacora, "Politische Aspekte der Verfassungsentwicklung in Österreich seit 1970," in *Österreichisches Jahrbuch für Politik* 1978, pp. 82-84.

16. Some insiders argue that the second argument holds true only for the judges who were nominated by the Socialists. Those nominated by the ÖVP have traditionally acted less cohesively in the court and are said to have displayed more party loyalty in recent years.

17. See *IMAS-report*, No. 12, May 1991.

18. Until 1992 the ÖVP had managed to maintain the position of the audit office's vice-president, an office which eventually was abolished in 1993. Though rather powerless within the audit office, the vice-president usually was well informed.

19. Another institution for the control of the administration is the ombudsman's office *(Volksanwaltschaft)*. Its three members are elected by the *Nationalrat* for a six year term. The ombudsman's office can be appealed to by any individual who feels unfairly treated by the administration. Though the administration is formally obliged to respond to the audit office, the latter cannot oblige the administration to change unreasonable albeit lawful behaviour. It can, however, suggest legal reform to the *Nationalrat*. The main political significance of the ombudsman's office is thus restricted to exercising public, or moral pressure on the administration.

20. On this, see the chapter by Herbert Dachs in this volume.

21. The suspensive *Bundesrat* veto proved to be relevant only in those rare situations where the majority in the *Nationalrat* and/or the party composition of government had changed before the bill was put again before the *Nationalrat*.

22. See the chapter by Herbert Dachs in this volume.

References

Adamovich, Ludwig. 1973. "Die Koordinationskompetenz des Bundeskanzlers in verfassungsrechtlicher Sicht." *Juristische Blätter* 95: 234-242.

Berchtold, Klaus. 1969. *Der Bundespräsident*. Vienna: Springer.

___. 1974. "Die Regierung," in Heinz Fischer, ed., *Das politische System Österreichs*. Pp. 151-179. Vienna: Europaverlag.

___. 1988. *Die Verhandlungen zum Forderungsprogramm der Bundesländer seit 1956*. Vienna: Braumüller.

Dachs, Herbert, Peter Gerlich, and Wolfgang C. Müller, eds., 1995. *Die Politiker*. Vienna: Manz.

Engelmann, Frederick C. 1962. "Haggling for the Equilibrium: The Renegotiation of the Austrian Coalition." *American Political Science Review* 56: 651-662.

___. 1966. "Austria: The Pooling of Opposition," in Robert A.Dahl, ed., *Political Opposition in Western Democracies*. Pp. 260-283. New Haven: Yale University Press.

Ermacora, Felix. 1978. "Politische Aspekte der Verfassungsentwicklung in Österreich seit 1970," in Andreas Khol et al., eds., *Österreichisches Jahrbuch für Politik 1976*. Pp. 59-84. Vienna: Verlag für Geschichte und Politik.

Fischer, Heinz. 1991. "Das Parlament," in Herbert Dachs et al., eds., *Handbuch des politischen Systems Österreichs*. Pp. 88-109. Vienna: Manz.

Gerlich, Peter. 1973. *Parlamentarische Kontrolle im politischen System*, Vienna: Springer.

___. 1994. "Österreichs politisches System und die Europäische Union," in Peter Gerlich, and Heinrich Neisser, eds., *Europa als Herausforderung*. Pp. 7-41. Vienna: Signum.

Gerlich, Peter, and Wolfgang C. Müller. 1988. "Austria: Routine and Ritual," in Jean Blondel, and Ferdinand Müller-Rommel, eds., *Cabinets in Western Europe*. Pp. 138-150. London: Macmillan.

Gerlich, Peter, Wolfgang C. Müller, and Wilfried Philipp. 1988. "Potentials and Limitations of Executive Leadership: the Austrian Cabinet since 1945." *European Journal of Political Research* 16: 191-205.

Heinrich, Hans-Georg, and Manfried Welan. 1991. "Gerichtsbarkeit, Verwaltungs- und Verfassungsgericht," in Herbert Dachs et al., eds., *Handbuch des politischen Systems Österreichs*. Pp. 145-155. Vienna: Manz.

Hengstschläger, Johannes. 1982. *Der Rechnungshof*. Berlin: Duncker & Humblot.

Kathrein, Irmgard. 1986. "Der Bundesrat," in Herbert Schambeck, ed., *Österreichs Parlamentarismus*. Pp. 337-401. Berlin: Duncker & Humblot.

Keller, Heinz. 1974. "Die Justiz als Staat im Staate?," in Heinz Fischer, ed., *Das politische System Österreichs*. Pp. 317-336. Vienna: Europaverlag.

Kirchheimer, Otto. 1957. "The Waning of Opposition in Parliamentary Regimes." *Social Research* 24: 127-156.

Kneucker, Roul F. 1973. "Austria: An Administrative State." *Österreichische Zeitschrift für Politikwissenschaft* 2: 95-127.

___. 1981. "Public Administration: The Business of Government," in Kurt Steiner, ed., *Modern Austria*. Pp. 261-278. Palo Alto: SPOSS.

Koja, Friedrich. 1967. "Der Parlamentarismus in Österreich." *Zeitschrift für Politik* 14: 333-351.

___. 1969. "Die Vertretung der Länderinteressen im Bund," in *Bundesstaat auf der Waage*. Pp. 9-31. Salzburg: Pustet.

Kollmann, Eric C. 1973. *Theodor Körner. Militär und Politik*. Vienna: Verlag für Geschichte und Politik.

Leser, Norbert. 1963. "Recht und Gesellschaft," in Jacques Hannak, ed., *Bestandsaufnahme Österreich 1945-1963*. Pp. 186-230. Vienna: Forum Verlag.

Luther, Kurt Richard. 1986. "The Revitalization of Austrian Federalism," in Michael Burgess, ed., *Federalism and Federation in Western Europe*. Pp. 154-186. London: Croom Helm.

___. 1987. "Austria's Future and Waldheim's Past: The Significance of the 1986 Elections." *West European Politics* 10(3): 376-399.

___. 1989. "Dimensions of Party System Change: The Case of Austria." *West European Politics* 12(4): 3-27.

___. 1991. "Bund-Länder Beziehungen: Formal- und Realverfassung," in Herbert Dachs et al., eds., *Handbuch des politischen Systems Österreichs*. Pp. 816-826. Vienna: Manz.

Markel, Ernst. 1984. "Sicherung der richterlichen Unabhängigkeit." *Österreichische Richterzeitung* 62: 162-169.

Meth-Cohn, Delia, and Wolfgang C. Müller. 1991. "Leaders Count: The Austrian Election of October 1990." *West European Politics* 14(2): 183-188.

Michalitsch, Michael. 1990. "Die geänderte, realverfassungsändernde Rechtsprechung des Verfassungsgerichtshofes," in Andreas Khol et al., eds., *Österreichisches Jahrbuch für Politik 1989*. Pp. 197-207. Vienna: Verlag für Geschichte und Politik.

Müller, Wolfgang C. 1986. "Vom Zusammenhang von politischen Entscheidungsmustern und Politikergebnissen am Beispiel der Witwerpension," in Andreas Khol et al., eds., *Österreichisches Jahrbuch für Politik 1985*. Pp. 397-416. Vienna: Verlag für Geschichte und Politik.

___. 1988. "Die neue große Koalition in Österreich." *Österreichische Zeitschrift für Politikwissenschaft* 17: 321-347.

___. 1989. "Party Patronage in Austria," in Anton Pelinka, and Fritz Plasser, eds., *The Austrian Party System*. Pp. 327-356. Boulder: Westview Press.

___. 1991. "Persönlichkeitswahl bei der Nationalratswahl 1990," in Andreas Khol et al., eds., *Österreichisches Jahrbuch für Politik 1990*. Pp. 261-282. Vienna: Verlag für Geschichte und Politik.

___. 1991a. "Regierung und Kabinettsystem," in Herbert Dachs et al., eds., *Handbuch des politischen Systems Österreichs*. Pp. 110-125. Vienna: Manz.

___. 1992. "Austrian Governmental Institutions: Do They Matter?" *West European Politics* 15(1): 99-131.

___. 1993. "Executive-Legislative Relations in Austria: 1945-1992." *Legislative Studies Quarterly* 18: 467-494.

___. 1994. "Models of Government and the Austrian Cabinet," in Michael Laver, and Kenneth A. Shepsle, eds., *Cabinet Ministers and Parliamentary Government*. Pp. 15-34. Cambridge: Cambridge University Press.

Müller, Wolfgang C., and Heidemarie A. Bubendorfer. 1989. "Rule-Breaking in the Austrian Cabinet: Its Management and Its Consequences." *Corruption and Reform* 4: 131-145.

Naßmacher, Karl-Heinz. 1968. *Das österreichische Regierungssystem*. Cologne: Westdeutscher Verlag.

Neisser, Heinrich. 1974. "Die Rolle der Bürokratie," in Heinz Fischer, ed., *Das politische System Österreichs*. Pp. 233-270. Vienna: Europaverlag.

___. 1991. "Die Verwaltung," in Herbert Dachs et al., eds., *Handbuch des politischen Systems Österreichs*. Pp. 132-144. Vienna: Manz.

___. 1994. "Parlamentsreform und EU-Beitritt," in Peter Gerlich, and Heinrich Neisser, eds., *Europa als Herausforderung*. Pp. 43-69. Vienna: Signum.

Nevlacsil, Anton. 1984. "Regierung und Opposition im parlamentarischen Prozeß," in Andreas Khol et al., eds., *Österreichisches Jahrbuch für Politik 1983*. Pp. 209-257. Vienna: Verlag für Geschichte und Politik.

___. 1987. "Der Nationalrat in der XVI.GP," in Andreas Khol et al., eds., *Österreichisches Jahrbuch für Politik 1986*. Pp. 465-494. Vienna: Verlag für Geschichte und Politik.

___. 1991. "Der Nationalrat in der XVII. GP," in Andreas Khol et al., eds., *Österreichisches Jahrbuch für Politik 1990*. Pp. 431-459. Vieanna: Verlg für Geschichte und Politik.

Nick, Rainer. 1989. "The States and the Austrian Party System," in Anton Pelinka, and Fritz Plasser, eds., *The Austrian Party System*. Pp. 309-326. Boulder: Westview Press.

Öhlinger, Theo. 1995. "Das Scheitern der Bundesstaatsreform," in Andreas Khol et al., eds., *Österreichisches Jahrbuch für Politik 1994*. Pp. 543-558. Vienna: Verlag für Geschichte und Politik.

Pelinka, Anton, ed., 1995. *EU-Referendum*. Vienna: Signum.

___, and Manfried Welan. 1971. *Demokratie und Verfassung in Österreich*. Vienna: Europa Verlag.

Pernthaler, Peter. 1992. "Föderalistische Verfassungsreform: Ihre Voraussetzungen und Wirkungsbedingungen in Österreich." *Österreichische Zeitschrift für Politikwissenschaft* 21: 365-388.

___, and Gert Schernthanner. 1995. "Bundesstaatsreform 1994," in Andreas Khol et al., eds., *Österreichisches Jahrbuch für Politik 1994*. Pp. 559-595. Vienna: Verlag für Geschichte und Politik.

Pesendorfer, Wolfgang. 1986. *Der Landeshauptmann*. Vienna: Springer.

Preston, R. 1957. "Austrian Parliamentary Democracy." *Parliamentary Affairs* 10: 344-352.

Pulzer, Peter. 1969. "The Legitimizing Role of Political Parties: The Second Austrian Republic." *Government and Opposition* 4: 324-344.

Rudzio, Wolfgang. 1971. "Entscheidungszentrum Koalitionsausschuß--Zur Realverfassung Österreichs unter der großen Koalition." *Politische Vierteljahresschrift* 12: 87-118.

Secher, Herbert P. 1958. "Coalition Government: The Case of the Second Austrian Republic." *American Political Science Review* 52: 791-809.

___. 1960. "Representative Democracy or 'Chamber State': The Ambiguous Role of Interest Groups in Austrian Politics." *Western Political Quarterly* 13: 890-909.

Stadler, Karl R. 1982. *Adolf Schärf. Mensch--Politiker--Staatsmann*. Vienna: Europaverlag.

Steiner, Kurt. 1972. *Politics in Austria*. Boston: Little, Brown and Co.

Ucakar, Karl. 1985. *Demokratie und Wahlrecht in Österreich*. Vienna: Verlag für Gesellschaftskritik.

Walter, Robert. 1969. "Der Bundesrat," in *Bundesstaat auf der Waage*. Pp. 199-290. Salzburg: Pustet.

___. 1972. *Österreichisches Bundesverfassungsrecht*. Vienna: Manz.

Weber, Karl. 1987. *Die mittelbare Bundesverwaltung*. Vienna: Braumüller.

___. 1992. "Macht im Schatten?" *Österreichische Zeitschrift für Politikwissenschaft* 21: 405-418.

Weissensteiner, Friedrich, ed., 1982. *Die österreichischen Bundespräsidenten*. Vienna: Österreichischer Bundesverlag.

Welan, Manfried. 1974. "Der Verfassungsgerichtshof--eine Nebenregierung?," in Heinz Fischer, ed., *Das politische System Österreichs*. Pp. 271-315. Vienna: Europaverlag.

___. 1976. "Die Kanzlerdemokratie in Österreich," in Andreas Khol, Robert Prantner, and Alfred Stirnemann, eds., *Um Parlament und Partei*. Pp. 169-180. Graz: Styria.

___. 1986. *Das österreichische Staatsoberhaupt*. Vienna: Verlag für Geschichte und Politik.

___. 1988. "Constitutional Review and Legislation in Austria," in Christine Landfried, ed., *Constitutional Review and Legislation*. Pp. 63-80. Baden-Baden: Nomos.

___. 1992. *Der Bundespräsident. Kein Kaiser in der Republik*. Vienna: Böhlau.

Welan, Manfried, and Heinrich Neisser. 1971. *Der Bundeskanzler im österreichischen Verfassungsgefüge*. Vienna: Hollinek.

Werndl, Josef. 1984. *Die Kompetenzverteilung zwischen Bund und Ländern*. Vienna: Braumüller.

Widder, Helmut. 1979. *Parlamentarische Strukturen im politischen System*. Berlin: Duncker & Humblot.

___. 1986. "Der Nationalrat," in Herbert Schambeck, ed., *Österreichs Parlamentarismus. Werden und System*. Pp. 261-336. Berlin: Duncker & Humblot.

___. 1991. "Rechnungshof und Volksanwaltschaft," in Herbert Dachs et al., eds., *Handbuch des politischen Systems Österreichs*. Pp. 156-165. Vienna: Manz.

Wittmann, Heinz. 1978. "Regierung und Opposition im parlamentarischen Prozeß," in Andreas Khol et al., eds., *Österreichisches Jahrbuch für Politik 1977.* Pp. 21-90. Vienna: Verlag für Geschichte und Politik.

___ . 1980. "Regierung und Opposition im parlamentarischen Prozeß--Struktur und Arbeit des Parlaments in der XIV. Gesetzgebungsperiode 1975-1979," in Andreas Khol et al., eds., *Österreichisches Jahrbuch für Politik 1979.* Pp. 39-68. Vienna: Verlag für Geschichte und Politik.

Wohnout, Helmut. 1995. "Politische Bilanz der XVIII. Gesetzgebungsperiode des Nationalrates," in Andreas Khol et al., eds., *Österreichisches Jahrbuch für Politik 1994.* Pp. 737-768. Vienna: Verlag für Geschichte und Politik.

Wögerbauer, Harald. 1993. "Die Rechnungshofreformen und die Wahl des Rechnungshofpräsidenten im Lichte der Erfahrungen des Jahres 1992," in Andreas Khol et al., eds., *Österreichisches Jahrbuch für Politik 1992.* Pp. 415-430. Vienna: Verlag für Geschichte und Politik.

3

Political Parties

Wolfgang C. Müller

Introduction

Austrian political parties have long been recognized internationally to have a number of specific features. These include their historical continuity through all the upheavals of the 20th century (including several regime changes), their enormous size, their penetration of civil society and the state. The party system has also received attention for its stability and concentration. Moreover, Austria is a particular good example of a "party state," with all elections (with the partial exception of local elections in small communities) being structured by parties and all office holders in the representative institutions being party nominees and, in almost all cases, also party members and functionaries.

This chapter reviews these and other features over the post-war period, with an emphasis on the 1980s and 1990s. In this period, many features of Austrian party politics went through a thorough change, which tended to diminish Austrian peculiarities. Nevertheless, from a comparative perspective, Austrian party politics still bears unique features, which makes it interesting for the comparativist.

The next section of this chapter introduces the parties that were relevant during the post-war period and outlines their development. A section then follows that briefly summarizes important changes in the party environment that took place during the post-war period, in particular over the last two decades, which constitute challenges to the parties. The bulk of this chapter then analyzes the development of parties and the party system along several dimensions. The conclusion draws together the various strands and tries to assess the extent of change in Austrian party politics.

Origin and History of the Parties

Lipset and Rokkan (1967, 50) concluded their famous survey of Western European cleavages by stating that "the party systems of the 1960s reflect, with few but significant exceptions, the cleavage structures of the 1920s" (see also Bartolini and Mair 1990). A similar position, although related exclusively to Austria, had been adopted more than a decade earlier by the historian Adam Wandruszka. He viewed continuity as the dominant feature in the history of Austrian parties, or *Lager* (camps). Since 1918 the Catholic-conservative, the Socialist and the German-national-liberal *Lager* remained so stable throughout all the upheavals "that one could quite easily speak of a 'natural or God-given division of Austria into three groups'" (Wandruszka 1954, 291). For most observers this still seemed to apply to Austria as late as the early 1980s (Plasser et al. 1987).

The traditional cleavages between the three *Lager* were socio-economic and religious. While the socio-economic cleavage divided the Socialist *Lager* from the other two, the religious cleavage separated the Catholic-conservatives and the other two *Lager*.

The central institution of the Socialist *Lager* in the Monarchy and the inter-war period was the Socialdemocratic Workers' Party (*Sozial-Demokratische Arbeiterpartei, SDAP*). It was founded in 1889 by uniting the different tendencies of the workers' movement at the Hainfeld party congress. After years of opposition, it took the lead in setting up the Republic between 1918 and 1920. For the remainder of the First Republic, the *SDAP* was reduced to being a permanent opposition party. Despite the foundation of the Communist Party of Austria (KPÖ) in 1918, the supremacy of the Social Democrats in representing the Austrian left was never in question. Only after the breakdown of Austrian democracy in 1934 and the banning of all organizations of the left did the KPÖ gain in relative importance. Also in 1934, the Revolutionary Socialists (*Revolutionäre Sozialisten, RS*) established themselves as a break-away party of the *SDAP*, mainly consisting of its left wing and its younger members. The KPÖ and the *RS* engaged in clandestine activities for which these parties, with their cell structure, were better suited than the classical mass party *SDAP*. In 1945, the representatives of the *SDAP* and the *RS* reunited and formed the Socialist Party of Austria (*Sozialistische Partei Österreichs*, SPÖ), which is the official successor to the *SDAP*. Although the KPÖ was stronger than ever before in its history at the beginning of the Second Republic, the supremacy of the SPÖ within the left was not in question. The close relationship between the KPÖ and the Soviet occupation power helped the KPÖ to participate in the government (until 1947) and to build up a relatively large party organization, but it also made the party unpopular. After the withdrawal of the occupation forces in 1955 the KPÖ lost its parliamentary representation and since 1966, when it recommended to its adherents to vote for the SPÖ, it has ceased to be an electorally relevant party by any standards (Ehmer 1991). In contrast to the inter-war period, the Social Democrats have become a permanent government party, having spent only four years in opposition so far. In 1991, whilst maintaining its initials, the SPÖ changed its name into *Sozialdemokratische Partei Österreichs.*[1]

In the Monarchy and the First Republic, the party political expression of the Catholic-conservative *Lager* was the Christian Social Party (*Christlichsoziale Partei, CSP*) (Boyer 1981; Pulzer 1988). Although the bishops were sceptical initially about this party and thought the interests of the Catholic Church could best be served by a special relationship with the House of Habsburg and the aristocracy, it soon became the political arm of the Church who wanted to defend its strong position in schools and society against the onslaught of the liberals and, later, the Social Democrats. During the First Republic, in various coalitions (first with the *SDAP* and then with the parties of the German-national-liberal *Lager*), the *CSP* was the permanent governing party. In 1933 the *CSP* leadership abandoned its commitment to parliamentary democracy and in 1934 set up a dictatorship, the self-styled corporatist *Ständestaat.* While the parties of the left were outlawed, the *CSP* dissolved itself. When democracy was reestablished after the period of Nazi rule (1938-45), the Catholic-conservative *Lager* did not revive the *CSP* but founded the Austrian People's Party (*Österreichische Volkspartei,* ÖVP). The ÖVP initially claimed to be a new party rather than the successor of the *CSP.* It wanted to distinguish itself from the *CSP* in particular by an unambiguous commitment to parliamentary democracy and by bearing no confessional label, thus appealing to a broader constituency. Indeed, the ÖVP managed to integrate large parts of the Agrarian League (*Landbund, LB*), which had been the farmers' party of the German-national-liberal *Lager* during the First Republic. Though the continuities of the ÖVP with the *CSP* were overwhelming in terms of personnel, social structure of members and voters, as well as ideology, the new concept of a non-socialist catch-all party proved to be successful: until 1970 the ÖVP was the strongest party electorally and the dominant force within the old grand coalition with the SPÖ. Since 1970, however, the ÖVP has faced a series of electoral defeats at the national level and spent seventeen years in opposition. Since 1987 it has been in government as the SPÖ's junior partner in the new grand coalition, at the price however of losing further electoral support.[2]

The third *Lager* is German-national-liberal. The combination of liberalism and (at times extreme right-wing) nationalism is due to historical developments, the most important of which was the emergence of nationalism as a major cleavage in the multi-national Habsburg monarchy in the second half of the 19th century. Once a liberal movement in the revolution of 1848, it increasingly stressed its German-National side during the nationality conflict later on. This *Lager* expressed itself in a variety of parties. In the First Republic there existed the Greater German People's Party (*Großdeutsche Volkspartei, GDVP*) and the *LB*, both of which participated in numerous coalitions with the *CSP*. While the *LB* increasingly leaned towards the *CSP*, the *GDVP* was undermined by the rise of the Nazi party, to which most of the German-Nationals deserted. In 1945 the *LB* was not revived and, because of denazification rules, the German-Nationals did not have a genuine representation by a political party of their own. In 1949 however, the League of Independents (*Verband der Unabhängigen*, VdU) was founded for that purpose (Riedelsperger 1978). Though under liberal leadership, it appealed to the German-National constituency by its main programmatic issue, namely the abolition of denazification rules. After this was achieved and after the Allied occupation forces had left Austria, the VdU was replaced by the Freedom Party of Austria (*Freiheitliche Partei Österreichs*, FPÖ), which mainly comprised the core of the German-National *Lager*, i.e. those who had been active in Nazi organizations. The FPÖ started as a ghetto party but gradually managed to move towards the center and to become acceptable to the other parties. This resulted in government participation (with the SPÖ) between 1983 and 1986. Since then the FPÖ, under a new leadership, has assumed the role of a populist protest party. This has improved its electoral fortunes but until now excluded it from government participation at the national level.[3] Most recently, the FPÖ has moved further to the right again. As a consequence, its liberal wing broke away in 1993, constituting a new party, the Liberal Forum (*Liberales Forum*, LF).

In the 1980s the Greens came to supplement the Austrian party system. In 1986 the most important green groupings joined forces for the general election and established themselves in parliament. The development of a common party organization, the Green Alternative (*Grüne Alternative*, GA), was carried out only after winning parliamentary representation. One of the more important members of the electoral alliance however, the United Greens of Austria (*Vereinte Grüne Österreichs*, VGÖ) did not integrate itself into the new party as a group. The VGÖ maintained a seperate party organization and constituted a relevant competition for the GA in the 1990 parliamentary election.[4] In 1993, attempts to reunite the two green parties almost succeeded until it turned out that the VGÖ had not only approached the GA but also the FPÖ. This led the GA's party executive to withdraw from the agreement with the VGÖ and provoked a serious split inside the VGÖ, with large parts deserting to the GA. The 1994 elections demonstrated that the VGÖ has ceased to exist as a relatively viable party.

The Challenge to Political Parties

During the post-war period the environment of political parties has changed enormously.[5] The changes that have occurred include the following:

Changes in the citizenry. Economic change, including industrialization and the growth of the tertiary sector, has brought a thorough transformation of social structure and culture. Citizens have experienced unprecedented affluence, they enjoy higher education, more leisure time (and a greater range of respective offers) and better welfare services than ever before. In short, citizens' resources have expanded considerably during this period. Citizens' preferences have also changed. *Inter alia*, traditional bread-and-butter issues were supplemented by environmental concerns and the desire for increasing political participation.

Changes in the political community. In the first two post-war decades political parties and the interest groups linked to the major parties monopolized the channelling of demands to the political system. This monopoly has been increasingly undermined by alternative organizations and movements since the late 1960s. These include citizen initiatives concerned with local issues such as preventing the construction of a specific road. Many of these local groups are loosely linked to social movements which promote broader goals, most importantly the ecology and anti-nuclear movement, the women's movement, the peace movement and the Third World movement (Gottweis 1991). These have more diffuse organizational structures, but nevertheless have been able to generate considerable political activism. Since the advent of social movements, politics is no longer an activity limited to professional politicians and the traditional organizations of representation.

Technological change. While technological change has been overwhelming in the post-war period, its genuinely political aspect consists in the transformation of the media system and the revolution in communication technologies. Changes in the mass media include the rise of TV and its establishment in the 1960s as the most important means of mass communication. More recently, the introduction of satellite and cable TV undermined the monopoly of the public broadcasting corporation. While the earlier of these changes constituted a challenge to the effectiveness of parties' communication styles, the latter is challenging their capacity to reach their audience at all.

Institutional change. The institutional framework in which political parties operate has changed considerably, if in a piecemeal fashion, in the post-war period. The role of political parties in Austrian politics has been affected by an expansion of direct democracy, a greater role for those governmental institutions where partisan control is relatively weak, and greater autonomy from party organizations for politicians in representative institutions. (See the chapter on "Political Institutions" in this volume and the section on the electoral system below.)

All these changes constitute challenges to traditional party politics. The bulk of this chapter will analyze how parties have responded to these challenges. In principle, they have three options: (1) remain passive and do nothing, (2) adapt to the changing environment, (3) try to control or manipulate environmental changes. The potential for control varies greatly according to the dimension of the party environment. Socio-economic and cultural change, for instance, are long-term and more difficult to control by political parties than the institutional framework under which they operate (Müller 1993b). Consequently, parties can be expected to try to adapt themselves to socio-economic, cultural and technological change. As to their institutional environment, however, parties may rather attempt to adapt it to their own needs rather than *vice versa*. Moreover, parties may try to use their capacity to manipulate the institutional environment to compensate for changes in the other dimensions, a possibility obviously reserved to only few parties who, as a result, enjoy a competitive advantage.

Legal and Financial Status of Parties

Legal regulation of parties [6]

Despite the fact that political parties have dominated Austrian politics since 1918, the foundation and life of party organizations outside parliament had not been subject to any specific legal regulations until 1975. Only one reference is made to them in the constitution as amended in 1929, and this is a negative one: the exclusion of party functionaries and employees from the Constitutional Court. However, courts and legal scholars have always argued that the existence of political parties was simply assumed by the constitution and necessary for its functioning. According to this interpretation, parties did not have to conform to any of the organizational forms defined by law. The Party Law of 1975 provided a new legal basis for political parties. Its adoption was not due to the concerns of legal scholars, who for a long time had been demanding an explicit legal basis for political parties, but came as a necessary prerequisite for the introduction of state financing for party organizations. All relevant regulations of their legal status are contained in its first article, which has constitutional status. It states that "The existence and variety of political parties are essential parts of the democratic order of the Republic of Austria." Without claiming to define fully the functions of political parties, Article I especially mentions their participation in the *politische Willensbildung* (i.e., to serve as channels of political expression). According to this law, political parties may be freely founded as long as no other legal provisions with constitutional status are violated. (In fact there is only one: the prohibition of Nazi activities.) Founding a party only requires depositing the party statute with the Department of the Interior, with the latter having no legal right to reject that statute. Only the courts may determine whether a party violates constitutional law (and may consequently outlaw it). The activities of parties may not be restricted by ordinary laws.

In 1975 all parties, by depositing their statutes with the Department of the Interior, changed their status in order to fall under this new liberal law and, in particular, to become eligible for state funding. In fact, some associations disguise themselves as parties because of the advantages of being a party rather than an association (*Verein*) which, unlike political parties, is subject to oversight and regulation by the authorities. Before 1975, the actual legal form of the existing parties differed and depended de facto on political power relations. Three parties, the SPÖ, the ÖVP and the KPÖ, were sure that they could afford to have an extra-constitutional status. They had signed the declaration of independence from Nazi Germany in April 1945 and thus had founded the Second Republic. Later these three parties were the only ones to be licensed by the Allied powers. As opposed to these "historic parties," more recently founded parties such as the VdU and the FPÖ assumed the legal form of an association (*Verein*) in order to avoid any risk resulting from their extra-constitutional status. Thus for the "historic parties," the party law did not change the status quo, but it made life easier for the others.

Of course, the party law is not the only statute which is relevant for political parties. The constitution, the electoral law (see below), the parliamentary rules of procedure and all statutes which affect the economic activities of political parties may prove relevant. The parliamentary *Fraktion* is briefly mentioned in the constitution. Since 1961, the main legal source of the parliamentary *Fraktion* has been the parliamentary rules of procedure. MPs (members of parliament) of the same electoral party may form a *Fraktion* which is officially recognized (as a parliamentary *Klub*) when it has at least five MPs. This status opens access to parliamentary resources (finance, personnel, office space) and parliamentary committees. MPs of different electoral parties may form a common parliamentary *Klub* only if the majority of the *Nationalrat* accepts it. Parliamentary activity beyond voting and speechmaking requires that MPs belong to a parliamentary *Fraktion*. Resources for individual MPs were not provided before 1992.

State subsidies for parties

State subsidies started to be given to the parliamentary *Fraktions* in the early 1960s, when these were the only party institutions positively recognized by law. However, amounts remained small, not even enough to provide for the minimum requirements of a parliamentary *Fraktion*. These resources were increased by unanimous decisions of the parliament once its role in the political process increased. State financing of the party organizations had been under discussion since 1959, but it was not implemented until the 1970s. The first step was made in 1972 when the training of party activists and functionaries was transferred from the party organizations themselves to the parties' newly created political education institutions, which were now funded by the state. Since this form of public funding was accepted by the media and the public, in 1975 the parties had enough self-confidence to introduce public financing for themselves. Their need for additional finance resulted from the new and expensive campaign techniques which began to spread in the late 1960s, and from the need to modernize and professionalize the party organizations. The more immediate cause for the parties' desire to fill their coffers with public money was a series of five cost-intensive national election campaigns in the first half of the 1970s. In order to introduce state funding, they first had to regulate their legal status (see above). This, however, was only a by-product of the desire for public money. Consequently, only one paragraph of the party law is devoted to the legal status of parties while thirteen others are concerned with financial aspects. Again political controversy was avoided and the decision was made unanimously. In order to encourage positive press coverage the Party Law was accepted by parliament at the same time as a rather generous scheme for press subsidies.

Since 1975, all parties that poll more than one percent of the vote have been entitled to receive state party finance in election years while the parties represented in the *Nationalrat* are entitled to receive these funds permanently. Parties with at least five MPs receive a fixed amount of money, the remaining funds are distributed according to the parties' share of the vote. Public party finance increased considerably in real terms since the 1970s. It is currently the single most important source of income for all parties and by far the dominant one for the FPÖ, the Greens and the Liberal Forum. In 1992 public party finance, consisting of contributions to the party organizations, the parliamentary *Fraktions* and the political education institutions, amounted to more than half a billion Schillings at the national level (Müller 1994a).

Not all decisions concerning public party finance were made unanimously. Controversies arose concerning the taxation of donations, the publication of the names of donors, the size of the fixed amount which goes to each parliamentary party irrespective of its size and, more recently, the size of public party finance itself. Until the 1970s donations to political parties were tax deductible; this proved favorable for parties with support from business. This tax privilege was abolished under the Social Democratic government in the 1970s. The SPÖ also required the publication of the names of donors but later, under the pressure of both trade unions and the opposition parties, gave in on this issue. Now a party is only required to report donors' names to the president of the audit office who, in the case of suspected corruption, can investigate. Controversies about the size of the fixed amount of public money which goes to each parliamentary party have emerged over its variation from Sch 4 million in 1975 to 14 million in 1982 and back to 3 million since 1987. The higher the fixed amount, the better off the small parties are. As long as the FPÖ was required as an actual or potential coalition partner by the SPÖ, the dominating party during the relevant period, the fixed amount increased. After the grand coalition of SPÖ and ÖVP was formed in 1987 and the Greens had established themselves in parliament, the fixed amount was reduced to its all-time low. On the one hand there was no intention of favoring the FPÖ, which was not required for coalitions any longer under its new aggressive leadership; on the other hand, maintaining the old rules would have led to a substantial reduction of state funding for SPÖ and ÖVP since now a fourth party was represented in parliament (Sickinger and Nick 1990, 76-78). Of course, the major parties could have solved the latter problem by increasing the total amount of state party finance, but this did not seem appropriate at a time of budgetary restraint. More recently, the FPÖ has criticised and voted against the further increase of public party finance in the form of campaign subsidies. The governing parties responded by introducing a clause that parties do not automatically get this money, but have to demand it formally before the election--something that the FPÖ indeed refrained from doing once (Müller 1992a).

Until 1992, all public funds were allocated to institutions (the party organization, the parliamentary *Fraktion* and the political education institution). Individual parliamentary candidates or MPs did not receive public funds before 1992. In that year a new law provided individual MPs with financial resources to be used for personal staff. Each MP can spend a relatively modest amount for this purpose. The law leaves it up to the individual MP how many staff members he or she wants to hire and whether these work in parliament or the electoral district.

The principle of allocating funds only to organizations still applies at the *Land* (regional) level, where public funds are allocated to the *Land* party organizations, the *Land* diet *Fraktionen*, the regional party press, etc. In contrast to public party finance at the national level, which in its entirety is based on specific laws, several of the *Land* subsidies to parties have been granted on the basis of ad hoc decisions by the respective *Land* diet (i.e. regional parliament) or *Land* government and thus have received less publicity (Dachs 1986; 1993). The *Land* level, however, is of greater importance than the national level. Between 1979 and 1990, the *Länder* spent almost three times as much on political parties than the central state (despite having less than half the total budget) (Dachs 1986; 1993; Müller 1992a; 1994a). Additional public funds for political parties are provided at the local level. No systematic information is available on this, but it can be assumed that it is considerably less important than public party finance at the national and *Land* levels.

The Electoral System

In order to be listed on the ballot sheet, an electoral party must be supported by the signatures of a number of voters specified by the electoral law and must contribute to the costs of the election. The number of signatures for a nation-wide candidacy has varied from 2,500 (1945 - 58) to 2,800 (since 1971) to 5,000 (1959 - 70). The signatures must be made in the presence of the electoral authorities. Alternatively a candidacy can also be supported by three MPs since 1969. The financial contribution was introduced along with official ballots in 1959; these relieved the parties from printing and distributing their own ballots, which had been quite expensive. At that time a nation-wide candidacy cost Sch 50,000, since 1971 54,000. This fee is also meant to avoid candidacies which are not serious.

The constitution only specifies that elections at all levels have to be general, equal, free and secret. All the other provisions regarding elections are contained in ordinary statutes. They can therefore be altered by a simple parliamentary majority as long as constitutional principles are not violated. Elections to the first chamber of parliament, the *Nationalrat*, are to be held every four years or earlier if the *Nationalrat* so decides.[7] Voters are automatically registered on the basis of their declaration of residence. Voting in *Nationalrat* elections can be made compulsory by *Land* statute, a possibility used by three *Länder*. Since 1945, the voting age has been lowered three times, from age twenty-one (1945-49) to twenty (1949-68) to nineteen (1968-92) to eighteen (since 1992). Other changes to the electoral law included the possibility to vote at places other than where one is registered, even abroad (since 1990).

The requirement of equality in elections has been interpreted as necessitating some form of proportional representation. While respecting this principle, several changes to the electoral law have been made since 1945. The most important of them affected the mechanism by which votes are translated into seats. Accordingly, the post-war period can be sub-divided into three phases.

From 1945 until 1970, twenty-five electoral districts existed. 165 seats were distributed among the parties participating in the election in two stages, the first of which operated within the electoral districts. In the second round the electoral districts were aggregated into four units and the unused votes entered the second stage of seat distribution, provided that the respective parties had received at least one seat in the first stage (a *Grundmandat*). Three aspects tended to make this electoral system a *relatively* "strong" one (cf. Sartori 1986). First, the electoral system worked against small parties since it included a substantial threshold for parliamentary representation by the requirement to win a seat in at least one of the twenty-five relatively small electoral districts. This resulted in parties failing to win parliamentary representation despite the fact that they had received more than 140,000 votes, while a seat for the major parties corresponded to only about 25,000 votes (Müller 1991b). Second, because of the constitutional principle that seats be distributed among electoral districts on the basis of inhabitants rather than voters, the electoral system contained a bias in favor of rural areas (and hence the ÖVP), which as a rule include a higher proportion of children. Third, the fact that the seats distributed in the first stage required a smaller number of votes than those distributed in the second stage[8] favored the big parties since they received a higher proportion of their seats in the first stage. This electoral system thus served the interests of the two major parties, effectively shielding them against competitors, and the ÖVP in particular, which owed its plurality in 1953 and 1959 and its majority in 1966 to the electoral system.

In 1970, the SPÖ and FPÖ joined forces to pass a new electoral law which became effective for the first time in 1971. The number of electoral districts was reduced to nine, identical with the *Länder*. The number of seats was increased from 165 to 183 and the electoral districts were aggregated into only two units in the second stage of seat distribution.

Not surprisingly, this reform benefitted the two parties that had introduced it and also new parties (which faced the same problem as the FPÖ). It first lowered the threshold of representation by reducing the number of electoral districts and increasing the number of seats. Second, it reduced the importance of inhabitants (rather than voters) by combining rural and urban areas in larger electoral districts. Third, it removed the advantage for those parties which receive a larger proportion of their seats in the first stage of seat distribution (i.e., the big parties) by making these seats more expensive in terms of votes.[9]

In 1992, the SPÖ and ÖVP, which have been governing together since 1987, introduced a new electoral law. It sub-divided the nine electoral districts into forty-three regional electoral districts (*Regional-Wahlkreise*). The seats are distributed among the candidates and parties participating in the election in three stages. In the first stage, seats are distributed at the regional district level. In the second stage, seats are distributed at the *Land* level. The cost of seats in these two stages is the same and is calculated for each *Land*. In the third stage, seats are distributed at the national level. Parties take part in the second and third stage only if they have won at least one seat at the regional electoral district level or have received at least 4 percent of the valid votes nationwide. Seats already distributed at the regional and *Land* levels are deducted from the number of seats calculated at the national level. The 4 percent-clause has raised the threshold for parliamentary representation and thus tends to favour those parties which have no problem in crossing this mark. The 1992 electoral system was first used in the 1994 general election.

Electoral laws are also important for political parties because they determine which candidates will take seats in parliament. In a pure list system, all discretionary power rests with the party organization; voters of a particular party have no influence over who should represent them in parliament. This was the case in 1945. In 1949, the possibility of intra-party preference voting was introduced. Until 1970, a potentially very powerful system, i.e. a system which gave relatively small numbers of voters the opportunity to change the party lists, was in operation but was little used. In 1971, it was replaced by a system in which the name of the preferred candidate has to be written on the ballot paper. To be elected, a candidate who is not ranked among the "eligible" places of the party list could be moved up by preference votes. This system proved relevant only once in electing a candidate to parliament (in 1983) (Müller 1984) and in 1990 was used partly to transform the parliamentary election into a chancellor election (Müller 1991; Müller and Plasser 1992). The preference voting system was changed in the 1992 electoral reform, the official goal of which was to personalize elections and hence to improve the relationship between citizens and their representatives. To win a seat at the regional electoral district level it is sufficient for a candidate to receive half as many preference votes as votes required for a seat, or to collect preference votes amounting to a sixth of the party vote, provided that the party received enough votes for a seat in this regional electoral district. In the 1994 election, fifteen candidates received enough preference votes in the regional electoral districts to win seats. However, all of them led their respective party lists. The preference vote therefore did not change anything (Müller and Scheucher 1995; 1995a). In summary, it can be said that until 1992 the party organization were almost free to determine who would obtain a seat in parliament. The 1992 reform certainly has reduced this capacity. It also has led to changes in the nomination of candidates, with the SPÖ and ÖVP holding primaries and all parties giving more weight to nominating popular candidates (Nick 1995).

Parties in the Electorate

The notion of *Lager* parties involved life-long loyalty of supporters and even inter-generational party loyalty. Ideology and subcultural ties ensured the cohesion and maintainance of the *Lager*. The subcultural ties were provided by the homogeneous social composition of each *Lager* and by the vast network of *Lager* organizations which made it possible to spend one's life within the boundaries of one particular *Lager* from the cradle to the grave.

All these factors weakened considerably over the post-war period. Changes in the social structure eroded the social bases of the *Lager* parties. The parties' core groups, the self-employed and the farmers in the case of the ÖVP and blue-collar workers in the case of the SPÖ, shrunk considerably. The share of white-collar workers in the population increased sharply. This last group is not inclined to a particular political party; it can be approached by both major parties, but also the FPÖ, the Greens and, more recently, the Liberal Forum. As a consequence of this development, political parties no longer have the clear class profile which was a prominent feature of *Lager* parties.

Figure 3.1 shows the social structure of declared party supporters in the 1980s and 1990s. The SPÖ still has more blue-collar workers among its voters than any other party, the ÖVP still appeals to the bulk of the farmers, and the self-employed and managers continue to vote for the ÖVP or FPÖ. Yet the original class profile of the parties is only rudimentarily reflected in the support structure of parties in the 1980s and 1990s.[10]

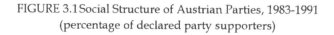

FIGURE 3.1 Social Structure of Austrian Parties, 1983-1991
(percentage of declared party supporters)

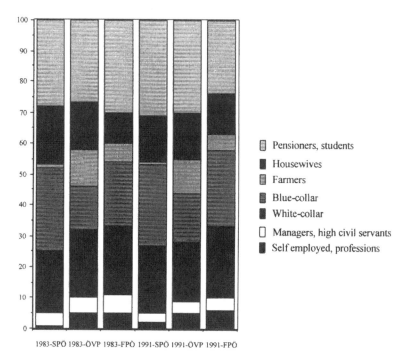

Sources: Representative surveys of the Dr. Fessel + GfK Institut.

Turning to the capacities of political parties to establish and maintain loyalty, we now look at party identification. According to figure 3.2 party identification declined considerably over the post-war period. While in 1954 almost three quarters of the population identified with a party, in 1994 only 44 percent of the respondents did so.

Electoral behaviour until the 1980s was remarkably stable. First, citizens went to the ballot box with a sense of civic duty: electoral participation was above 90 percent before 1990, though it had been gradually declining since the 1950s. Second, aggregate electoral behavior was stable with an average Pedersen index of aggregate electoral volatility of merely 2.9 percent for the 1953-83 period (Haerpfer 1991, 480). Accordingly, the strength of the parties did not experience dramatic changes (table 3.1). Third, electoral behavior was stable not only at the aggregate but also at the individual level (Blecha et al. 1964; Engelmann and Schwartz 1974a and 1974b; Haerpfer 1985).[11]

FIGURE 3.2 Party Identification, 1954-1992

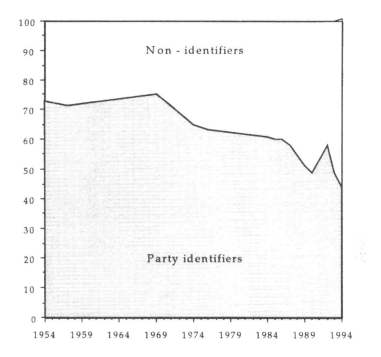

Sources: Plasser et al. 1992; Plasser and Ulram 1992; Plasser and Ulram 1995a.

In recent years, social structure changes, the decline of party identification and the ideological convergence of the post-war period (see below the section on Ideology) caught up with electoral behavior. First, participation continues to decline. In the 1994 election, only 81.9 percent of the potential electorate--4.2 percent less than in the previous election--went to the ballot box. Aggregate volatility changed more gradually since the beginning of the 1980s, with the Pedersen index reaching its all-time high of 14.2 percent in the 1994 election. Individual volatility peaked in the 1986, 1990 and 1994 elections with almost a sixth of the voters switching to another party since the previous election (table 3.2).

TABLE 3.1 Austrian Parliamentary Elections, 1945-1994

	Percentage of votes				Seats in Parliament[1]			
	ÖVP	SPÖ	FPÖ[2]	others[3]	ÖVP	SPÖ	FPÖ[2]	others[4]
1945	49.79	44.59	-	5.6	85	76	-	4
1949	44.03	38.71	11.66	5.6	77	67	16	5
1953	41.25	42.10	10.94	5.7	74	73	14	4
1956	45.95	43.04	6.52	4.5	82	74	6	3
1959	44.19	44.78	7.70	3.3	79	78	8	-
1962	45.43	43.99	7.04	3.5	81	76	8	-
1966	48.34	42.56	5.35	3.7	85	74	6	-
1970	44.69	48.42	5.52	1.4	78	81	6	-
1971	43.11	50.03	5.45	1.4	80	93	10	-
1975	42.94	50.42	5.40	1.2	80	93	10	-
1979	41.90	51.02	6.06	1.0	77	95	11	-
1983	43.22	47.65	4.98	4.2	81	90	12	-
1986	41.29	43.12	9.73	5.9	77	80	18	8
1990	32.06	42.80	16.63	8.5	60	80	33	10
1994	27.67	34.92	22.50	14.5	52	65	42	24

[1] 1945-70: 165 seats; 1971-90: 183 seats.
[2] Before 1956 VdU (*Verband der Unabhängigen*).
[3] 1945-62 mainly Communist Party (KPÖ; 1966 mainly *DFP*, a splinter group from the SPÖ; 1970-79 mainly Communist Party; 1983-90 mainly green parties; 1994 Greens (7.31%) and Liberal Forum (5.97%).
[4] 1945-56: Communist Party; 1986 and 1990: Green Alternative; 1994: Greens (13 seats) and Liberal Forum (11 seats).
Sources: Dachs et al. 1991; official result of 1994 election.

According to survey evidence, the share of voters stating that their choice of a party is based on ideological grounds dropped from 59 percent in 1972 to 37 percent in 1990 (Plasser et al. 1992, 24). In contrast, issues and personalities have won ground as factors influencing the voting decision. Another indicator of decreasing party loyalty is that about a sixth of the voters do not make their electoral decision until just before election day. Thus campaigns increasingly matter (Müller and Plasser 1992; Schaller and Vretscha 1995).

TABLE 3.2 Party Loyalty in Elections, 1979-1994

% of total electorate of parliamentary elections	1979	1983	1986	1990	1994
Turnout	92.2	91.3	90.5	86.1	81.9
Net-volatility (Pedersen index)	1.3	3.0	6.4	9.3	14.2
Floating voters[1]	7	10	16	17	19
Late deciders[2]	9	8	16	14	18

[1] Percentage of declared party-shifters on representative post-election survey, or exit poll.
[2] Percentage of those voters who made a definitive voting decision just before election day.
Sources: Haerpfer 1991; Plasser et al. 1992; Plasser and Ulram 1995a.

There is another factor which has contributed to recent changes in Austrian electoral behavior, i.e., growing disenchantment with the main political actors, the parties and politicians. Despite the peaceful development of post-war Austria, its good international standing, excellent economic performance and extensive welfare system, survey evidence shows that popular disenchantment with political parties and politicians increased since the late 1970s and has reached considerable levels (see table 3.3). It is worth noting that young people (under twenty-five years) demonstrate an even greater alienation from traditional party politics. This mood in the population, which has been nourished by a number of political scandals, has been skilfully exploited by the Greens and in particular by the FPÖ since 1986 under Haider.

TABLE 3.3 Popular Disenchantment with Parties and Politicians, 1979-1989

% of population who	1979 or 1981	1984 or 1985	1989
have recently been angry about political parties	43	68	-
agree that politicians are corrupt and open to bribery	38	49	69

Sources: Plasser et al. 1992, p. 27; Plasser and Ulram 1991, p. 136.

Party Organizations

Organizational structures

All Austrian parties have a relatively complex organizational structure. With the exception of the ÖVP, which has both a territorial and a functional organization, their organization is territorial and follows the state structure in its hierarchical levels, thus having local, district, *Land* and national organizations. In the SPÖ and FPÖ, internal representation is based first and foremost on members; in the ÖVP; it is based on both members and voters. Representation within the Greens is based on the population, giving each *Land* organization a share of the national congress delegates which is proportional to that *Land's* share in the Austrian population, irrespective of the organizational or electoral strength of the Greens in the *Land* concerned. To some extent the systems of representation in all parties reflect the federal character of Austria: as a rule each *Land* party organization has a fixed quota in many party bodies (Müller 1992a).

The most fundamental organizational feature distinguishing Austrian parties is the way in which members are organized: it is *indirect* in the case of the ÖVP and *direct* in the case of all other parties (Duverger 1954). In the SPÖ and the FPÖ the local party organizations recruit and organize the members. In the ÖVP this task is carried out by the three Leagues (*Bünde*) and three special organizations for women, young people and the elderly. All six have formally the same status and are referred to as the ÖVP's constituent organizations. In practice, however,

Political Parties

the three Leagues have been much more important than the others. They are the Farmers' League (*Bauernbund*, ÖBB), the Business League (*Wirtschaftsbund*, ÖWB) and the Workers' and Employees' League (*Arbeiter- und Angestelltenbund*, ÖAAB). They exist at all levels of the party, accounting for a high level of factionalism, but are also the main non-socialist players in the major interest groups. Winning up to 85 percent of the seats in the respective chambers, the Farmers' and the Business Leagues dominate two of the four large interest organizations set up by law with compulsory membership (see figure 3.3).

FIGURE 3.3 Organizational Links Between the Major Parties and Interest Groups in Austria

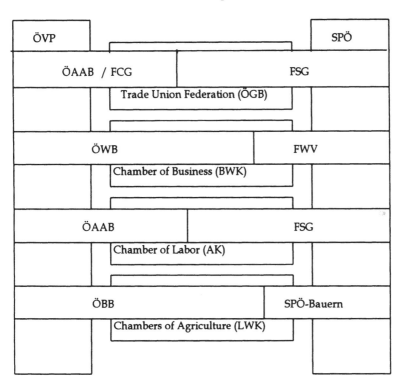

Abbreviations:
FCG/ Fraktion Christlicher Gewerkschafter/ Christian Trade Unionists
FSG/ Fraktion Sozialistischer Gewerkschafter/ Socialist Trade Unionists
FWV/ Freier Wirtschaftsverband/ Free Business Association
ÖAAB/ Österreichischer Arbeiter- und Angestelltenbund/ League of Workers and Employees
ÖBB/ Österreichischer Bauernbund/ Farmers' League
ÖWB/ Österreichischer Wirtschaftsbund/ Business League
SPÖ-Bauern/ SPÖ Farmers

For the Leagues, the ÖVP is one important instrument of their interest politics; however, there are others as well. The best way to serve these interests is a combination of party political and interest group activities. A precondition for both is the organizational capacity of the Leagues. Within the chambers this is the guarantee of electoral domination, within the party it is important for the power distribution between the Leagues. The intra-party strength of both Leagues rests on the number of members, their finacial capacity and the fact that they can rely on the large resources of the chamber organizations (Müller 1991a; Müller and Steininger 1994a and 1994b).

The organizational rationale of the Worker's and Employees' League is, in principle, the same as for the Farmers and the Business Leagues. There is, however, a major difference concerning its position within the respective chamber, the Chamber of Labor, and in the Trade Union Federation; in both organizations it occupies a permanent minority position vis-à-vis the socialist trade unionists (*Fraktion Sozialistischer Gewerkschafter, FSG*). Thus, the Workers' and Employees' League and its closely associated group in the Trade Union Federation, the Christian Trade Unionists (*Fraktion Christlicher Gewerkschafter, FCG*), have only little influence on these interest groups. Consequently, the *ÖAAB* is the most party-oriented of the Leagues--and since the vast majority of the electorate has become its potential clientele, it claims that what is good for this League is also good for the ÖVP. In practice, however, this League has been much more successful in appealing to civil servants than to blue- and white-collar workers in the private sector. Although the public sector grew considerably during the last decades, its members remained a minority, with demands quite different from those of the private sector.

According to figure 3.3, the position of the Socialist Trade Unionists (*FSG*), the SPÖ Farmers and the Free Business Association (*FWV*) within the SPÖ is similar to that of the Leagues within the ÖVP. However, this analogy is misleading. The FWV and the SPÖ Farmers are small organizations and are powerful neither within the party nor within the respective interest organizations. In contrast, the *FSG* is powerful within the party and dominates the two labor interest organizations but, unlike the ÖVP Leagues, it does not control party membership or have a majority in any of the party bodies. Not even together do the three socialist interest organizations exercise control over the party. Moreover, the *FSG* and the SPÖ traditionally had identical or similar positions on most issues. It is only since the second half of the 1980s that conflicts between the *FSG* and the SPÖ have become a more regular feature of Austrian politics.

The ÖVP belongs to the family of Christian Democratic parties. However, it has no official organizational relations with the Catholic Church, which in 1945 reconfirmed its 1933 decision to withdraw from party politics. Accordingly, priests are not allowed to accept political mandates and even the official lay organization, the *Katholische Aktion*, does not allow its functionaries to hold parliamentary seats at the national and *Land* levels or leading positions in political parties. At a more informal level, however, there are important links between the ÖVP and the Catholic Church. Many leading ÖVP politicians have held functions in the lay organizations of the Church before or after their political career (Steger 1985, 69). The Church provided organizational help for setting up the party in 1945 and supported the ÖVP in election campaigns until the 1960s. At that time the relationship between the Catholic Church and the ÖVP's main competitor, the SPÖ, normalized, with the SPÖ accepting many of the Church's demands on the state. The Catholic Church never practiced an "equidistance" with the two main political parties; however, when in the 1970s the SPÖ government's abortion and divorce reforms brought the party into open conflict with the Church, both sides took care not to let the conflict escalate into a *Kulturkampf* (Leitner 1988). The network of Catholic organizations united in the *Arbeitsgemeinschaft Katholischer Verbände* is very important for the ÖVP. They include the Catholic student fraternity (*Cartellverband der katholischen österreichischen Studenten-Verbindungen, CV*), to which many university graduates among the ÖVP leaders belong (Welan 1985), and a variety of social organizations, e.g., the Catholic Family Association (*Katholischer Familienverband*) and the largest federation of sport clubs, the *Turn- und Sportunion*. Although no formal organizational links between the party and these organizations exist, they de facto serve as a functional equivalent to the Social Democrats' extensive network of auxiliary organizations.

The network of SPÖ forefield organizations in the 1980s and 1990s comprised a membership of more than two million (Müller 1995). This is more than four times as much as the SPÖ's membership and considerably more than the party's number of voters. Although a great number of individuals are counted several times due to membership in more than one of the SPÖ's affiliated organizations, this figure indicates a high penetration of civil society by that party. In the case of the ÖVP, the constituent organizations fulfill many of the functions served by the SPÖ's affiliated organizations. Their total membership, again with considerable overlap, was about 1.2 million in the 1980s. Together with the parties' own affilliated organizations and the large network of Catholic organizations, the Catholic-conservative camp does not lag behind the socialist one in terms of societal penetration.

The FPÖ has its own forefield organizations and there is also a network of German-National cultural organizations. Their role in society is limited, but the latter in particular were occasionally influential in intra-party politics, resisting liberalism and holding up the flag of pan-Germanism. Currently the FPÖ is trying to change its party organization according to the rules of party competition in the 1990s. This meant that the word "party" was eliminated from the official name (now "The Freedomites") and a new type of associate membership was offered to all those who do not want to become members of a political party.

The large public sector provides plenty of opportunities for patronage by the two major parties, which are extensively used (Dobler 1983; Müller 1989). Jobs in the administration, schools, nationalized industries, state-controlled media and the central bank were traditionally filled with party loyalists, and party membership proved useful for getting public housing and government contracts.

In sum, civil society is heavily penetrated by political parties. Parties, or, more precisely, party factions, dominate the major socio-economic interest groups. Most of the other interest groups and cultural organizations belong to the forefield of political parties, mostly resulting in "red" and "black" organizations for the same purpose. While these organizations continue to dominate Austrian civil society, they have become less overtly partisan over the years.

The Greens started as the antithesis of "traditional" political parties (Dachs 1991). They carefully avoid the word "party" in favour of "movement" or just "the Greens" or "the Green Alternative." They also stress their openness, meaning that participation does not require formal membership (a *Parteibuch*) and the payment of a fixed membership fee. Internal democracy is claimed to be more substantive than in other parties. A more powerful and frequent party congress, strict rules of incompatability between different party functions and between party functions and elected offices, restrictions in the number of terms in office and other provisions of the statutes were intended to bypass Michels' (1962) "iron law of oligarchy." In order to promote democracy in the polity, the constitutional principle of the "free mandate" is upheld against the principle of party democracy. Moreover, the Greens claim to be the most transparent party (in terms of party finance, internal decision-making, etc.). Finally, gender relations within the Greens are characterized by total equality, resulting in the aim of achieving parity between men and women in party and elective offices. However, not all these claims could be upheld since some of them tended to be a liability in party competition. Thus the Greens have relaxed their standards of internal democracy and have come to accept the value of professional experience even of politicians. In sum, they are moving in the direction of becoming a "normal" party.

Parties as membership organizations

Both major parties have truly nationwide organizations with branches in practically all local communities. All Austrian parties were extremely effective in recruiting members. Despite the fact that Austria is a small country, the SPÖ and ÖVP outnumber most of their respective sister parties in Western Europe in membership terms. Indeed, party organizations which comprise about half a million people can hardly be found elsewhere (Katz and Mair 1992). In any case, the major parties have an organizational density which is several times higher than that achieved by political parties in other West European countries.

TABLE 3.4 Party Members and Organizational Density, 1945-1994

Year	Party members (in 1000)			Degree of organization (party members in % of the potential electorate)			Total degree of organization[2]
	SPÖ	ÖVP[1]	FPÖ	SPÖ	ÖVP	FPÖ	
1945	358	441	-	10,4	12,8	-	23,9
1949	614	439	-	14,0	10,0	-	27,9
1953	657	441	-	14,3	9,6	-	27,4
1956	688	498	11	14,9	10,8	0,2	27,7
1959	727	509	20	15,2	10,8	0,4	27,8
1962	699	532	27	14,5	11,1	0,6	27,0
1966	699	543	27	14,3	11,1	0,6	26,7
1970	719	561	28	14,3	11,1	0,6	26,5
1971	703	564	29	14,1	11,3	0,6	26,4
1975	693	562	32	13,8	11,2	0,6	25,9
1979	721	560	37	13,9	10,8	0,7	25,7
1983	695	552	37	13,1	10,4	0,7	24,4
1986	669	528	37	12,3	9,7	0,7	22,8
1990	605	488	42	10,7	8,7	0,8	20,2
1994	518	433	42	9,0	7,5	0,7	17,2

1. Minimum number of members, excluding "family members."
2. Including estimates of the members of the Communist Party (based on Ehmer 1991) and the League of Independents (VdU).
   Source: Müller 1992a; 1995; Müller et al. 1995a.

The degree of organization as reported in table 3.4 is measured in terms of party members as percentage of the potential electorate. Over the whole post-war period, the SPÖ has organized more than 13 percent of the electorate. The respective figure of the ÖVP is above 10 percent and the ÖVP would match the SPÖ if its "family members" who pay only symbolic membership fees were included. Even the FPÖ's organizational degree is high if compared to liberal parties elsewhere.

Table 3.4 includes a column which adds up party memberships in Austria. In addition to the parties listed in the table, it includes estimates of the membership of the Communist Party, which in the early post-war years organized up to 150,000 members (Ehmer 1991), and of the League of Independents, the predecessor of the FPÖ (1949-56), which did not organize masses of members but certainly had as many as the FPÖ in its beginning. Other parties, including the Greens, have not had a relevant impact on the dimension of the overall degree of party organization. According to table 3.4, more than a quarter of the adult population was organized in political parties for most of the post-war period. In recent years the overall degree of party membership has dropped significantly. In the early 1990s it amounts to one fifth of the adult population. This is still extremely high compared to other Western democracies.

What accounts for the high level of party membership in Austria and what are the causes of its decline in recent years? Its extraordinarily high level cannot be explained by a higher level of political interest: comparative data demonstrate that Austria in this respect occupies a middle-of-the-road-position (Verba et al. 1978, 348; Plasser 1987, 283f; Plasser and Ulram 1991b). It is rather family tradition, the desire for social contacts and in particular for patronage which account for the extremely high level of party membership. According to survey evidence collected between 1969 and 1985, all these motives are relevant. Allowing for multiple responses, each of them (with the exception of one year) is reported as a motive for party membership by more than 40 percent of party members (table 3.5). Unfortunately the survey questions and the answer categories have been varied considerably and thus do not allow comparison over time. Table 3.5 therefore should not be read as indicating an increase in the importance of ideology for joining a party between the 1960s and the 1980s (Müller 1989). Nevertheless, ideology figures as the single most important motive in all surveys. However, these data represent the self-portraits of party members. If they are asked about the motives for which other people join, this results in patronage being identified as the single most important motive (Deiser and Winkler 1982, 94-98). Deiser and Winkler have construed this discrepancy as a projection, i.e., one's own socially unacceptable ways of thinking and behaving are attributed to others, and they claim that the "projected statements adequately describe reality."

TABLE 3.5 Motives for Joining a Party, 1969-1985

(Multiple responses possible. The wording of the questions in the three surveys differed and different categories were offered for the responses. Therefore the table is *not* to be read as a time series.)

	1969[1]	1980[1]	1985[1]	1980[2]
Patronage	43	49	37	78
Ideology	50	79	64	61
Family tradition	n.a.	65	53	60
Social contacts	n.a.	53	32	31

1. Party members' own motives.
2. Party members' assumptions about the motives of other party members.
n.a. = not asked
   Source: Deiser and Winkler 1982; Müller 1989.

Indeed, parties have provided these patronage services on a large scale in the post-war period. In recent years however, they have become more sceptical about both the effectiveness of patronage to create loyalty and the net effect of an extensive patronage system. Without being accompanied by other sources of loyalty, in particular a sense of subcultural belonging which still was strong in the first post-war decades, patronage may create long-term loyalty only if it is needed over a lengthy period. Thus only those clients that need *permanent* patronage (e.g., promotion during a career in the public service) are likely to maintain their party membership while those who do not may quit it once they have received what they wanted (e.g., public housing). The net effect of an extensive patronage system also has to include the reactions of those citizens who do not receive patronage benefits or who actually suffer from it (in not being promoted, not receiving public housing, etc.). Political parties in recent years came to realize that more and more citizens are alienated by patronage, which thus may not produce a net benefit (Müller 1989). Moreover, patronage resources have become more scarce due to privatization and budgetary restraint. As a consequence of these developments, political parties have become more reluctant in providing patronage, at least openly, since the 1980s. Thus the Vienna *Land* executive of the SPÖ decided that party membership will no longer be relevant for the allocation of public housing. Needless to say that so far not all functionaries of those parties that can avail themselves of patronage resources believe in such a policy.

Party membership decline can be explained first and foremost by the failure of major parties to adapt to change. Changes in the economic and social structure, as well as cultural change, substantially reduced the number of people who are relatively easy to organize. Although extensive welfare services also created new dependencies, their overwhelming effect--in combination with the new affluence--was to reduce the relevance of politics for individual "life chances." Moreover, new demands such as environmental protection and political participation, which the "established" political parties have rather neglected, became more prominent in recent years. These developments reduced the barriers for exit and made recruitment of new members more difficult. In addition, political parties contributed to their own decline by their bureaucratic aspects and their involvement in scandals. Finally, as already indicated, political parties have become more reluctant in applying methods of membership recruitment which previously proved particularly effective, especially patronage.

If the figures on which this section is based are not an artefact of a delay in reporting membership decline, the SPÖ has been affected earlier and more severely than the ÖVP. Four specific factors may account for this: the declining attractiveness of socialism and the rise of neo-conservative ideas in the West since the late 1970s, government or opposition status, organizational efforts, and involvement in scandals. The organizational decline of the SPÖ began once it came to be the sole governing party for almost a decade and continued when it became the major party of government. To the younger generations, the SPÖ, therefore, is no longer associated with its heritage of representing the underprivileged but rather is an epitome of the political establishment. In the 1980-90 period, the SPÖ or individual SPÖ politicians were involved in numerous scandals, some of which were not significant in absolute terms but had a major impact on the organization by revealing an enormous distance between the rank and file and "workers" representatives' who had maximized their own income by the accumulation of paid political positions and/or the abuse of party or public money. Moreover, the SPÖ has become less concerned about maintaining or even expanding the size of its organization at almost any price. In contrast, the ÖVP was in opposition from 1970 to 1987 and the only opposition party in parliament between 1983 and 1986. Opposition status made the ÖVP less vulnerable to party scepticism. The party was also less involved in scandals and, similar to the German CDU, made greater organizational efforts during its opposition years. These differences disappeared in recent years, when both major parties were affected by substantial membership decline.

In a more general way, the decline of party membership and its impact on the political behaviour of members can be explained in terms of Michael Hechter's (1987, 46f) theory of group solidarity. According to this theory, the extent of group solidarity is determined by four elements, (1) the supply of close substitutes, (2) information about alternatives, (3) costs of moving, and (4) the strength of personal ties.

1. Group solidarity will decline when there is an ample supply of close substitutes to group membership. The convergence in parties' programmes and policies, the changes in the political community which have provided substitutes to party membership for those who are particularly concerned about single issues and/or political participation, and finally the declining importance of political parties for satisfying urgent personal needs increased the number of substitutes considerably.
2. Group solidarity will decline with increasing information about alternatives. Higher levels of education, the emergence of non-party controlled information sources and, conversely, the decline in the parties' capacities to shield their members from other influences provided an information surplus.
3. Group solidarity will decline as the cost of moving between groups decreases. Austrian parties are no longer communities of faith that burden their members with enormous exit costs. Likewise, the importance of the parties' non-political services has declined in recent years. Moreover, due to a wide range of citizen initiatives and social movements, party members do not need to desert to other parties if they want to maintain political acitvity.
4. Group solidarity will decline as personal ties among group members become weaker. Personal ties are probably high among many party activists, but an Austrian saying ranks enemies as: enemy, mortal enemy, "party friend" (*Parteifreund*). Ordinary party members are normally only marginally affected by personal ties.

In the light of Hechter's theory and the above discussion it appears that the Austrian case supports an argument put forward by Richard S. Katz (1990, 158): the costs and benefits of party membership have shifted and this shift has made membership less attractive for both party elites and ordinary citizens.

Intra-Party Power Relations

Intra-party power relations can be discussed in at least three different dimensions: first, between leaders and the rank and file; second, among the national leadership; and third, between the national and sub-national levels, in particular the *Land* level (Müller 1994a). Compared to party leaderships elsewhere in Western Europe, Austrian party leaders have enjoyed a great deal of autonomy from their rank and file. The traditional encapsulation of the political subcultures (Luther 1992, 65-71) left the rank and file without much information or a realistic assessment of the "outside" world. It also allowed the leaders to combine a constructive negotiating relationship with other parties' elites with polemics, in the intra-party arena, directed against the very same elites. Mutual hostility increased support for the leaders who represented the party in the day-to-day fights in the parliamentary, governmental and interest group arenas. Being under fire from other parties tends to silence intra-party critique. The prominence of patronage and social contacts as motives for party membership has provided the major parties with a rank and file ready to accept ideological or policy maneoevering as long as these advantages are forthcoming. Similarly, party activists are preoccupied with maintaining the party organization (for many of them, in particular in the SPÖ, this has become a goal in itself) and with extracting patronage resources from office holders of their respective party and allocating them among the rank and file (Müller 1989). Party leaders have also been very effective in limiting intra-party democracy, resulting in long tenures and the absence of rank and file revolts against party leaders (Müller and Meth-Cohn 1991; Müller et al. 1992).

In all traditional parties, the party chairman is the most powerful leader, who normally combines party office with the most powerful public office the party has at its disposal. Thus the chairmen of SPÖ, ÖVP and FPÖ have held the positions of Chancellor or Vice-Chancellor when these parties took part in the government. In addition, the chairmen served as top candidates in general elections and became increasingly important for the outcome of elections (Plasser 1993). This tended to make them more powerful as long as they deliver, but also more vulnerable once they could not. However, there are differences between the parties. In the ÖVP, the party leader is constrained by faction leaders, the most important of which have their power-base in one of the Leagues, or at the *Land* level by the party leaders and governors (*Landeshauptleute*) (Müller 1991a). The FPÖ party leader has broad powers according to the party statute; incumbent leader Jörg Haider, who is *the* electoral asset of his party (Stirnemann 1992), is the first however who manages to make full use of them (Luther 1991). All his predecessors were severely constrained by the barons of the *Land* party organizations. The SPÖ party statute provides for the most markedly collective leadership; in practice, however, the party chairman usually acted as chief. While the first post-war chairman, Adolf Schärf, did so by the skilful management of the party executive, his two most important successors--Bruno Kreisky and Franz Vranitzky--capitalized on their appeal to the electorate.

In the 1940s, 1950s and even the 1960s, important issues of *Land* party politics were decided in the national executives of the major parties. This has gradually changed. Nowadays national party leaders of the ÖVP and SPÖ largely refrain from intervening at the *Land* level and if they occasionally do, there is no guarantee that they will prevail. As mentioned above, *Land* party leaders currently play an important role in national party politics, in particular in the ÖVP. In the FPÖ however, things evolved in the opposite direction. Since the mid-1980s, the national leader has been able not only to free himself from interventions by the barons of the *Land* party organizations into national politics, but to exercise considerable control over the *Land* organizations as well. The Greens have subscribed to the idea of complete autonomy of their *Land* party organizations. In practice, the central party may have had some influence on the weaker *Land* party organizations when these depended on resources provided by the central party.

Party Ideology

During their long history, each of the traditional *Lager* parties travelled a wide ideological distance. The Socialists started out with the goal of replacing capitalism by socialism. Socialism was to be achieved in a democratic way, by exercising influence in parliament and government. In the early years of the inter-war period, and in particular in the post-war period, the Socialists succeeded in introducing policies that added up to a substantial change of society. Reforms included large-scale nationalization,[12] the building-up of the welfare state and the introduction of elements of "economic democracy," in particular at the supra-firm level in the form of corporatist institutions. All this allowed the party to identify more and more with the status quo. Socialism as the final goal withered away. Indeed, the SPÖ proved to be pragmatic and accommodating throughout the Second Republic and functioned as a case study from which Kirchheimer's (1966) "catch-all party" was derived (Müller 1992b). Although the SPÖ continued to have a reform agenda and maintains that it is the party's permanent task to work for the underprivileged, to some extent it has become not only an established party but also a party of the establishment. In recent years, like several other European social democratic parties, the SPÖ has become more sceptical about traditional forms of state interventionism and has learned to love the market (Müller 1994b).

After a radical beginning the predecessor of the ÖVP, the Christian Social Party, became a defender of the status quo as early as 1907, when it incorporated the Conservatives (Wandruszka 1954). The ÖVP, as a non-socialist catch-all party (*bürgerliche Sammlungspartei*), wants to represent all groups and individuals who are not socialist. In ideological terms this means the incorporation of elements from several democratic non-socialist ideologies, i.e., Catholic social doctrine, conservatism and liberalism (Müller 1988; 1991a; Müller and Steininger 1994b). The emphasis of the various ideological elements has varied over time, with the ÖVP being remarkably flexible and pragmatic. In principle, it always subscribed to a pro-market approach. Traditionally this was qualified by the party's claim for social responsibility, thus leading the ÖVP to promote the "social market economy" as its ideal. More recently, when environmental protection became the most important political goal for the population, the ÖVP developed the vision of the so-called "eco-social market economy." Concerning moral issues, the ÖVP traditionally assumed a conservative position, roughly along the lines taken by the Catholic Church. Likewise, the ÖVP supported the Church in questions of state-church relations.

The parties of the third *Lager*, the VdU and the FPÖ, shared with the ÖVP the reliance on the free market. However, they were anti-clerical and found themselves on the same side with the SPÖ concerning issues which affected state-church relations. More recently however, the FPÖ has pushed its traditional anti-clericalism into the background and has sided with the most conservative bishops on a number of issues. Another line of division was the question of an Austrian nation. In the inter-war period, all parties were in favor of incorporating rump-Austria, i.e. what was left of the Habsburg empire, into Germany. This was prevented by the victors of the World War I but nevertheless remained a goal of all parties until Hitler assumed power in Germany. Unlike Social Democrats and Christian Socials, the German-Nationals continued to maintain this goal and wholeheartedly supported the *Anschluss*, which eventually occurred in 1938. Given the post-1938 history and the success story of the Second Republic, the parties of the third *Lager* did not find it appropriate to express their desire for pan-Germanism in its strongest form, i.e. the *Anschluss*. The FPÖ has come to accept the existence of an independent Austrian state but has insisted on Austrians and Germans constituting one nation in terms of culture (*Kulturnation*). This conviction has come to constitute a gulf, in the Second Republic, between the Third *Lager* on the one hand and the socialist and Catholic conservative *Lagers* on the other. SPÖ and ÖVP have subscribed to the idea of an independent Austrian nation--a feeling which now is shared by the overwhelming majority of the Austrian population.[13] In order to leave this electoral handicap behind, FPÖ leader Haider in 1995 began to disassociate himself and his party from the previous commitment to the German nation.

In the inter-war period, ideological conflicts between the *Lager* were intense. The break-down of democracy in the 1930s led to a discrediting and truncation of both ends of the left-right continuum in the Second Republic. Nevertheless, the major parties, in the early postwar period, had very distinctive ideologies. Over the years, however, the gap between the SPÖ and ÖVP in terms of party programs, electoral platforms and positions in the main policy areas narrowed considerably (Kadan and Pelinka 1979; Horner 1987 and 1991; Müller et al. 1995; Thomas 1979). As a consequence, citizens find it increasingly difficult to place SPÖ and ÖVP into the traditional left-right pattern (Ulram 1990).

The parties' moves towards the ideological center have their equivalent in an increasing concentration of the electorate in the political center; the left-right scale is losing more and more of its significance for understanding politics. Beginning the mid 1970s, those citizens who described themselves as either left or right dropped from 45 percent to 27 percent in 1989. Those who located themselves in the political center increased from 40 percent to 44 percent of the respondents, while those who did not place themselves on the left-right scale increased from 15 percent to 28 percent during the same period (Plasser et al. 1992, 24). The concentration of the electorate in the ideological center in Austria is not matched by any other Europen country (Falter and Schumann 1993, 196-197).

The catch-all ideologies of the major parties and--up to 1986--of the FPÖ opened up space at the fringes. On the left, the Communists were unable to exploit this since they were one of the most Moscow-oriented communist parties. The lack of appeal of communist ideas is not too surprising in a country which bordered on the iron curtain by more than a thousand kilometers and had experienced ten years of Soviet occupation after the Second World War. However, when the Greens emerged on the political scene, they not only positioned themselves along a new political cleavage, promoting post-materialism, but assumed positions on the left on many socio-economic questions. Since this particular combination of political positions does not appeal to the bulk of social democratic voters, the SPÖ's drive to the center has not had a major impact on the behavior of left-wing voters. In contrast, the open space at the right end of the ideological spectrum has proved more important for party competition. In 1986, the FPÖ abandoned its long-term strategy of moving towards the political center and building up the image of a party suitable for government. In the beginning of this new phase of party history, the FPÖ assumed a protest position, exploiting political scandals and the unpopularity of government policy. Most of its policy proposals could still be derived from liberal values (e.g., its protest against the "chamber state," political patronage, etc.). More recently, however, the FPÖ has moved towards the right in ideological terms (Bailer and Neugebauer 1993). In particular, the wave of immigration to Austria following the break-down of Communism in Eastern Europe has provided the FPÖ with a theme which allows the party to bring together law and order issues, economic questions (unemployment caused by Eastern workers, problems in the housing market) and even racial-biological arguments (*"Umvolkung"*) (Plasser and Ulram 1995b). This move of the FPÖ to the right in turn caused the break-away of its liberal wing, which then established the Liberal Forum. This party subscribes to a truly liberal program, in economics and politics as well as on moral issues.

The Party System

Party systems can be classified according to the number and relative size of parties. According to the Austrian party law, several hundred parties exist; however, the vast majority of them do not participate in elections which after all is the major criterion distinguishing political parties from other types of political organizations. The first column of table 3.6 contains the number of those parties that participated in elections and received a minimum support of 1,000 votes (which is considerably less than the number of signatures required for participation in the election). The second column reports the number of parties that won parliamentary seats.

In 1945, only the three parties that had been licensed by the allied powers at the federal level won parliamentary representation: the ÖVP, SPÖ and KPÖ. In 1949, when the German-national-liberal camp reestablished itself in the VdU, it had no problem winning parliamentary representation, which was maintained after the VdU had been transformed into the FPÖ in 1956. The Communists lost parliamentary representation after the end of Soviet presence in the eastern part of Austria, leaving three parliamentary parties, the ÖVP, SPÖ and FPÖ. Austrian politics remained a three-party politics for more than a quarter of a century. Only in the mid 1980s did the parliamentary battle ground become more crowded. In 1986, the Greens entered parliament and in 1993, five MPs left the FPÖ to establish the Liberal Forum, thus creating a five-party parliament, which was confirmed in the 1994 election.

Political Parties

TABLE 3.6 The Austrian Party System, 1945-1994

Year	Number of Parties Candi- dacies[1]	in Parli- ament	Combined shares of the two major parties Seats	Votes	Poten- tial Voters	Fractionaliza- tion of the party system (Rae) Votes (Fa)	Seats (Fp)	Number of parties according to Rae[2]	Blon- del	Sartori
1945	4	3	97.6	94.4	88.0	0.55	0.52	2	2	3
1947	7	4	87.3	82.7	79.0	0.64	0.61	3	2½	3
1953	10	4	89.1	83.4	78.5	0.64	0.60	3	2½	3
1956	5	4	94.5	89.0	83.9	0.60	0.55	2½	2½	3
1959	5	3	95.2	89.0	82.7	0.60	0.54	2	2½	3
1962	5	3	95.2	89.4	82.9	0.59	0.54	2	2½	3
1966	6	3	96.4	90.9	84.3	0.58	0.53	2	2	3
1970	6	3	96.4	93.1	84.7	0.56	0.53	2	2	3
1971	5	3	94.5	93.2	85.2	0.56	0.55	2½	2	3
1975	5	3	94.5	94.0	85.8	0.55	0.55	2½	2	3
1979	5	3	94.0	92.9	84.7	0.56	0.55	2½	2	3
1983	8	3	93.4	90.8	83.0	0.58	0.56	2½	2	3
1986	8	4	85.8	84.4	75.0	0.63	0.62	3	2½	4
1990	11	4	76.5	74.9	62.6	0.68	0.67	3½	3	4
1993	-	5	76.5	74.9	62.6	0.68	0.67	3½	3	5
1994	11	5	63.9	62.6	50.2	0.74	0.73	4	3½	5

1. Parties which recieved more than 1,000 votes.
2. Based on seats (Fp).

Table 3.6 also reports the combined shares of the two major parties, the SPÖ and ÖVP, in terms of votes, seats and potential voters. Over the post-war period their share fell from close to 100 percent to about three quarters of the votes and seats in the early 1990s, and to only a little over 60 percent currently. Again it is the period since the mid-1980s which accounts for the rather dramatic loss of support of the major parties. Table 3.6 not only reports the numbers of parties represented in parliament, but also applies the measures of Rae (1971) and Blondel (1968) which are based on a calculation of the relative strength of parties. These again show the same development of a deconcentration of the party system.

Finally, table 3.6 contains the number of parties according to the counting rules of Sartori (1976, 121-125). In contrast to the other measures, they are not mechanical but are based on a qualitative assessment of the role of the respective parties in the political system. Only relevant parties are counted. A party qualifies as being relevant whenever it has coalition or blackmail potential. In applying these rules, the SPÖ, ÖVP, VdU or FPÖ, the Greens and the Liberal Forum were counted as relevant parties throughout their existence, and the KPÖ was counted as relevant from 1945 to 1949. According to this measure, the change of the party system is more dramatic than according to the indices of Rae and Blondel but it occurred during the same period.

FIGURE 3.4   The Mechanics of Party Competition, 1945-1995

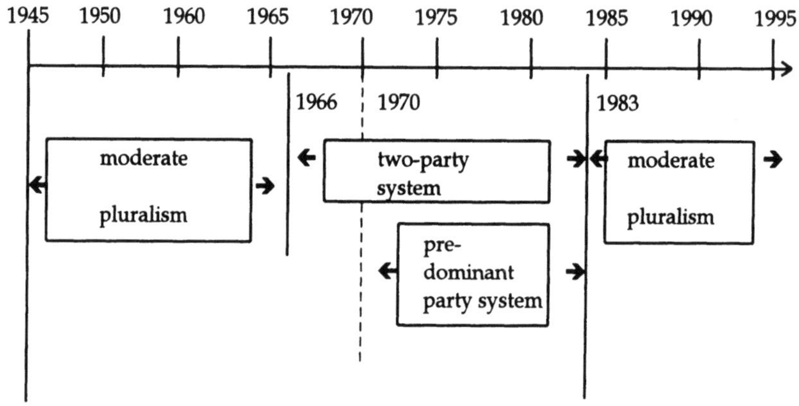

Having established the number of relevant parties, it is possible to turn towards the mechanics of the party system, i.e. the pattern of party competition. According to Sartori (1976, 131-216), three main types of party systems can be distinguished: two-party systems (including the special case of predominant-party systems), moderate pluralism and polarized pluralism. In two-party systems (such as the USA and the UK), more than two parties may exist without preventing the two major parties from governing alone and alternating in power. A two-party system is classified as predominant when a party succeeds in winning an absolute majority of seats in three successive elections or is at least able to form stable minority governments over this period (Sartori 1976, 196, 199). Moderate pluralism is characterized by three to five relevant parties none of which is able to win a majority. Therefore, government is based on coalitions which alternate in power. Party competition is bipolar and competition is centripetal. Polarized pluralism is characterized by more than five parties, including anti-system parties. One or more parties cover the center ground and form the government, but there are opposition parties on both left and right. Party competition is ideologically patterned and centrifugal forces are stronger than centripetal ones.

Post-war Austria did not experience polarized pluralism, but went through periods of the other types or sub-types of party systems. Figure 3.4 summarizes the development and distinguishes three periods. While the first two post-war decades fall into the category of moderate pluralism, the roughly two decades that followed saw a two-party system, which in 1983 was replaced by moderate pluralism again.

Conclusion

This chapter argues that parties and the party system in Austria changed considerably over the post-war years and particularly since the 1980s. In changing their ideology, strategy and organization, traditional political parties tried to adapt to changes in their environment. The emergence of new parties indicates that the adaptation of traditional parties has not been or could not be sufficient to maintain a "closed club." The considerable changes in the fortunes of the traditional parties suggest that they differed in their capacity and willingness to adapt. In recent years, the FPÖ undoubtedly went furthest in changing itself in order to exploit changes in the party environment. As the sections on party finance and the electoral system show, those parties that were in the position to change their environment did so. The introduction of public party finance in the 1970s certainly had a major impact on all parties. Changing the system of state funding of political parties, and particularly changing the electoral system, reshuffled the cards among the parties, but had only a limited impact on the development of the party system itself.

Some aspects of party system change can easily be measured and are therefore comparable to party and party system change elsewhere. However, it is considerably more difficult to assess the overall amount of change in a comparative perspective. Probably the best possible way is to take up the four category scheme of change proposed by Gordon Smith (1989). Accordingly, party *system* change can be classified as: mere *fluctuations*, which are not permanent; *restricted change*, which is permanent but in which most of the relevant dimensions of a party system remain unaltered; *general change*, which in contrast means that "several of these changes take place at the same time or follow on quickly;" finally *transformation*, meaning that one or more dimension of the party system are so radically transformed "that any continuities are swamped."

The previous section has shown that the number and relative size of parties have changed, as have the mechanics of the party system. Other sections have mapped out important changes in the more relevant dimensions of the party system over the post-war period but particularly since the 1980s. Accordingly, ideological change has been considerable. The old cleavages have become weaker and a new cleavage--materialism vs. post-materialism--has been added. Likewise, the government-opposition status of political parties has changed, i.e., the three largest parties have experienced both government participation and opposition (see the chapter on Political Institutions). In the 1990s, there are more *potential* governing parties than ever before. As this and other chapters of this book make clear, the relative importance of political arenas went through considerable change as well. The arena of party politics increased its importance vis-à-vis the corporatist arena, and within the individual parties power was shifted between the federal and the *Land* levels. Finally, the parties' mass organizations have not only become weaker in terms of members but also in determining party strategy and policy. This is an impressive list of relevant changes and it allows the development of the Austrian party system since the beginning of the 1980s to be classified as *general change*.

Notes

1. On the history of the social democrats see Knapp (1980), Shell (1962), Sully (1982), Leser (1988), Pelinka and Steger (1988), Ucakar (1991) and Maderthaner and Müller (1995).

2. On the ÖVP see Reichhold (1975), Gottweis (1983), Pelinka (1983), Müller (1988) and (1991a) and Müller and Steininger (1994b).

3. On the FPÖ see Piringer (1982), Perchinig (1983), Luther (1988) and (1991), Bailer-Galander and Neugebauer (1993), and Plasser and Ulram (1995b).

4. On the Greens see Haerpfer (1989), Dachs (1989) and (1991).

5. See Strøm and Svåsand (1995) for an excellent general discussion of these factors.

6. See Schaden (1983), Raschauer (1989) and Müller (1991b).

7. Other constitutional means to reduce the term of the Nationalrat exist but have not proved relevant.

8. Until 1970 in the first round in each electoral district the number of votes required for a seat was calculated by the Hagenbach-Bischoff system while the d'Hondt system was used in the second round.

9. Since 1971 seats in the first round have been distributed by the Hare system, while the d'Hondt system was still being used in the second (or, since 1992, third) round.

10. The class profile of parties would be sharper if housewives were included in the class of their husbands and pensioners counted according to their former profession. See Müller and Ulram (1995).

11. The elections of 1966 and in particular of 1970 (with the ÖVP winning an absolute majority in terms of seats in 1966, and the SPÖ winning a plurality of votes and seats in 1970) constituted exceptions. In the 1966 election 11 percent of the voters changed their voting behavior compared to the last election. The respective figure for the 1970 election is 12 percent (Haerpfer 1985, 274).

12. Nationalization was introduced by an all-party government when the ÖVP held an absolute majority in parliament. Although nationalization fulfilled the ideological desires of Socialists, it was carried out on pragmatic grounds. First, few private entrepreneurs would have been willing to rebuild the firms largely destroyed during the Second World War. Second, nationalization was an attempt to prevent the Allied Powers from taking over these firms, which were seen as "German property."

13. In 1990 74 percent of the Austrians agreed that Austria is a nation and additional 20 percent stated that Austria is beginning to feel like a nation. Only 5 percent explicitly rejected the idea of an Austrian nation. (See Plasser et al. 1992, 22).

References

Bailer, Brigitte, and Wolfgang Neugebauer. 1993. "Die FPÖ: Vom Liberalismus zum Rechtsextremismus," in Dokumentationsarchiv des österreichischen Widerstandes, ed., *Handbuch des österreichischen Rechtsextremismus*. Pp. 327-428. Vienna: Deuticke.

Bartolini, Stefano, and Peter Mair. 1990. *Identity, Competition, and Electoral Availability*. Cambridge: Cambridge University Press.

Blecha, Karl, Rupert Gmoser, and Heinz Kienzl. 1964. *Der durchleuchtete Wähler*. Vienna: Europa Verlag.

Blondel, Jean. 1968. "Party Systems and Patterns of Government in Western Democracies." *Canadian Journal of Political Science* 1: 180-203.

Boyer, John W. 1981. *Political Radicalism in Late Imperial Vienna. Origins of the Christian Social Movement 1848-1897*. Chicago: University of Chicago Press.

Dachs, Herbert. 1986. "Öffentliche Parteienfinanzierung in den österreichischen Bundesländern," in Andreas Khol et al., eds., *Österreichisches Jahrbuch für Politik 1985*. Pp. 439-454. Vienna: Verlag für Geschichte und Politik.

___. 1989. "Citizen Lists and Green-Alternative Parties in Austria," in Anton Pelinka, and Fritz Plasser, eds., *The Austrian Party System*. Pp. 173-196. Boulder: Westview Press.

___. 1991. "Grünalternative Parteien," in Herbert Dachs et al., eds., *Handbuch des politischen Systems Österreichs*. Pp. 263-274. Vienna: Manz.

___, ed., 1992. *Parteien und Wahlen in Österreichs Bundesländern 1945-1991*. Vienna. Verlag für Geschichte und Politik.

___. 1993. "Vom öffentlichen Parteiengeld in Österreichs Bundesländern," in Andreas Khol et al., eds., *Österreichisches Jahrbuch für Politik 1992*. Pp. 695-723. Vienna: Verlag für Geschichte und Politik.

Dachs, Herbert, Peter Gerlich, Herbert Gottweis, Franz Horner, Helmut Kramer, Volkmar Lauber, Wolfgang C. Müller, and Emmerich Tálos, eds., 1991. *Handbuch des politischen Systems Österreichs*. Vienna: Manz.

Deiser, Roland, and Norbert Winkler. 1982. *Das politische Handeln der Österreicher*. Vienna: Verlag für Gesellschaftskritik.

Dobler, Helmut. 1983. "Der persistente Proporz: Parteien und verstaatlichte Industrie," in Peter Gerlich, and Wolfgang C. Müller, eds., *Zwischen Koalition und Konkurrenz. Österreichs Parteien seit 1945*. Pp. 317-333. Vienna: Braumüller.

Duverger, Maurice. 1954. *Political Parties. Their Organization and Activity in the Modern State*. London: Methuen.

Ehmer, Josef. 1991. "Die Kommunistische Partei Österreichs," in Herbert Dachs et al., eds., *Handbuch des politischen Systems Österreichs*. Pp. 275-285. Vienna: Manz.

Engelmann, Frederick C., and Mildred A. Schwartz. 1974a. "Partisan Stability and the Continuity of a Segmented Society: The Case of Austria." *American Journal of Sociology* 79: 948-966.

___. 1974b. "Austria's Consistent Voters." *American Behavioral Scientist* 18: 97-110.

Falter, Jürgen W., and Siegfried Schumann. 1993. "Politische Konflikte, Wählerverhalten und die Struktur des Parteienwettbewerbs," in Oskar W. Gabriel, ed., *Die EG-Staaten im Vergleich*. Pp. 192-219. Opladen: Westdeutscher Verlag.

Gerlich, Peter. 1987. "Consociationalism to Competition: the Austrian Party System since 1945," in Hans Daalder, ed., *Party Systems in Denmark, Austria, Switzerland, the Netherlands and Belgium*. Pp. 61-106. London: Francis Pinter.

___, and Wolfgang C. Müller, eds., 1983. *Zwischen Koalition und Konkurrenz. Österreichs Parteien seit 1945*. Vienna: Braumüller.

Gottweis, Herbert. 1983. "Zur Entwicklung der ÖVP: Zwischen Interessenpolitik und Massenintegration," in Peter Gerlich, and Wolfgang C. Müller, eds., *Zwischen Koalition und Konkurrenz. Österreichs Parteien seit 1945*. Pp. 53-68. Vienna: Braumüller.

___. 1991. "Neue soziale Bewegungen in Österreich," in Herbert Dachs et al., eds., *Handbuch des politischen Systems Österreichs*. Pp. 309-324. Vienna: Manz.

Haerpfer, Christian. 1985. "Austria," in Ivor Crewe, and David Denver, eds., *Electoral Change in Western Democracies*. Pp. 264-286. London: Croom Helm.

___. 1991. "Wahlverhalten," in Herbert Dachs et al., eds., *Handbuch des politischen Systems Österreichs*. Pp. 475-492. Vienna: Manz.

Hechter, Michael. 1987. *Principles of Group Solidarity*. Berkeley: University of California Press.

Hölzl, Norbert. 1974. *Propagandaschlachten. Die österreichischen Wahlkämpfe 1945-1971*. Vienna: Verlag für Geschichte und Politik.

Horner, Franz. 1987. "Austria 1949-1979," in Ian Budge, David Robertson, and Derek Hearl, eds., *Ideology, Strategy and Party Change: Spatial Analyses of Post-War Election Programmes in 19 Democracies*. Pp. 270-293. Cambridge: Cambridge University Press.

___. 1991. "Programme - Ideologien: Dissens oder Konsens," in Herbert Dachs et al., eds., *Handbuch des politischen Systems Österreichs*. Pp. 197-209. Vienna: Manz.

Houska, Joseph J. 1985. *Influencing Mass Political Behavior. Elites and Political Subcultures in the Netherlands and Austria*. Berkeley: Institute for International Studies.

Kadan, Albert, and Anton Pelinka. 1979. *Die Grundsatzprogramme der österreichischen Parteien*. St.Pölten: Verlag Niederösterreichisches Pressehaus.

Katz, Richard S. 1990. "Party as Linkage? A Vestigial Function?." *European Journal of Political Research* 18: 143-161.

___, and Mair, Peter, eds., 1992. *Party Organizations. A Data Handbook on Party Organizations in Western Democracies, 1960-90*. London: Sage.

Kirchheimer, Otto. 1966. "The Transformation of the Western European Party Systems," in Joseph LaPalombara, and Myron Weiner, eds., *Political Parties and Political Development*. Pp. 177-200. Princeton: Princeton University Press.

Knapp, Vincent J. 1980. *Austrian Social Democracy, 1889-1914*. Washington: University Press of America.

Kofler, Toni. 1985. *Parteiengesellschaft im Umbruch*. Vienna: Böhlau.

Kriechbaumer, Robert. 1990. *Parteiprogramme im Widerstreit der Interessen*. Vienna: Verlag für Geschichte und Politik.

Leitner, Franz. 1988. *Kirche und Parteien in Österreich nach 1945*. Paderborn: Schöningh.

Leser, Norbert. 1988. *Salz der Gesellschaft. Wesen und Wandel des österreichischen Sozialismus*. Vienna: Orac.

Lijphart, Arend. 1980. *Democracy in Plural Societies*. New Haven: Yale University Press.

Lipset, Seymour M., and Stein Rokkan. 1967. "Cleavage Structures, Party Systems, and Voter Alignments: An Introduction," in Seymour M. Lipset, and Stein Rokkan, eds., *Party Systems and Voter Alignments*. Pp. 1-64. New York: Free Press.

Luther, Kurt Richard. 1988. "The Freiheitliche Partei Österreichs: Protest Party or Governing Party?," in Emil J. Kirchner, ed., *Liberal Parties in Western Europe*. Pp. 213-251. Cambridge: Cambridge University Press.

___. 1989. "Dimensions of Party System Change: The Case of Austria." *West European Politics* 12 (3): 3-27.

___. 1991. "Die Freiheitliche Partei Österreichs," in Herbert Dachs et al., eds., *Handbuch des politischen Systems Österreichs*. Pp. 247-262. Vienna: Manz.

___. 1992. "Consociationalism, Parties and the Party System in Austria." *West European Politics* 5 (1): 45-98.

___, and Wolfgang C. Müller, eds., 1992. *Politics in Austria. Still a Case of Consociationalism?* London: Frank Cass.

Maderthaner, Wolfgang, and Wolfgang C. Müller, eds., 1995. *Die Organisation der österreichischen Sozialdemokratie.* Vienna: Löcker.

Meth-Cohn, Delia, and Wolfgang C. Müller. 1994. "Looking Reality in the Eye: The Politics of Privatisation in Austria," in Vincent Wright, ed., *Privatisation in Western Europe. Programmes and Problems.* Pp. 160-179. London: Francis Pinter.

Michels, Robert. 1962. *Political Parties.* New York: Free Press.

Müller, Wolfgang C. 1983. "Parteien zwischen Öffentlichkeitsarbeit und Medienzwängen," in Peter Gerlich, and Wolfgang C. Müller, eds., *Zwischen Koalition und Konkurrenz. Österreichs Parteien seit 1945.* Pp. 281-315. Vienna: Braumüller.

___. 1984. "Direktwahl und Parteiensystem," in Andreas Kohl et al., eds., *Österreichisches Jahrbuch für Politik 1983.* Pp. 83-112. Vienna: Verlag für Geschichte und Politik.

___. 1985. "Die Rolle der Parteien bei Entstehung und Entwicklung der Sozialpartnerschaft," in Peter Gerlich, Edgar Grande, and Wolfgang C. Müller, eds., *Sozialpartnerschaft in der Krise.* Pp. 135-224. Vienna: Böhlau.

___. 1988. "Conservatism and the Transformation of the Austrian People's Party," in Brian Girvin, ed., *The Transformation of Contemporary Conservatism.* Pp. 98-119. London: Sage.

___. 1989. "Party Patronage in Austria," in Anton Pelinka, and Fritz Plasser, eds., *The Austrian Party System.* Pp. 327-356. Boulder: Westview Press.

___. 1991. "Persönlichkeitswahl bei der Nationalratswahl 1990," in Andreas Khol et al., eds., *Österreichisches Jahrbuch für Politik 1990.* Pp. 261-282. Vienna: Verlag für Geschichte und Politik.

___. 1991a. "Die Österreichische Volkspartei," in Herbert Dachs et al., eds., *Handbuch des politischen Systems Österreichs.* Pp. 227-246. Vienna: Manz.

___. 1991b. "Das Parteiensystem," in Herbert Dachs et al., eds., *Handbuch des politischen Systems Österreichs.* Pp. 181-196. Vienna: Manz.

___. 1992a. "Austria (1945-1990)," in Richard S. Katz, and Peter Mair, eds., *Party Organizations.* Pp. 21-120. London: Sage.

___. 1992b. "The Catch-All Party Thesis and the Austrian Social Democrats." *German Politics* 1 (2): 181-199.

___. 1993a. "After the 'Golden Age': Research into Austrian Political Parties since the 1980s." *European Journal of Political Research* 23: 439-463.

___. 1993b. "The Relevance of the State for Party System Change." *Journal of Theoretical Politics* 5: 419-454.

___. 1994a. "The Development of Austrian Party Organizations in the Post-War Period," in Richard S. Katz, and Peter Mair, eds., *How Parties Organize: Adaptation and Change in Party Organisations in Western Democracies.* Pp. 51-79. London: Sage.

___. 1994b. "Political Traditions and the Role of the State." *West European Politics* 17 (3): 32-51.

___. 1995. "Die Organisation der SPÖ, 1945-1994," in Wolfgang Maderthaner, and Wolfgang C. Müller, eds., *Die Organisation der österreichischen Sozialdemokratie 1889-1995.* Vienna: Löcker. (forthcoming)

___. 1996. "Decision for Opposition: The Austrian Socialist Party's Abandonment of Government Participation in 1966," in Wolfgang C. Müller, and Kaare Strøm, eds., *Policy, Office, or Votes? How Political Parties Make Hard Decisions.* (forthcoming).

___, and Delia Meth-Cohn. 1991. "The Selection of Party Chairmen in Austria: A Study of Intra-Party Decision-Making." *European Journal of Political Research* 20: 39-61.

___, and Wilfried Philipp. 1987. "Parteienregierung und Regierungsparteien in Österreich." *Österreichische Zeitschrift für Politikwissenschaft* 16: 277-302.

___, Wilfried Philipp, and Marcelo Jenny. 1995. "Ideologie und Strategie der österreichischen Parteien: Eine Analyse der Wahlprogramme 1949-1994," in Wolfgang C. Müller, Fritz Plasser, and Peter A. Ulram, eds., *Wählerverhalten und Parteienwettbewerb. Analysen zur Nationalratswahl 1994,* Pp. 119-166. Vienna: Signum.

___, Wilfried Philipp, and Barbara Steininger. 1992. "Wie oligarchisch sind Österreichs Parteien? Eine empirische Analyse 1945-1992." *Österreichische Zeitschrift für Politikwissenschaft* 21: 117-146.

___, and Fritz Plasser. 1992. "Austria: The 1990 Campaign," in Shoun Bowler, and David Farrell, eds., *The Campaign: Electoral Strategies and Political Marketing in Contemporary Elections.* Pp. 24-42. London: Macmillan.

___, Fritz Plasser, and Peter A. Ulram, eds., 1995. *Wählerverhalten und Parteienwettbewerb. Analyse der Nationalratswahl 1994.* Vienna: Signum.

___, Fritz Plasser, and Peter A. Ulram. 1995a. "Wähler und Mitglieder der ÖVP, 1945-1994," in Robert Kriechbaumer, and Franz Schausberger, eds., *Geschichte der ÖVP.* Pp. 605-642. Salzburg: IT-Verlag.

___, and Christian Scheucher. 1995. "Das verstärkte Vorzugsstimmensystem: Durchbruch zur Persönlichkeitswahl? Bilanz der Nationalratswahl 1994," in Wolfgang C. Müller, Fritz Plasser, and Peter A. Ulram, eds., *Wählerverhalten und Parteienwettbewerb. Analysen zur Nationalratswahl 1994,* Pp. 323-340. Vienna: Signum.

___, and Christian Scheucher. 1995a. "Persönlichkeitswahl bei der Nationalratswahl 1994," in Andreas Khol et al. eds., *Österreichisches Jahrbuch für Politik 1994.* Pp. 171-197. Vienna: Verlag für Geschichte und Politik.

___, and Barbara Steininger. 1994a. "Party Organisation and Party Competitiveness: the Case of the Austrian People's Party." *European Journal of Political Research* 26: 1-29.

___, and Barbara Steininger. 1994b. "Christian Democracy in Austria: the Austrian People's Party," in David Hanley, ed., *Christian Democracy in Europe.* Pp. 87-100. London: Francis Pinter.

___, and Peter A. Ulram. 1995. "The Social and Demographic Structure of Austrian Parties, 1945-1993." *Party Politics* 1: 145-160.

Pedersen, Mogens N. 1983. "Changing Patterns of Electoral Volatility in European Party Systems, 1948 - 1977: Explorations in Explanation," in Hans Daalder, and Peter Mair, eds., *West European Party Systems.* Pp. 29-66. London: Sage.

Pelinka, Anton. 1974. "Struktur und Funktion der politischen Parteien," in Heinz Fischer, ed., *Das politische System Österreichs.* Pp. 31-53. Vienna: Europaverlag.

___. 1983. "Die Österreichische Volkspartei," in Hans-Joachim Veen, ed., *Christlich-demokratische und konservative Parteien in Westeuropa,* Vol. 1. Pp. 195-265. Paderborn: Schöningh.

___, and Fritz Plasser. 1988. "Compared to What? The Austrian Party System in International Comparison," in Anton Pelinka, and Fritz Plasser, eds., *The Austrian Party System.* Pp. 21-40. Boulder: Westview Press.

___, and Fritz Plasser, eds., 1989. *The Austrian Party System.* Boulder: Westview Press.

Pelinka, Peter, and Gerhard Steger, eds., 1988. *Auf dem Weg zur Staatspartei. Zu Geschichte und Politik der SPÖ.* Vienna: Verlag für Gesellschaftskritik.

Plasser, Fritz. 1987a. *Parteien unter Streß.* Vienna: Böhlau.

___. 1988. "The Austrian Party System between Erosion and Innovation: An Empirical Long-term Analysis," in Anton Pelinka, and Fritz Plasser, eds., *The Austrian Party System.* Pp. 41-67. Boulder: Westview Press.

___. 1993. "Tele-Politik, Tele-Image und die Transformation demokratischer Führung." *Österreichische Zeitschrift für Politikwissenschaft* 22: 409-425.

___, and Peter A. Ulram. 1991a. "'Die Ausländer kommen!'", in Andreas Khol et al., eds., *Österreichisches Jahrbuch für Politik 1990.* Pp. 311-323. Vienna: Verlag für Geschichte und Politik.

___, and Peter A. Ulram, eds., 1991b. *Staatsbürger oder Untertanen? Politische Kultur Deutschlands, Österreichs und der Schweiz.* Frankfurt: Peter Lang.

___, and Peter A. Ulram. 1992. "Überdehnung, Erosion und rechtspopulistische Reaktion," *Österreichische Zeitschrift für Politikwissenschaft* 21: 147-164.

___, and Peter A. Ulram. 1995a. "Konstanz und Wandel im österreichischen Wählerverhalten," in Wolfgang C. Müller, Fritz Plasser, and Peter A. Ulram, eds., *Wählerverhalten und Parteienwettbewerb. Analysen zur Nationalratswahl 1994.* Pp. 341-406. Vienna: Signum.

___, and Peter A. Ulram. 1995b. "Wandel der politischen Konfliktdynamik: Radikaler Rechtspopulismus in Österreich," in Wolfgang C. Müller, Fritz Plasser, and Peter A. Ulram, eds., *Wählerverhalten und Parteienwettbewerb. Analysen zur Nationalratswahl 1994,* Pp. 471-503. Vienna: Signum.

___, Peter A. Ulram, and Alfred Grausgruber. 1987. "Vom Ende der Lagerparteien. Perspektivenwechsel in der österreichischen Parteien- und Wahlforschung." *Österreichische Zeitschrift für Politikwissenschaft* 16: 241-258.

___, Peter A. Ulram, and Alfred Grausgruber. 1992. "The Decline of '*Lager* Mentality' and the New Model of Electoral Competition in Austria." *West European Politics* 15 (1): 16-44.

Powell, G. Bingham. 1970. *Social Fragmentation and Political Hostility. An Austrian Case Study.* Stanford: Stanford University Press.
Pulzer, Peter. 1969. "Austria," in Stanley Henig, ed., *European Political Parties.* Pp. 282-319. New York: Praeger.
___. 1988. *The Rise of Political Anti-Semitism in Germany and Austria.* London: Peter Halban.
Rae, Douglas W. 1971. *The Electoral Consequences of Electoral Laws.* New Haven: Yale University Press.
Raschauer, Bernhard. 1988. "The Legal Status of Parties," in Anton Pelinka, and Fritz Plasser, eds., *The Austrian Party System.* Pp. 489-399. Boulder: Westview Press.
Reichhold, Ludwig. 1975. *Geschichte der ÖVP.* Graz: Styria.
Riedelsperger, Max. 1978. *The Lingering Shadow of Nazism: The Austrian Independent Party Movement since 1945.* Boulder: East European Quarterly.
Sartori, Giovanni. 1976. *Parties and Party Systems.* Cambridge: Cambridge University Press.
___. 1986. "The Influence of Electoral Systems: Faulty Laws or Faulty Method?," in Bernhard Grofman, and Arend Lijphart, eds., *Electoral Laws and Their Political Consequences.* Pp. 43-68. New York: Agathon Press.
Schaden, Michael. 1983. "Parteien und Rechtsordnung," in Peter Gerlich, and Wolfgang C. Müller, eds., *Zwischen Koalition und Konkurrenz. Österreichs Parteien seit 1945.* Pp. 225-247. Vienna: Braumüller.
Schaller, Christian. 1988/1989. "Zur Rolle von Kleinparteien im politischen System Österreichs seit 1960." *SWS-Rundschau* 28: 415-430 and 29: 5-25.
___, and Andreas Vretscha. 1995. "'Es geht um viel (mehr). Es geht um (ein demokratisches) Österreich!' - Der Nationalratswahlkampf 1994," in Wolfgang C. Müller, Fritz Plasser, and Peter A. Ulram, eds., *Wählerverhalten und Parteienwettbewerb. Analysen zur Nationalratswahl 1994,* pp. 167-225. Vienna: Signum.
Schwarz-bunter Vogel. Studien zu Programm, Politik und Struktur der ÖVP. 1985. Vienna: Junius.
Shell, Kurt L. 1962. *The Transformation of Austrian Socialism.* New York: State University of New York Press.
Sickinger, Hubert, and Rainer Nick. 1990. *Politisches Geld: Parteienfinanzierung in Österreich.* Thaur: Kulturverlag.
Smith, Gordon. 1989. "A System Perspective on Party System Change." *Journal of Theoretical Politics* 1: 349-363.
SPÖ - Was sonst? Die Linke in der SPÖ. Geschichte und Bilanz. 1983. Vienna: Junius.
Steger, Gerhard. 1985. "ÖVP, Kirchen und politischer Katholizismus," in *Schwarz-bunter Vogel.* Pp. 64-94. Vienna: Junius.
Steiner, Kurt. 1972. *Politics in Austria.* Boston: Little, Brown & Co.
Stiefbold, Rodney. 1975. "Elites and Elections in a Fragmented Political System." *Sozialwissenschaftliches Jahrbuch für Politik* 4: 119-227.

Stirnemann, Alfred. 1981. "Innerparteiliche Gruppenbildung am Beispiel der ÖVP," in Andreas Khol et al., eds., *Österreichisches Jahrbuch für Politik 1980.* Pp. 415-448. Vienna: Verlag für Geschichte und Politik.

___. 1989. "Recruitment and Recruitment Strategies," in Anton Pelinka, and Fritz Plasser, eds., *The Austrian Party System.* Pp. 401-427. Boulder: Westview Press.

___. 1992. "Gibt es einen Haider-Effekt?," in Andreas Khol et al., eds., *Österreichisches Jahrbuch für Politik 1991.* Pp. 137-185. Vienna: Verlag für Geschichte und Politik.

Strøm, Kaare, and Lars Svåsand. 1995. "Political Parties in Norway: Facing the Challenges of a New Society," in Kaare Strøm, and Lars Svåsand, eds., *Challenges to Political Parties: The Case of Norway.* Ann Arbor: University of Michigan Press. (forthcoming).

Sully, Melanie A. 1982. *Continuity and Change in Austrian Socialism.* Boulder: East European Monographs.

Thomas, John Clayton. 1979. "The Changing Nature of Partisan Division in the West: Trends in Domestic Policy Orientations in Ten Party Systems." *European Journal of Political Research* 7: 397-413.

Traar, Kurt, and Franz Birk. 1987. "Der durchleuchtete Wähler - in den achtziger Jahren." *Journal für Sozialforschung* 27: 3-74.

Ucakar, Karl. 1985. *Demokratie und Wahlrecht in Österreich.* Vienna: Verlag für Gesellschaftskritik.

___. 1991. "Die Sozialdemokratische Partei Österreichs," in Herbert Dachs et al., eds., *Handbuch des politischen Systems Österreichs.* Pp. 210-226. Vienna: Manz.

Ulram, Peter A. 1990. *Hegemonie und Erosion. Politische Kultur und politischer Wandel in Österreich.* Vienna: Böhlau.

Umdenken - Analysen grüner Politik in Österreich. 1984. Vienna: Junius.

Verba, Sidney, Norman H. Nie, and Jae-on Kim. 1978. *Participation and Political Equality.* Cambridge: Cambridge University Press.

Wandruszka, Adam. 1954. "Österreichs politische Struktur. Die Entwicklung der Parteien und politischen Bewegungen," in Heinrich Benedikt, ed., *Geschichte der Republik Österreich.* Pp. 289-486. Vienna: Verlag für Geschichte und Politik.

Weber, Fritz. 1986. *Der Kalte Krieg in der SPÖ.* Vienna: Verlag für Gesellschaftskritik.

Welan, Manfried. 1985. "CV und ÖVP," in *Schwarz-bunter Vogel.* Pp. 170-177. Vienna: Junius.

Zulehner, Paul M., Hermann Denz, Martina Beham, and Christian Friesl. 1991. *Vom Untertan zum Freiheitskünstler.* Vienna: Herder.

4

Corporatism - The Austrian Model

Emmerich Tálos

According to a well-known Austrian saying, "social partnership" (the usual expression for the Austrian form of corporatism) does not need to be explained to an Austrian and simply cannot be explained to a foreigner. In fact, neither the first nor the second part of the saying is true. In Austria a very superficial notion of social partnership has always been widespread. Attention from social scientists outside of Austria came mostly in the 1970s and 1980s. In view of the noticeable tendency towards erosion in corporatist interest politics (latest example: Sweden), the Austrian social partnership--despite all the changes still the most stable form of European corporatism--might become even more interesting to them.

After World War II, a distinct model of economic interest representation and intermediation was established in Austria, comprised of the trade unions, business associations and government. In this respect Austrian corporatism differs substantially from models of interest group politics in the USA, Canada or Australia. The plurality of interest groups that exists in those countries is in strong contrast to Austria. Highly concentrated, centrally organized and quasi-monopolistic interest associations[1] predominate in Austria. The relationship between interest associations on one hand, and the state bureaucracy, political parties and parliament on the other, is not simply one of delivering and receiving demands.[2] The interest associations that are involved in Austrian corporatism are a part of the political decision-making structure. Their activities are determined primarily by a spirit of cooperation and the desire to establish a balance of interests, not just by pressure group strategies.

This configuration of social partnership is not unique to Austria, as comparative studies have shown.[3] In countries such as Norway, Sweden and the Netherlands a specific form of organizing economic interest groups and their political activities, called neo-corporatism, has emerged in the last decades. Although there is considerable debate about definitions within the framework of the neo-corporatism discourse,[4] there is agreement on the two dimensions that constitute neo-corporatism. Schmitter has outlined its institutional dimension:

> Corporatism can be defined as a system of interest representation in which the constituent units are organized into a limited number of singular, compulsory, noncompetitive, hierarchically ordered and functionally differentiated categories, recognized or licensed (if not created) by the state and granted a deliberate representational monopoly within their respective categories in exchange for observing certain controls on their selection of leaders and articulation of demands and supports.[5]

Lehmbruch describes the political dimension of corporatism, often referred to as "concertation," as the inclusion of the large organizations of capital and labor in the process of formulating economic, financial and social policy.[6] In more or less pronounced forms this model also exists in other countries, but corporatism in Austria is considered not only to be distinct but also comparatively stable. Lijphart and Crepaz assert that "Austria is widely regarded as the 'paradigm case' of corporatism."[7] However, it has recently become apparent that changes are taking place in Austrian corporatism, as they are in other major institutions of Austria's political system.

The Austrian model of corporatism is the subject matter of this chapter. As a first point the organizational, ideological, political and economic preconditions will be described. Secondly, the historical development and structure of corporatist interest politics will be presented. The role of the interest associations in the political decision-making process and in shaping the political agenda will be explained subsequently. Finally, current tendencies towards change will be described. These changes do not necessarily portend an end to corporatism in Austria, but instead signify a noticeable difference in the erstwhile form of interest group politics in Austria.

The Preconditions for Corporatism in Austria

The varied history of the different "trends towards corporatist intermediation"[8] shows clearly that the potential for developing and maintaining corporatist interest group politics is largely dependent on historical preconditions. Austria, Sweden and the Netherlands are good examples of this.[9] An important precondition in Austria was the decisive role of the government, and the state bureaucracy in particular, in shaping economic and social policy in the nineteenth century. Administrative strategies in mediating conflicting social interests were developed.[10] Furthermore, the basis for Austria's specific form of regulating the interest associations, the chambers, was already established by the middle of the last century. This is particularly important for developments after 1945, since particularistic options and pressure group strategies remained the dominating features of interest group politics until 1933. (Between 1933-1938 and 1938-1945 there existed different forms of interest group politics, organized and structured in an authoritarian mode). The most important conditions for making the development and stability of Austrian corporatism possible were created after 1945.

Characteristics of Austria's Organized Interest Associations

In Austrian corporatism the most important representatives of labor (white and blue collar workers) are the Trade Union Federation (ÖGB) and the Federal Chamber of Labor (AK). The Federal Chamber of Business (BWK) is the primary representative of the businessmen, and farmers are represented by the Presidential Conference of the Chambers of Agriculture. These four economic interest associations do not represent all special interests in Austrian society, but they do have a particularly important position as a result of institutional and ideological characteristics that are an essential part of corporatism.

The organization of economic interests groups in Austria is highly concentrated. This is not only because of the small number of relevant interest associations, but also because to a large extent these groups have a monopoly in representing their constituents. The ÖGB has a de facto monopoly: for a long time it represented more than 60 percent of blue and white collar workers. The chambers, on the other hand, have a legal monopoly. Membership in the chambers is obligatory at the provincial level. The Chambers of Labor in the provinces include all employed white and blue collar workers (excluding civil servants). The Chambers of Business include all self-employed businessmen, with the exception of the professionals who have their own chambers (like notaries and physicians). Nearly all self-employed farmers are members of the Chambers of Agriculture. The financial resources of the chambers are legally guaranteed by means of compulsory dues.

Apart from concentration, the centralization within the interest associations is an important prerequisite for Austrian corporatism. The peak organizations (*Dachverbände*) of the chambers, i.e. the Federal Chambers mentioned above, are granted legal rights (according to its own constitution the ÖGB also has the right) to dispose of the personnel and financial resources of the members (i.e. the provincial chambers, or individual unions) and make decisions which are binding for them. The peak organizations have the further advantage of receiving state help in pressing sanctions as well as having the opportunity to participate in the decision-making process.

> Measured by the monopoly of representation (that is, the lack of competing interest associations within one category of interests) and the centralization of the peak organizations (*Dachverbände*), Austrian unions and Chambers of Business unquestionably rank at the top before Norway and Sweden.[11]

In many respects, this organizational structure is a beneficial and necessary prerequisite for social partnership. Through concentration and centralization, heterogeneous interests are forced to become integrated. This requires the balancing of interests. The necessity of defusing intra-organizational conflicts encourages a policy that in the long run will improve the position of all members.[12] This in turn encourages a policy of forced economic growth that requires the cooperation of both the interest associations and the government. In order to solve a second intra-organizational problem, namely the problem of keeping the loyalty of their membership, external help comes from the state for organization and sanctions.

Political Preconditions

The Economic Interest Associations' Self Image. In contrast to the inter-war years, there have been remarkable changes in goals and strategies after 1945. The earlier, particularistic, often incompatible goals and the conflict-orientated strategies lost most of their importance. In the program on economic, social and cultural policy during the ÖGB's fourth National Congress in 1959, this new perspective was well illustrated:

> Unions must influence the entire economic and social development today, because they have long since realized that not only the nominal size of wages is of importance, but also the whole economic and political situation. One of the most important features of a progressive union policy, one not always appreciated by the rank and file, but gaining more

acceptance among the leadership, is the responsibility it has towards the economy as a whole.[13]

Similarly, the Federal Chamber of Business goes beyond the particularistic agenda of an interest group in stating:

> The duties of modern interest group representatives are, while maintaining a responsible attitude towards the whole economy, to represent the members in dealing with the government, the administration, other interest groups, the political parties and the public...[14]

On the basis of their responsibility for public welfare, in some cases decisions must be made that

> ...require the immediate interests of individual economic groups to be subordinated to general economic goals...It is obvious that the individual trade groups try to push through their groups' interests, while the Chamber (of Business) as the representative of all businesses must attempt to balance interests. Group interests must be deferred for the sake of the whole economy.[15]

However, representing special interests while keeping the entire economy under consideration does not imply converging views about socio-political values, nor does it mean the end of conflicts and dissent. Yet this model is characterized by both widespread consensus on the main objectives for the entire economy (economic growth, low unemployment, stable currency, international competitiveness) that must be kept in mind while pursuing special interests, and the search for consensual problem-solving. This is known in Austria as the "class struggle at the negotiating table." Strikes and lock-outs have not been altogether abolished, but they are only used as a last resort in dealing with economic and social conflicts.

Surveys show that members of the interest associations support the attempt to avoid conflicts. In 1990 more than half of those questioned preferred to have economic and social decisions determined through negotiations between the state, business and labor groups. Only 3 percent supported decisions arrived at by active conflicts such as strikes.[16]

Beyond the institutional conditions and the responsibilities the interest associations felt they had, Austrian corporatism was also reinforced by the close relationship between the interest associations and the parties, and by the configuration of the party system itself.

Interest Associations and Parties. An important characteristic of the interest group system in the Second Republic is the close relationship between each of the large economic interest associations with one of the two major political parties (ÖVP and SPÖ). This is demonstrated by their extensive institutional links. For example, the Social Democratic faction in the ÖGB, the largest group within the union, is represented in the full party executive of the SPÖ. In the elections to the Chambers of Business and Agriculture, the parties compete for votes with specialized organizations of their own. The close relationship is underscored by the fact that often the same individual holds positions in the interest association and the party. It was also once common to find a large number of representatives of the interest associations among the deputies to the Austrian parliament (51.4 percent in 1973).[17]

The two major parties that produced the bi-polar party and government system in the first decades after the Second World War also left their mark on the composition of the economic interest associations. The Socialists dominate the ÖGB and the Chambers of Labor, while the People's Party dominates the Chambers of Business and Agriculture.

Under these circumstances, the long standing coalition between the two parties after 1945 was not the only factor that furthered cooperation among the economic interest associations. The perspectives of the economic interest associations coincided with those of the two major parties and the government: namely, the inclusion of the interest associations in the policy-making process and in the implementation of that policy, as well as the agreement on how to realize the necessary goals for the entire economy.

Economic Preconditions

There is a large share of nationalized companies in the industrial and banking sectors; otherwise, today as in the past, small and middle-sized firms dominate the economy. This has maintained the traditionally weak presence of private capital in the economy after 1945. Private capital is oriented towards cooperation with the unions and the government in order to safeguard its competitiveness. This position has been furthered by Austria's position as a small state economy.[18] The public sector does not only provide a framework for combining state and economic interests; as a result of its specific structure of ownership, public enterprises also provide an opportunity for the unions and the Socialist Party to exert economic influence. In addition, the relatively good economic developments in the years between the 1950s and the 1970s helped to make trade-offs in interest politics easier.

Development and Structure of Austrian Corporatism

Before 1945 voluntary cooperation between the economic interest associations and the government was limited in content and in time to the end of the First World War and the end of the 1920s. In the Second Republic it became the permanent form of interest politics.

Developments until the Early 1980s

The Austrian model of cooperative and concerted interest politics basically reached its present form by the end of the 1950s and in the early 1960s. The initial stages emerged in the years immediately after the Second World War. Several wage-price agreements were negotiated between the 'big four' interest associations and the government. These agreements regulated prices and restrained wage increases and social benefits[19] for the purpose of encouraging the economic recovery. This policy was not fully supported by the wage-earners themselves and led to a series of strikes in the autumn of 1950. These were the most serious, but also the last, significant manifestations of opposition to the co-operative-concerted politics in Austria. In any event, the cooperative forums established in the 1940s and the 1950s remained limited in time and content at first, to deal with the emergency which prevailed at that time.

After the economic recovery was completed, differences between the interest associations over budget, economic, social and employment policy increased. Particularistic interest strategies, especially those of the business associations, gained more importance.[20] The subcommittee of the coalition parties (ÖVP and SPÖ) became the decision-making center.[21]

At the end of the 1950s and in the early 1960s the cooperation between the interest associations was extended with the consent of the government. This enhanced their participation in the process of formulating public policy. The circumstances that led up to this development were, on the one hand, economic problems such as rising prices in the mid-1950s, problems of economic integration and competitiveness, signs of weak economic growth, an increasingly scarce supply of labor, and upward pressure on wages. On the other hand, the cooperation between the coalition parties in the government and parliament eroded, while the importance of the staffs of the interest associations in formulating policies increased.

The initiative for the institutionalization and expansion of the cooperation between the interest associations came primarily from the leadership of the ÖGB. Upon a recommendation from the Council of

Ministers, the Joint Commission for Wages and Prices was established in 1957 as a temporary instrument to further cooperation and agreement. In the following years the Commission became permanent. Its role was expanded, and cooperation with the government and the dominating interest associations in policy making and implementing was increased. This development can be seen in several agreements that furthered both economic stability and cooperation between the interest associations.

The expansion of the model of the cooperative-concerted interest politics was by no means undisputed.[22] The demand of the interest associations to be increasingly included in the decision-making process was also challenged. However, opposition dissipated quickly.[23] The expansion of social partnership in the early 1960s was supported by the government, which is represented in it, and by the coalition parties, which are closely connected with the interest associations.

The difference between the attempts and the realization of cooperative-concerted politics in other countries, for example, Germany or the Netherlands, is that the development of corporatism in Austria displayed exceptional continuity and stability. Neither the change from the grand coalition government to that of one-party governments (ÖVP from 1966 to 1970 and SPÖ from 1970 to 1983), nor the clearly increasing divergence of interests brought on by growing economic and social problems at the end of the 1970s and the early 1980s, led to any fundamental doubts about social partnership.

Until the second half of the 1970s cooperation among the interest associations was highly influential. Not only did they make a substantial contribution to stabilizing the economy and managing labor market problems, but several laws (the Works Constitution Act regulating codetermination and collective bargaining, the Employment Act, the Employment of Foreigners Act) could be passed largely because the conflicts had been resolved in agreements outside of parliament.

Even though as a whole the policy-making process in the first half of the 1970s displayed no uniform character,[24] the divergences became more obvious with time. On the one hand, dissent among the interest associations themselves as well as between them and the government intensified. Their positions became increasingly divergent and often agreements on social and economic issues could not be reached. Also, in some cases bills were initiated from the floor in parliament, which formally reduced the interest organizations' room for maneuvering. Analogous to the political power constellation until 1986, this was viewed critically by the business associations.

On the other hand, apart from laws regulating agricultural commodities which require consensus on account of the necessary two-thirds majority, social partnership as a process of achieving agreement between the interest associations and the government proved useful in working out a number of other laws (Sickness Benefits Act 1977, Amendment to the Works Constitution Bargaining Act 1986). When the FPÖ took part in the government from 1983 until 1986, the relationship between the government and the interest associations did not change substantially.

The Structure of Austrian Corporatism

Structurally, Austrian corporatism is made up of a complex network of formal and informal interactions among the large interest associations and between these and the government/state bureaucracy.

The relationship between the interest associations is institutionalized on several different levels. The central institution is the Joint Commission for Wages and Prices. The interweaving of the important interest associations is reflected in it in a special way.

In addition to the Federal Chancellor, who chairs the General Assembly of the Commission, three other members of the government (the Minister of Labor and Social Affairs, the Minister of Economic Affairs, and the Minister of Agriculture), the presidents and one or two vice presidents of the peak organizations of the four economic interest associations, as well as their secretary generals and staff, take part in the consultations, a total of about 25 to 30 people.[25] Since 1966 only the representatives of the four economic interest associations have had the right to vote. In that year the first one-party government took power after the long post-war phase of the grand coalition.

The principal structural elements of the Joint Commission include the parity of the interest associations (which the corresponding political parties duplicated in the years of the Grand coalition government), the principle of unanimity, and that of secrecy. In comparison to other forms of interaction between interest associations, the Joint Commission was not based on legislation but on the voluntary agreement of the associations involved.

Another important level of the social partnership network is the system of advisory councils, commissions and subcommittees. Between 1971 and 1987, the interest associations were represented in 223 such institutions.[26]

FIGURE 4.1 The Structure of the Joint Commission on Wages and Prices

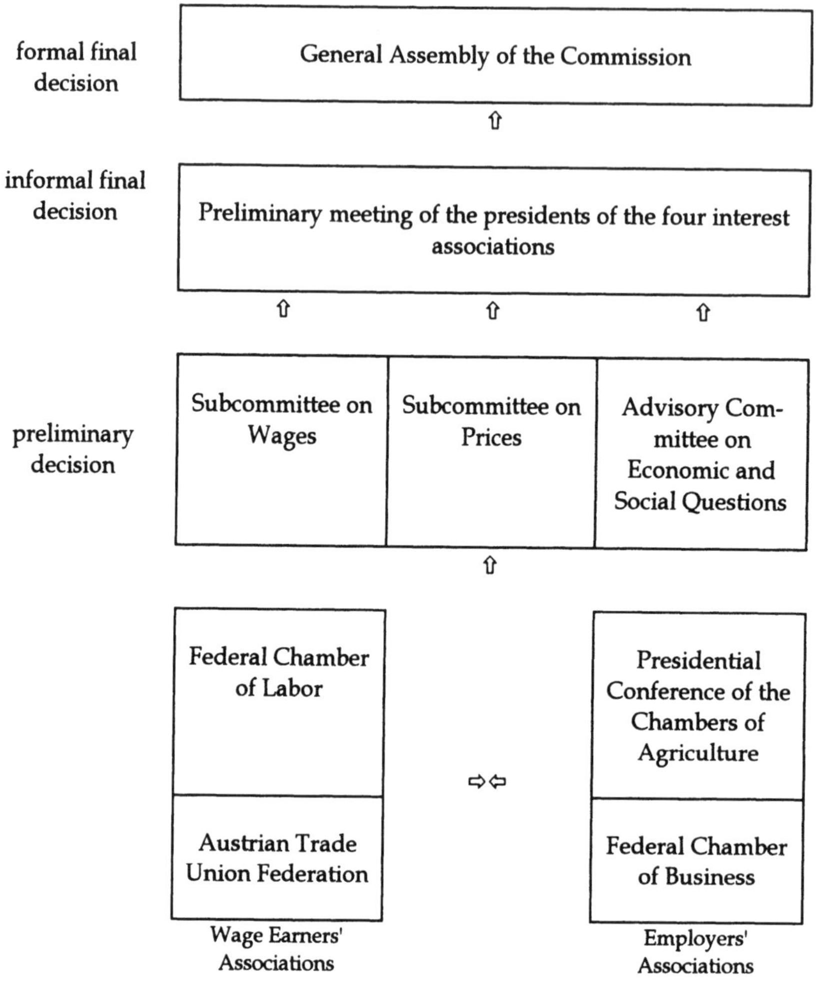

formal final decision	General Assembly of the Commission
informal final decision	Preliminary meeting of the presidents of the four interest associations
preliminary decision	Subcommittee on Wages | Subcommittee on Prices | Advisory Committee on Economic and Social Questions

Wage Earners' Associations	Employers' Associations
Federal Chamber of Labor	Presidential Conference of the Chambers of Agriculture
Austrian Trade Union Federation	Federal Chamber of Business

Source: Anton Pelinka, *Sozialpartnerschaft und Interessenverbände* (Vienna 1986), p. 21.

The interaction among the interest associations, as well as between them and the government, is also anchored in important economic and social institutions:

- Social Security: The representatives of the insured are chosen by the Chambers of Business, Agriculture and Labor and the ÖGB.
- Agricultural Funds for milk, cereals and meat: The interest associations play a dominant role in managing these resources.

- Money and Credit Policy: The interest associations are, by law, represented on the governing boards of the Austrian Post Office Savings Bank and of the Austrian National Bank. They are also involved in the activities of the European Recovery Program Credit Commission, a holdover of the Marshall Plan.

There are also several informal modes of cooperation that play an important role in the political decision-making process. These include informal contacts within the framework of the Joint Commission, negotiations on the level of the interest association experts, informal talks with the appropriate ministries and even so-called top talks of the presidents of the interest organizations among themselves and with the responsible minister.

The "heart" of Austrian corporatism, put briefly, consists in the cooperation and balancing of interests between the interest organizations and the government/state bureaucracy on the basis of a network of interaction and consensus on the options for the economy as a whole.

The Political Role of Austrian Corporatism

The Austrian version of corporatism is most effective on the macro level of interest politics. On the level of the provinces (the *Länder*[27]) and in individual branches of the economy[28] only some rudiments exist. The political relevance of corporatism is most obvious in the decision-making process in important political areas.

Corporatism and Political Decision-making

The extensive network of horizontal interaction and the above-mentioned privileges received from the government constitute the framework for the extraordinary amount of involvement the major economic interest associations have in consensus-building, decision-making, and policy implementation in Austria.[29]

Involvement in the formulation of policy takes place not only in the Joint Commission but also within the framework of diverse advisory councils and commissions. Social partnership negotiations settle all the decisive questions of a multitude of economic and social welfare laws before the bills even reach parliament. By this means a certain amount of influence can be exerted on the administration. It is also possible for the interest associations to participate in formulating policy while a bill is being considered in parliament, either through negotiations between the interest associations that run parallel to those in the parliamentary subcommittees or through the inclusion of the interest associations' own staff in the subcommittee deliberations.

In addition to the cooperative pursuit of goals that affect the whole economy, there is naturally also a need to safeguard the special interests of the individual pressure groups. This is made possible by the legal right of the chambers (and the de facto right of the ÖGB) to comment on draft bills and by the special relationship between each of the interest associations and the parties and ministers closely associated with them.

Fields and Extent of Activity of Austrian Corporatism

Contrary to Austrian popular opinion, the social partners are not by any means concerned with every political field. For example, the interest associations are not very involved in the fields of justice, education, arts, science or research.[30] However, they are represented in the administration of educational and research institutes.[31] Because of the practice of commenting on draft bills in such fields as primary and higher education as well as criminal justice, the statement that in "strongly corporatist countries with pronounced concertation the large interest associations tend to be involved at least formally in all important regulations in every political field"[32] also applies to Austria to a considerable extent.

Several areas in which the model of cooperative-concerted politics is of prime importance can be clearly identified: prices and incomes policy, economic policy and social welfare policy. These three main areas offer the corporatist actors a wide basis for possible exchanges in the pursuit of their special interests.

Incomes policy. The core of social partnership is the formulation of incomes policy in the Joint Commission. Wages, and to some extent prices, were included in the deliberations between the large economic interest associations, who also take into account the overall goals of economic policy. In practice, the regulation of wages and prices have different ranges. While the founders of the Joint Commission gave it extensive authority over prices, its actual influence has steadily decreased, as more prices have been exempted from the proceedings. By the end of the 1970s the Commission controlled approximately 50 percent of manufacturer's (wholesale) prices and less than 20 percent of consumer prices.[33] The importance of this form of price policy has declined in recent years because of generally of low inflation rates in Austria and among its most important trading partners, and also as a result of an increase in imported consumer goods.[34]

The Commission's influence over wages (which is exerted through a subcommittee) is more extensive, even though its official function is limited to giving the go-ahead for the collective bargaining of wages in the different sectors. The bargaining itself is done by the parties to the agreement (unions and sectoral subunits within the BWK). Wage drift within the factories is not addressed. By involving the ÖGB and by placing a representative of each of the four interest associations in the subcommittee on wages, a double filter is built in. According to Nowotny, this

> ...has the effect that the wage demands of the unions are subjected to a preliminary examination both of their extent and their timing. This increases the chances of achieving a wage policy that takes its orientation from the imperatives of solidarity and the national economy.[35]

The effects of that kind of concurrence in establishing wage policy in particular, and income policy in general, are the following: strengthening the position of the leadership of the interest associations,[36] stabilization of business expectations,[37] positive effects on employment,[38] the ability to manage inflation[39] and to mutually implement wage discipline, good industrial relations, and long term constancy in the distribution of the national income.

Until the mid-1980s the OECD ascribed Austria's relatively good economic performance to the interaction between the interest associations and the government in the field of incomes policy.[40] From 1953 to 1981, Austria boasted one of the lowest rates of inflation among Western industrial countries, ranking after Germany, Switzerland, Belgium and the United States.[41] Compared to other countries, Austria has a low level of labor conflict. Between 1980 and 1987, for every 1000 workers only two days of work were lost through strikes each year in Austria. This compared to 11 days in Japan, 35 in West Germany, 162 in the United States, 191 in Sweden and 719 in Greece.[42]

A stable distribution of incomes (stable share of wages in the national income) used to be viewed as a result of social partnership as well. However, this was no longer true in the 1980s. In addition, it is clear that the tacit understanding not to redistribute incomes either by wage or by price increases[43] is largely responsible for the continuation of existing economic inequalities. The wage policy of the last decades permitted both the traditional gender-related income inequality[44] as well as the largest wage differentials between individual branches in the European context to remain unchanged.[45]

Economic Policy. Cooperation between the interest associations and the government on economic policy (stimulating the economy, credit, fiscal, monetary and financial policy) attains different levels of intensity depending on the particular field. There is cooperation in regulating agricultural commodity markets, in allocating state subsidies for exports, in giving credits on favorable terms and in determining tax policy. But it is the policy of maintaining a "hard" currency that particularly demonstrates the consensus between the interest associations, the government and the National Bank. The hard currency policy followed by the Nationalbank, that is, pegging the Austrian schilling to the German mark, is combined with a consensual incomes policy, particularly concerning wages, in order to import stability and to weaken inflationary pressures. The hard currency policy, the wage policy agreed upon by the social partners, and the expansive budget (all characteristics of "Austro-Keynesianism") contributed to relatively favorable conditions in the labor market as well as to real growth until the end of the 1980s.[46] The hard currency policy and the incomes policy demonstrate that social partnership is not only used for crisis management, but also for the continuous supervision of economic problems. The high points of this policy are "big bargains", or package deals, whereby an incomes policy that is orientated towards the whole economy is balanced by tax policy,[47] the hard currency policy is softened by a moderate wage policy and competitiveness is encouraged by state subsidies and a productivity-oriented wage policy.

Social Welfare Policy. The social welfare policy of the Second Republic is to a large part the product of the interaction among interest associations, as well as between these associations and the government. The search for consensus and the bargains struck in the policy-making process do not exclude some fierce conflicts. While working conditions are usually the domain of the interest associations alone, the associations, government and the political parties determine labor market policy jointly. Decisions on social security require, in addition, the inclusion of the representatives of social welfare institutions and the *Länder* in the deliberations. The considerable expansion of the welfare state after 1945 is a result of this cooperation. This can be seen both in the expansion of labor law (reducing weekly and yearly working time, improving worker codetermination, assimilating white and blue collar workers) and in the expansion of social welfare with regard to benefits and recipients.

Problems on the labor market are managed in general terms by budgetary and macroeconomic policy, with active labor market policies used as supporting measures. The interest associations are not only involved in policy-making but also in its implementation, as in the case of regulating the employment of foreigners.

While social partnership is a coalition oriented towards general economic goals, it is also a coalition of employers and employees in the area of social welfare and as such represents--not without selectivity--the interests of the active working population. In this way the interest associations serve as "guardians" of a social welfare system established in the nineteenth century to address the needs of the working population. As a result, it clings to a structure that largely reproduces income inequalities, especially between genders, within the welfare state and tends to ignore those who are not integrated in the labor market.

Social Partnership since the 1980s

Change

Current economic developments, such as increasing internationalization, more competitive pressure and lower growth rates, have restricted the ability of the state to influence the economy. Restructuring in business firms created not only new tasks, but also new problems for the interest associations. The diversification of the work force and the greater importance of the firms themselves with regard to labor relations have changed the conditions for interest aggregation.[48] These changes are reflected on the macro level in different priorities and options (consolidating the budget, departure from Keynesian demand-side management, orientation towards supply-side economics), and on the micro level in more flexibility and decentralization. Altogether, these changes have made compromises within and between the interest associations more difficult to find. Also, the increase in unemployment and the departure from state regulated demand have shifted the power relationships to the disadvantage of the labor unions.[49]

No less important are the political changes. The party system in Austria is experiencing a period of intense change. The erosion of the two large parties is indicated by declining party identification and membership ties (in the context of the eroding traditional social milieu[50]), the decline in the traditional political polarization, and the shift in political themes.[51] The resulting increase in importance of the three smaller parties (Freedom Party, Green-Alternative Party and Liberal Forum) has widened the possibilities for building coalitions. The traditionally close ties between the two major parties and the interest associations have been loosened with the mounting competition among the political parties. There is increased divergence on ecological, social and economic questions. On the institutional level there are fewer representatives of the interest associations in the *Nationalrat* and reduced involvement in the decision-making process, as became evident in the preparation of the 1995 budget (see the chapter on Economic Policy in this volume).

The change in the party system was accompanied by a change in the attitudes of the Austrians towards social partnership and the special nature of its institutions. In particular, the compulsory membership in the chambers has been sharply criticized. Also, the interest associations themselves and their top officials have been subjected to increasing and popular criticism. The members themselves are sometimes more uncomfortable with the interest associations than the general population. Fewer members take part in the elections in the chambers, and ÖGB membership is declining. The chambers are criticized for being too bureaucratic, for not giving its members a voice in the decision-making process, for their sluggishness and lack of innovation. As a result of changes in their environment, the relations between the officials of the interest associations have come under pressure; this is increased by pressure from within the associations. In view of the interest associations' declining ability to integrate the interests of their membership, they must compensate internal problems of loyalty by success in their relations to the other associations. As conflict among social partners is rising, their calculability is declining.

The changes in the external and internal conditions of interest politics is particularly revealing in one of the central functions of social partnership: shaping political decision-making. Compared to the heyday of the 1960s and 1970s, the interest association's ability to find compromises in the fields of wages or in economic and social policy is declining. Furthermore, the particularistic options and strategies are gaining in importance. This augments the importance of the interrelation between the interest associations and the parties closely associated with them in the decision-making process. The increased competition among the parties and the growing challenge to the parties' competence to solve problems is reflected in the headway they are making into the traditional domain of the interest associations. For this reason, it has become less likely that parliament simply gives its rubber-stamp approval, as it had in the past, to legislation negotiated in advance by the interest associations.

Continuity

Despite the changes within social partnership and in the conditions surrounding it, this mainstay of the Austrian political system is in no danger of collapsing, nor does it lack continuity. Both the organizational setup (including the domination by men and the underrepresentation of women) and the institutional infrastructure of the interest associations remain unchanged. The extensive network of horizontal and vertical interaction between the interest associations, the government/state bureaucracy, major political parties and parliament has been gradually and not drastically curtailed (for example, changing the tasks of the

Subcommittee for Prices). The same is true for the wide range of possibilities of interest associations to take part in the political decision-making process. The large interest associations want to maintain essential institutional requirements such as compulsory membership and central cooperative forums like the Joint Commission. This was emphasized in an agreement by the presidents of the peak organizations in November 1992. The agreement states that in the future the Joint Commission should become the special arena for talks between the government and the social partners. It also states that the Subcommittee for Prices, since its original role has been reduced, should acquire new and different tasks such as investigating the state of competition within the various markets. A Subcommittee for International Affairs has also been established.

Finding compromises has become more difficult as a result of the increasing divergence of interests. However, basic consensus on the willingness to search for common ground and to pursue overall economic goals has continued. The aforementioned agreement effectively confirms the desire for a continuation of consensus among the interest associations.

In recent economic and social policy, the economic interest associations have not been limited in the last years to simply giving advice. Their representatives were often involved in the negotiations of the coalition parties as well as in those of the federal bureaucracy. They also played an important role in the preparation of the 1994 EU referendum, during which they closely cooperated with the government. The contents of a number of recent bills are to a large degree influenced by compromises made by the interest associations. The 1993 reorganization of the state agencies for employment and retraining is a clear example of the fact that the three-sided model of interest politics has not reached its end. On the contrary, within the framework of this reorganization, the influence of the interest associations has been upgraded and extended.

While Austrians are uneasy with and critical of the individual interest associations, they do not question the existence of the corporatist system itself,[52] although there is an undeniably serious problem of legitimacy regarding its actors, i.e. the interest associations. Social partnership is still seen as an important and desirable part of the political system. It is deemed to be useful, efficient and beneficial for the overall economy. Its rules are generally accepted.

Even with all the acknowledged tendencies towards change, social partnership still shows a considerable amount of continuity. Compared internationally--most recently, for example, with Sweden--it is still stable.

It may continue into the future, in a changed environment and with further modifications.

In the face of increasing internationalization, a corporatist model of interest politics can protect a small country like Austria from extreme external shocks. Social scientists have made it clear that this model will only survive if it adjusts its functions to the changing economic conditions: in the direction of supply-side economic management and by bearing in mind qualitative aspects like training, technology and investments.[53] Traxler called this the "transition from demand-side to supply-side corporatism."[54] According to Traxler and Unger, these functional changes imply further changes in the institutional structure. In concrete terms this means decentralizing decision-making and increasing the participation of the individual members while decreasing the autonomy of the leadership. Central control would not become completely obsolete, but it would primarily consist of giving guidelines for overall policy on the macro level.

On the whole this author, unlike Gerlich,[55] does not believe that the dissolution of the Austrian model of corporatist interest politics is a realistic possibility in the near future. However, it will become less important because the range and weight of activities will be smaller with regard to political decisions, and also because of the functional and structural changes which result from Austria's accession to the European Union.[56] Thus the EU decision-making process is characterized by interaction with particularistic interests and their lobbying strategies; cooperation between Europe-wide federations of labor unions and employer organizations exists only marginally. As a result, the particularities of the Austrian social partnership could be weakened, or, in other words, the Austrian model may come to resemble other more "moderate" models of corporatist interest politics.

Notes and References

1. The term interest association rather than interest group is used to stress the high level of interest aggregation achieved by the groups under discussion.

2. Gabriel A. Almond and G.Bingham Powell, *Comparative Politics* (Boston 1966). Jürgen Hartmann, *Verbände in der westlichen Industriegesellschaft* Frankfurt/New York 1985).

3. Gerhard Lehmbruch, "New Corporatism in Comparative Perspective," in Gerhard Lehmbruch and Philippe C. Schmitter, eds., *Pattern of Corporatist Policy Making* (London 1982). Pp. 1-28, p. 16f. Gerhard Lehmbruch, "Sozialpartner-schaft in der vergleichenden Politikforschung," in Peter Gerlich et al., eds., *Sozialpartnerschaft in der Krise* (Vienna 1985). Pp. 85-107, p. 90. Arend Lijphart and Markus L. Crepaz, "Corporatism and Consensus Democracy in

Eighteen Countries-Conceptual and Empirical Linkages," in *British Journal of Political Science*, Vol. 21, No. 2, 1991. Pp. 235-246, p. 238f.

4. In recent articles the use of the concept "policy network" for the diversity of the interchange between the state and the associations has developed. (e.g. see Frans v. Waarden, "Dimensions and types of policy networks," in *European Journal of Political Research*, Vol. 21, No. 1-2, 1992. Pp. 29-52; Grant Jordan and Klaus Schubert, "A preliminary ordering of policy network labels," in *European Journal of Political Research*, Vol. 21, No. 1-2, 1992. *Pp.* 7-27. Corporatism as well as pressure pluralism, clientelism or iron triangles are all seen as types of policy networks.

5. Philippe C. Schmitter, "Still the Century of Corporatism?" in Philippe C. Schmitter and Gerhard Lehmbruch, eds., *Trends Towards Coporatist Intermediation* (London-Beverly Hills 1979). Pp. 7-52, p. 13.

6. Lehmbruch, "Sozialpartnerschaft," p. 89.

7. Lijphart and Crepaz, "Corporatism and Consensus Democracy," p. 241.

8. Schmitter, *Trends Towards Corporatist Intermediation.*

9. Lehmbruch, "The Organization of Society, Administrative Strategies and Policy Networks," in Roland M. Czada and Adrienne Windhoff-Heritier, eds., *Political Choice* (Frankfurt 1991). Pp. 121-158.

10. Emmerich Tálos, "Entwicklung, Kontinuität und Wandel der Sozialpartnerschaft," in Emmerich Tálos, ed., *Sozialpartnerschaft. Kontinuität und Wandel eines Modells* (Vienna 1993). Pp. 11-34. Emmerich Tálos and Bernhard Kittel, "Roots of Austrocorporatism: Institutional Preconditions and Cooperation Before and After 1945," in *Contemporary Austrian Studies*, Vol. 4, 1995. Pp. 147-185.

11. Lehmbruch, "Sozialpartnerschaft," p. 99.

12. Franz Traxler, "Gewerkschaften und Unternehmerverbände in Österreichs politischem System," in Herbert Dachs, Peter Gerlich, Herbert Gottweis, Franz Horner, Helmut Kramer, Volkmar Lauber, Wolfgang C. Müller, and Emmerich Tálos, eds., *Handbuch des politischen Systems Österreichs* (Vienna 1991). Pp. 335-352.

13. ÖGB, *Stellungnahme zur Wirtschaftspolitik, Sozialpolitik, Kulturpolitik. 4. Gewerkschaftskongreß* (Wien 1959), p. 5f.

14. *Jahrbuch der Bundeskammer der Gewerblichen Wirtschaft* 1970, p. 156.

15. Ibid.. Pp. 160-161.

16. *Sozialwissenschaftliche Studiengesellschaft* FP 269, 1990.

17. Anton Pelinka, *Modellfall Österreich?* (Vienna 1981), p. 18.

18. Franz Traxler, "Klassenstruktur, Korporatismus und Krise," in *Politische Vierteljahresschrift*, Vol. 28, No. 1, 1987. Pp. 59-79.

19. Emmerich Tálos, "Sozialpolitik und Arbeiterschaft 1945 bis 1950," in Michael Ludwig et al., eds., *Der Oktoberstreik 1950* (Vienna 1991). Pp. 25-40.

20. Ibid.

21. Wolfgang Rudzio, "Entscheidungszentrum Koalitionsausschuß. Zur Realverfassung Österreichs unter der Großen Koalition," in *Politische Vierteljahreschrift*, Vol. 12, No. 1, 1971. Pp. 87-118.

22. Emmerich Tálos, "Sozialpartnerschaft: Zur Entwicklungsdynamik kooperativ-konzertierter Politik in Österreich," in Peter Gerlich et al., eds., *Sozialpartnerschaft in der Krise* (Vienna 1985). Pp. 41-83, p. 72f.

23. Gertrude Neuhauser, "Die verbandsmäßige Organisation der österreichischen Wirtschaft," in Theodor Putz, ed., *Verbände und Wirtschaftspolitik in Österreich* (Berlin 1966). Pp. 3-132, p. 80.

24. Wolfgang C. Müller, Die Rolle der Parteien bei Entstehung und Entwicklung der Sozialpartnerschaft," in Peter Gerlich et al., eds., *Sozialpartnerschaft in der Krise* (Vienna 1985). Pp. 135-224.

25. Johann Farnleitner, *Die Paritätische Kommission* (Eisenstadt 1977).

26. Ilse Bulda, Martin Hengel, and Wolfgang C. Müller, "Das österreichische Beiratssystem in den 70er und 80er Jahren," in Andreas Khol et al., eds., *Österreichisches Jahrbuch für Politik 1989* (Vienna 1990). Pp. 763-787.

27. Christian Schaller, "Verbände und Sozialpartnerschaft," in Herbert Dachs et al., eds., *Handbuch des politischen Systems Österreichs* (Vienna 1991). Pp. 804-815.

28. Bernd Marin, *Unternehmerorganisationen im Verbändestaat. Politik der Bauwirtschaft in Österreich* (Vienna 1986).

29. Emmerich Tálos, Kai Leichsenring, and Ernst Zeiner, "Verbände und politischer Entscheidungsprozeß," in: Emmerich Tálos, ed., *Sozialpartnerschaft. Kontinuität und Wandel eines Modells* (Vienna 1993). Pp. 147-185.

30. Ilse Bulda et al., "Beiratssystem," Pp. 776-779.

31. Egon Matzner, "Sozialpartnerschaft," in Heinz Fischer, ed., *Das politische System Österreichs* (Vienna 1982). Pp. 429-451, p. 434.

32. Gerhard Lehmbruch, "Sozialpartnerschaft," p. 94.

33. Bernd Marin, *Die Paritätische Kommission* (Vienna 1982), p. 197.

34. Ewald Nowotny, "Institutionelle Grundlagen, Akteure und Entscheidungsverhältnisse in der österreichischen Wirtschaftspolitik," in Hanns Abele et al., eds., *Handbuch der österreichischen Wirtschaftspolitik* (Vienna 1989). Pp. 125-148, p. 139.

35. Ibid., p. 139ff.

36. Ibid.

37. Georg Winckler, "Der Austrokeynesianismus und sein Ende," in *Österreichische Zeitschrift für Politikwissenschaft*, Vol. 17, No. 3, 1988. Pp. 221-230.

38. Georg Winckler, "Sozialpartnerschaft und ökonomische Effizienz," in Peter Gerlich et al., eds., *Sozialpartnerschaft in der Krise* (Vienna 1985). Pp. 295-312.

39. Wolfgang Blaas, and Alois Guger, "Arbeitsbeziehungen und makroökonomische Stabilität im internationalen Vergleich," in Peter Gerlich et al., eds., *Sozialpartnerschaft in der Krise* (Vienna 1985). Pp. 255-277.

40. Volkmar Lauber, "Changing Priorities in Austrian Economic Policy," in Kurt R. Luther, and Wolfgang C. Müller, eds., *Politics in Austria* (London 1992). Pp. 147-172.

41. Blaas and Guger, "Arbeitsbeziehungen," p. 266.

42. *Der Standard*, May 7, 1990.

43. Georg Winckler, "Sozialpartnerschaft," p. 301.

44. Emmerich Tálos, and Gerda Falkner, "Politik und Lebensbedingungen von Frauen," in Emmerich Tálos, ed., *Der geforderte Wohlfahrtsstaat* (Vienna 1992), pp. 195-234, pp. 282-294.

45. Alois Guger, "Einkommensverteilung und Verteilungspolitik in Österreich," in Hanns Abele et al., eds., *Handbuch der österreichischen Wirtschaftspolitik* (Vienna 1989). Pp. 183-202, p. 186f.

46. Georg Winckler, "Sozialpartnerschaft," p. 300f, and Volkmar Lauber, "Changing Priorities," p. 149 ff.

47. Ewald Nowotny, "Wirtschaft- und Sozialpartnerschaft und Finanzpolitik," in Peter Gerlich et al., eds., *Sozialpartnerschaft in der Krise* (Vienna 1985). Pp. 313-329, p. 326.

48. Gerd Schienstock, "Neue Produktions- und Arbeitskonzepte als Herausforderung an die Sozialpartnerschaft," in Emmerich Tálos, ed., *Sozialpartnerschaft. Kontinuität und Wandel* (Vienna 1993). Pp. 51-68.

49. Wolfgang Fach and Gerd Gierszewski, "Vom 'sanften' zum 'strengen' Korporatismus," in Peter Gerlich et al., eds., *Sozialpartnerschaft in der Krise* (Vienna 1985). Pp. 279-294, p. 292ff.

50. Fritz Plasser and Peter Ulram, "Politisch-kultureller Wandel in Österreich," in Fritz Plasser and Peter Ulram, eds., *Staatsbürger oder Untertanen?* (Frankfurt 1991). Pp. 103-155, p. 121ff.

51. Peter Ulram, "Politische Kultur der Bevölkerung," in Herbert Dachs et al., eds., *Handbuch des politischen Systems Österreichs* (Vienna 1991). Pp. 466-474.

52. Peter Ulram, "Die Österreicher und die Sozialpartner(schaft)," in Emmerich Tálos, ed., *Sozialpartnerschaft. Kontinuität und Wandel eines Modells* (Vienna 1993). Pp. 131-145.

53. Brigitte Unger, "Internationalisierung und Veränderung der Wettbewerbsbedingungen," in Emmerich Tálos, ed., *Sozialpartnerschaft. Kontinuität und Wandel eines Modells* (Vienna 1993), Pp. 35-50.

54. Franz Traxler, "Vom Nachfrage- zum Angebotkorporatismus?," in Emmerich Tálos, ed., *Sozialpartnerschaft. Kontinuität und Wandel eines Modells* (Vienna 1993). Pp. 103-116.

55. Peter Gerlich, "A Farewell to Corporatism," in Kurt Luther, and Wolfgang C. Müller, eds., *Politics in Austria* (London 1992). Pp. 132-146.

56. Emmerich Tálos, "Interessenvermittlung und Interessenkonzertierung," in Peter Gerlich, and Heinrich Neisser, eds., *Europa als Herausforderung* (Vienna 1994). Pp. 159-183, p. 175f.

5

Economic Policy

Volkmar Lauber

Introduction

With regard to the performance of its economy, Austria appears as one of the most successful countries of Europe since the Second World War. This performance places it today among the wealthiest countries worldwide--not only in terms of per capita GDP, but also in terms of stability of the currency, low unemployment, comprehensive social welfare, and high environmental quality. Somewhat surprisingly, it is also characterized currently (i.e., 1995) by bitter controversy over how to reduce a record budget deficit. The economic record of the Second Republic contrasts strikingly with that of the interwar years. Between the two World Wars, the Austrian economy--except for a few years--did not even reach the output levels of the last year before the First World War; in fact, the GDP of 1937 was lower than that of 1913.[1]

There are many reasons for the economic success since 1945; it originated in different economic and political conditions, internationally and within Austria; in a new economic and political behavior on the part of Austrian society (discussed in other chapters of this book); and finally in a specific orientation of economic policy which showed a high degree of continuity over the decades.

This chapter will sketch the development of the Austrian economy and place it in the context of the new conditions that prevailed since the Second World War. It will describe how certain principles of economic policy evolved during those decades, securing a rapidly growing prosperity. The recent policy of stabilization (to reduce the budget deficit) will be discussed, and finally the prospects of the Austrian economy in the years to come will be assessed. Indeed, there are important changes ahead. Austria, after joining the European Economic Area, has become a member of the European Union. At the same time, exchanges with Eastern Europe are expanding rapidly, and the world economy itself will become more open as a result of the recent GATT negotiations. A reflection on Austria's strategies to deal with those changes will conclude the present chapter.

Difficult Transitions: From the Monarchy to the Second Republic

Industrialization set in comparatively late in the Austro-Hungarian Empire, and the state took an active role to make up for the deficiency of private enterprise. Heavy industry was concentrated in Bohemia and Moravia (today the Czech Republic). Only part of the territory of contemporary Austria was industrialized then, mostly to the East (Vienna, Lower Austria and Styria), and there was a predominance of small and medium-sized enterprises in light industry and manufacturing which depended on basic products and markets from the other parts of the empire that were (except for Bohemia and Moravia) still less developed.[2] The First World War shifted production on the Austrian territory towards armaments while at the same time depleting other sectors.

After this war, the new countries arising from the dismembered monarchy were eager to gain autarky and built up barriers against imports from the other successor states.[3] As a result, Austrian exports to those areas declined dramatically; at the same time, Austrian firms were not yet sufficiently competitive to be very successful in West European markets. The adjustment resulting from this situation amounted to a net de-industrialization of the country; even in the boom year of 1929 Austrian industrial production was still 2 percent below the level of 1913 (in the United States, the increase during the same time period amounted to 81.8 percent).[4] The world economic crisis slashed Austrian exports in half (between 1929 and 1932) and ruined several large banks. When the government came to their rescue, it needed funds equivalent to roughly one third of the federal budget. These sums could only be obtained by incurring a large foreign debt, which was granted in exchange for a strict policy of deflation, budgetary balance and monetary stability. As a result, unemployment climbed from around 9 percent in the years 1923-1929 to about 24 percent between 1932 and 1937. Political antagonisms increased even further and led to the termination of democratic rule in 1933 and to a brief civil war in 1934.

The economic plight of the First Republic seemed to validate the belief--widespread in 1918--that Austria could not survive on its own. In fact, the Austrian parliament had decided in 1918 that Austria would become part of Germany; the allies formally prohibited this choice and also defeated a later attempt at a German-Austrian customs union. By 1938, this belief in the non-viability of an Austrian state helped to smoothe the *Anschluss*, the incorporation into the Third Reich.

The Anschluss was followed by a wave of industrialization, with German firms setting up large plants, often in the area of heavy industry where Austria had been deficient: Iron and steel, aluminum, basic chemicals etc. This was accompanied by large infrastructure projects; electric production from hydraulic dams was doubled; oil production was increased more than thirtyfold.[5] Unemployment receded as the new boom continued well into the Second World War. Austrian production was now oriented towards the wartime needs of the Reich and dominated by German capital whose share in Austrian stock corporations rose, from 9 percent in 1938, to 57 percent in 1945.[6]

Three Postwar Decades: The Establishment of Austro-Keynesianism

Austro-Keynesianism emerged in the first three postwar decades out of several pragmatic responses to the economic problems and opportunities of that time. The war led to new geopolitical realities. Austria was carved up into four zones, each of which was occupied by one of the great powers, with the Soviet zone experiencing an economic development quite different from that of the rest of the country, due to reparation claims and general business insecurity. The Cold War strongly reduced trade relations with countries beyond the iron curtain; at the same time, it made Austria (which was particularly exposed from the Western perspective) one of the chief recipients of Marshall Plan aid on a per capita basis, with about half of this aid going to public sector industry.[7] Against this background, an economic policy was developed whose assumptions were quite different from those prevailing in the First Republic.

It is usually argued that Austro-Keynesianism rests on two preconditions and four different elements. The preconditions are a large public sector and close cooperation between the major interest groups. The four elements consist of, first, the commitment to a hard-currency policy and to trade liberalisation; second, the promotion of investment and savings (supply-side measures); third, the depoliticisation of incomes policy (and to some extent even of business cycle policy); and fourth, the stabilization of demand in times of recession by deficit spending. These preconditions and elements were established at different times; only in retrospect were they viewed together as elements of a coherent design. The overall goal of this policy consisted in promoting stable and favorable conditions for growth and, in particular, for investments, as a response to the Keynesian assumption that investment decisions are characterized by insecurity and instability, in order to achieve the optimal use of resources and production factors.

A Large Public Sector

The period of Nazi rule left Austria with a substantial industrial base (damaged by the war) whose status was quite uncertain in the first years of the Second Republic. In principle, former German property was subject to the reparation claims of the allies. In addition, it was an open question among policy makers at the time whether those industries were not oversized for a small country. Soon an important decision was made: German-owned enterprises in Austria were nationalized--mostly to protect them against reparation claims (here the Soviet Union was most persistant), but also because private capital able and willing to invest the necessary amount was lacking in Austria, and finally for ideological reasons on the part of the Socialists, one of the two large parties in power. As a result, Austria now had one of the largest nationalized industrial sectors of any Western country. This greatly strengthened the position of the labor unions, since these are particularly well organized in the nationalized industries. Their top representatives were powerful not only within their own firms; often they were active politicians (e.g., members of parliament) and enjoyed direct access to the government, at least until the mid-1980s.

Corporatist Cooperation

This quite unusual pattern of close cooperation between the top organizations of labor, business and agriculture is described in greater detail in chapter 4 of this book. The first steps towards cooperation between those groups were taken between 1947 and 1951, when several yearly wage and price agreements were negotiated between the peak associations of business and labor. In one of those years there was a very large strike movement (initiated from below) against the outcome of one such negotiation. The leadership of the labor movement stuck to the agreement however, and the strike collapsed. From then on, incomes policy never again became the object of intense political strife. The cooperative behavior of interest associations lapsed for a few years during the early 1950s, but it was revived in 1956, as will be shown below.

The large role played by labor in this cooperation is usually explained by the absence of significant private capital. Large industrial firms in Austria are either in the public sector or foreign-owned subsidiaries. The peak organization of business is thus dominated by small and medium-sized firms producing largely for the domestic market and divided internally, whereas the large industrial enterprises (oriented towards exports) are often labor strongholds, particularly in the public sector (see the chapter on corporatism in this volume). The labor movement soon identified with the success of exports as a condition for improved welfare and as a result became a valuable partner of the state in its drive for modernization and structural change, with business often considerably more hesitant.[8]

Hard Currency Policy and Trade Liberalization

After a few years of strong state intervention which was unable to contain inflationary pressures, the government undertook the stabilization of the currency in 1952. Inflation was stopped very suddenly. This led to the highest level of unemployment experienced during the Second Republic, close to 9 percent at one point. But the stabilization was successful and the hard currency policy (not yet termed this way) became a central tenet of Austrian economic policy, with only brief deviations. This policy forced export-oriented industries to focus on productivity increases as the chief means to improve their competitiveness and held down the cost of imports, which in turn helped to moderate wage demands. Labor unions also came to accept productivity gains as the main criterion for wage increases. In 1959, the Austrian schilling became fully convertible.

Also in the early 1950s, Austria began to follow a trade-oriented growth strategy and progressively liberalized its import and capital flow regimes. Because of Soviet objection, Austria could not join the newly created European Community (the Soviet government viewed this as contrary to the spirit of Austrian neutrality); however, in 1960 it became a founding member of the European Free Trade Association (EFTA). Since then it also liberalized its trade in the context of several GATT rounds.[9] The resulting international competition promoted a rapid shift of resources into high-productivity lines of production and led to a pace of technological progress above the OECD average. Since 1960, Austria's current external account was close to balance, with a large trade deficit of 4-5 percent of the GDP balanced by a large surplus from tourism. (The real trade balance deteriorated between 1960 and 1973, reflecting insufficient industrial restructuring and the discrimination on the markets of the European Community). The hard currency policy, the increasingly liberal capital flow regime and other elements of Austro-Keynesianism also led to a net inflow of investment capital.[10]

Supply-side Measures

After the succes of stabilization in 1952, the government gave priority to supply-side measures (as they came to be called later on). These encompassed a business and income tax cut of about one third, reducing in just one year the share of taxes in the GDP by more than 10 percent; in addition, the government introduced tax promotion of investments (most importantly an accelerated tax write-off of 50 percent) and savings. It was argued that the growth and employment effects of the tax cut would more than offset the shortfall in revenue; this was confirmed by subsequent developments.[11] Investments rose to a high level and remained there; export increased rapidly. Already Austria was becoming one of the most successful countries of the OECD.

Depoliticization of Incomes/Business Cycle Policy

This boom led to renewed inflationary pressures. The urgent need for an incomes policy was realized by both major parties; at the same time, the achievement of political independance in 1955 removed one fundamental reason for the close cooperation they had been practicing since the war. In this situation the government decided to reactivate the institutions of interest cooperation. The *Paritätische Kommission* (Joint Commission) was set up,[12] a body that consisted of representatives of the four large interest groups plus certain representatives of the federal government, to decide jointly and according to the principle of unanimity on wage and (to a lesser extent) on price increases. The commitment by the trade union federation to act as a strongly moderating influence on wage increases was decisive in creating this institution in 1957 and in making it permanent later on. Since that time, incomes policy did not give rise to significant political conflict; an important source of inflationary tensions was thus brought under control. This proved to be a highly valuable asset in later years.

In the early 1960s the functions of the Joint Commission were expanded to include all major economic issues and to make recommendations thereon to the government. In practice this meant that most of the management of the economy and its business cycle was transferred from the government to the *Paritätische Kommission* and the *Beirat für Wirtschafts- und Sozialfragen* (Advisory Council on Economic and Social Affairs) established in 1963. These bodies concentrated Austrian expertise on economic policy and clearly outmanned the government in this respect; their culture of expertise helped to insulate economic policy-making from the daily political struggles and further enhanced stability.

When the first grand coalition government came to an end in 1966,[13] these institutions became even more important.[14] The government (whose representatives in these bodies now came from the ÖVP only) renounced its right to vote and thereby demonstrated that it would not try to upset the carefully designed balance within the institutions of social partnership.

Deficit Spending

The stabilization of demand by deficit spending in times of recession is most easily viewed as Keynesian today. When, in 1957-58, the international recession came to affect Austria as it did other countries, ÖVP finance minister Kamitz (in office since 1952) chose a response that was quite innovative in Europe, at least outside Scandinavia. In order to stabilize the business cycle, he accepted a rapid and substantial increase of the budget deficit which reached 4 percent of the GDP in 1958. Part of this was due to automatic stabilizers (the automatic shortfall of revenue resulting from the declining tax receipts on business profits). The deficit was used anti-cyclically, and within three years the budget was nearly in balance again. Anti-cyclical budgets came to be an accepted element of Austro-Keynesianism.

The assumption was that deficits in recession years should be reduced quickly and would be offset by surpluses in boom years in such a way as to maintain the level of public debt in absolute terms and to reduce it over the years in terms of percent of GDP.[15] Surpluses were never achieved, but in good years the budget was nearly in balance, and deficits did not surpass the 3 percent mark until the world recession of the mid-1970s.[16]

While the budget deficit principally served to maintain demand in the face of recession, it was also used repeatedly as an instrument against inflation. Thus in the recession of 1967-68 (the most serious since 1958), the government increased the deficit by reducing tax receipts (through lower income tax rates) and by stepping up social welfare spending, but only in exchange for a commitment by organized labor to moderate wage demands. The agreement was a success and the "big bargain" procedure was resorted to repeatedly thereafter.[17]

The Essence of Austro-Keynesianism

In this way, Austrian economic policy from the mid-1950s until the mid-1970s consisted of measures designed to stimulate economic growth and simultaneously to contain inflationary pressures. The incentives to investment and savings helped to contain increases in consumption; Austria developed a very high domestic savings rate and one of the highest investment ratios in the OECD without any significant recourse to foreign borrowing except during 1973-81.[18] The hard currency policy limited profits in exports-oriented industry and thus served to moderate wage demands in that sector. Even the budget deficit was used for anti-inflationary purposes thanks to the "big bargain" procedure described above.

What was Keynesian about early Austro-Keynesianism? Keynes' main concern was with the destabilizing effects of subjective expectations and collective moods which subject a market economy to erratic ups and downs. A downward phase could easily become self-reinforcing, leading to the sub-optimal use of productive capacities.[19] Economic policy in this view should counteract these destructive tendencies by providing a stable environment favorable to business investment and thus to long-term growth.

This is what Austrian economic policy tried to achieve. It provided low and stable interest rates for business; promotion of investment via the tax system; a stable currency linked to the German mark; low rates of inflation and unemployment; and a very stable incomes policy with almost no strikes at all. Economic activity was regulated mostly with the help of automatic stabilizers built into the tax system which reacted quickly and strongly to business cycle variations; in emergencies deficit spending and other forms of demand-side management were also used, with discretionary budget deficits focusing mainly on investment programs and less on social transfers than in many other countries.[20] The large public sector could be counted upon to support government policy. In short, Austria tried to become an investor's paradise while making sure that labor would benefit symmetrically from the resulting growth.

1975-1986: Full Employment by Increasing the Public Debt

In 1970 the Socialists came to power and soon made an effort to become less dependent on the experts from both the corporatist interest groups (even those of labor) and of the finance ministry, who often sympathized with the ÖVP (a similar development occurred in the ÖVP about ten years later). Because of internal disagreements, the Advisory Council on Economic and Social Affairs of the Joint Commission also declined in importance at that time. Corporatist influence was maintained however in the field of wages and prices.[21] In 1972 Austria achieved a free trade agreement with the European Community; membership in EFTA had turned out to be a handicap, since most trade was with Germany and Italy. This agreement, the general international boom of those years and gains in manufacturing competitiveness due to industrial restructuring improved Austria's real trade balance.[22]

TABLE 5.1   Public Debt as Percentage of GDP 1974-1991:
An International Comparison

Austria - Federal Republic of Germany- France - United Kingdom - Sweden - Netherlands - Japan - United States of America

Year	Austria	FRG	France	UK	SWE	NL	Jap.	USA
1974	17.6	19.6	24.7	69.5	30.5	41.3	18.0	40.1
1975	23.9	25.0	25.8	65.2	29.6	41.3	22.5	43.3
1979	36.0	30.7	26.2	55.6	39.6	42.7	47.6	37.8
1980	37.2	31.7	17.6	56.7	51.8	45.3	40.9	45.0
1981	39.3	35.3	17.1	54.9	59.4	50.3	44.9	44.3
1982	41.6	38.7	30.2	54.6	67.5	55.6	72.1	44.9
1983	46.0	40.3	31.8	55.3	72.1	61.9	77.9	49.3
1984	47.9	41.0	34.4	56.7	73.9	66.1	79.5	51.6
1985	49.6	41.7	36.3	54.6	75.1	69.6	80.9	57.6
1986	53.8	41.6	36.9	52.8	72.9	71.3	82.1	61.6
1987	57.3	42.6	38.6	50.4	66.8	75.2	79.5	64.0
1988	57.8	43.1	38.5	42.7	60.2	77.5	76.6	64.9
1989	57.2	41.8	38.1	37.4	54.2	77.8	73.1	67.7
1990	56.4	43.6	36.1	35.4	51.3	76.5	66.5	68.4
1991	57.1	41.9	36.2	36.5	53.9	76.4	63.9	74.6
1994*	64.5	50.1	48.5	52.5	79.1	78.3		

* according to Maastricht definition

Source: OECD, *Economic Surveys 1985-1986: Austria* (Paris, 1986), p. 26. (for the years 1974, 1975, 1979) and ÖSTAT, *Statistisches Jahrbuch für die Republik Österreich 1992* (Vienna, 1993), p. 478 and Österreichische Postsparkasse, *Bericht der österreichischen Postsparkasse über die Finanzschuld des Bundes 1992* (Vienna, 1993), p. 45 (for the years 1990 and 1991) and *WIFO-Monatsberichte*, 8/95, p. 550 (for 1994).

The big challenge came with the two oil crises and the resulting international recession. In order to stabilize demand, the budget deficit in 1975 was set at 4.5 percent of GDP, and at almost 5 percent in 1976. This prevented a sharp decline of investments as it occurred in Germany.[23] To control inflation, the Austrian currency was formally pegged to the *Deutsche Mark*; the hard currency strategy thus became institutionalized.[24] When hopes for a brief recession evaporated, the budget deficit was gradually reduced, but it still came close to 3 percent in 1981. Never before had deficit spending occurred for such a long period. The goal of this policy was to maintain full employment until the recession would be over, at the cost of substantially increasing the public debt (see table 1). Remarkably, most of the deficit spending was used for investments, particularly infrastructure investments.

This policy of deficit spending soon raised questions about the strength of the Austrian currency. Between 1974 and 1978, the Austrian inflation rate was persistently higher than that of Germany, and in 1977 the current account deficit rose to 4.5 percent of GDP. In this situation, OECD and IMF officials questioned the Austrian hard currency strategy; within Austria they were supported by the Federal Business Chamber and the Federation of Industrialists. Chancellor Kreisky was also inclined in favor of devaluation; remarkably the labor unions were opposed to it. In 1978, the new governor of the Austrian National Bank (Koren), the president of the Trade Union Federation (Benya) and the Finance Minister (Androsch) jointly decided to make the hard currency policy stick. Their opportunity came in September 1979, when the Austrian schilling was in fact revalued against the German mark; together with the subsequent appreciation which lasted until 1981, the gain amounted to 4.5 percent. Since that time the hard currency strategy was never questioned again,[25] and the exchange rate with the *Deutsche Mark* remained constant.

As a result, not only was the value of the currency maintained; the policy of full employment was also quite successful, largely because of the wage moderation practiced by the labor unions to secure competitive prices for exports. Public sector industry also maintained a high level of employment until about 1980. In private industry there was considerable labor shedding starting in 1973, but most of this was compensated by expansion in the service sector. As a result, unemployment in 1980 stood only at 2 percent in Austria, compared with an average of about 6 percent in the European member countries of OECD (see Graph 5.1). This was probably the high point of prestige for Austrian economic policy.

The second oil crisis considerably modified the picture. Both public and private industry reacted with substantial reductions of the work force. Unemployment went up steeply, though even in 1985 it amounted to less than half the average of OECD Europe. The government stepped up subsidies (especially to large public sector firms) and promoted early retirement, thus shifting the problem from the labor market to the social security system whose deficit promptly increased.[26] The budget deficit reached a new record level in 1983 (about 5.5 percent); the public debt increased by another large jump.

Economic Policy

Faced with these developments, chancellor Kreisky, during the 1983 electoral campaign, proposed new taxes on wages and capital incomes, as well as cutbacks in the social security system. The top associations of business and labor were willing to support these proposals. However, the ÖVP--in opposition since 1970, short on economic ideas of its own but looking with increasing frustration for a theme on which it could challenge the government--decided to make a populist issue out of the proposed package of relative austerity and posed as the advocate of the "little people." This was a rare instance when economic policy was politicized. Party competition indeed did not produce superior results. The government did not dare to stick to its proposals and took a step backwards. Even so the Socialists lost their parliamentary majority in the election, and Kreisky retired.

GRAPH 5.1   Unemployment in Austria, Germany and OECD Europe Since 1974 (percentage)

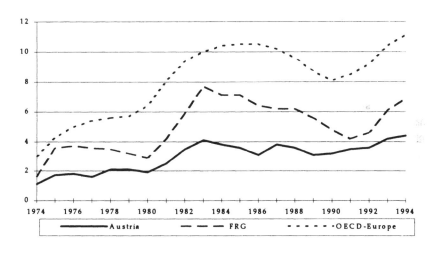

Sources: OECD, *Quarterly Labour Force Statistics*, No. 1, 1995 (for FRG and OECD-Europe 1974-1991); *Statistische Übersichten. Beilage zu Statistische Nachrichten*, No. 7, 1995 (for FRG and OECD-Europe 1992-1994); OECD, *Labour Force Statistics 1970-1990* (Paris, 1992) (for Austria 1974-1990); *Statistische Übersichten. Beilage zu Statistische Nachrichten*, No. 7, 1995, table 16.4 (for Austria 1991-1994).

Preparing the Turnabout. Between 1983 and 1986, Austria was governed by a coalition between the SPÖ and FPÖ (the latter was a party with a liberal orientation at that time; see chapter 3 of this book). The government realized the need for budget consolidation but did not want to incur its political costs in the face of ÖVP criticism. There were some new taxes and some cuts in expenditures, and finance minister Vranitzky announced a restriction on subsidies to public sector industry. When in late 1985 VOEST (the largest nationalized firm, engaged mostly in steel production) suffered a financial debacle, public sector minister Lacina dismissed all of its chief managers and stressed the importance of profitability. In a major reform, public sector industry was placed on a new legal basis.

Having played a role as a motor of industrialization in the first two post-war decades (e.g., by providing the economy with cheap basic materials), and as a stabilizing factor in the business cycle until the 1970s, the public sector lost its dynamism towards the end of that decade.[27] This was partly due to the fact that many of its productions were in decline just as in other industrial countries (especially iron and steel). But nationalized industries had also become the playground of the two big political parties, whose patronage consisted in the appointment of managers and in granting security of employment to the work force; of shop stewards and labor unions; and of economic interests (investment goods and construction sector, banks). Major organizational innovations that spread among private corporations were simply ignored; there was no strategic planning. Highly centralized structures were administered rather than managed.

The small coalition government operated a major reform by placing the nationalized industrial sector on a new legal basis and by curbing the practice of political appointees to chief management positions. The new chairman of the ÖIAG (Austrian Industrial Holding Corporation) introduced modern management principles; the new board reduced employment by 20 percent (about 20,000 people) within three years, and without strikes. But the law still contained no clear statement on corporate goals and responsibilities.[28] As early as 1985, Vranitzky declared that the SPÖ was quite open to the idea of privatizations and viewed this a a purely pragmatic matter.

In mid-1986, Vranitzky became chancellor, broke with the FPÖ when it elected Haider as its new leader and called a snap election. Before that election Vranitzky presented his own economic program. Its core consisted in a strong reduction of the federal budget deficit from about 5 percent in 1986 to 2.8 percent by 1991, mostly by cutting back expenditures. Privatizations would be carried out where it made sense for pragmatic reasons, to raise funds or to improve performance. This was presented as a contrast to the ÖVP, which in its 1985 program made privatizations an electoral and ideological issue.[29] Vranitzky--also for electoral reasons--played the part of the serious manager.

In this way Vranitzky integrated the neo-conservative policy reorientation more quickly even than the conservative ÖVP, who was now deprived of opportunities for criticism. With remarkable speed, Vranitzky also set a sometimes reluctant SPÖ on this new course. In the election of 1986, the SPÖ emphasized the consolidation of the budget, structural reforms and privatizations for the public sector. From past experience (in 1983) it was clear that budget consolidation, and to some extent structural reform, called for a grand coalition with the ÖVP. In fact, Vranitzky was clearly preparing such a course.[30]

1987-1993: Half-Hearted Consolidation and Restructuring

The new grand coalition government between the SPÖ and ÖVP was formed in early 1987. It drew its legitimacy from the widely recognized need to consolidate public finance and to improve the structure of production by acting on the supply-side, and from the idea that only a government with a very strong and solid majority, acting over two legislative terms (i.e., eight years), could implement such a policy which would invariably meet with resistance from different corners. Consolidation was required to prevent public finance being dominated by the debt problem; if the previous policy were continued, interest payments and debt amortisation would soon crowd out other budget items.[31] Restructuring was necessary because, in the early 1980s, Austrian competitiveness had declined and economic growth rates fallen below the average of OECD-Europe, despite unemployment rates that were substancially lower. The reasons for this were seen in the insufficient adjustment of Austria's economic structure to changing international markets.

Budget consolidation

The budget policy announced by the new government in 1987 set itself the goal of reducing the federal budget deficit gradually to 2.5 percent by 1992 and to stabilize the gross debt around 50 percent of the GDP. This goal was to be reached by expenditure cuts, privatizations and a reform of the tax system. A lengthy period of austerity was envisioned.

Consolidation as it was practiced followed a somewhat different pattern. Expenditure cuts were decided rather quickly and brought down federal outlays from 33 percent of GDP in 1986 to 30 percent in 1990. But in fact, austerity lasted for only two years. The unexpected boom of 1988 brought higher revenues than anticipated, and in 1991 the federal budget deficit was increased once more. Since then it has not been reduced. Already in 1990, the consolidation target of 2.5 percent of the GDP originally set for 1992 was shifted to 1994.[32] Financial discipline was relaxed for several reasons. First, the boom which started in 1988 was (mistakenly) expected to last in Austria (despite the beginning worldwide recession) and to produce increased revenues. Second, the ÖVP was so weakened politically by competition from the FPÖ that it did not dare to impose the planned sacrifices upon its traditional constituencies. Third, new programs for social welfare were introduced; also, the fall of the iron curtain required new expenditures such as infrastructure investments in transports or public assistance to refugees. Fourth, even though fiscal policy was tightened again in 1992, the recession which started to affect Austria in mid-1992 reduced tax receipts and by 1993 even led the government to give a small stimulus to the economy.

Until the onset of the 1993 recession, the overall picture of the public sector deficit was more positive than this enumeration would make it seem to be. The general government account (on a national account basis) covers the federal, state and local governments and the social security system; its financial balance is a better measure than the federal deficit alone, even though the latter dominates public discussion in Austria. The general government financial deficit declined steadily between 1987 and 1992, with the exception of 1991 when a slight increase was registered. In 1992, its level was below 2 percent of the GDP, less than half of what it had been in 1987. By international comparison, this deficit (in terms of GDP) was one of the lowest in the OECD area in recent years.[33]

After 1987, budget consolidation succeeded in moving the primary financial balance of the general government (i.e., the budget balance net of interest payments on the public debt) into surplus. From 1988 until 1992, this surplus was larger than the level required to stabilize the debt ratio of the GDP. As a result, the debt/GDP ratio reached a level which is close to the OECD average. In 1993 however, due to the large budget deficit at the federal level, indebtedness for the first time exceeded the criteria laid down at Maastricht.[34]

Privatizations and tax reforms were part of the coalition agreement concluded in early 1987. The privatizations helped to reduce the budget deficit by about 40 billion Austrian schillings until 1990; from 1991 to 1993, their volume was insignificant.

Structural reform

The grand coalition agreement of 1987 included a structural policy package to act on the supply side, in order to strengthen competitiveness throughout the economy (not just in industry). Concern about structural deficiencies of the Austrian economy had reemerged with the poor growth performance of the early 1980s; this concern was intensified by the prospect of stepped-up European integration. It rested on the assumption that Austrian firms were insufficiently dynamic in their adaptation to changing international conditions. This deficiency in turn was seen to result from insufficient incentives to performance (insufficient rewards for risk-taking, excessive taxation of profits) or even from practices and regulations that provided certain sectors of the economy with a comfortable existence despite a suboptimal performance.

Tax reform. The tax reform of 1989 was one of the most sweeping in the history of the Second Republic; its main goal was to act on the supply side by considerably lowering income and corporate tax rates and by suppressing incentives to low risk/low yield forms of investments and savings. This was meant to reorient resources towards business ventures promising high profits rather than tax avoidance. Financial resources for business were to be provided in the future by an effective capital market, not by special tax incentives or subsidies. While many traditional tax deductions and investment premiums were abolished, the corporate tax rate was lowered to only 30 percent (one of the lowest in Europe; the German corporate tax rate was 50 percent at that time) to promote profitablity and to attract new firms to Austria. On the revenue side, the tax reform was meant to make the automatic stabilizers more responsive again to GDP growth and to stop the erosion of the tax base by closing loopholes; in the short run, however, the reform reduced revenue due to the tax reductions mentioned above.[35]

A second tax reform in 1994 also lowered taxation (partly to stimulate demand) on both wage-earners and business. Business also benefits from an exceptional tax break on investment, and generally from a significant administrative simplification of its taxes. With the two tax reforms, Austria, which once had quite high taxes on business, became a country with remarkably low business taxation; in 1994, the total tax burden on business will amount to less than two thirds of its equivalent in Germany (estimated at 39.5 percent and 61.6 percent respectively).

Public sector restructuring and privatization. The main steps to restructure the nationalized industries were taken by the small coalition government in 1986. The grand coalition added to this its program of privatizations. The SPÖ/ÖVP coalition agreement of early 1987 and a more detailed program at the end of that year provided for the state to keep enterprises of vital importance and to privatize by issuing shares for only a minority of the capital (the last point was due to the pressure of the labor unions on the SPÖ). In this way, a number of enterprises were partially privatized until 1990: the National Oil Corporation

(OMV), the country's two largest banks (Creditanstalt-Bankverein and Länderbank) who have extensive industrial holdings of their own, the Federal Electric Utility Corporation, Austrian Airlines, and a large number of smaller firms plus real estate holdings sold purely for revenue purposes. These privatizations were meant to terminate a practice of state subsidies (especially to obsolescent productions), to stress management responsibility and to create a constituency of shareholders that would counterbalance the influence of the labor unions and militate for greater profitability.

As to the core of public sector industry, the branch holdings grouped together in Austrian Industries and for whom ÖIAG now served as financial holding, privatization was postponed for the time being upon the insistance of the SPÖ in order to prepare an "Austrian solution", i.e., an arrangement that would create an Austrian "national champion" (large corporations in Austria are either nationalized or subsidiaries of foreign multinationals, and it is often argued that Austria should have "champions" of its own to confront integration in the world market). Shares were to be issued only in the early 1990s.[36] During the boom of 1989-1991, the restructuring of the public sector seemed highly successful; even the national steel maker (VOEST) returned to profitability. But in 1992, the situation deteriorated due to competition from Eastern European countries in traditional sectors (metals, cement), the persistance of structural problems, and management errors especially in the aluminum sector (AMAG). In 1993, this reached crisis proportions, with AMAG close to bankruptcy. This crisis upset the original concept of an Austrian national champion; at ÖVP insistence the different firms that form Austrian Industries will be privatized individually.

Even before the 1990 elections, the SPÖ had given up the principle that the state had to retain the majority of shares in case of privatization. Finance minister Lacina even declared that he could well imagine total privatization of the two largest banks (Creditanstalt and Länderbank), provided that they remained in Austrian hands and that the structural problems of the bank sector were settled at the same time by the creation of the larger units.[37] Even these conditions were at least partially abandoned in the coalition negotiations in late 1994. By mid-1995, both large banks are still looking for partners, even though Länderbank had merged with Vienna Central Savings Bank to form Bank Austria.

The sheltered sector. By OECD estimates, in the late 1980s about half of Austria's GDP was produced in sectors sheltered from competition. This concerned above all the large numbers of small and medium-sized firms (mostly outside the secondary sector) which are subject to the Trade Regulations Law (Gewerbeordnung) and to similar legislation that supposedly ensure the quality of goods and services by a tight control of competition and market access. Such regulations were successfully lobbied for by corporatist business organizations.[38] In addition, the protected sector includes the liberal professions, transportation, telecommunications, banking and insurance, and the marketing of agricultural commodities. In several areas, measures were taken to step up competition, with limited success so far.[39] It is widely agreed among the top leadership of the two large parties and the large interests groups that a major productivity reserve is at stake here, but because of the expected electoral costs involved, there is great reluctance to take direct and effective measures. The government and the large parties and interest groups were counting on European Community/European Union membership to solve this problem by the resulting intensification of competition and various legal challenges.[40]

Perspectives of the Austrian Economy Today

The international recession of the early 1990s affected Austria lightly in comparative terms. In the monetary turbulences of 1992/93, the Austrian currency was revalued along with the *Deutsche Mark*. Exports to several European countries were adversely affected by revaluation and recession, but those to North America, East Central Europe and East Asia increased. This shift was confirmed when exports recovered again in 1994.[41]

In mid-1995, the outlook for the Austrian economy was again quite favorable. To be sure, there were problem areas. Unemployment was still low in comparative terms (with close to 4.5 percent in 1994 it stood at less than half the EU average), but it is rising in a long-term trend.[42] Part of it is hidden by early retirement; few people are still in the workforce by the age of sixty, fewer than in any other OECD country. Receipts from tourism seem to be embarked on a decline. The sheltered sector still resists competition and is insufficiently dynamic. At the same time several developments are likely to enhance productivity and income, perhaps even employment: the opening of Eastern Europe; accession to the European Union; and the expansion of trade with other parts of the world. In economic policy, many of the preconditions of Austro-Keynesianism seem about to disappear.

The Opening of Eastern Europe

As a result of the opening of the borders, Austria moved from a position at the edge of the European economy towards what may well be the centre of a future European growth area. It may thus become a highly attractive location for industry, commerce, and for financial and corporate headquarters of multinational corporations doing business in that area. Increased Austrian trade with the eastern neighbours led to substantial benefits. Between 1988 and 1994, exports to Hungary, the Czech Republic, Slovakia and Slovenia increased at an average annual rate of 20 percent (imports: 15 percent), leading to a considerable surplus which replaced the earlier trade deficit. In 1994, Austria supplied nearly 12 percent of all OECD exports to Eastern Europe.[43]

Eastern Europe also attracts Austrian direct investment. At the end of 1992, Austrian firms participated in about 11 percent of foreign joint ventures in those countries (in East-Central Europe--Poland, Czech Republic, Slovakia, Hungary this share even amounted to 18 percent). The flow of Austrian investments to that area multiplied after 1989 and represents a considerable share of all Austrian direct investments abroad.[44] Austrian industry is in the process of shifting a significant part of its total production to Eastern countries to become more competitive by taking advantage of low production cost there (labor, energy etc.).[45]

Open borders with Eastern Europe also put pressure on traditional resource- and/or labor-intensive productions and thus imposes industrial restructuring; the share of these productions in Austrian industry is generally considered to be too large, while that of science-based products stand at less than half of OECD (or world) average, though growing extremely rapidly.[46] Import competition in the more traditional sectors already led to stepped-up calls for protection, despite the fact that, so far, Austria has been a net beneficiary of trade with Eastern Europe.[47]

Finally, open borders brought an inflow of cheap labor from Eastern Europe. Because of growing unemployment in Austria and an increasing politicisation of this issue, expecially by the FPÖ and its leader, yearly quotas for foreign workers were established beginning in 1993. Officially, foreign workers represented close to 10 percent of the work force in 1995; to this figure "underground" foreign labor, estimated at several percentage points, must be added.[48]

European Integration

The idea of a European Economic Area (EEA)--i.e., a special association of EFTA-countries with the European community--was launched before 1989, partly to offer an attractive option to countries who otherwise might have reservations about membership due to their neutral status. After the demise of Soviet power in Eastern Europe, those reservations fell by the wayside and the EEA served as preparation for membership in the European Community, renamed European Union. The EEA started in 1994 and was expected to enhance competitive pressures and productivity in the service sector, and particularly in Austria's sheltered sector. Productivity in these domestically oriented sectors had stagnated of late, while it had been rising exceptionally fast (in relation to most OECD-countries) in the export and import-competing sectors.[49]

In 1989 Austria applied for membership in the EC. The *avis* of the European Commission was highly positive and stressed Austria's likely contribution to the Community: an economic performance and dynamism above average, public finances meeting the Maastricht convergence criteria (a rare feat among European countries)[50] and a high level of political stability. The problems the Commission perceived related to the structural trade balance deficit (usually compensated by tourism; this sector produces about 8 percent of the GDP and is the strongest in the world in per capita terms[51]); the large share of resource-/labor-intensive productions; the relatively high influence of government on business; the lack of large Austrian corporations; the existence of a large sheltered sector; and considerable agricultural surpluses.[52] The biggest economic impact of EU membership in the medium term is expected in the sheltered sector, in the form of stepped-up competition. This process is now under way. If the Economic and Monetary Union (Maastricht) should establish an area of monetary stability in Europe, this should not present problems for the Austrian economy; in particular there should be no deflationary shock. However, there may be serious problems due to the current budget deficit. At the same time it will become more difficult to conduct economic policy at the national level.

Changing Preconditions for Economic Policy-Making

In the first postwar decades, Austro-Keynesianism seemed to steer the country from success to success. In the mid-1970s, a series of significant budget deficits, lasting more than a decade, appeared to indicate the abandonment of that strategy. Did 1986 bring the return to earlier concepts and prescriptions? Do current conditions and policies offer similar promises of success?

The large public sector has shrunk, and will clearly shrink some more due to additional privatizations. In any case it has lost much of its earlier significance. Due to labor shedding and structural change it lost in relative importance; and its labor representatives no longer enjoy the position they once had. This may have a significant impact in political terms. Strong labor unions represented one of the pillars of corporatist interest group cooperation at top levels. Because a larger share of economic policy was turned over to the market since 1986, social partnership itself lost in importance. Growing unemployment, structural change in the traditional sectors and the difficulty of organizing labor in the service sector compounds the situation of the trade unions. By promoting the mobility of capital, the EU will further weaken labor's position; trade union hopes for corporatist cooperation in Brussels seem unwarranted at this time.[53]

This growing asymmetry may threaten social partnership, the other precondition of Austro-Keynesianism. It is hard to predict how a diminished role of labor organizations will affect the politics of incomes and business cycle policies, and more generally, political and economic stability, at a time when full employment no longer seems possible. One probable consequence is that the share of wages in the national income will fall. Austrian labor unions played an important role in organizing wage restraint (in exchange for full employment), in making wage increases dependent on productivity increases and in containing wage-and-price spirals. It may well be that the tradition of wage restraint and the reliance on productivity gains to determine wage increases will persist for some time, particularly in an environment of intensified competition; but this tradition is likely to erode and to give way to particularistic strategies of the various groups. The rancorous discussions surrounding the austerity packages in 1994 and 1995 may represent a foretaste of things to come, although in those years the intense controversy resulted primarily from the logic of party competition.

Another element of Austro-Keynesianism consisted in the (supply-side) promotion of investment and savings. Here important changes took place in 1986. Investments are now promoted, and foreign investors attracted, by low business taxes on profits rather than by tax deductions on investments. Savings are not similarly promoted anymore but instead are left to the capital market, which since 1991 is one of the most liberal of the OECD.[54]

As to the hard currency strategy, it is likely to last and to merge with the policy of the European Economic and Monetary Union. However, this depends on a successful budget consolidation over the next four years. Increasing the budget deficit in difficult times--the last element of Austro-Keynesianism--was no longer considered an acceptable policy from 1986 to 1993, when it was practiced again under the impact of the crisis (mostly as a result of automatic stabilizers). Most likely there will be a gradual return to greater financial discipline over the next few years, accompanied by considerable strife over distributing the costs of austerity among the different groups. Depoliticization of incomes and business cycle policies is clearly a thing of the past.

The New Fiscal Crisis (1993 and After)

The consolidation of the budget, which had progressed (albeit more slowly than expected) from 1987 to 1991, came to a halt in 1992. 1993 brought a massive setback as a result of the international recession which by then had reached Austria. The dramatic increase in the federal budget deficit was mostly due to the operation of the automatic stabilizers; in addition, a tax deduction to promote investments was granted on a temporary basis. For the first time, Austria no longer met the Maastricht criteria for membership in the economic and monetary union (budget deficit below 3 percent, state debt below 60 percent of the GDP).

The next two years saw a further deterioration of the situation. In 1994, a tax reform was enacted which reduced taxation both on wage-earners and business. In an important departure from the past, this reform made Austria a country with a remarkably low business taxation (amounting to only about two thirds of the corresponding taxation in Germany).[55] On the other hand, the diminished receipts enhanced the 1994 deficit. Austria's accession to the EU in 1995, which beyond the regular contribution entailed an exceptional, one-time payment, produced a similar effect. The budget deficit, calculated according to EU standards, now reached about 5.5 percent of the GDP. This was one of the biggest deficits since the beginnings of Austro-Keynesianism.

New measures to consolidate the economy and the budget began in 1993. In the fall of that year, yet another "big bargain" was struck: The 1993 tax reform was invoked to induce moderation in the area of wage and price increases. A lowering of the interest rate and other credit costs and a ban on new taxes and on increases of charges and fees levied by local and regional government were also part of the bargain. All this was intended to strengthen business competitiveness. In fact, the recession began to lift towards the end of 1993.

After the 1994 parliamentary election, the government took to drawing up a new medium-term austerity program. Its first formulation was somewhat more ambitious than the previous program for the 1987-1992 period. Consolidation was to be reached predominantly through cuts in expenditure (civil service, welfare payments, investments, subsidies). But the agreement negotiated between the two parties of the governmental coalition, without social partner involvement, met with unexpectedly strong resistance. The representatives of labor strongly protested against the one-sided burdens on wage earners and announced their determination to fight the implementation of this program. As a result, the planned cuts were almost halved subsequently; this was compensated for partly by tax increases (a measure which the ÖVP had originally opposed very strongly). In the end, this will lead to a record deficit which, if it were repeated next year, would endanger Austria's triple A rating on international capital markets (which in turn would mean bigger interest payments on the debt). The difficult political battle about austerity induced the government to ask the social partners to participate in the preparation of the next austerity package (for the fiscal year 1996), returning to the practice of the previous decades. But there was no ready consensus when the results became known in the late summer of 1995.

The two big parties could not agree on implementing this package; in addition, the deficit seemed to be larger than envisioned at first. As a result, conflict broke out with renewed intensity. Between 1986 and 1994, the ÖVP had been rather lukewarm about austerity, fearing that parts of its electorate might then go over to the FPÖ. By 1995 the SPÖ was constrained by a similar fear and seems to have drawn a line on cutbacks affecting its own clientele. By contrast, Wolfgang Schüssel, the ÖVP's new leader and now vice-chancellor, seemed eager to bring the conflict to a head and pushed for further cuts with increasing determination. He drew encouragement from public opinion surveys which showed him to be Austria's most popular political leader (something that no ÖVP politician had achieved for many years), and he was egged on by Haider who was eager to characterize any ÖVP concession to the Social Democrats as a sell-out. In October 1995, the ÖVP somewhat surprisingly announced that budget negotiations had foundered and called for new elections. This is where things stood at the time of this writing.

Under these circumstances, the near future is characterized by an unusual degree of uncertainty. Over the decades, economic policy has contributed to making Austria, one of Europe's poorer states during the interwar period, a member of the leading group of industrial countries with regard to economic performance, standards of social welfare and environmental quality.[56] Austria is one of a few countries that form the bloc of monetary stability in Europe. But it is not certain now whether it will be able to meet the Maastricht criteria by 1998, especially with regard to state debt.[57] Exceptional political stability was an important asset in the past. This stability is now under question.

Notes and References

1. Fritz Weber, "Die wirtschaftliche Entwicklung," in Herbert Dachs et al., eds., *Handbuch des politischen Systems Österreichs*, (Vienna, 1991). Pp. 20-36, p. 34.

2. Ibid. at pp. 23-25.

3. Helmut Kramer, *The Impact of the Opening-Up of the East on the Austrian Economy--A First Quantitative Assessment*, Österreichische Nationalbank/ Auslandsanalyseabteilung Working Paper no. 11 (March 1993), p. 4.

4. See table 5.1 in Fritz Weber, "Die wirtschaftliche Entwicklung," op.cit., p. 25.

5. Stephan Koren, "Struktur und Nutzung der Energiequellen Österreichs," in Wilhelm Weber, ed., *Österreichs Wirtschaftsstruktur gestern, heute, morgen* (Berlin, 1961). Pp. 159-222.

6. Fritz Weber, "Die wirtschaftliche Entwicklung," op.cit., p. 31.

7. Ibid., p. 32.

8. Franz Traxler, "Interests, Politics, and European Integration," in *European Journal of Political Research*, Vol. 22, No. 2, 1992. Pp. 193-217.

9. OECD, *Economic Surveys 1992-1993: Austria* (Paris, 1993), p. 58.

10. Ibid., pp. 45-51.

11. Karl Aiginger, "Die wirtschaftsprogrammatischen Vorstellungen der ÖVP 1945-1985," in *Schwarz-bunter Vogel* (Vienna, 1985), pp. 98-100.

12. See chapter 4 of this volume.

13. See chapter 3 of this volume.

14. Wolfgang C. Müller, "Die Rolle der Parteien bei Entstehung und Entwicklung der Sozialpartnerschaft," in Peter Gerlich, Edgar Grande, and Wolfgang C. Müller, eds., *Sozialpartnerschaft in der Krise* (Vienna, 1985). Pp. 162-175; E. Talos, "Sozialpartnerschaft: Zur Entwicklung und Entwicklungsdynamik kooperativ-konzertierter Politik in Österreich," in Peter Gerlich, Edgar Grande, and Wolfgang C. Müller, eds., *Sozialpartnerschaft*. Pp. 67-81.

15. Stefan Koren, "Monetary and Budget Policy," in Kurt Steiner, ed., *Modern Austria* (Palo Alto, 1981), p. 180.

16. For details see the table by Manfred Hellrigl in Volkmar Lauber, "Changing Priorities in Austrian Economic Policy," in *West European Politics*, Vol. 15, No. 1, 1992. Pp. 147-172, p. 151.

17. Ewald Nowotny, "Wirtschafts- und Sozialpartnerschaft und Finanzpolitik," in Peter Gerlich, Edgar Grande, and Wolfgang C. Müller, eds., *Sozialpartnerschaft*. Pp. 313-329, at pp. 326-327.

18. OECD, *Economic Surveys 1992-93: Austria* (Paris, 1993), pp. 45-47.

19. Gunther Tichy, "Austro-Keynesianismus gibt's den? Angewandte Psychologie als Konjunkturpolitik," in *Wirtschaftspolitische Blätter*, Vol. 29, No. 3, 1982. Pp. 50-64, at pp. 57-60.

20. Erich Streissler, "Die Fiktion des Austro-Keynesianismus. Zum realexistierenden 'Keynesianismus' im Schrifttum von Hans Seidel," in *Wirtschaftspolitische Blätter*, Vol. 3, No. 5-6, 1987. Pp. 714-725, at p. 720.

21. Wolfgang C. Müller, "Die Rolle der Parteien," Pp. 180-193; Nowotny, "Wirtschafts- und Sozialpartnerschaft," p. 323.

22. OECD, *Economic Surveys 1992-93: Austria* (Paris, 1993), p. 51.

23. Wilhelm Hankel, *Prosperity Amidst Crisis* (Boulder, 1981), p. 182.

24. Eduard Hochreiter, and Georg Winckler, *Signaling a Hard Currency Strategy: The Case of Austria*. Österreichische Nationalbank/ Auslands-

analyseabteilung, Working Paper no. 10, November 1992, introduction and chapter 1.

25. Ibid, chapters 4.3 and 5. In August 1993 there was a brief bout of speculations against the Schilling, but it could be handled easily.

26. Ewald Nowotny, "Prozesse und Institutionen der finanzpolitischen Willensbildung," in Wolfgang Weigel, Eckhard Leitner, and Rupert Windisch, eds., *Handbuch der österreichischen Finanzpolitik* (Vienna, 1991). Pp. 226-229; Emmerich Tálos, "Arbeitslosigkeit und beschäftigungspolitische Steuerung," in Emmerich Tálos, and M. Wiederschwinger, eds., *Arbeitslosigkeit. Österreichs Vollbeschäftigung am Ende?* (Vienna, 1987). Pp. 91-166.

27. Karl Aiginger, "Eine zukunftsorientierte Industriepolitik vor dem Hintergrund der Verstaatlichten-Krise," in Andreas Khol, Günther Ofner, and Andreas Stirnemann, eds., *Österreichisches Jahrbuch für Politik 1992* (Vienna, 1993). Pp. 487-503 at p. 499.

28. Karl Aiginger, "Industriepolitik," in Herbert Dachs et al., eds., *Handbuch des politischen Systems Österreichs*. Pp. 513-524, at pp. 518-519.

29. Delia Meth-Cohn, and Wolfgang C. Müller, "La réalité en face: Les politiques de privatization en Autriche," in Vincent Wright, ed., *Les privatisations en Europe* (Arles, 1993). Pp. 209-269, at pp. 213-214.

30. Manfred Hellrigl, *Paradigmen und Wirtschaftspolitik. Die Rolle von Policy-Paradigmen in der Wirtschaftspolitik der Zweiten Republik*. Research project supported by the Jubiläumsfonds of the Austrian National Bank, Project No. 3551 (Salzburg, 1990).

31. OECD, *Economic Surveys 1987-88: Austria* (Paris, 1988), p. 19.

32. OECD, *Economic Surveys 1992-93: Austria* (Paris, 1993), p. 34; Gerhard Lehner, "Die Budgetkonsolidierung--eine Notwendigkeit", in Andreas Khol, Günther Ofner, and Alfred Stirnemann, *Österreichisches Jahrbuch für Politik 1991* (Vienna 1992), p. 557; *Salzburger Nachrichten*, June 14, 1994.

33. OECD, *Economic Survey 1992-93: Austria* (Paris, 1993), pp. 36-37.

34. According to the Maastricht Treaty, those EU countries who meet specified economic criteria should set up the core of a European currency by 1997. One of the criteria regards government debt, which should not exceed sixty percent of GDP. M.J. Artis, "The Maastricht Road to Monetary Union," in *Journal of Common Market Studies*, Vol. 30, No. 3, 1992. Pp. 299-309.

35. Gerhard Lehner, "Ökonomische und steuerpolitische Auswirkungen der Steuerreform 1988," in Andreas Khol, Günther Ofner, and Alfred Stirnemann, eds., *Österreichisches Jahrbuch für Politik 1988* (Vienna 1989). Pp. 591-613. Ewald Nowotny, "Die große Steuerreform 1988--Analyse und Bewertung," in Andreas Khol, Günther Ofner, and Alfred Stirnemann, eds., *Österreichisches Jahrbuch für Politik 1988* (Vienna 1989). Pp. 571-589.

36. Delia Meth-Cohn, and Wolfgang C. Müller, "La réalité en face: Les politiques de privatization en Autriche," op.cit., pp. 220-226.

37. Ibid., pp. 226-227.

38. OECD, *Economic Surveys 1989-90: Austria* (Paris, 1990), p. 59; OECD, *Economic Surveys 1992-93: Austria* (Paris, 1993), p. 64.

39. OECD, *Economic Surveys 1995: Austria* (Paris, 1995). Pp. 86-96.
40. Franz Traxler, "Interests, Politics, and European Integration," op.cit., pp. 205-207.
41. *Der Standard*, August 7/8, 1993; OECD 1994 (op.cit.), pp. 30-31; OECD 1995 (op.cit.), p. 5.
42. Ibid., pp. 42-43.
43. Jan Stankovsky, "Die wirtschaftliche Bedeutung der Transformation in Osteuropa für Österreich," in Andreas Khol, Günther Ofner, and Alfred Stirnemann, eds., *Österreichisches Jahrbuch für Politik 1991* (Vienna 1992). Pp. 469-489; Jan Stankovsky, "Marktstellung in Ost-Mitteleuropa bedroht," in *WIFO-Monatsberichte*, June 1993. Pp. 322-328; Helmut Kramer, "The Impact of the Opening-Up of the East on the Austrian Economy," op.cit., p. 488; OECD, *Economic Surveys 1992-93: Austria* (Paris, 1993), p. 89; OECD, *Economic Surveys 1995: Austria* (Paris 1995), pp. 81-83.
44. OECD 1993 (op.cit.), p. 26; Jan Stankovsky, "Marktstellung in Ost-Mitteleuropa bedroht," op.cit., p. 327. Austrian direct investment abroad increased steadily from about Sch13 billion in early 1989 to about 60 billion in 1994; nearly a third of this sum went to Eastern Europe (*Salzburger Nachrichten*, August 16, 1995).
45. OECD, *Economic Surveys 1992-93: Austria* (Paris, 1993), p. 73.
46. Ibid., pp.74-76; Karl Aiginger, "Wirtschaftsstandort Österreich," in Andreas Khol, Günther Ofner, and Alfred Stirnemann, eds., *Österreichisches Jahrbuch für Politik 1994* (Vienna 1995), pp. 491-92.
47. Helmut Kramer, "The Impact of the Opening-Up of the East on the Austrian Economy," op.cit., pp. 13-14; and comments by Andreas Wörgötter in the same volume, pp. 24-29.
48. Figures from the Bundesministerium für Arbeit und Soziales 1995.
49. OECD, *Economic Surveys 1992-93: Austria* (Paris, 1993), p. 17; Aiginger, "Eine zukunftsorientierte Industriepolitik," op.cit., p. 492. Also Jan Stankovsky, "Die Bedeutung des EWR für Österreich," in *WIFO-Monatsberichte*, December 1991. Pp. 666-670.
50. Franz Nauschnigg, "Die EG auf dem Weg zur Wirtschafts- und Währungsunion--Auswirkungen auf Österreich," in *Wirtschaft und Gesellschaft*, Vol. 18, No. 3, 1992. Pp. 341-355.
51. OECD, *Economic Surveys 1992-93: Austria* (Paris, 1993), pp. 54 and 82.
52. Helmut Kramer, "Strukturprobleme aus der Sicht des Avis der EG-Kommission," in *WIFO-Monatsberichte*, September 1991, pp. 519-521.
53. Franz Traxler, "Interests, Politics, and European Integration," op.cit., p. 209.
54. OECD, *Economic Surveys 1992-93: Austria* (Paris, 1993), p. 63.
55. Undersecretary of the Treasury Ditz in *Salzburger Nachrichten*, June 17, 1993.
56. Karl Aiginger, "Eine zukunftsorientierte Industriepolitik," op.cit., p. 493.

57.OECD, *Economic Surveys 1995: Austria* (Paris, 1995), p. 38; Fritz Breuss, and Fritz Schebeck, "Budgetkonsolidierung in kurz- und mittelfristiger Sicht," in *WIFO-Monatsberichte*, April 1995. Pp. 270-274.

6

Foreign Policy

Helmut Kramer

Introduction

Austrian foreign policy in the Second Republic (since 1945) can be considered and described from several perspectives.[1] First, in this fifty year period, it is the foreign policy of a country that worked its way up from an initially difficult economic and political position to that of one of the economically most successful and politically most stable industrial countries in Europe. With good reason, one could say that Austria's flexible and enterprising foreign policy, which always carefully considered the international situation as well as national interests, contributed significantly to this "success story" (described in detail in other chapters of this book). Austria's international and foreign policy status in the Second Republic stands in marked contrast to the experiences in the period between the First and Second World War, when Austria was "a state no one wanted" and in which political and economic sovereignty was restricted to a minimum by massive pressures and interventions on the part of foreign powers (see chapter 1 of this book). Second, Austria's foreign policy since 1955 has been the foreign policy of a neutral country. Its policy of neutrality was conceived from the start as "active." Austria played an active role in international organizations, in particular in the United Nations, it started and supported foreign policy initiatives to reduce military and political tensions in the international system and it offered "good offices" through conference diplomacy in mediating conflicts and by being the seat of international organizations (Vienna as the third center of the UN). Third, Austria's foreign policy can be seen and interpreted as the foreign policy of an (industrially developed) smaller state.[2] Small states try to compensate for their relative weakness in power and foreign policy resources and their dependence on the external environment by diversifying the focus and the level of the foreign policy strategies. On the other side, they attempt to concentrate on international domains and foreign policy questions which are important to them and less important to the bigger and to the very big actors in the international system, thus taking advantage of the "difference in the distribution of attention" (Frei 1977, 213; Elgström 1983) and of opportunities for "free-riding"-strategies.[3] Like the other European neutral small(er) states, Austria was very active in multilateral foreign policy, notably in the UN and in other international organizations where small states tend to take part as an equal actor and partner. These multilateral activities of small states can be also seen as contributions towards transforming the international system into a more democratic and more stable order, one more suitable for the realization of their foreign policy needs and interests. Another important small-state-strategy is to invest in "like-mindedness", by seeking out arrangements and cooperation with countries that have similar or complementary interests (e.g. the neutral and non-aligned states within the framework of the CSCE-process). Fourth, a study and description of Austria's foreign policy from the end of the Second World War to the mid-1990s cannot ignore the structural changes in the international system and in international politics. Above all, in the last decades the nation-state and the traditional foreign policy decision-makers had to reckon with a considerable number of new partners and new spheres of action in the international system. Public opinion and grassroot groups have a growing interest in and an increasing influence on foreign policy. With the end of the East-West conflict and the democratic revolution in Eastern Europe, the structural break in 1989 decisively increased the complexity of the international system (Rosenau 1990; Camilleri and Falk 1992; Laidi 1992). These changes in the international environment and the political-organizational set-up of foreign policy-making have been forcing Austria, now rising economically to a "middle power", to a revision of its former foreign policy and security strategies.

In the following description of the development of Austrian foreign policy, five main periods or phases will be distinguished in the 1945-1995 timespan. They show significant differences regarding issues, the regional concentration of activity and, due to the changing international environment, the potential for success in achieving goals. The last foreign policy period starts with the collapse of the Communist system in Eastern Europe in the autumn of 1989 and ends on January 1, 1995 when

Austria together with Finland and Sweden acceded to the European Union.

From the End of World War II to the Austrian State Treaty
(1945-1955)

Until Austria regained full independence in the year 1955, Austrian foreign policy was to a very high degree limited by the decisions and interests of the four allied occupying powers (United States, Soviet Union, Britain, France). In the first years after the war it thus was imperative for the Austrian government to restrict the extensive control the Allies had (Cronin 1986). An important step here was the second Control Agreement in June 1946 that limited the veto rights of the occupation authorities. This success was, to a large extent, the result of the Austrian government's skillful negotiating tactics (Steiner 1977, 172; Cronin 1986, 38; Rauchensteiner 1987, 82f). By reacting flexibly to the negotiating positions of (and the disagreement among) the occupying powers, an optimum could be achieved in crucial questions affecting the country's economic and political recovery. As a result, Austria could take part in the American Marshall Plan (European Recovery Program, ERP) without any major objections on the part of the Soviet Union. Austria was the only country under partial Soviet occupation that received Marshall Plan Funds (Mähr 1989, 82; Tweraser 1995). It received the highest per capita allocations of all the countries benefitting from ERP funds (962 million dollars from June 1948 until December 1953). The Austrian economy was subject to extensive control by the Economic Cooperation Agency (ECA) which was set up by the USA to implement the Marshall Plan. Nonetheless, a skillful and flexible strategy made it possible to use the economic aid as the Austrians themselves saw fit.

In establishing this flexible policy in the difficult political constellation after the war, Austria tried to follow a clear course of action. It tried "to model itself on Switzerland...to have good friends everywhere and not to bind itself to one side" (President Theodor Körner in February 1952, quoted by Stourzh 1981,74). This active and flexible strategy proved particularly successful in the period from 1953 onwards, particularly in 1955, the year of the Austrian State Treaty (Rathkolb 1995a, 130f). With the change in Soviet foreign policy under Khrushchev and the willingness of the Eisenhower administration to make concessions, it was possible to attain full sovereignty on rather favorable terms. The Austrian State Treaty, which was signed on May 15, 1955 in Vienna, and the Declaration of Permanent Neutrality that followed a few months later on October 26, were both great achievements for Austria, its interests and its foreign policy, and at the same time "also an internationally important touchstone of success: the State Treaty as the first sign of surmounting the Cold War" (Plaschka 1981,47; Stourzh 1975 and 1988; Verdross 1978; Larson 1987; Bischof 1988; Gehler 1994).

An important prerequisite of this "shrewd foreign policy" (Verosta 1975, 56) was the broad domestic political consensus on the basic goals and the general orientation of domestic and foreign policy. To be sure, there were at times clashes and tensions between the two governing parties, the ÖVP and the SPÖ, over tactical questions and decisions, such as the issue of South Tyrol (Bischof 1995, 111f), or with regard to the assessment of the leeway available to secure a policy for the completion of the State Treaty (Schärf 1955, 132f). In the SPÖ, there was also displeasure at the fact that, as in the First Republic, the diplomatic apparatus was largely dominated by officials associated with the conservative *Lager.* (Denk and Kramer 1988, 269; Rathkolb 1990, 499). But as Adolf Schärf, the SPÖ party chairman and Vice-Chancellor at the time, stated, there was "agreement on the principle that there should be a bipartisan foreign policy" (Schärf 1955, 132; Denk and Kramer 1988, 272).

This far-reaching political agreement between the two major parties and their efforts to be politically united in order to achieve national independence also produced less enviable results. Because they wanted to put Austria in the best light possible, the Austrian political elites argued that Austria bore no blame or responsibility for National Socialist crimes. Most Austrians did not face up to the pernicious role many of their countrymen had played under Hitler. This was also reflected in the meager compensation for the Jewish victims of National Socialism and in the lack of sensitivity and support, for those emigrants who wished to return after the war, on the part of the government and other institutions such as universities (Knight 1988 and 1991; Sternfeld 1990).

Besides attempting to settle the question of South Tyrol and other contentious problems in its relations with its neighbors, Austria's foreign policy made an effort to establish diplomatic relations with as many states and international personalities as possible. The following table (table 6.1) documents the development of the Austrian diplomatic service after the Second World War.

At the end of 1945, there was only one Austrian diplomatic mission, the *Amt des Bevollmächtigten* (Office of the Plenipotentiary) in Prague. In 1946, political missions were established in Moscow, Washington, Paris and London. By 1950, there were twenty-five diplomatic missions abroad (Steiner 1977; Bielka 1983).

TABLE 6.1 Austrian Diplomatic Missions

	1950	1955	1959	1966	1970	1979	1983	1989	1994
West	9	14	16	17	18	18	18	18	18
Eastern Europe	7	7	7	7	7	8	8	8	12
European Neutrals	2	2	3	3	3	3	3	3	3
Asia	2	4	5	9	11	17	20	19	22
Africa	1	1	1	7	8	13	16	12	11
Latin America	4	4	5	6	7	9	10	8	11
Total	25	32	39	49	54	68	75	68	76

Source: Amtskalender der Republik Österreich, Außenpolitischer Bericht, Jahrbuch der österreichischen Außenpolitik (various issues).

Parallel to this diplomatic offensive on the state level, the ÖVP and the SPÖ were active in the international associations of their respective political groupings (European Union of Christian Democrats, Socialist International) (Demblin 1984; Denk and Kramer 1988). Even before it had achieved full sovereignty, Austria successfully applied for membership in important international organizations such as GATT, the International Monetary Fund and the World Bank, as well as in the specialized agencies of the UN (ILO, WHO, FAO, and UNESCO). Austria's admission to the UN was thwarted at first by a Soviet veto. With the support of the USA, the Austrian government again applied for membership on July 2, 1947, and was also supported by Brazil and other developing countries. Admission finally came after the State Treaty in 1955. Active participation in international organizations provided the opportunity to participate in the work of the community of states as an equal partner. Making its mark in multilateral diplomacy also meant "increasing its importance internationally" (Strasser 1967, 7; Quendler 1991), a useful asset in the context of its struggle for national independence. Austria also actively strove for maximum participation in European integration. It was a founding member of the OEEC (1948), the forerunner of the OECD that played an important role in Europe's economic recovery after 1945. Austria also tried to keep a close relationship to the Council of Europe (Burtscher 1988) before becoming a member in 1956.

For the many foreign policy tasks however, there was a relatively small amount of resources and personnel available. As before 1938 there was no independent Foreign Ministry (such a ministry was established only in 1959). It had been abolished in 1923, as part of the austerity policy forced by the Geneva Stabilization Agreement. At that time Austria had to downgrade the Foreign Ministry to a division of the Chancellor's office.

From 1945 to 1955, the central foreign policy goal was certainly to regain complete independence. But there were also other very difficult and highly charged problems to solve, especially in the relations with two neighboring countries, i.e. Italy and Yugoslavia. From the day the war was over, Austria attempted to regain South Tyrol from Italy (the predominantly German-speaking South Tyrol had to be ceded to Italy in 1919). However, the allied powers did not support this claim. After lengthy negotiations the Gruber-de Gasperi Agreement was signed in September 1946 (Karl Gruber and Alcide de Gasperi were foreign ministers of Austria and Italy, respectively). It provided for a certain amount of autonomy in school matters and in legislation and established a system of ethnic proportionality for public offices in South Tyrol (Ermacora 1984). Another problem for Austria was the Yugoslav claim to parts of Carinthia and Styria. The allied powers agreed in 1949 to leave Austria's southern border unchanged. After his break with the Soviet Union the Yugoslav leader, Tito, was interested in good relations with his Western neighbors. He dropped his claim and relations with Austria were normalized (Bielka 1983, 198).

Foreign Policy and Neutrality: Integration and Emancipation (1955-1968/70)

The Austrian State Treaty and the Declaration of Permanent Neutrality brought to its end a period in which attaining independence had largely dominated the foreign policy agenda. Though Austria declared its neutral status on its own accord, this decision was to an important extent a political necessity due to the new international constellation of the Cold War. It was now imperative to define this neutrality--a task that the Austrian government and population were hardly prepared for (Rauchensteiner 1987, 322). The Moscow Memorandum of April 1955 specified that after signing the State Treaty, Austria would make a declaration that would commit it "to a permanent neutrality as practiced by Switzerland" (Stourzh 1975, 164).Austria's history and geo-political position differed, of course, from those of its western neighbor. Austrian foreign policy makers decided from the very beginning that they would follow a policy of neutrality that "would take more risks and be more dynamic" than Swiss policy (Bonjour 1980, 80). The goal of the Austrian government was "to do everything possible to make its contribution to international understanding in active cooperation in organizations encompassing the whole world" (Declaration of Foreign Minister Figl at the signing of the State Treaty, quoted by Csaky 1980, 409). In contrast to Switzerland, Austria became member of the United Nations in December 1955. It was also admitted to the Council of Europe in 1956 and became a signatory of its European Convention on Human Rights.

"Though East-West Crises are"--according to the Finnish political scientist Harto Hakovirta in his study on the European Neutrals in the East-West conflict--"tests of neutrality, their consequences for neutral states are not always negative; crises also provide the opportunity to demonstrate what neutrality means in practice" (Hakovirta 1988, 144). The events of late autumn 1956, the uprising of the Hungarian population against the communist regime and its bloody repression by the Soviet army, were to become the first major test of Austrian neutrality. As Reiner Eger points out, Austria's behavior during the Hungarian uprising was "courageous" and even "provocative" towards the Soviet Union, especially when compared to the restraint of the West, which was tied down by the Suez Crisis (Eger 1981,34; Hakovirta 1988, 208). The "firm and clear position taken by the Austrian government" (Steiner 1977, 184), the decisive measures taken to secure the borders and to safeguard neutrality, were fully supported by the Austrian population (Steiner 1977, 184; Rauchensteiner 1987, 342,354; Eger 1981). The extremely positive international image in the West and the international community, on account of what the United Nations called Austria's "exemplary achievement" in absorbing and caring for the Hungarian refugees (Eger 1981, 68), was above all due to the spontaneous outpour of help on the part of the Austrian population. This "foreign policy from below" clearly shaped the government's decision to speak out without reservations against any form of ideological neutrality. The decision was made after initial caution motivated by the concern that a public opinion highly critical of the Soviet Union might endanger Austria's neutrality. However, according to witnesses, "the mood was such that the government simply had to go along with it" (*Profil* May 8, 1990).

As a result, the Hungarian crisis of 1956 seriously strained the relationship between Austria and the Soviet Union. However, the Soviet Union's anti-Austrian campaign, which was concerned that the Austrian model of neutrality could spread to its East European satellites, subsided surprisingly soon. The visit of Deputy Prime Minister Mikoyan to Vienna in April 1957 initiated a new phase of intensive contacts and positive dialogue between the Soviet Union and Austria. As in the case of Soviet policy towards Finland after 1956/57, the relations to neutral Austria were shaped to fit with Moscow's new foreign policy course of "peaceful coexistence" between different social systems, between superpowers and small states, to ease tensions in Europe and the world (Harkovirta 1988, 59f). Austrian neutrality was to be interpreted and practiced as the Austrians themselves decided; this was made clear to an Austrian government delegation that visited Moscow in July 1958. Austria's self-determined neutrality was seen by Khrushchev and other leading Soviet politicians as an important factor for stability, helpful for reducing tension in Central Europe (Zemanek 1984, 20; Neuhold 1986, 92f). The link between an active foreign and neutrality policy and détente was expressed by Bruno Kreisky in an article in *Foreign Affairs*:

> At no time have we been in doubt that Austrian neutrality is only a function of an international equilibrium, and that it would be in grave danger if this equilibrium is disturbed. It follows, then, that Austrian foreign policy must always aim to help maintain the balance of power by contributing in all ways possible toward lessening international tensions (Kreisky 1959, 277).

Shaping Austria's policy of neutrality called for a considerable amount of diplomatic finesse and political sensitivity. Austria's security as a neutral state depended decisively "on how much interest the powers in the East and West--above all the Soviet Union and the United States--attributed to maintaining Austria's special status and to the usefulness of the policy of this neutral country situated between East and West of seeking consent and preserving peace" (Haymerle 1983, 150). Rather inevitably though, the process of strengthening Austria's self-confidence in foreign affairs and its emancipation from the four signatory powers of the State Treaty brought about some turbulence and foreign policy discord with the United States, a country to which the Austrian government and people felt obliged as a result of support rendered after the war. The instrument of neutrality seemed to collide with the strict friend-enemy formula of US "containment" policy. On its side the Austrian government, despite clearly emphasizing its affiliation to the West, was not prepared to make itself available for the *cordon sanitaire* built by the United States around the Soviet Union (Kremenyuk 1984, 97). The government in Washington and particularly the U.S. military, worried about the strategic disadvantages resulting from the existence of a "neutral bolt" (Austria, Finland) across Europe. Even before the signing of the State Treaty such apprehensions about an Austrian "neutralistic course" had been made public (Luchak 1987, 315f; Rathkolb 1995b). Tension between the United States and Austria reached its peak in 1958 during the Lebanon Crisis. U.S. transport planes flew over Austrian territory without authorization from the Austrian government, which reacted with a diplomatic protest. Furthermore, the United States was not happy that Austria joined the Danube Convention (in which only Warsaw Pact states and Yugoslavia were full members) without consulting any of the Western signatory powers. In the early 1960s, relations between the United States and Austria improved noticeably. Washington had begun to concentrate its foreign policy increasingly on areas outside of Europe--in Latin America, the Middle East, and Indochina. The United States valued Austria and Vienna highly as a meeting place for summit conferences and superpower dialogues, but otherwise in the 1960s Austria received significantly less attention from U.S. foreign policy than it had in the 1940s and 1950s (Luchak 1987).

Austria (and Vienna) became, along with Switzerland (and Geneva), one of the most important "meeting places of coexistence" (Kreisky 1981, 551). Particularly important in this respect were the international organizations that settled in Vienna, such as the International Atomic Energy Agency (IAEA) in 1957, OPEC in 1965 and UNIDO in 1967. Important international conferences, and in particular the summit meeting between Khrushchev and Kennedy in June 1961, did much to enhance the image of Austria and Vienna. Neutral Austria could highlight its international usefulness also by participation in peace-keeping-operations of the UN that started in the early 1960s (Congo 1960-1963, Cyprus 1964, Middle East since 1967; Caytas 1982). This active role made it easier for the Austrian government to find support in the UN for its own foreign political interests (in the South Tyrol question and in developing Vienna into one of the UN's three official seats; Michal-Misak 1990).

In 1959 Foreign Affairs was set up as an independent ministry. For the first time in the Second Republic a Socialist--Bruno Kreisky--was in charge of Austria's foreign policy. Undoubtedly, this administrative expansion was also an expression of newly-won self-confidence and of a development in which "the foreign policy of Austria found its specific rhythm" (Haymerle 1983, 169).

In the area of bilateral foreign policy Austria made efforts to establish diplomatic relations with a maximum number of countries. Diplomatic contacts were intensified, Austrian government officials made state visits abroad and foreign dignitaries came to Austria; new embassies were established in the Third World, especially in Africa (table 6.1). Of particular importance was Austria's *Besuchsdiplomatie* ("diplomacy of state visits") in Eastern Europe. Kreisky was the second Western foreign minister to visit Poland (March 1960), and the first in Romania (July 1963), Hungary (October 1964) and Bulgaria (July 1965). Austrian foreign policy, which was "emulated by the whole West" (Kreisky quoted in Skuhra 1987b, 124), continued to be a "window to the Eastern world" (Chancellor Klaus 1966, quoted in Meier-Walser 1988, 158) even during the years in which the ÖVP governed alone (1966-1970). It was not difficult for Austria's foreign policy elite to understand the specific and differing positions of their Eastern and Southeastern European neighbors, given their long historical association with this region. Austria's foreign policy emphasized its close attachment to Western pluralistic political principles in its contacts to its Communist neighbors in the East, and the frequent contacts fulfilled an important function in the "normalization" of East-West relations (Bielka 1983; Haymerle 1983).

The two most important and most difficult foreign policy issues in the 1960s were the problem of South Tyrol and Austria's relationship to the European Economic Community, founded in 1957. The question of South Tyrol was only settled towards the end of the 1960s. The Austrian government felt it was compelled to internationalize the problem after Italy circumvented and undermined the agreement negotiated in 1946, which granted partial autonomy to South Tyrol. The autonomy statutes were applied by Rome not only to this area, but to the whole region Trentino/South Tyrol in which the Italian speaking population had a majority. Foreign Minister Kreisky addressed this issue at the General Assembly of the UN in 1959 and 1960. Tension between Austria and Italy increased when South Tyrolean activists carried out bomb attacks in Italy. The Austrian army was deployed to close the border to terrorists acting from Austrian territory. The acts of violence subsided, and when government posts in Rome were taken over by politicians like Aldo Moro, who was more sympathetic to minority rights, a "package" of measures to protect the rights of the German-speaking South Tyroleans was negotiated. In 1969, an agreement was reached on an "operational calendar" to carry out the negotiated measures (Alcock 1970 and 1982; Meier-Walser 1988, 243f).

With regard to its relations to the dynamic ally evolving European Economic Community (EEC, later EC) Austria--like Sweden, Switzerland and Finland--found itself in a painful dilemma. It had to reconcile its neutral status with participation in economic integration (Katzenstein 1975; Hakovirta 1988; Luif 1988). After the EEC was founded by Germany, France, Italy and the Benelux countries (March 1957), Austria supported Great Britain's proposal of a large European free trade area. When this initiative failed, the European Free Trade Association (EFTA) was established. Austria and the other neutrals (with the exception of

Finland, which became an associated EFTA member only in 1961) were founding members. After membership in the EC was ruled out on the grounds of Austria's neutrality and once the attempt to build a multilateral link between the EEC and EFTA had failed, Austria attempted to negotiate a broad association agreement with the EEC. Initially this was done together with Sweden and Switzerland. Warnings and *démarches* were repeatedly sent by the Soviet government indicating that any more extensive Austrian economic arrangements with the EC would mean a "renunciation of the State Treaty and the neutral course that has proven so effective" (Soviet President Podgorny 1966 during a visit in Vienna, quoted by Luif 1988, 115; Meier-Walser 1988, 214f). The negotiations with the EC broke down in 1967 due to an Italian veto (because of the conflict over South Tyrol) and French opposition (Maier-Walser 1988, 235).

The EC question also produced the first cracks in the bipartisan consensus on foreign policy in the 1960s. It was not just disagreement on tactics as in the 1940s and 1950s, but rather diverging designs for European, economic and social policy that were at stake in the serious differences of opinions between the ÖVP--the majority of which preferred closer economic ties to the EC--and the SPÖ. For the first time in the Second Republic, foreign policy became an important controversial question as was shown in the negotiations for a new coalition government. After the 1962 parliamentary elections the ÖVP claimed the foreign ministry for itself. The ÖVP did not succeed and Kreisky remained Foreign Minister. But responsibility for negotiations on economic integration was transferred to the Minister of Trade, Fritz Bock of the ÖVP (Rauchensteiner 1987, 447f).

During the years when the ÖVP governed alone (1966-70), the narrower political basis for active foreign and neutrality policy became obvious during the Czechoslovak Crisis in the late summer and fall of 1968. According to the opinion of the mass media and opposition parties, the government under Chancellor Josef Klaus did not react decisively enough, in speaking out against the military intervention of the Soviet Union and other Warsaw Pact states, during this recurrent "test of neutrality" (Klaus, quoted in Schlesinger 1972, 53). "Serious shortcomings and mistakes in the decision-making process and in the cooperation between the political and military leadership" were sharply criticized by the opposition (Meier-Walser 1988, 434; Eger 1981). At the end of the 1960s, a veritable crisis of legitimacy developed in Austria's armed forces. It can be said generally that the political status and the social acceptance of the military in Austria is clearly lower than in other European countries. This is the result of the historical experiences of the Austrians--the Austrian military has been on the losing side every time for over a century by now--and the realistic assessment that neutral Austria, surrounded by NATO and the Warsaw Pact, would have little chance to effectively deter an attack. Furthermore, the Austrian State Treaty prohibited the Austrian army from acquiring long-range artillery and--decisively--missiles. As a result, and despite its commitment in the Declaration of Neutrality to maintain and defend its neutrality "with all the means at her disposal," Austria has economized on defense spending. On average, little more than 1 percent of the GDP has been spent on the military over the years (on average 1.2 percent in the years 1960-1989). The other neutrals, particularly Switzerland and Sweden, have spent between 2 percent and 3 percent of their GDP on defense (Vetschera 1990; Unterberger 1992).

Globalization of Foreign and Neutrality Policy (1968/70-1983/84)

The phase of global orientation in foreign and neutrality policy that began when the SPÖ under Chancellor Kreisky formed the government in Spring 1970 had already been prepared by Kurt Waldheim, Foreign Minister in the Klaus cabinet. Waldheim, who before taking over the Foreign Ministry in January 1968 was the Austrian representative at the United Nations, anticipated the essential elements of Kreisky's foreign policy concept by equating foreign policy with neutrality policy and by reducing the importance of the military dimension in national security policy (Meier-Walser 1988, 93, 383, 444; Höll 1994, 37). The general global (and domestic social) conditions at the end of the 1960s and in the early 1970s fostered Austria's new course. Détente between the United States and the Soviet Union permitted an expansion of the scope of action for neutral and small states (Hakovirta 1988). Also, the economic and political weight of the Third World, particularly the OPEC countries, became stronger. The activation of Austria's foreign policy, the attempts to offer "services which to be sure were restricted in their global significance, but still useful for international politics" (Kreisky quoted in *Arbeiterzeitung*, October 29, 1983) were further supported by the process of modernization and the opening of Austrian society, reflected by the increase in educational levels and the incorporation of the Austrians in the unfolding "world society" (foreign travel, foreign trade, the oil shock of 1973). The characteristic post-war syndrome of shutting themselves off from the world in terms of awareness and information on international affairs made way for more cosmopolitan attitudes (Kicker et al. 1983; Kramer 1984; Höll 1994).

In the first years of the SPÖ government, the main focus of foreign policy was still Europe. In 1972, the Austrian government succeeded in concluding an extensive Free Trade Agreement with the EC. These agreements--the EC signed similar agreements with Switzerland, Finland, and Sweden--were compatible with Austria's status of neutrality. The Soviet Union, which took a negative attitude towards the EC in the early 1970s, softened its position somewhat after concluding the *Ostverträge* (Eastern Treaties) with West Germany and raised no objections. The Free Trade Agreement, from which agricultural products were excluded, meant that until 1977 in most areas of foreign trade with EC countries (Luif 1988, 131f; Schultz 1992) customs and trade barriers for commercial and industrial goods were completely abolished. Graph 6.1 shows the increase in trade between Austria and the EC countries during the 1970s and 1980s.

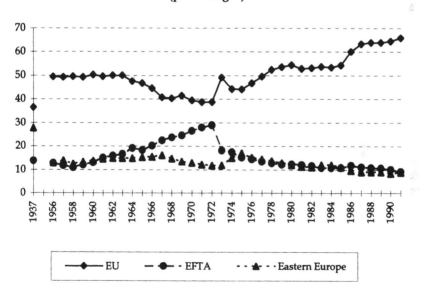

GRAPH 6.1 Austrian Exports to the EU, EFTA and Eastern Europe (percentages)

Source: Luif 1992, p. 41 (updated by Luif)

Regarding its neighbors, Austria's relations to Italy were normalized as a result of the agreement on the question of South Tyrol. In November 1971, Franz Jonas was the first Austrian head of state to officially visit Italy since the Republic of Austria was founded in 1918. At that time turbulences developed with Yugoslavia. In the early 1970s, the conflict over the Slovenian minority in Carinthia flared up. In several diplomatic protests the Yugoslav government accused the Austrian government, which had been unable or unwilling to prevent activists of the German nationalist *Kärntner Heimatdienst* (Carinthian Patriotic Front) from dismantling the bilingual topographic inscriptions, of violating the State Treaty on the issue of minority rights. By the mid-1970s, however, contacts between Kreisky and Tito, particularly within the framework of their attempts to ease tensions in Europe, had helped to fully re-establish good neighborly relations (Bielka 1983, 213f; Höll 1988).

Together with the other European neutrals, especially Finland, Austria contributed decisively to the Final Act of the CSCE (Conference for Security and Cooperation in Europe) which was signed in August 1975 in Helsinki (Höll 1986; Lehne 1991). The Austrian government concentrated its efforts on persuading the United States and other western countries, which at first displayed little interest in the political project of a CSCE-process, to take an active part in it. Within the framework of the CSCE follow-up conferences in Belgrade 1977-78, in Madrid 1980-83, and in Vienna 1986-89 and of several special conferences, the European neutrals--in cooperation with the non-aligned countries in Europe (N + N Group)--made themselves available for technical and political "good offices" to ensure the successful continuation of the CSCE-process and to safeguard and reinforce détente and stability in Europe. By "actively using their independence from existing blocs and groups in setting up communication between opposing interests and in supporting the search for solutions" (Zemanek 1984, 20), the neutral and non-aligned states could negotiate their own security interests in the context of the CSCE as equal partners to the larger states and the world powers, i.e. the United States and the Soviet Union. At the same time they could help establish and strengthen general positive international norms in the community of states (Birnbaum 1987, 150f; du Bois 1984; Lehne 1991).

Austria was most active and enjoyed its greatest reputation in the United Nations during the 1970s. Kurt Waldheim was elected Secretary General of the United Nations in 1971 and confirmed in office for another term in 1976. Austrian representatives served as chairmen of important UN-commissions. In October 1972, Austria was elected by the General Assembly (by 115 out of 118 votes) to one of the non-permanent seats in the Security Council. Austrians were thus able to have an impact upon international politics and to collect valuable foreign policy experience in the handling of global crises (Middle East War, Cyprus Conflict, Southern Africa; Jankowitsch 1975). Analyses of the UN voting record show that by aligning itself with like-minded countries Austria, together with Sweden, developed its own independent position at the end of the 1970s (Dolman 1981). Austria was also active in the Council of Europe, which is apparent from numerous initiatives and the election of the Austrian representative Karl Czernetz as president of the Parliamentary Assembly (1975-1978) and of Franz Karasek as secretary-general of the organization in 1979.

Besides these activities in the field of multilateral diplomacy and in the United Nations, the SPÖ government under Bruno Kreisky began increasingly to develop its own independent initiatives. An attempt was made to use the status and political independence of a neutral country to contribute to the reduction of differences and tensions in the world, particularly in the North-South conflict. The Austrian government did not avoid confrontation or political risks. Austria was after Finland the first European neutral participating with a guest status at the 1970 summit conference of the Movement of Non-Aligned Countries in Lusaka. It was among the first Western countries to establish diplomatic relations with the People's Republic of China in May 1971 and with the German Democratic Republic (East Germany) in December 1972. Among the political activities that contributed to Austria's good reputation in many Third World countries (President Kaunda of Zambia praised "Austria's positive neutrality policy"; *Arbeiterzeitung,* May 1, 1981) were, above all, Bruno Kreisky's initiatives in the conflict between Israel and the Palestinians. In three Fact Finding Missions of the Socialist International which he directed in March 1974, February 1975, and March 1976, Kreisky attempted to contribute to solving this conflict. In November 1974 Kreisky, who took a more and more critical view of the Israeli government, declared before the United Nations General Assembly that for a peaceful solution it was essential "that the intricate problem of bringing peace to the Middle East cannot be solved without taking into account the legitimate aspirations of the Palestinian people" and that the PLO and its political leader, Arafat, be recognized as the most important partner in the peace talks (Kreisky 1981, Vol. II.455; Thalberg 1983).

Austria's active position in supporting the Third World also had the goal of "distinguishing itself in the eyes of the developing countries by being open to and showing solidarity for their interests in order to win their support for Austria's international ambitions" (Michal-Misak 1985, 83). The enhancement of Vienna's position as the third seat of the UN is to an important extent the result of the improvement of Austria's reputation in the Third World. After building a large UN Center in Vienna that was handed over to the the UN and the IAEA in 1979, a number of important UN agencies were transferred (International Drug Control Programme, Centre for Social Development and Humanitarian Affairs, Commission for International Trade Law) from New York and Geneva to Vienna. The number of UN employees in the Vienna

International Center rose from approximately 3,200 at the end of the 1970s to more than 4,000 in the 1980s. Austria's active policy of bringing international organizations to Vienna was seen by the government and by the population as a way of protecting their national security, as "a necessary investment for safeguarding neutrality" (Neuhold and Zemanek 1968, 23). As expressed by Kreisky: "International Organizations based in Austria are important from a security and political point of view. They are as valuable as big stores of arms which might never be used" (Kreisky quoted in *Financial Times*, August 21, 1979).

From 1974/75 onwards, the policy of actively supporting the Palestinians' right to self-determination led to growing differences of opinions between Washington and Vienna. In his first years as Chancellor, Kreisky restrained from critically commenting on US policy in areas of conflict in the Third World (Kramer 1986, 188; Luchak 1987, 343), which was in clear contrast to the Swedish government under Olof Palme, whose sharp criticism of the US intervention in Vietnam led to the temporary suspension of diplomatic relations between the United States and Sweden. Kreisky can be regarded a "true 'Atlanticist' ... who appreciated the democratic achievements of the US society and accepted the hegemonic position of the United States" (Höll 1994, 40; Rathkolb 1994). However, in the second half of the 1970s, Kreisky became more radical in his position on the Middle East. At the UN in October 1979, Kreisky declared that he considered the PLO the legitimate representative of the Palestinian people. In March 1980 Austria officially recognized the PLO, which set up an office in Vienna. In the US Congress, this unusual form of diplomatically recognizing the PLO was called "the misguided effort of a small neutral country to put itself on the map" (quoted by Luchak 1987, 398). The US displeasure over Kreisky's initiatives increased when Kreisky invited the Libyan dictator Gadhafi to Vienna and criticized the Reagan Administration's Middle East policy. Austria also did not take part in the Carter Administration's economic boycott of Iran. Like Switzerland, the Austrian government let the Austrian participants and officials decide for themselves whether to take part in the Moscow Olympics (the United States and other Western countries boycotted the games to protest against the Soviet military intervention in Afghanistan in December 1979). Austria attempted to mediate when American diplomats were taken hostage by the Khomeini regime in Iran and again in the Afghanistan conflict, but was unsuccessful in both cases.

The international conditions for a foreign policy of "active neutrality" deteriorated at the end of the 1970s and in the early 1980s as the Cold War intensified and the political and economic importance of the Third

World decreased. The SPÖ government's foreign policy--conceived and represented abroad above all by Chancellor Kreisky--was now increasingly criticized in Austria by the opposition in parliament. Kreisky's Third World policy was rebuked by the ÖVP as a dangerous trend towards "anti-Americanism," as "neutralism," and as "equidistance" between the USA and the Soviet Union, and in any case not very beneficial for Austria's interests. The views of the SPÖ government on neutrality, the concept of an "active" and "dynamic" neutrality and foreign policy similar to that of Sweden, were rejected as the inadmissable "total equation of foreign policy with neutrality policy" (Khol 1981, 114). In 1982, the ÖVP initiated a petition for a referendum against building an international conference center in the complex of the Vienna International Center of the United Nations that had been opened in 1979; this petition was supported by more than 1.3 million voters. When the Austrian government was accused by the US government of permitting illegal technology transfer to Warsaw Pact states, the Secretary General of the ÖVP, Michael Graff, put the blame "exclusively on the neutralistic foreign policy" of the Kreisky government (*Die Presse*, December 15, 1982). The issue of Austrian transfers of technology to the Communist bloc was finally resolved after very difficult negotiations and several amendments to Austria's foreign trade laws.[4] However, in view of his reputation as an international statesman, in the election campaign of 1983 the ÖVP avoided criticizing Kreisky on questions of foreign policy. Kreisky tried to improve relations to the Reagan Administration by visiting the United States in February 1983 (Luchak 1987, 426f).

With the loss of the SPÖ's absolute majority in the parliamentary elections of 1983, the "Kreisky era" of Austrian foreign policy came to an end. Many of Kreisky's attempts to find peaceful solutions to the Middle East conflict and other crises of the Third World remained unsuccessful at the time because the positions of the conflicting parties allowed for no real rapprochement or agreement (Zemanek 1984, 20; Hakovirta 1988, 221f). That "Kreisky's political passions exceeded his possibilities" (thus Henry Kissinger) is evidenced by the fact that his verbal support for the Third World was at odds with Austria's development aid expenditures. In its thirteen years in power the SPÖ under Kreisky neglected to increase its development aid to the level of the OECD average and in particular to that of the Scandinavian countries (table 6.2). Also, the quality of development aid left much to be desired, as the grant element, the portion of the poorest countries selected and the tying of aid to Austrian products indicate (Höll 1991).

TABLE 6.2 Development Aid by Country in International Comparison
(percent of GDP)

	1960	1965	1970	1975	1980	1985	1990	1991	1992	1993*	1994*
Austria	0	0.34	0.07	0.21	0.23	0.38	0.25	0.34	0.30	0.30	0.29
Belgium	0.88	0.59	0.46	0.59	0.50	0.55	0.45	0.41	0.39	0.39	0.30
Denmark	0.09	0.13	0.38	0.58	0.74	0.80	0.93	0.96	1.02	1.03	1.03
Finland	n.d.a.	n.d.a.	0.06	0.18	0.22	0.40	0.64	0.78	0.62	0.45	0.31
France	1.38	0.75	0.66	0.62	0.64	0.78	0.55	0.62	0.63	0.63	0.64
Germany	0.33	0.38	0.33	0.40	0.44	0.47	0.42	0.40	0.39	0.36	0.33
Ireland	0.05	0.04	0.03	0.08	0.19	0.24	0.16	0.19	0.16	0.20	0.24
Italy	0.27	0.15	0.16	0.11	0.17	0.31	0.32	0.30	0.34	0.31	0.20
Netherlands	0.31	0.36	0.61	0.75	1.03	0.91	0.94	0.88	0.86	0.82	0.76
Norway	0.11	0.16	0.32	0.66	0.85	1.03	1.17	1.13	1.16	1.01	1.05
Spain	n.d.a.	n.d.a.	n.d.a.	n.d.a.	0.07	n.d.a.	n.d.a.	0.14	0.26	0.25	0.26
Sweden	0.05	0.19	0.38	0.82	0.79	0.86	0.90	0.90	1.03	0.99	0.90
Switzerland	0.04	0.08	0.15	0.19	0.24	0.31	0.31	0.36	0.46	0.33	0.36
United Kingdom	0.56	0.48	0.39	0.39	0.35	0.34	0.27	0.32	0.31	0.31	0.30
Australia	0.38	0.52	0.62	0.65	0.48	0.49	0.34	0.38	0.35	0.35	0.38
Canada	0.19	0.19	0.41	0.54	0.43	0.49	0.44	0.45	0.46	0.45	0.42
Japan	0.24	0.28	0.23	0.23	0.32	0.29	0.31	0.32	0.30	0.27	0.29
New Zealand	-	-	0.23	0.52	0.33	0.25	0.22	0.25	0.26	0.25	0.24
USA	0.53	0.51	0.32	0.27	0.27	0.24	0.20	0.20	0.20	0.16	0.15
DAC-Countries (total)	0.52	0.46	0.34	0.36	0.38	0.35	0.35	0.33	0.33	0.31	0.29

* preliminary figures

Source: *OECD Report. Development Cooperation. Efforts and Policies of the Members of the Development Assistance Committee*, various issues; *OECD Press Realease on Financial Flows to developing countries in 1994* (June 21, 1995).

The ambivalence and inconsistency of Austria's "mediating position in the North-South conflict" (Benedek 1983, 332) become obvious if one considers Austria's position in the negotiations for the New International Economic Order demanded by developing countries. The declamatory and programmatic openness and the initiatives such as Kreisky's "New Marshall Plan for the Third World", as well as the attempts to resume the

North-South dialogue in the early 1980s, which led to the Cancún Conference in October 1981, stand in contrast to the economic reserve the Austrian government displayed when it came to translating the demands into action (Skuhra 1984). Another dark spot in the Third World policy under Kreisky was the increase in arms exports in the mid-1970s to dictatorial regimes in the Third World such as Argentina, Bolivia and Chile, and to the crisis region of the Middle East, where arms were delivered to both Iraq and Iran in the first Gulf War (Pilz 1982; Skuhra 1991).

Even considering the contradictions and failures of Kreisky's foreign policy,[5] its over-all balance and its international image was very positive. In the years when he was chancellor, the positive expectations of the international community towards Austria as a neutral state increased markedly, and "particularly because of its high reputation in the Third World ... the international community readily accepts its help" (UN Secretary General Perez de Cuellar, *Der Standard*, June 1, 1990). Taking the whole foreign policy picture into account, one can say that Kreisky, portrayed by Kissinger "as a shrewd and perceptive chancellor, who had parlayed his country's formal neutrality into a position of influence beyond its strength" (Kissinger 1979, 1204) succeeded in his main goal of enlarging Austria's recognition and presence in Europe and in the world. Asked what he thought to be his most important achievement in foreign policy, Kreisky answered that it was "the systematic claim to a role of Austria in the world" (Basta 1989/12, 50). In this perspective, Kreisky can be regarded as a "transformational leader" in the foreign policy arena whose political activities and political influence was oriented towards changing his society and raising its politics to a higher level, thus "producing social change that will satisfy followers' authentic needs" (Burns 1978, 4).

"Realistic Foreign and Neutrality Policy" (1983/84-1989)

In the period of the SPÖ/FPÖ coalition government (1983-1986) a fundamental change in the focus and priorities of Austria's foreign policy began to emerge. In the context of important structure changes in Austria's international environment which closed the "windows of opportunity" for active neutrality policy, the focus of foreign policy was turned on Austria's neighbors and Europe (the EC). Its central aim was now to "assert a regional rather than global line of vision" and to make a "change in emphasis towards its immediate environment" (Luchak 1987, 229-330). This change in priorities and scope was strengthened when the

SPÖ and the ÖVP formed the coalition government in early 1987 and Alois Mock ÖVP leader took over the Foreign Ministry (Kramer 1988).

The foreign policy of the SPÖ/FPÖ government under Chancellor Sinowatz showed signs of a readjustment towards "interest politics," "defending the status quo" (Khol 1984, 461) and "natural self-restraint" (Mock in *AZ*, February 3, 1987) demanded by the ÖVP. Fred Sinowatz, Kreisky's successor as chancellor in Spring 1983, was much less interested than his predecessor in global foreign political activities and initiatives. His foreign political philosophy and his assessment of Austria's role in world politics coincided in important points with the foreign policy concept of the ÖVP. Both wanted a return to a "realistic" foreign and neutrality policy with emphasis on a narrower European sphere.

The break with Kreisky's foreign policy became more obvious when Leopold Gratz replaced Erwin Lanc as foreign minister in September 1984. Lanc, who in the 1970s was a minister in several of Kreisky's cabinets, tried to maintain Kreisky's foreign policy course even though the conditions for a globally-oriented active neutrality policy had changed. In contrast, Gratz made it clear from the beginning that he did not believe it was in Austria's interests to start controversial initiatives that would cause it to fall out of favor with other countries (particularly the USA). Gratz argued that Austria would otherwise be "open to the reproach of being a small state that wants to be, so to speak, the schoolmaster of the world and give out grades in morality" (Gratz in International 1985/3, 34). The increasing restraint shown in statements and initiatives on international issues led to the noticeable weakening of Austria's political profile in the Middle East conflict and in other areas of activities of the Kreisky government (Kramer 1988, 126). Furthermore, Austria's active role at the United Nations clearly decreased, as reflected in the loss of leading administrative positions and in the reduction of political initiatives (Michal-Misak 1990, 394).

The "narrower interpretation of Austrian neutrality" (Luchak 1987, 229) was also expressed in a somewhat stronger emphasis on the military component of Austria's security policy. The Defense Ministry, which was directed by an FPÖ minister, was able to get government approval for the purchase of new interceptor aircraft and anti-tank missiles. However, due to the economic and budgetary difficulties faced by the government in the mid-1980s, the defense budget was not increased in a significant way (Vetschera 1990; Skuhra 1991).

The policy of concentrating on the narrower European issues was also reflected in Foreign Minister Peter Jankowitsch's term of office (June to December 1986). He continued the foreign policy of his predecessor Gratz, which had been praised by the ÖVP, in the opposition at the time, as one of "skillful moderation" (*Die Presse*, October 20, 1986). The transition from Jankowitsch to Mock, when in the Grand Coalition government the ÖVP took over the Foreign Ministry in January 1987, was a "changing of the guard but not a turning point. Kreisky's great design had been abandoned long ago behind the rhetorical smoke screen of 'continuity' by Socialists like Gratz and Jankowitsch" (Heinz Nußbaumer in *Kurier*, January 21, 1987).

The new foreign minister Alois Mock, party leader of the ÖVP since 1979, whose rise to power in his party was very much enhanced by his record of being active in international affairs and foreign policy (Schaller 1994, 47),[6] finally provided a new definition of Austria´s foreign policy guidelines: "realistic neutrality policy". The emphasis was now on a foreign policy "based on Austria's real interests" (Andreas Khol, foreign policy spokesman of the ÖVP), on "non-intervention in international conflicts" (Mock) and a strengthening of the military dimension in foreign policy (Kramer 1988, 122f.). This conception of Austrian foreign policy was a distinctive change from the former optimistic and activist approach to international affairs and the foreign policy opportunities of Austria in the Kreisky era to a more pessimistic perspective on the international system and Austria's role in it. In one of his first interviews as foreign minister Mock, declared, echoing the basic tenets of the "realists" in international relations theory, that "international relations are basically a jungle, a sort of wilderness ('Wildwuchs')" (International 1987/ 1, 5).

The major reorientation of Austria's foreign policy that started in 1983/84 took place, as pointed out, within the context of external conditions which were obviously different from the 1970s. In addition to the crisis in the relationship between the United States and the Soviet Union and the shrinking importance of the Third World, Austria's "integration environment" (Väyrynen 1987, 37; Hakovirta 1988, 121f; Luif 1988) had been considerably rearranged. The increased economic and political momentum of the EC, particularly the Single Market project scheduled for completion in the early 1990s, caused Austria to reconsider its relationship to the EC.

At a time when the other European neutrals--Finland, Sweden, and Switzerland--still maintained that their neutral status was incompatible with membership in the EC, Austria decided in 1989 to "go on its own to Brussels" (Schneider 1990; Schaller 1994). On July 17, 1989, Foreign Minister Alois Mock submitted the Austrian application for EC membership. That Austria was caught up in the economic and political maelstrom of the EC earlier and more intensely than the other European neutrals can also be explained by specific internal factors. Austria, which by international standards had a very successful economy in the 1970s, was faced from 1983/84 on with a recession, rising unemployment, and structural crisis in the nationalized industries. "Becoming a member of the European Community as soon as possible is seen (by Vienna) as a kind of panacea for all the economic and political misfortunes of the country," was the commentary of the *Neue Zürcher Zeitung* on the hopes of the SPÖ-ÖVP government and the Austrian business community that closer contacts to the EC would bring about the modernization that could not be accomplished without that kind of external *deus ex machina* (*Neue Zürcher Zeitung*, August 31, 1988; Schneider 1990, 104f).

Besides the economic problems, there was also a serious image and identity crisis which led to a rather agitated and emotional EC-debate in Austria. During the Second Republic, Austria could always count on a very good international image as an asset. A series of scandals (wine scandal, Reder affair, illegal arms exports) and the international debate on the wartime record of Kurt Waldheim, who was elected president in June 1986 and was now refused entry into the United States, brought Austria "the worst image abroad that any state in Europe was confronted with lately" (*Die Presse*, February 11, 1988). The consequences of the "Waldheim affair" became a serious burden for Austrian foreign policy (Giller 1989, 104; Unterberger 1992). The number of official state visits in Vienna sank drastically after Waldheim took office; meetings with foreign ministers of the West had to be moved to provincial capitals, "because that way the foreign guests could avoid paying the obligatory visit to the president" (*Die Presse*, July 6, 1988).[7]

Austria's international image crisis and dimensions of the troubled political-psychological identity of the Austrians and its political and economic elites became mixed with the EC-issue:

> One did believe to be a fully accepted, even loved member in the community of the Western European states. As a consequence of the presidential election campaign--but also as result of various other scandals--one now experienced indignant rejection or amused surprise in the democratic states. The more urgent was the wish to convince oneself and others that one *truly* belonged to the family of prosperous and democratic states and to insist on the confirmation of a Western European identity (Nowotny 1987, 23).

But the development and the change in Austria's foreign policy in the mid 1980s can also be seen and explained as a "crisis of normalization" (which did not affect domestic policy in Austria until the end of the 1980s). Austria's foreign policy trade-mark as small-state strategy lost much of its unique character, its mission-mindedness and its former self-confidence by being successful and achieving its international and economic goals. This change became apparent in the rather suprisingly deferential attitudes and statements by Austria's foreign policy actors during the negotiations for European Union membership.[8]

Crucial to the decision of the government and the social partners to revise the relationship to the EC and then to request admission was the fear of being excluded from the dynamic economic developments resulting from the EC Single Market, to be put into effect by January 1993. Austrian exports to the EC increased considerably in the 1980s, as graph 6.1 shows. Austrian business, particularly industrialists from the western provinces and the Austrian Association of Industrialists, in which the representatives of foreign companies based in Austria are also influential, had already been pressing for full EC membership in 1987. In the first phase of the EC discussion in Austria, the government's aim was mere participation in the Single Market of the EC and not full membership. By taking a "global approach" in which negotiations were made in conjunction with the other EFTA countries, but also by making bilateral agreements and by extensively adapting its legal system to that of the EC, discrimination against the Austrian economy was to be avoided (Schultz 1992, 184f). However, when the EC and Commission President Delors made it more or less clear that taking part in the Community's decision-making process could only be achieved by joining the EC as a member, the ÖVP and the large corporatist interest groups decided to opt for full membership. Vranitzky had already called for "quasi-membership" in the EC when he became chancellor in 1986. Even though by 1987/88 his party had again become more cautious on EC membership, it gave the go-ahead in April 1989. The SPÖ insisted, however, that the application for membership must explicitly include a clause to safeguard neutrality, which read as follows:

> Austria is making this application on the assumption that its internationally recognized status of permanent neutrality, based on the Federal Constitutional Law of October 26, 1955, will be maintained and that, as a member of the European Community by virtue of the Treaty of Accession, it will be able to fulfil its legal obligations arising out of its status as a permanently neutral State and to continue its policy of neutrality as a specific contribution towards the maintenance of peace and security in Europe (Österreichische außenpolitische Dokumentation, January 1990, 68).

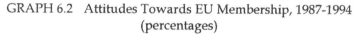

GRAPH 6.2 Attitudes Towards EU Membership, 1987-1994 (percentages)

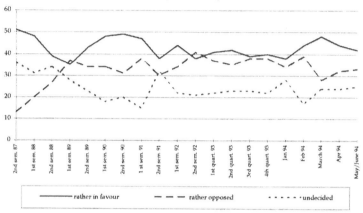

Source: Fessel+GfK Surveys, 1987 to 1994, N = 1,000 to 2,000 interviews per survey

The SPÖ under Vranitzky insisted on this clause in order to fend off objections by the Soviet Union, which were still likely at that time, but also because of the high value the Austrian people assign to neutrality (cf. graph 6.3) and because of other reservations among citizens. The ÖVP under party chairman Alois Mock, strongly in favor of EC membership, had to acknowledge this after the provincial diet elections in Salzburg, Carinthia and Tyrol in March 1989. The ÖVP lost heavily in Tyrol, one of its traditional bastions, and the debate over transit traffic (trucks travelling between Germany and Italy)--one of the main issues between Austria and the EC--played a large role here. Mock stayed on as foreign minister but was replaced as party chairman and vice-chancellor by the representative of the *Bauernbund* (the ÖVP faction in the Chamber of Agriculture), former Minister of Agriculture Josef Riegler, whose approach to EC matters was a more cautious one (Kramer 1991). Graph 6.2 shows that in the first months of 1989 opinions on EC membership were equally balanced.

In the 1980s, interest in foreign policy debates increased among Austrians. The EC discussion, the new area of international environmental affairs and and the problem of transit traffic had become relevant to domestic politics, even in the electoral context (Kramer 1991; Neuhold and Luif 1992). Opinion polls showed a growing interest in foreign policy. A growing number of Austrians believed that foreign policy and international issues directly affected them (see tables 6.3 and 6.4).

TABLE 6.3 Interest in Foreign Policy Issues (percentages)

Question: In general, are you interested in foreign policy issues?

	very interested	somewhat interested	moderately interested	slightly interested	not interested	don't know
1981	10	15	27	24	24	-
1990	29	27	23	13	6	1

Source: Fessel + GFK Oct./Nov. 1981, n = 1500, SWS March 1990, n = 1886.

TABLE 6.4 Sense of Being Affected by Foreign Policy (percentages)

Question: Do you believe that foreign policy decisions affect you personally?

	yes, a great deal	yes, but only slightly	no, not at all	don't know
1981	7	22	35	36
1990	20	46	23	11

Source: Fessel + GFK Oct./Nov. 1981, n = 1500, SWS March 1990, n = 1886.

The Road to EU Membership (1989-1994/95)

The developments in Europe which began in 1989 (the collapse of the communist regimes in Eastern Europe, the reunification of Germany in October 1990 and the disintegration of the Soviet Union into fifteen successor states in late 1991) substantially changed the international environment of Austrian foreign policy. The de facto end of the East-West Conflict, in the context of which Austrian neutrality had been developed by allowing Austria to adopt a mere leniant and flexible interpretation of ist neutrality status, improved the chances for Austrian membership in the EC. Due to its geographical position and close cultural and historical ties to Eastern and Southeastern Europe, Austria was, in the transformation process in Eastern Europe, a particularly active partner from the start, especially in the economic area. The disintegration of Yugoslavia with its tragic consequences, the military conflict between Serbia, Slovenia, and Croatia in 1991 and, since 1992, in Bosnia-Hercegovina had serious consequences for Austria's foreign and security policy and brought thousands of war refugees to Austria. A further important change was brought about by the United Nations when it began to actively use its collective security function, as laid down in the UN Charter, during the Gulf War against Iraq. Austria, which was a non-permanent member of the Security Council from 1991 to 1992, took part not only in the economic sanctions against Iraq, but also allowed the US-led alliance against Iraqi dictator Saddam Hussein to transport war material across Austria. Giving precedence to UN law over the law of neutrality signified a substantial change in the interpretation of Austrian neutrality and can be seen as the transition from an "integral" to a "differentiated" concept of neutrality (Rotter 1991; Zemanek 1991).

Austria and the European Community

In Europe's "new political architecture," which began to develop in 1989, the EC had become not only the most important economic, but increasingly also political, center of gravity between the Atlantic and the Ural Mountains. This is demonstrated in the attempts of the new democracies in Eastern Europe to seek economic association with Brussels as quickly as possible. Limited free trade agreements between the EC and Poland, Czechoslovakia, and Hungary were concluded in December 1991. The most promising candidates in the EC strategy to enlarge the community in the new situation in Europe were, without a doubt, the prosperous neutral countries Sweden, Finland, Switzerland and Austria as well as Norway. In view of their close economic interaction with the EC countries and their expected net contributions to the EC budget, no insurmountable problems were to be envisaged in the negotiations for membership. The reactions of the governments in Bern, Stockholm and Helsinki were rather reserved when the Austrians dashed ahead in the question of EC membership in 1989. At the time, those governments believed their neutrality to be incompatible with EC membership. For this reason they favored multilateral links between EC and EFTA. But it became clear later on that any extension of economic cooperation would result in the EC unilaterally deciding upon rules and regulations for the EFTA countries (i.e. without those countries participating in the decision making process). In addition, Sweden and Finland developed serious economic problems which led them to reconsider their position (Luif 1995).

In October 1990 the Swedish government, confronted with a severe economic recession and a major crisis of the "Swedish Model" (low unemployment, active social policy and strong role for the State), came out for the first time in favor of applying for membership in the EC. In June 1991, an overwhelming majority of the Swedish parliament voted to start negotiations with Brussels, and in the application there was no reservation concerning neutrality. The Finnish government had to fight an even more disastrous economic collapse (Finland's GDP dropped by more than 5 percent in 1991). Traditionally, Finland had been forced to act more cautiously on account of its special relationship to its neighbor in the East. After the breakdown of the Soviet Union at the end of 1991 and the conclusion of a new treaty with the Russian Federation, an application for EC membership was passed by the Finnish parliament in March 1992 with the votes of all the major political parties--with the exception of the agrarian Center Party--again without mentioning neutrality as a problem. Finally, at the end of May 1992 Switzerland followed after its citizens had voted in a referendum in favor of membership in the International Monetary Fund and World Bank. The decision of the Swiss government to start negotiations with the EC was very close (four votes to three--most of the members from the German-speaking cantons voted against; Luif 1995).

Thus, after a certain period of isolation on the EC question, Austria was once again in line with the European neutrals. The Austrian government could point out to its EFTA partners that it had understood the rapidly changing international situation better and earlier and that the historical developments proved its 1989 decision to be correct (Khol 1993, 116f). As mentioned above, Moscow had gradually eased its objections to Austrian (and Finnish) membership. In August 1989, soon after Vienna had handed in its EC membership application, the Soviet government still had notified the Austrians of its concern in a memorandum. Subsequently however, in the course of a trip to Finland, Gorbachev, who was highly interested in improved relations with the EC and the West, reacted more obligingly. During a visit by Chancellor Vranitzky to Moscow in September 1991, Gorbachev affirmed Moscow's intention not to raise any more obstacles to Austrian EC membership. The Soviet leader assured Vranitzky that earlier objections and the constant references to neutrality were no longer issues in Moscow and that Austria itself must decide if it wanted to become a member of the EC (*Die Presse*, October 1, 1991).

At the time when the other neutrals were just revising their position towards EC membership, Austria had already received a favorable opinion (*avis*) on its application for membership from the EC Commission. In this report, the product of a two-year examining procedure and sent to the Austrian government on July 31, 1991, the Commisssion emphasized that Austria's case for membership, based on the country's economic strength, its intensive economic interaction with the EC and the fact that it had already taken over many EC regulations and laws, was viewed very positively. Problems in the area of agriculture and traffic (especially in the question of transit traffic across Austria) and in other areas were mentioned, but these were expected to be solved without any great difficulties in the course of negotiations. With respect to the Austrian government's goal of maintaining its status as a neutral country, Brussels conceded that this would in principle be possible. However, the Commission argued that there was an obvious strain between the duties of an EC member and those of a permanently neutral country. During the negotiations Austria would therefore either have to make a declaration, binding under international law, that its neutrality had been redefined, or a special, mutually acceptable formula must be included in the membership treaty. It was explicitly pointed out that the EC must receive a clear guarantee from Austria that it would be prepared to take over responsiblities in the EC´s common foreign and security policy (Außenpolitischer Bericht 1991, 22f).

The willingness of the EC Commission to make compromises on the question of neutrality in the *avis* of July 31, 1991 would not have been possible without the vigorous support the British and the Danish members of the Commission, who favored an expanded EC. Certainly, the fact that the Austrian government substantially modified its interpretation of neutrality with respect to the economic and military sanctions imposed by the UN Security Council in a way favored by the EC and the USA helped considerably. Austria joined the UN economic sanctions against Iraq--the Austrian representative in the Security Council was the chairman of the Iraq Sanctions Committee--and allowed military supplies to be transported across Austrian territory. These actions were justified by the government and parliament as collective security measures, defined as a "police action". Austria could not stand aside--according to the government in Vienna--when acts of aggression are committed and when international law is violated, and as a small state it must be particularly interested in establishing and securing international relations that are determined by law rather than by power (Freudenschuß 1993, 26; Skuhra 1995). The precedence of UN law over the law of neutrality was further corroborated when parliament passed an amendment to the War Materials Law on January 17, 1991. Though it prohibits the movement of arms through Austrian territory in general, this does not apply if a relevant decision is taken by the UN Security Council (Rotter 1991).

According to Foreign Minister Mock, the changed international situation required that "neutrality develops in the direction of solidarity" (*Kurier*, March 3, 1992). This could be done by actively participating in the creation of stable peace structures in Europe. With the summit conference in Maastricht in December 1991--the Treaty was signed February 7, 1992 and ratification was completed on November 1, 1993--the tasks of the EC--renamed "European Union" (EU)--were expanded to include also defense. Since the high expectations with respect to the CSCE as a European security system had not been fulfilled, those responsible for Austrian foreign affairs and national security maintained that the EC had become "the point of reference and the anchor of stability" and the "cornerstone of any future system of European security." (Ernst Sucharipa, at the time Political Director of the Foreign Ministry, *Der Standard*, February 2, 1992). The Austrian government declared its complete support for the planned Common Foreign and Security Policy of the Maastricht Treaty. In several aide-memoires and public statements made by members of the government and other top officials, it was affirmed that Austria as a future EC member would work "on the creation and the functioning of a new European security order within the framework of the European Union and, beyond that, would cooperate in a spirit of solidarity" (Außenpolitischer Bericht 1992, 49). The Austrian side argued that Austria's inclusion in the Common Foreign and Security Policy would not be a serious problem because in recent years its foreign policy position had been strongly and increasingly in agreement with the EC countries in the United Nations, in the CSCE and also in bilateral foreign policy (Österreichische außenpolitische Dokumentation, October 1992, 51). In organizational terms, the intensive political dialogue that the Austrian authorities had with the EC within the framework of European Political Cooperation (EPC) structure was also deepened. Since 1989, contact talks have been held twice a year with the EC presidency as well as with the foreign ministers and the political directors of the foreign ministries.

In the domestic debate on integration which began in the autumn and winter of 1991, the government increasingly emphasized that aside from economic arguments, national security considerations strongly favored Austria's speedy entrance into the EC. Strategically, as Foreign Minister Mock emphasized, Austria was no longer "in a calm zone between the two blocs," but was, as the conflict in the former Yugoslavia and the increasing instability in Eastern Europe showed, "on the edge of a storm front" and had to protect itself against it (*Die Presse*, November 22, 1992). "Austria's security is greater with EC membership than without it" (*Die Presse*, January 30, 1993) because with rapid world integration, new non-military security problems such as international crime, migration and refugee flows and environmental problems have developed, and clearly such issues cannot be dealt with efficiently within the framework of traditional strategies of the nation-state (Gärtner 1992).

In its attempt to avoid conflict with Brussels and particularly within Austria on the compatibility of Austrian neutrality with the EC/EU's common foreign and security policy agreed upon in Maastricht, the Austrian government has insisted that for the time being membership in the West European Union (WEU) and in NATO were not on the agenda. However, ÖVP members of the government and their foreign policy spokesman increasingly spoke out in favor of rethinking Austria's position towards WEU and NATO in view of the changed situation in Europe. Behind the coalition consensus on foreign policy there were in fact very different opinions and positions that surfaced at regular intervals in a way confusing to the public. The SPÖ, especially Chancellor Vranitzky and Heinz Fischer, president of the *Nationalrat*, repeatedly joined the debate. They emphasized that even though it is necessary to rethink Austria's neutrality as a foreign and security policy instrument and to limit it to its military content, as of yet no stable new security structure has developed in Europe. Neutrality has been viewed very positively by the Austrian population since 1955 and has even "become a part of Austria's identity" (Vranitzky in *Der Standard*, September 16, 1990, cf. graph 6.3). Therefore, according to the SPÖ, it should not be rashly thrown overboard in an era characterized by so much insecurity and uncertainty.

ÖVP views on neutrality were substantially different. In the opinion of Andreas Khol, its foreign policy spokesman in parliament, neutrality had outlived its usefulness as an instrument of national security in Europe and had to be replaced by solidarity. Erhard Busek, ÖVP party chairman and vice-chancellor since 1991, criticized the SPÖ for clinging to neutrality in a way that "mythologized" and "fossilized" the concept (*Der Standard*, October 20, 1992). In addition to Foreign Minister Mock, President Thomas Klestil, who was nominated by the ÖVP and had succeeded Kurt Waldheim in the presidential office in June 1992, also pleaded for the gradual abandonment of neutrality and for "the step forward from neutrality to solidarity" (interview with Klestil in *Newsweek*, July 6, 1992).

In 1991 and 1992, the Austrian government made great efforts--by direct contact with leading Social Democratic and Christian Democratic politicians of the EC countries and official aide-memoires of the foreign ministry--to hasten the start of the official membership negotiations with Brussels. As a result of developments within the EC, especially the delays of the ratification process of the Maastricht Treaty, negotiations with Finland, Sweden and Austria did not start until early 1993. In a situation

Foreign Policy

in which it was not foreseeable how long it would take Austria and the other EFTA countries to become members of the EC, the government and big business placed their hopes on maximum participation in the EC internal market that had been created in 1993. Since 1990 EC and the EFTA countries had been negotiating an agreement on the European Economic Area (EEA), which was to extend the internal market to the EFTA countries.

GRAPH 6.3 Neutrality or EU Membership: Preferences in Public Opinion Polls (percentages)

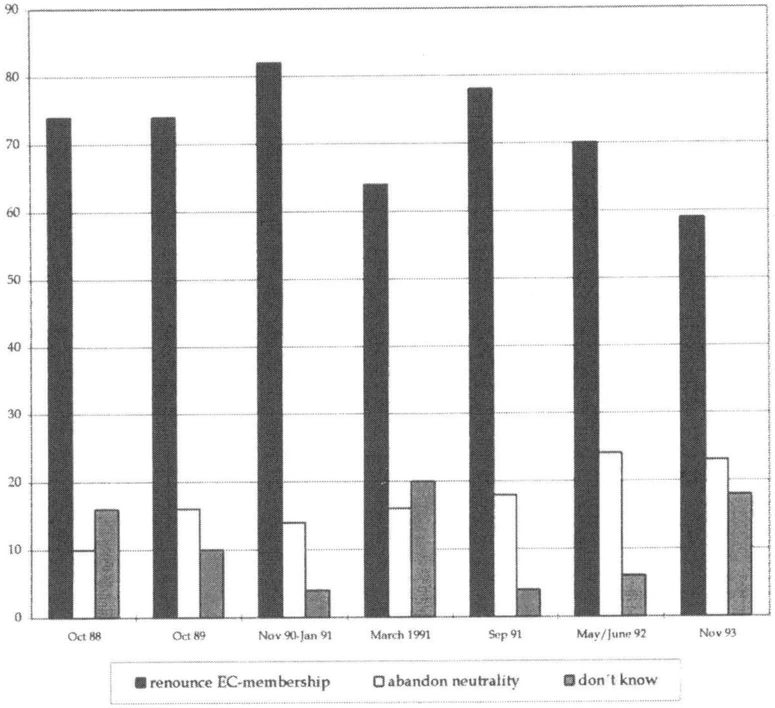

Answers referring to the question: "Suppose that accession of Austria to the EC would only be possible in case Austria were to abandon neutrality, should Austria then (1) rather renounce EC-membership or (2) rather abandon neutrality?"

Source: Neuhold and Luif 1992, p. 102; *Zukunft*, No. 2, 1993, p. 13; *Der Standard*, November 11/12, 1993.

The EEA Treaty, by which the EFTA countries were to take over a large part of the *acquis communautaire*, the common body of law of the

EC, was seen by the government and the Social Partners as an important intermediate stage and as a "kind of training camp" (Mock in *Die Presse*, November 13, 1991) for full membership. The negotiations were extremely difficult; little by little the EFTA countries had to take back their initial positions (equal participation in the law-making process, exemptions and protective clauses). In May 1992, the EEA Treaty was finally signed. Austria was the first country to ratify the treaty in both chambers of parliament. There were fierce confrontations on this subject between representatives of the governing parties and those of the parliamentary opposition (FPÖ and Greens). In addition to the content of the treaty, the opposition parties particularly criticized that the obligations to adopt a large part of EC law implied far-reaching alterations of the Austrian legal and constitutional order and would in fact eliminate parliament from the law-making process. The Greens in particular argued that, according to the constitution, such a step required a referendum (*Der Standard*, September 8, 1992). The ratification of the EEA Treaty by all the parties concerned was delayed until the end of 1993 by the negative result of the EEA referendum in Switzerland and by various objections of EC countries. The EEA Treaty led to nearly complete mobility of goods, people, services and capital in a market of more than 370 million people. However, EFTA countries were exempted from the community regime in the areas of agriculture, common foreign trade and customs policy, as well as commitments in the areas of transportation and energy. By participating in the EEA, Austria has accepted approximately two thirds of the existing EU-legislation. Also, the treaty included close cooperation in the so-called "supporting political areas" (research and development, environment, education and social policy). The EEA finally came into force in January 1994 (Außenpolitischer Bericht 1994, 47).

The start of the membership negotiations with the EC was set for February 1, 1993, after the EC Council summit in Edinburgh in December 1992 had decided to begin such negotiations with the applicants from the EFTA countries Finland, Austria and Sweden before the end of the Maastricht Treaty ratification process. In the opening session in Brussels, Foreign Minister Mock declared that "Austria is ready to accept the principles of the European Union and to adopt its laws (Acquis). Austria declares its complete support for the entire contents of the Treaty on the European Union" (Österreichische außenpolitische Dokumentation, March 1993, 48). The governing parties agreed that Austria would not raise the issue of neutrality at the opening session. However, in a statement made by the government in Vienna, it was clarified (in the words of Chancellor Vranitzky) that "Austria is entering the negotiations as a neutral country and will join as a neutral" (*Kurier*, January 1, 1993).

Foreign Policy

GRAPH 6.4 Results of the National Referenda on EU Membership in Austria, Finland, Sweden and Norway (percentages)

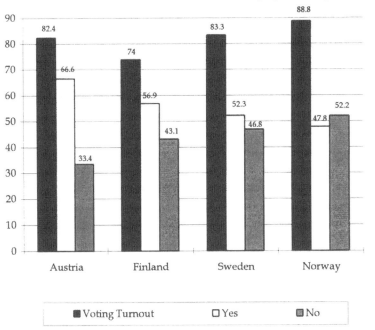

Source: Kaiser 1995

The membership negotiations between Austria, the other EFTA countries (Norway entered the membership negotiations on April 5, 1993) and the EC were intense and took place on several levels--the foreign minister level (four meetings in the year 1993) and the level of their "representatives" (ambassadors), as well as that of working groups and experts. By June 1993, twelve out of a total of twenty-nine items were settled. By the end of 1993, agreement was achieved on classification of economic regions in Austria, and a compromise formula was devised for neutrality. On the regulation of agriculture, the question of transit traffic and of secondary residences, the parties reached agreement only in the last days of the negotiations. Truck traffic across Austria posed a particularly difficult problem. Austria had signed a twelve-year agreement on this subject with the EC in December 1991. There was strong domestic resistance against EC attempts to void this treaty during the membership negotiations. Differences on this issue were one of the main reasons why opinion for and against EC-membership was fairly balanced until the final round of negotiations.

After a three-day marathon meeting, negotiations were concluded in Brussels in early March and the results approved by the European Parliament on May 4. Since membership of the European Union affected fundamental principles of the Austrian constitution, the law on accession passed by parliament in May had to be submitted to a national referendum. This referendum was held on June 12, with a majority of 66.6 percent in favor of joining the EU (with 82.4 percent of the Austrian voters participating). The national referenda in Finland and Sweden in the fall of 1994 resulted in majorities of 56.9 percent and 52.3 percent respectively, while in Norway a majority of 52.5 percent rejected EU membership (cf. graph 6.4). According to public opinion analyses, the main motives for the impressive two-thirds majority in Austria's national referendum were expectations of economic advantages, the fear of being isolated politically and economically outside the EU, as well as positive attitudes towards the idea of Europe and European unification (Plasser and Ulram 1994).

The formal signing of the treaty of accession and of the final act took place on June 24 at the European Council in Korfu.[9] From this date on Austria acted as an "active observer" in the EU, participating in the Council of Ministers, in the Commission and in the framework of the Common Foreign and Security Policy, until after the ratification of their treaty of accession by the national parliaments of the twelve member states. Austria, together with Finland and Sweden, became a member of the EU on January 1, 1995. Austria has four votes in the Council of the European Union, sends 21 delegates to the European Parliament and nominates one member of the European Commission.

Relations with Eastern Europe

The second main concern of Austrian foreign policy after the major changes in 1989 was to activate the relations with countries in Eastern and Southeastern Europe (Sucharipa and Lehne 1991). For Austria, which until 1989 due to its geographic position "had been pressed to the edge of the Western world, the reform process in the East (offered) an historical chance to move into the center of a united Europe" (Klestil 1989, 156). The fact that Austria could "use its experiences and connections to its neighbors in Central and Eastern Europe for common European interests" was explicitly mentioned in the *avis* of the EC Commission as an Austrian asset (Österreichische außenpolitische Dokumentation, January 1994, 14). Austria tried to rise to this challenge by intensifying and readjusting its policy towards its neighbors and by making a contribution to the democratization process. Trade and direct investment increased. Financial and technical assistance was substantial.

The new democracies in Eastern and Southeastern Europe, notably Hungary, Slovakia and Slovenia, expressed their hope that Austria, once a member of the EU, would open the door (Hungary's Foreign Minister Laszlo Kovacs in *Die Presse*, August 5, 1994) and act as a "mentor and escort" (Slovakian President Michal Kovac in *Die Presse*, May 17, 1994) in the negotiations on the accession of these reform countries to the EU.

Austrian foreign trade with Eastern Europe has expanded considerably since 1989 (especially exports). This is particularly true for those countries in East Central Europe with which Austria could reestablish relations that date back to a common past under the Habsburg Monarchy. The percentage of total Austrian exports that went to the East rose from 8.6 percent in 1988 to 12.7 percent in 1993. The share of Hungary, Poland, the Czech Republic and Slovakia in Austrian exports amounted to 8.1 percent, which was nearly as much as was exported to EFTA countries (8.7 percent in 1993). Austria's share of OECD exports to the East rose from 7.3 percent in 1989 to 10.3 percent in 1992. Imports grew by a somewhat smaller amount (from 7.2 percent to 9.2 percent). Even more impressive was the increase in the rate of Austrian direct investments in East Central European countries (see the chapter on economic policy in this volume).

Since Austria had a strong economic and national security interest in the rapid and smooth transformation of the former communist countries into democratic societies with market economies, it is understandable that the Austrian government made a particular effort to persuade OECD countries to give generous and effective aid to Eastern Europe. In numerous initiatives and appeals at international conferences, in international organizations and during visits to the Western capitals, Austrian government officials promoted the idea of granting economic aid to the East along the lines of the Marshall Plan that had been so decisive for Austria's reconstruction and development after the Second World War. Austria was not only an advocate (thus former President Rudolf Kirchschläger, *Der Standard*, June 4, 1992) for politically farsighted and effective economic aid to Eastern Europe and for the rapid integration of these countries into the Western financial and economic institutions; it also took on a disproportionate share of economic aid to Eastern Europe within the framework of the G-24 Aid Program of the OECD. Austria's share in overall OECD wealth is about 1 percent. Its share in OECD bilateral credits to transition countries, however, amounted to 4.7 percent in the years 1990-1992. This reflects the highest aid-to-GDP ratio of any OECD country (0.21 percent in 1993). A considerable amount of this economic aid is made up of export credits and investment guarantees for Austrian companies and banks and therefore, directly or indirectly, benefits the Austrian economy as well.

Another form of economic aid--the main recipients being once again the neighboring countries Hungary, the Czech Republic, Slovakia and Slovenia--is the technical assistance administered by the Federal Chancellor's Office. These projects--with a yearly budget of Sch300 to 400 million--serve to promote the development of modern administrative and political structures. The main objective is "to reintegrate Eastern Europe into the world economy, which should also be in Austria's own interest" (Georg Lennkh, Head of Development and Eastern European Aid in the Federal Chancellor's Office, *Wiener Zeitung*, October 29,1993).[10]

Austria's interest in a rapid and successful economic and social tranformation in Eastern and Southeastern Europe is motivated, aside from economics and from concern about environmental damages as well as safety problems of nuclear power plants in Eastern Europe, above all by the concern that if the reform process fails in the former communist countries, the region near Austria could become a zone of instability for a long period of time. Recent developments concerning refugees and migrant workers provide an indication of this. Table 6.5 shows that the number of refugees asking for political asylum in Austria has risen considerably since 1988/89. In 1991 more than 27,000 asked for asylum-- most of them from Romania or Yugoslavia--nearly as much as in the peak year 1981, when martial law was declared in Poland and more than 30,000 refugees came to Austria.

With the introduction of extremely restrictive legislation and harsh administrative practices--in 1992 and 1993 the asylum, residency and alien laws were all amended--the number of refugees sank considerably. Not included in the numbers in table 6.5 are war refugees from the former Yugoslavia. Under public pressure, the government decided to grant war refugees from Croatia and then, in particular, from Bosnia-Hercegovina temporary assistance without asylum procedures (de facto refugees). People from the war zones received the right of residency, health insurance and a food allowance. At the end of 1992, more than 60,000 refugees that had fled the war in Bosnia-Hercegovina were in Austria. (3,900 requesting asylum were in federal care, 42,500 were de facto refugees in the care of the federal government and the *Länder*, and about 20,000 were cared for by friends and relatives) (Außenpolitischer Bericht 1992, 121).

The reform of the refugee and alien laws was made in step with the countries of the European Union ("Fortress Europe") and led to intense domestic controversy. The number of people asking for asylum dropped; so did the number of migrant workers from Eastern and Southeastern Europe, which had increased rapidly after the fall of the "Iron Curtain" (from about 60,000 in 1989 and 120,000 in 1990 the annual increase went down to the pre-1989 level of about 20,000). Since September 1990 the Austrian army has been deployed on the border to Hungary to prevent illegal immigration. Austria's practices of restricting asylum and refugee status and of expelling applicants even led to criticism by human rights groups such as Amnesty International and by the UN High Commissioner of Refugees (*Der Standard*, March 4/5, 1994).

TABLE 6.5 Number of Persons Requesting and
Number of Persons Granted Official Refugee Status, 1982-1994

Year	Number of Persons Requesting Refugee Status (New Inflow)							Total Number of People Granted Official Refugee Status
	Total	(Ex-) CSFR	Poland	Hungary	Romania	(Ex-) Yugoslavia	Turkey	
1982	6,314	1,975	1,870	922	737	74	54	17,361[1]
1983	5,868	1,651	1,823	961	502	116	39	2,678
1984	7,208	1,941	2,466	1,229	501	158	31	2,053
1985	6,724	2,333	662	1,642	890	410	56	1,876
1986	8,639	2,147	568	2,220	2,329	488	163	1,430
1987	11,406	2,705	667	4,689	1,460	402	408	1,115
1988	15,790	1,728	6,670	2,610	2,134	477	644	1,785
1989	21,882	3,307	2,107	364	7,932	634	3,263	2,879
1990	22,789	176	132	46	12,199	768	1,862	864
1991	27,306	12	19	6	7,506	6,436	2,252	2,469
1992	16,238	10	10	0	2,609	7,410	1,251	2,289
1993	4,744	15	17	9	293	1,851	342	1,193
1.-10. 1994	4,092	0	14	8	135	441	280	499

War refugees are not included
[1] Due to backlog from 1981.

Source: Bundesministerium für Inneres, Österreichisches Statistisches Zentralamt.

The greatest challenge to Austrian security came from the crisis in former Yugoslavia, beginning in 1991/1992 (Siegl 1993). After the Communist Party in Yugoslavia was dissolved, control over federal agencies and the well-equipped People's Army, which had been under strong Serbian influence in the past, was arrogated by Slobodan Milosevic. He had become the leader of the Serbian Communist Party in 1987. With his concept of a Greater Serbia, Milosevic was able to convert the nationalistic feelings of the Serbian population into political support and remained in power after the first free elections in 1990. In the Republics of Slovenia and Croatia, however, the former communist politicians and parties were voted out of office and the oppositional middle-class parties took over the governments in Zagreb and Ljubljana. As a result the movement to break free from Belgrade became unstoppable in the northwestern republics. On June 25, 1991, Slovenia and Croatia declared their independence. Belgrade answered with armed action by the Yugoslav army. This was the first time since the crisis in Hungary in 1956 that there were military clashes on Austria's borders. Austria's airspace was also violated repeatedly. To protect the population near the border and to prevent armed groups from crossing over into Austrian territory, a contingent of the Austrian army was transferred to the area on the Slovenian border (Außenpolitischer Bericht 1991, 125f).

From the beginning of the Yugoslavian crisis, the Austrian government attempted to call the international community's attention to the dangers of destabilization in this region. They made suggestions on how to resolve the conflict and supported attempts at mediation. Austria's Foreign Minister Alois Mock reacted in August 1990 to the endangered rights of the ethnic Albanians in Kosovo by using Step One of the Human Dimension of the CSCE Mechanism against Yugoslavia. (Step two of the CSCE Mechanism was activated by Austria in May 1991). As the fighting escalated, Foreign Minister Mock suggested appointing a European Council of Wise Men to help bring about a dialogue between the conflict parties and develop new security mechanisms to prevent the use of force. As a non-permanent member of the Security Council in 1991 and 1992, Austria was the first country to advocate dealing with the Yugoslavian crisis in that forum (Skuhra 1995).[11]

In spring and summer 1991, Austria and "Vienna were the turntable for crisis management and a target for Belgrade" (*Der Standard*, July 1, 1991). The Austrian government, but also the governments of some of the *Länder* such as Styria and Carinthia, built up intensive communication networks with Slovenia and Croatia. The governor of Styria, Krainer, said that Austria "should be, without any false obtrusiveness, the interpreter and solicitor for Slovenia and Croatia in the West" (*Kurier*, July 8, 1991). Foreign Minister Mock and leading representatives of the ÖVP pressed for recognizing the Republics of Slovenia and Croatia as soon as possible. Austria, according to Foreign Minister Mock, had "taken over the role as a forerunner to actively recruit support for recognition, which Austria had already decided to grant." (*Der Standard*, August 8, 1991). The Foreign Minister explained before parliament that such a step would be a lever to internationalize the crisis. The conflict in the former Yugoslavia could then "no longer be qualified as an internal affair. As a result, more favorable conditions for the direct use of additional international mechanisms of crisis management would be created" (Außenpolitischer Bericht 1991, 129).[12]

Besides drawing accusations from Belgrade of supporting separatism in the region and of trying, along with Germany, to destabilize Yugoslavia, Austria's Yugoslavia policy was also more or less openly criticized by other Western countries, especially France, but also by the government in Moscow. Under these circumstances, Chancellor Vranitzky declared that since the efforts of the Austrian government "to internationalize the Yugoslavian crisis...have not brought the desired success," Austria would still reserve the right to use the "political instrument of recognizing Slovenia and Croatia. However, it is senseless for Austria to take this step alone." (Österreichische aussenpolitische Dokumentation, Sonderdruck Jugoslawische Krise 1992, 87) In contrast to the ÖVP, Vranitzky argued that Austria must "proceed in step with the international community... acting on its own is out of the question" (*Der Standard*, September 3, 1991). As in the areas of neutrality, the EC, and the revision of the State Treaty, there were thus clear differences of opinion in the coalition government, and they were discussed in public. This disagreement was finally settled when the EC countries recognized Croatia and Slovenia on January 15, 1992; on the same day Austria granted the new republics diplomatic recognition.

The "active role of Vienna in the Balkan conflict" (US Ambassador to Bosnia-Hercegovina Jackovich in *Die Presse*, February 24, 1994) was continued in the years 1992 and 1993. The political director of the Foreign Ministry, Sucharipa, said in an interview that "Yugoslavia took 30 percent to 35 percent of our time, if not more" (*Die Presse*, September 2, 1993). In view of the tragic events in Bosnia-Hercegovina, the Austrian government attempted to find peaceful solutions and contributed extensive humanitarian relief. It started international initiatives for this purpose at different levels. These included the CSCE, the Security Council of the UN, the Central European Initiative (which in 1993 included Austria, Slovakia, the Czech Republic, Slovenia, Hungary, Italy, Poland, Croatia, Bosnia-Hercegovina and Macedonia) and bilateral talks with other countries. Very early on in the conflict Foreign Minister Mock suggested sending UN Peacekeeping Forces into the combat areas of the Balkans. Since spring 1992 Austria has supported sweeping economic and political sanctions against Serbia. Austria suggested setting up safe havens and security zones in Sarajevo and other contested areas similar to those made by the UN Security Council for protecting the Kurds in northern Iraq in 1991. This was reflected in Security Council Resolutions in 1992 and 1993 (Österreichische aussenpolitische Dokumentation, July

1993, 56f and December 1993, 110). The aid given by Austria to the suffering in Bosnia-Hercegovina and other conflict areas in ex-Yugoslavia by the campaign "Neighbor in Need" amounted to nearly Sch1 billion by mid-1995, more than two-thirds of which were individual donations.

Austria's foreign policy after 1989, with its emphasis on the EC/EU accession, the transformation in East Europe, the conflict in ex-Yugoslavia, and on activities in CSCE as well as in the Central European Initiative (CEI), continued and deepened the "concentration of foreign policy on the immediate environment" (Foreign Minister Mock in *Oberösterreichische Nachrichten*, July 6, 1993). One of the domains in international politics where Austria could maintain its presence was the question of protection of human rights and the rights of minorities. The UN Conference on Human Rights in June 1993 assembled more than 7000 representatives from 171 different countries and numerous non-governmental organizations in Vienna. The outcome of this conference, the largest international conference that ever took place in Austria, was the "Vienna Declaration", a program of action which significantly expanded the protection of human rights by international law and created a High Commissioner on Human Rights to be appointed by the General Assembly and the Secretary General of the United Nations. Another important event in the field of human rights and the protection of minorities was the Council of Europe's Summit of Heads of State and Government of its member countries in Vienna in October 1993. In the final document, a reform of the Strasbourg human rights control mechanism and an important political guideline for the protection of minorities were unanimously adopted (Außenpolitischer Bericht 1994, 53).

The Austrian government and its foreign minister argue that Austria is still able and willing to combine an active European strategy with the continuation of a global engagement (Außenpolitischer Bericht 1994, XV; Alois Mock in *Die Presse*, April 19, 1995). However, Austria's difficulty in recent years in maintaining an active and independent strategy in the UN shows the difficulties and the dilemma Austria faces there. As a result of the harmonization of Austria's positions with EU policy in the UN, a development which already set in before Austria's EU membership, it has become much more difficult than in the past to get political credit and distinction for initiatives and independent activities. The fact that Austria has a very small diplomatic staff at the UN--of all EU-member states, only Luxemburg has a smaller UN-staff--restricts its influence in the formulation of common EU-positions in the General Assembly; on the other side, it reduces informal contacts with other UN members which, in the past, made Austria a well-accepted go-between and mediator between various countries and interests in the UN (Quendler and Schachner 1995). Another indicator for the less active political role and the waning political interest of Austria in the UN is the decrease of Austria's participation in the peacekeeping operations. While Austria used to be one of the major contributors in this domain in the 1980s--in 1988 it furnished about 10 percent of all personnel of UN operations--the respective percentage has been reduced considerably in the 1990s. At the end of 1994 Austria contributes, with approximately 900 soldiers, less than 2 percent of the currently approximately 70,000 UN peacekeepers (Außenpolitischer Bericht 1994, 211f; Ernst Sucharipa, Austria's UN ambassador in *Die Presse*, July 10, 1995). Thus, in 1992, the government rejected a UN request for blue helmets for the UN mission in Somalia.

Another indicator of Austria's difficulties in living up to its internationalistic rhetoric in the UN is that Austria is far behind comparable UN members in voluntary contribution payments to the UN. Austria contributes 0.75 percent of the regular UN budget, but only about 0.2 percent for UN organizations such as UNICEF, UNRWA, UNHCR and others, which is less than non-member Switzerland (Mock in *Die Presse*, December 4, 1994; Quendler and Schachner 1995). This lack of financial magnanimity in UN matters which manifests itself also in the area of development aid (cf. table 6.2) seems hardly wise at a time when as a result of financial and organizational reform measures the UN's Vienna International Center is faced with personnel reductions and plans to move agencies from Vienna to New York and Geneva (Quendler and Schachner 1995).

This reluctance to devote adequate resources to its UN policy reflects a mind-set which maintains that an active policy towards the international environment is needed, but at the same time is not prepared to give it the necessary material support. Funding for the foreign ministry has been parsimonious since its establishment in 1959. In recent years, this situation has even worsened and the Foreign Ministry rightly complains that it is provided with one of the lowest operational budgets of all European states (0.37 percent of the national budget in 1992, comparing with Finland's 0.85 percent and Sweden's 0.87 percent; Neuhold 1993, 41; Außenpolitischer Bericht 1994, XVI).[13] Under these conditions, a discourse between practitioners and universities or research institutes, in many countries an important base for a systematic and competent preparation and reflection of foreign policy decisions and foreign policy options, is not easy and rather the exception (Quendler 1994).

Another example of the low amount of financial investment in foreign policy and security matters is Austria's defense budget. As a percentage of GDP, it is the lowest among all EU member states with the exception of Luxembourg. In 1993/94, Austria spent 0.95 percent of its GDP on military defense, while the other two new EU-members Finland and Sweden spent 1.38 percent and 2.12 percent respectively (International Institute for Strategic Studies 1993, 72, 88f). However, military outlays can probably buy and guarantee security far less than in the past, in an international constellation in which non-military threats and dangers are becoming ever more important.

Conclusion

Austria´s foreign policy can be summed up as follows:
- In the period until 1955, a flexible and successful political strategy was developed to attain national independence and to safeguard the integrity of Austria's territory in the difficult international context of the Cold War years.
- This was followed by the development of an active foreign policy outlook after 1955 based on the international status of neutrality. It secured the main goals of foreign policy and led to greater activities through participation in the international organizations and by rendering "good offices" to the international community (conflict mediation, conference diplomacy).
- After that a "crisis of normalization" set in which started in the late 1970s and was accentuated in the mid 1980s, when the international and domestic base for the former small state strategies narrowed considerably, forcing Austria to revise the foundations of its political and economic independence as well as the main lines of security and neutrality policy. This eventually led to the accession to the European Union, a step which opened up a wholly new page in Austria's international relations.

Notes

1. More detailed information can be found in the respective chapters in the complete German version of the *Handbuch des politischen Systems Österreichs* (Kramer 1991; Skuhra 1991; Luif 1991; Höll 1991 and Quendler 1991). I would like to thank Otmar Höll, Thomas Nowotny, Franz Quendler, Anselm Skuhra, and Helmut Szpott for their comments.

2. There is a vivid and on-going discussion on the operational definition of "small states" in International Relations (Höll 1983; Waschkuhn 1994).

3. "Free-riding" strategies take on either a positive form, i.e. when small states use their wider room to maneuver in specific constellations for bold policy moves and policy initiatives and contribute to the easing of political tensions and

the prospects of international mediation or a rather problematic form by circumventing or outwitting existing rules and standards for international behavior (as in the case of economic sanctions, or by not fulfilling international standards in the field of development aid).

4. "Just as Vienna has been a center for the passing of intelligence secrets, for years it has been a major staging area for moving restricted American technology behind the Iron Curtain." (*Business Week*, April 4, 1983 quoted in Paul Luif. 1985. "USA-Österreich: Der Konflikt um den Technologietransfer," in *Die Zukunft*, No. 12, 1985, p. 17).

5. Policies and initiatives judged by contemporaries as "failures" may appear in a much more positive light in historical perspective and as a result of new developments and political breakthroughs. Bruno Kreisky's attempts in the 1970s to establish communication lines between Israel, the PLO and the USA--according to Yair Hirshfeld, one of the main actors in the secret negotiations leading to the mutual recognition of Israel and the PLO in September 1993 in Oslo--did help to prepare ground for the peace accord reached in Norway and signed in Washington (cited in the French magazine *Le Globe*, July 27, 1993, quoted in Thomas Nowotny, *Le chancelier Kreisky vu par les hommes politiques français*, Austriaca, Cahiers Universitaires d'Information sur l'Autriche 40, forthcoming).

6. Mock was President of the European Democratic Union and also President of the International Democratic Union, the international association of conservative parties, created in 1983 (Demblin 1984).

7. During the last four years of the second term of Rudolf Kirchschläger, Kurt Waldheim's predecessor as President (1981-1985), thirteen heads of state paid official visits to Austria, whereas in the first four years of the presidency of Kurt Waldheim (1986-1991) only three heads of state did so (and none of a Western country).

8. There have been numerous declarations and interviews by Foreign Minister Alois Mock in which he claimed that if Austria remained outside of the EC/EU it would without any doubt become a "second class country" (*Kurier*, May 31, 1994), "a country with colonial status" (*Profil*, February 2, 1992 and *Kurier*, November 10, 1993). Peter Jankowitsch of the SPÖ, at the time Secretary of State for European Integration, argued the same way (*Der Standard*, September 13, 1991).

9. The conflict between the SPÖ and Foreign Minister Mock, later on also between the SPÖ and President Klestil (supported by the ÖVP) about the constitutional roles of the president, the chancellor and the foreign minister in foreign policy decision making and the representation of Austria at international summits and in the EU reached its climax in the quarrel over who would be signing the EU-accession treaty in Corfu (*Salzburger Nachrichten*, July 26 and July 27, 1993; *Die Presse*, February 24, 1994; *Die Presse*, June 18/19, 1994). In the end, the treaty was signed by Chancellor Vranitzky, Foreign Minister Mock, two civil servants, but not by State Secretary Brigitte Ederer of the SPÖ, formally in charge of European integration matters. President Klestil was present but did not participate in the European Council meeting there (*Profil*, June 27, 1994).

10. On some occasions Austria's actual behavior towards the new democracies contrasted sharply with its proclaimed goals. Austria slowed down the conclusion of free trade treaties between EFTA and Eastern European countries in 1993 and 1994 as it was concerned that trade liberalization with the East might have negative effects on its agriculture and protected sectors of industry (Jan Stankovsky, head of the Eastern European section in the Austrian Institute for Economic Research in *Die Presse*, July 7, 1994 and *Der Standard*, September 9, 1994).

11. The Austrian line in the Security Council with its active support of sanctions and punitive measures against Serbia in the Balkan conflict--e.g. Austria's initiative in July 1992, which was not accepted by the Security Council--was "certainly the clearest articulation to date of a foreign policy position with military implications" (Helmut Freudenschuß, deputy head of the Austrian delegation to the Security Council in a report in 1993, Freudenschuß 1993, 30; Skuhra 1995). This policy position in the Security council which was orchestrated by Foreign Minister Mock was criticized quite harshly by Austrian experts on neutrality and by former diplomats (as by one of the leading academic experts on neutrality, Felix Ermacora, *Der Standard*, March 7/8, 1992).

12. It is interesting that Foreign Minister Alois Mock, in his years as opposition leader and when taking up the foreign ministry in 1986/87, sharply criticized Kreisky's foreign policy as "unrealistic", "moralistic" and "missionary" (Khol 1993, 9)--cf. part 4 of this chapter--but on account of the conflict in ex-Yugoslavia changed his foreign policy views towards a more active, interventionist foreign policy outlook with an explicitely "idealistic" basis ("Foreign policy is a tightrope act between ideals and 'Realpolitik'," Mock in *Oberösterreichische Nachrichten*, July 7, 1993; cf. the commentary of Gerfried Sperl in *Der Standard*, September 11, 1992).

13. The meager operational budget for Austria's cultural affairs abroad--Sch 86 million in 1994 (Außenpolitischer Bericht 1994, 355)--contrasts sharply with the wish and the claim of Austria to operate as a "big cultural power in the EU ('EU-Kulturgroßmacht')"--Andreas Khol in *Standard*, June 28, 1994).

References

Alcock, Anthony E. 1970. *The History of the South Tyrol Question*. London.
___. 1982. *Geschichte der Südtirolfrage. Südtirol seit dem Pakte 1970-1980*. Vienna.
Außenpolitischer Bericht des Bundesministers für auswärtige Angelegenheiten. Vienna (annual report).
Bielka, Erich. 1983. "Österreich und seine volksdemokratischen Nachbarn," in Erich Bielka et al., eds., *Die Ära Kreisky. Aspekte österreichischer Außenpolitik*. Pp. 195-231. Vienna.
Birnbaum, Karl. 1987. "The Neutral and Non-Aligned States in the CSCE Process," in Bengt Sundelius, ed., *The Neutral Democracies and the New Cold War*. Pp. 148-159. Boulder.

Bischof, Günter. 1988. "The Anglo-American Powers and Austrian Neutrality 1953-1955." *Mitteilungen des Österreichischen Staatsarchivs* 42: 368-393.

___. 1995. "The Making of a Cold Warrior: Karl Gruber and Austrian Foreign Policy." *Austrian History Yearbook* 26: 99-127.

Bonjour, Edgar. 1980. "Österreichische und schweizerische Neutralität. Zwei Leitbilder konvergieren." *Schweizer Monatshefte* 10: 79-91.

Burns, James M. 1978. *Leadership*. New York.

Burtscher, Wolfgang. 1988. "Österreichs Annäherung an den Europarat von 1949 bis zur Vollmitgliedschaft im Jahre 1956," in Waldemar Hummer, and Gerhard Wagner, eds., *Österreich im Europarat 1956-1986. Bilanz einer 30jährigen Mitgliedschaft*. Pp. 37-52. Vienna.

Camilleri, Joseph A., and Jim Falk. 1992. *The End of Sovereignty? The Politics of a Shrinking and Fragmenting World*. Aldershot-Brookfield.

Caytas, Ivo. 1982. *Internationale kollektive Friedenssicherung. 20 Jahre österreichische Praxis*. Berlin.

Cronin, Andrey. 1986. *Great Power Politics and the Struggle over Austria, 1945-1955*. Ithaca.

Csaky, Eva Maria. 1980. *Der Weg zur Freiheit und Neutralität. Dokumentation zur österreichischen Außenpolitik 1945-1955*. Vienna.

Demblin, Alexander. 1984. "Die ÖVP in internationalen Organisationen—EDU, IDU," in Andreas Kohl et al., eds., *Österreichisches Jahrbuch für Politik 1983*. Pp. 243-255. Vienna.

Denk, Herbert, and Helmut Kramer. 1988. "Außenpolitik und internationale Solidarität. Die Außenpolitik der SPÖ von 1945-1986," in Peter Pelinka, and Gerhard Steger, eds., *Auf dem Weg zur Staatspartei. Zur Geschichte und Politik der SPÖ seit 1945*. Pp. 267-292. Vienna.

Dolman, Anthony. 1981. "The Like-Minded-Countries and the North-South-Conflict." *Österreichische Zeitschrift für Politikwissenschaft* 10: 153-163.

Du Bois, Pierre. 1984. "Neutrality and Political Good Offices: The Case of Switzerland," in Hanspeter Neuhold, and Hans Thalberg, eds., *The European Neutrals in International Affairs*. Pp. 7-16.Vienna.

Eger, Reiner. 1981. *Krisen an Österreichs Grenzen*. Vienna.

Elgström, Ole. 1983. "Active Foreign Policy as a Preventive Strategy Against Dependence," in Otmar Höll, ed., *Small States in Europe and Dependence*. Pp. 262-280. Laxenburg.

Ermacora, Felix. 1984. *Südtirol und das Vaterland Österreich*. Vienna.

Frei, Daniel. 1977. "Kleinstaatliche Außenpolitik als Umgang mit Abhängigkeit," in Daniel Frei, ed., *Die Schweiz in einer sich wandelnden Welt*. Pp. 201-225. Zürich.

Freudenschuß, Helmut. 1993. "Von der Neutralitätspolitik zur Solidaritätspolitik? Österreich im Sicherheitsrat der Vereinten Nationen 1991/92-Versuch einer Bilanz." *International* 1993(2-3): 25-31.

Gärtner, Heinz. 1992. "Challenges and Opportunities in New Political Scenarios for Europe: An Austrian Perspective," in Hanspeter Neuhold, ed., *The European Neutrals in the 1990s*. Pp. 17-30. Boulder-San Francisco-Oxford.

Gehler, Michael. 1994. "State Treaty and Neutrality." *Contemporary Austrian Studies* 2: 39-78.
Giller, Joachim. 1989. "Insel der Seligen? Bedrohungsbewußtsein und Friedenskultur im neutralen Kleinstaat Österreich," in Wilhelm R. Vogt, ed., *Angst vor Frieden. Über die Schwierigkeiten der Friedensentwicklung für das Jahr 2000.* Pp. 154-166. Darmstadt.
Hakovirta, Harto. 1988. *East-West Conflict and European Neutrality*. Oxford.
Haymerle, Heinrich. 1983. "Die Beziehungen zur Großmacht im Osten," in Erich Bielka et al., eds., *Die Ära Kreisky. Schwerpunkte der österreichischen Außenpolitik.* Pp. 143-193. Vienna.
Höll, Otmar, ed., 1983. *Small States and Dependence in Europe*. Boulder.
___ . 1985. "Abhängigkeit oder Autonomie: Österreich im Internationalisierungsprozeß," in *Österreichisches Jahrbuch für Internationale Politik 1984*. Pp. 26-63.
___ . 1986. "Kleinstaaten im Entspannungsprozeß. Am Beispiel der neutralen und nichtpaktgebundenen Staaten in der KSZE." *Österreichische Zeitschrift für Politikwissenschaft* 15: 293-310.
___ , ed., 1988. *Österreich-Jugoslawien: Determinationen und Perspektiven ihrer Beziehungen.* Vienna.
___ . 1991. "Entwicklungspolitik," in Herbert Dachs et al., eds., *Handbuch des politischen Systems Österreichs.* Pp. 690-704. Vienna.
___ . 1994. "The Foreign Policy of the Kreisky Era." *Contemporary Austrian Studies* 2: 32-71.
International Institute for Strategic Studies, ed., 1993. *The Military Balance 1993/94.* London.
Jankowitsch, Peter. 1975. "Österreich im Sicherheitsrat." *Österreichische Zeitschrift für Außenpolitik* 15: 67-85.
Kaiser, Wolfram et al. 1995. *Die EU-Volksabstimmungen in Österreich, Finnland, Schweden und Norwegen: Verlauf, Ergebnisse, Motive und Folgen.* Research Memorandum 23. Institute for Advanced Studies. Vienna.
Katzenstein, Peter J. 1975. "Trends and Oscillations in Austrian Integration Policy Since 1955." *Journal of Common Market Studies* 14: 171-197.
Khol, Andreas. 1981. "Zur Kritik und Bestandsaufnahme der österreichischen Außenpolitik." *Europäische Rundschau* 3: 111-118.
___ . 1984. "Außenpolitik als Realutopie. Kanten einer neuen Außenpolitik," in Stephan Koren et al., eds., *Politik für die Zukunft. Festschrift für Alois Mock.* Pp. 457-476. Vienna.
___ . 1993. "Vorwort," in Andreas Khol, ed., *Neue Außenpolitik in einer neuen Welt. Ergebnisse des Symposions der Politischen Akademie in Zusammenarbeit mit der Vereinigung Österreichischer Industrieller vom 19. Oktober 1992.* Pp. 5-13. Vienna.
Kissinger, Henry. 1979. *The White House Years*. Boston.
Klestil, Thomas. 1989. "Die Entwicklung aus österreichischer Sicht," in *Österreichisches Jahrbuch für Internationale Politik 1989*. Pp. 156-161.

Knight, Robert, ed., 1988. *'Ich bin dafür, die Sache in die Länge zu ziehen.'* Die Wortprotokolle der österreichischen Bundesregierung von 1945 bis 1952 über die Entschädigung der Juden. Frankfurt.

___. 1991. "Restitution and Legitimacy in Post-War Austria 1945-1953," in *Leo Baeck Institute Yearbook* 36. Pp. 413-440.

Kramer, Helmut. 1984. "Zur Rolle der öffentlichen Meinung in der Außenpolitik." *Österreichische Zeitschrift für Politikwissenschaft* 13: 141-164.

___. 1986. "Aspekte der österreichischen Außenpolitik (1970-1985)," in Erich Fröschl, and Helge Zoitl, eds., *Der österreichische Weg 1970-1985. Fünfzehn Jahre, die Österreich verändert haben.* Pp. 187-199. Vienna.

___. 1988. "'Wende' in der österreichischen Außenpolitik? Zur Außenpolitik der SPÖ-ÖVP-Koalition." *Österreichische Zeitschrift für Politikwissenschaft* 17: 117-131.

___. 1991. "Öffentliche Meinung und die österreichische EG-Entscheidung im Jahre 1989." *SWS-Rundschau* 31: 191-202.

___. 1991. "Strukturentwicklung der Außenpolitik (1945-1990)," in Herbert Dachs et al., eds., *Handbuch des politischen Systems Österreichs*. Pp. 637-657. Vienna.

Kreisky, Bruno. 1959. "Austria Draws the Balance." *Foreign Affairs* 38: 269-281.

___. 1981. *Reden*. 2 vols. Vienna.

Kremenyuk, Viktor A. 1984. "The European Neutrals and Soviet-American Relations," in Hanspeter Neuhold, and Hans Thalberg, eds., *The European Neutrals in International Affairs*. Pp. 93-104. Vienna.

Laidi, Zaki, ed., 1992. *L'ordre mondial relaché. Sens et puissance après la guerre froide.* Paris.

Larson, Welch L. 1987. "Crisis prevention and the Austrian State Treaty." *International Organization* 41: 27-64.

Lehne, Stefan. 1991. *The Vienna Meeting of the Conference on Security and Cooperation in Europe.* Boulder.

Luchak, John Michael. 1987. *Amerikanisch-österreichische Beziehungen von 1955 bis 1985. Neutralität und der Ost-West-Konflikt*. Doctoral dissertation. University of Vienna.

Luif, Paul. 1988. *Neutrale in die EG? Die wirtschaftliche Integration in Westeuropa und die neutralen Staaten.* Vienna.

___. 1991. "Außenwirtschaftspolitik," in Herbert Dachs et al., eds., *Handbuch des politischen System Österreichs*. Pp. 674-689. Vienna.

___. 1992. "Die Österreichische Integrationspolitik," in Hanspeter Neuhold, and Paul Luif, eds., *Das außenpolitische Bewußtsein der Österreicher.* Pp. 37-86. Vienna.

___. 1995. *On the Road to Brussels. The Political Dimension of Austria's, Finland's and Sweden's Accession to the European Union.* Vienna.

Mähr, Wilfried. 1989. *Der Marshallplan in Österreich.* Graz.

Meier-Walser, Reinhard. 1988. *Die Außenpolitik der monocoloren Regierung Klaus in Österreich 1966-1970.* Munich.

Michal-Misak, Silvia. 1985. *Die österreichische UNO-Politik in den siebziger Jahren,* doctoral dissertation. University of Vienna.

___. 1990. "Österreich in den Vereinten Nationen." *Österreichische Zeitschrift für Politikwissenschaft* 19: 379-395.

Neuhold, Hanspeter. 1986. "Austria and the Soviet Union," in Bo Huldt, and Atis Lejins, eds., *European Neutrals and the Soviet Union.* Pp. 83-118. Stockholm.

___. 1993. *Internationaler Strukturwandel und staatliche Außenpolitik. Das österreichische Außenministerium vor neuen Herausforderungen.* Vienna-Laxenburg.

___, and Paul Luif, eds., 1992. *Das außenpolitische Bewußtsein der Österreicher.* Vienna.

___, and Karl Zemanek. 1968. "Die österreichische Neutralität im Jahre 1967." *Österreichische Zeitschrift für Außenpolitik* 8:14-32.

Nowotny, Thomas. 1987. "Österreich und die EG. Die politische Dimension." *International* 1987 (4): 21-26.

___. 1988. "Identitätskrise der Diplomaten." *Österreichische Zeitschrift für Politikwissenschaft* 17:183-199.

Pilz, Peter. 1982. *Die Panzermacher. Die österreichische Rüstungsindustrie und ihre Exporte.* Vienna.

Plaschka, Richard G.. 1981. "Selbstverständnis und Kriterien nationaler Integration in Österreich: Impulse 1918 und 1945/55," in Österreichische Akademie der Wissenschaften, ed., *25 Jahre österreichischer Staatsvertrag.* Pp. 39-50. Vienna.

Plasser, Fritz, and Ulram Peter A. 1994. "Meinungstrends, Mobilisierung und Motivlagen bei der Volksabstimmung über den EU-Beitritt," in Anton Pelinka, ed., *EU-Referendum. Zur Praxis direkter Demokratie in Österreich.* Pp. 87-119. Vienna.

Quendler, Franz. 1991. "Österreich in internationalen Organisationen," in Herbert Dachs et al., eds., *Handbuch des politischen System Österreichs.* Pp. 705-718. Vienna.

___. 1994. "Bridging the gap: The Austrian case," in Michel Girard et al., eds., *Theory and Practice in Foreign Policy-Making. National Perspectives on Academics and Professionals in International Relations.* Pp. 136-152. London-New York.

___, and Maria Ponholzer-Schachner. 1995. "Der UN-Sitz Wien im Kontext sich verändernder Rahmenbedingungen der österreichischen Außenpolitik." *Österreichische Zeitschrift für Politikwissenschaft* 24: (forthcoming).

Rathkolb, Oliver. 1990. "Sozialistische Außenpolitik(er) in Österreich 1945 bis 1959," in Erich Fröschl, and Helge Zoitl, eds., *Die Bewegung, 100 Jahre Sozialdemokratie.* Pp. 499-514. Vienna.

___. 1994. "Bruno Kreisky: Perspectives of Top-Level U.S. Foreign Policy Decision Makers, 1959-1983." *Contemporary Austrian Studies* 2: 130-151.

___. 1995a. "Austria's 'Ostpolitik' in the 1950s and 1960s: Honest Broker or Double Agent?" *Austrian Yearbook* 26: 129-145.

___. 1995b. "The Foreign Relations between the U.S.A. and Austria in the late 1950s." *Contemporary Austrian Studies* 3: 24-38.

Rauchensteiner, Manfried. 1987. *Die Zwei. Die Große Koalition in Österreich 1945-1966.* Vienna.
Rosenau, James. 1990. *Turbulence in World Politics. A Theory of Change and Continuity.* Princeton.
Rotter, Manfred. 1991. "Von der integralen zur differentiellen Neutralität." *Europäische Rundschau* 18: 25-35.
Schaller, Christian. 1994. "Die innenpolitische EG-Diskussion seit den 80er Jahren," in Anton Pelinka et al., *Ausweg EG? Innenpolitische Motive einer außenpolitischen Umorientierung.* Pp. 27-269. Vienna-Cologne-Graz.
Schärf, Adolf. 1955. *Österreichs Erneuerung 1945-1955. Das erste Jahrzehnt der Zweiten Republik.* Vienna.
Schlesinger, Thomas O. 1972. *Austrian Neutrality in Postwar Europe. The Domestic Roots of a Foreign Policy.* Vienna.
Schneider, Heinrich. 1990. *Alleingang nach Brüssel. Österreichs EG-Politik.* Bonn.
Schultz, Mark D. 1992. "Austria in the International Arena: Neutrality, European Integration and Consociationalism," in Kurt R. Luther, and Wolfgang C. Müller, eds., *Politics in Austria.* Pp. 173-200. London.
Siegl, Walter. 1993. "Die österreichische Jugoslawienpolitik," in Andreas Kohl et al., eds., *Österreichisches Jahrbuch für Politik 1992.* Pp. 825-842. Vienna.
Skuhra, Anselm. 1984. "Austrian Aid: Policy and Performance," in Olaf Stokke, ed., *European Development Assistance, Vol. 1: Policies and Performance.* Pp. 65-87. Oslo.
___ . 1987. "Austria and the New Cold War," in Bengt Sundelius, ed., *The Neutral Democracies and the New Cold War.* Pp. 117-147. Boulder.
___ . 1991. "Österreichische Sicherheitspolitik," in Herbert Dachs et al., eds., *Handbuch des politischen Systems Österreichs.* Pp. 658-673. Vienna.
___ . 1995. "Österreich im Sicherheitsrat der Vereinten Nationen 1991-92." *Österreichische Zeitschrift für Politikwissenschaft* 24: (forthcoming).
Steiner, Ludwig. 1977. "Zur Außenpolitik der Zweiten Republik," in Erich Zöllner, ed., *Diplomatie und Außenpolitik Österreichs.* Pp. 169-188. Vienna.
Sternfeld, Albert. 1990. *Betrifft: Österreich. Von Österreich betroffen.* Vienna.
Stourzh, Gerald. 1975. *Kleine Geschichte des Staatsvertrages.* Graz.
___ . 1981. "Der österreichische Staatsvertrag und die Voraussetzungen seines Zustandekommens," in Österreichische Akademie der Wissenschaften, ed., *25 Jahre österreichischer Staatsvertrag.* Pp. 65-76. Vienna.
___ . 1988. "The Origins of Austrian Neutrality," in Alan T. Leonhard, ed., *Neutrality, Changing Concepts and Practices.* Pp. 35-57. Lanham-New York-London.
Strasser, Wolfgang. 1967. *Österreich und die Vereinten Nationen. Eine Bestandsaufnahme von 10 Jahren Mitgliedschaft.* Vienna.
Sucharipa, Ernst, and Stefan Lehne. 1991. "Die Ostpolitik Österreichs vor und nach der Wende." *Österreichische Zeitschrift für Politikwissenschaft* 20: 301-312.
Thalberg, Hans. 1983. "Die Nahostpolitik," in Erich Bielka, Peter Jankowitsch, and Hans Thalberg, eds., *Die Ära Kreisky--Schwerpunkte der österreichischen Außenpolitik.* Pp. 293-321. Vienna.

Tweraser, Kurt K. 1995. "The Politics of Productivity and Corporatism: The Late Marshall Plan in Austria, 1950-54." *Contemporary Austrian Studies* 3: 91-115.

Unterberger, Andreas. 1992. "Die außenpolitische Entwicklung," in Wolfgang Mantl, ed., *Politik in Österreich. Die Zweite Republik*. Pp. 204-239. Vienna.

Väyrynen, Raimo. 1987. "Adaption of a Small Power to International Tensions: The Case of Finland," in Bengt Sundelius, ed., *The Neutral Democracies and the New Cold War*. Pp. 33-56. Boulder.

Verdross, Alfred. 1978. *The Permanent Neutrality of Austria*. Vienna.

Verosta, Stephan. 1975. "Außenpolitik," in Erika Weinzierl, and Kurt Skalnik, ed., *Das neue Österreich. Geschichte der Zweiten Republik*. Pp. 85-151. Graz.

Vetschera, Heinz. 1990. "Austria," in Richard E. Bissel, and Curt Gasteyger, eds., *The Missing Link. West European Neutrals and Regional Security*. Pp. 59-77. Durham.

Waschkuhn, Arno. 1994. "Small State Theory and Microstates," in Frank Pfetsch, ed., *International Relations and Pan-Europe. Theoretical Approaches and Empirical Findings*. Pp. 149-158. Münster, Hamburg.

Zemanek, Karl. 1984. "Austria's Policy of Neutrality: Constants and Variables," in Hanspeter Neuhold, and Hans Thalberg, ed., *The European Neutrals in International Affairs*. Pp. 17-22. Vienna.

___ . 1991. "The Changing International System: A new look at Collective Security and Permanent Neutrality." *Austrian Journal of Public and International Law* 42: 277-294.

7

Environmental Politics and Policy

Volkmar Lauber

Career of the Environmental Issue

Economic development is always paralleled by a modification of the environment. The relationship is complex. On the one hand, economic growth usually leads to greater resource use and (at least at first) to more pollution; on the other, it may also lead to new demands for "quality of life" and "sustainable development." This theme is usually expressed by environmental activists before being taken up by governmental actors whose main concern is economic growth.

Austria's industrialization came relatively late. Most of its heavy industry (steel, chemicals, paper and cellulose, cement, etc.), was set up after the incorporation into the Third Reich. The progressive shift to light industries and services, and the declining demand for most products of heavy industry, contributed to reducing visible pollution in recent decades. Economic success often created environmental problems which were at first neglected because they seemed unimportant to a generation that had experienced so much economic hardship.

It was only in the mid-1970s, in the wake of the oil crises, that the environment became a political issue in its own right, due to a new political activism whose legitimacy was, at best, reluctantly acknowledged by government, the bureaucracy, the established political parties and the major interest groups, i.e., the central actors of economic policy.

In reaction to the oil crisis of 1973/1974, the Austrian government--as many others--planned among other things to significantly expand its program of atomic energy. The first nuclear power plant (built in

Zwentendorf) met with increasing resistance, and soon opposition to nuclear power became the rallying ground for the nascent environmental movement. The issue was politicized to such a degree that Chancellor Kreisky decided to hold a referendum on the subject. In November 1978, nuclear power was rejected by a slim majority and soon afterwards banned by a special law. There were efforts--especially among the social partners--to have the law repealed, but they were unsuccessful.[1] (The Chernobyl accident in 1986 put an end to these efforts). As a result of this struggle, the environmentalists had acquired new clout and a fairly high degree of organization.

Even though the goals of the environmental movement were manifold, the second great wave of mobilization took place over yet another power plant, a hydraulic dam at Hainburg on the Danube which would have destroyed rare wetland areas. Once more the utility industry--at that time wholly within the public sector--pushed its project with dire warnings of imminent crisis in the power supply, in contradiction to information leaked from inside the industry that showed that there was, in fact, a large surplus of generating capacity at that time and that the utilities' main worry was with marketing this surplus. When construction of the plant was about to start in December 1984, several thousand activists occupied the site. The attempts to dislodge them with the help of the police, and a threat by the large construction worker union to "counterdemonstrate" on the site, only led to a wave of support for the obstructionists. Once again, the country seemed intensely polarized. After a cooling-off period, the project was put off indefinitely by the government. Many other, smaller hydraulic projects throughout the country were also stopped after intense controversies.[2] Environmentalists argued that government and utilities should focus on energy savings rather than keep expanding supply.

By the mid-1980s, another theme gripped public opinion. Acid rain had produced *waldsterben* (a steadily declining state of health of the forests) which seemed to progress at alarming rates. The government passed very strict legislation on air pollution and, in 1985, required catalytic converters for gasoline-powered automobiles, in fact taking over US standards. Given the delay of the European Community in this area, this was one instance where Austria took the lead in Europe, along with Sweden and Switzerland. The measure was considered necessary to pacify public opinion; on the other hand, the EC was expected to follow suit (in fact it did so only after a decade).

By the late 1980s, the environmental movement was quite differentiated. It could count on many different organizations, ranging from the older nature protection societies to new organizations such as Greenpeace, WWF or Global 2000. The big themes of that time were transit traffic (essentially trucks crossing the Alps) and the threat from nuclear power installations in neighboring countries. But there was also a multitude of domestic issues, and many substantive laws were passed during that period until the onset of the recession in the early 1990s. Public opinion surveys regularly showed that the environment was viewed as the most urgent problem facing the country.

The recession, the influx of refugees from Eastern and Southeastern Europe and the preparation of European Union membership changed this picture. Economic priorities came to the fore again. In the new climate, business and industrial associations were successful in holding back additional environmental reforms with the argument that Austria was already one of the leading countries in Europe in this respect and that further reforms would threaten competitiveness and thus employment. For several years these arguments were successful, even if they were not necessarily correct (there is much evidence to show that countries with strict environmental legislation are leading in the development of new technologies and benefit from their lead through exports).

In 1994/95, the mood seemed to swing back again, as evidenced by the discussion of an ecological tax reform (see below). Surveys showed strong public support for such a measure. In general, there seems to be a widespread willingness to resort to economic instruments in the field of environmental policy, something which in Austria has not been used much so far.

Ecological Modernization of the State

Before the subject of ecology was taken up by the environmental movement, there were very modest responses to environmental deterioration. After the first United Nations Conference on the Environment in Stockholm in 1972, a Federal Ministry of Public Health and Environmental Protection was created. Its resources in the evironmental area were tiny, and it had no power to initiate environmental legislation (laws or decrees). Such legislation could come forth only from other federal ministries (government departments) with an economic focus such as Construction, Trade, Agriculture, etc.; due to their general orientation and clientele, these ministries had no great interest either in formulating strict environmental laws or in making sure that they were actually applied.[3] Thus, the function of the new Ministry of Environmental Protection was largely symbolic, at best preparatory.

Things changed in the 1980s. Some major laws were passed then, most importantly to combat air pollution. Second, there were important institutional changes at both the federal and *Land* levels. Finally, the environmental movement organized itself politically by the creation of the Green Party (see chapter 3) and thus forced the other parties to respond.

Major institutional innovations in the public management of the environment were made in the second half of the 1980s. The experience of Hainburg in particular led to concern about the fact that, within the political and administrative system, environmental interests were not represented with any degree of authority, thereby legitimizing unorthodox forms of activism. In most *Länder* this led to the creation of an Office of the Environmental Advocate (*Umweltanwalt*). The person heading this office was appointed by the *Landeshauptmann* without being bound to direct political instructions and was to look after the environmental interests in all administrative preceedings before the *Land* authorities (this excluded most industrial permit procedures, which were federal matters). However, he or she also had to take into account the economic interests of the *Land* and to strive for compromise solutions. As a result, the office was marked by ambiguity. It was set up to show that the government was concerned about the environment, and that for this reason, political activism by citizens would not be necessary any longer, all the more so since the advocate would be an expert and not an amateur. At the same time, it was intended to ward off demands for stronger citizen participation in administrative preceedings and thus fits under the frequent Austrian pattern of administrative paternalism.[4] Even so, no Environmental Advocate was created at the federal level. A new agency created in 1985 (the *Umweltbundesamt*) was at first intended to play that role, but was restricted to monitoring environmental data and similar tasks.[5]

At the federal level, a reform gave the Ministry of the Environment (now joined with Youth and Family) at least modest powers and also increased personnel; control over certain expenditures was added. Still it was clearly a junior ministry. In any case, the ministry became more activist, proposing legislation in several areas; in fact, it often clashed with the Ministry of the Economy, also held by the ÖVP since 1986 and supported by a strong clientele of its own. While most ministries enjoy the support of such a clientele, the Environment Ministry is an exception.[6] The environmental movement would represent its natural constituency. However, partly because of the anti-state, anti-interest group orientation of this movement and partly because of the ministry's need to compromise with the more powerful economic departments, the environmental movement often turned against its "own" ministry for "betraying the cause." This led to efforts to create a more supportive environmentalist constituency in the first half of the 1990s. In 1993/94, the idea of an "environmentalist chamber" was discussed, a peak organization of the various environmentalist organizations to link those groups with the ministry. However, no action was taken, and the idea was opposed by some of the major environmentalist groups.[7]

Also, as a result of Hainburg, work started on several bills to allow the participation of citizens in environmentally relevant administrative preceedings. The idea was to transfer conflicts from the construction site to the negotiating table, and in the process, to reduce unconventional participation. Some drafts provided for the participation of citizens, but only if they represented a certain percentage of the local population; environmentalist organizations were to be granted standing if they existed at least ten years and were active throughout Austria. However, the years went by and until 1991 no bill was sent to parliament. Taking advantage of the recession, the coalition parties in 1993 passed a law which differed quite substantially from the original intentions. A fairly elaborate environmental impact procedure was set up, partly to comply with a EU guideline, but it was restricted to certain large-scale projects (it was estimated that a few dozen at most would have to be decided each year). Also, the whole procedure was greatly simplified in order to speed up the process. The environmental interests in the proceedings would be represented by the neighboring communes, the environmental advocate and citizen initiatives numbering at least 200 persons from the area; these parties would be entitled to challenge administrative decisions before the highest courts. The law only became operative in mid-1994, so it is too early to judge its effect. In any case, it is obvious that when compared to the US, where "any citizen" may bring a suit under most environmental laws, the Austrian regulation is very restrictive in granting standing.[8]

Beginning in 1980, and particularly from the middle of the decade onwards, a series of laws was passed to improve the environmental situation. Within approximately a decade, this made Austria one of the leading countries of Europe with regard to environment-related expenditure. Also, in several areas Austrian regulations were stricter than those prevailing in the EC (see also the next subchapter). However, with the recession of the early 1990s and the adaptation of

Austrian law to that of the European Community/European Union, a new mood set in. Demands to cut back on environmental regulations and bureaucracy in the name of efficiency and of attracting new industrial plant to Austria became more vocal and were reflected in the legislative process, resulting in a setback for environmental reform.

The Environmental Situation Today

The picture is necessarily a mixed one. Austria has undoubtedly made great efforts to improve its environmental situation. There are some areas of success; at the same time, increasing wealth most often leads to increased consumption of limited and non-renewable resources.

With regard to the "classical" pollutants, progress is fairly clear. Austria has successfully cleaned up its lakes and most of its rivers. Lead has been eliminated from gasoline and sulphur dioxide emissions were reduced dramatically, more so than in any other European country (by about 82 percent between 1980 and 1993). Nitrogen oxide emissions were also reduced, but (mostly due to increased car traffic) by only about 26 percent during the same time period.[9] However, even though the acid rain problem has diminished, acidity in soils (with its negative consequences for plant growth) is still building up, though at a reduced rate of accumulation. Ground-level ozone is exceptionally high in the European context. Since the pollutants are partially imported, Austria in recent years made efforts to curb pollution from power plants in the neighboring Czech Republic and Slovenia, often by funding (and furnishing) pollution control equipment.

The problem of waste has at least partly been tackled by recycling. Household waste has to be divided into several components which are recycled separately. Glass and paper are collected and recycled for more than a decade by now, and recycling ratios are already very high (about 75 percent in 1994). Recycling of metals and plastics is more recent, its success more doubtful. Organic waste (kitchen leftovers, grass clippings etc.) are also sorted out and composted. Opening new waste dumps is politically highly sensitive. The construction of waste incineration plants has become even more difficult, especially with regard to toxic waste. In most cases, strong local opposition prevented projects from being realized.

Modern agriculture with its heavy reliance on chemicals is a major environmental problem in many countries. From an environmental perspective, organic-biological agriculture is a desirable alternative. For a long time such production was practiced only by relatively few pioneers. In the first half of the 1990s however, organic-biological production increased extremely rapidly in Austria, mostly due to government subsidies set aside for this purpose, bot also due to rapidly increasing demand.[10] In 1995, about 10 percent of the farms (and about 8 percent of arable land) are cultivated according to organic-biological methods, the highest rate in Europe. Even so demand keeps exceeding supply. Despite this recent increase, most agricultural produce will continue to come from mass production. In any case, the Ministry of Agriculture and many farmers feel that improved quality production may be the best way to improve the chances of Austrian farmers in the European Union.

Traffic became an important issue in the 1980s. Some areas of the country (primarily in Tyrol) witnessed a veritable uprising of citizens against the steady increase of heavy truck transit which polluted sensitive Alpine valleys. For a long time the government did not take any measures to restrict this traffic; attempts to introduce generalized toll charges were repeatedly withdrawn upon protests from abroad, mostly from Germany (even though France and Italy levy tolls for their superhighways). In order to prevent a further deterioration of the situation and after heavy protest voting in elections in Tyrol (see chapter 10 of this volume), the government negotiated a transit freight traffic agreement with the European Community in 1992 to reduce pollution from trucks by 60 percent over a period of twelve years. This was supposed to be achieved by a combination of technical improvements and numerical limitations on trucks and by shifting part of the freight to rail transport. In the membership negotiations with the European Union, this agreement had to be watered down, but this has to be viewed against the background of the European Union's dogma of the free flow of goods and the expected increase of truck traffic (doubling or more by the year 2010). In 1993 only 31 percent of all goods crossed Austria by train. This is a higher share than on the French/Italian border (there too the Alps must be crossed), but much less than in Switzerland, where about 80 percent of merchandise transit is handled by rail and where after a referendum in early 1994 all truck transit must come to an end by 2004. Even today Italy and Germany are pressing for the construction of yet another superhighway across the Austrian Alps.

Energy consumption rose steadily in Austria; long-term demand growth was interrupted only briefly from 1973 to 1975 and from 1980 to 1983. Between 1973 and 1991, energy consumption increased by about 25 percent. Despite two oil crises, the emphasis of energy policy lay on the expansion of supply. It is true that these crises also generated a spate of ideas about a more efficient use of energy (better housing isolation, cogeneration, district heating, consumption standards for household appliances or cars, etc.), but only in recent years have demand-side management and least cost planning become accepted by official rhetoric, and very rarely have they been put into practice (mostly in large cities). These ideas of the 1970s seem to find their practical expression only with a delay of twenty years. Only district heating was promoted fairly steadily, but its share is still modest (9 percent in 1992). About two thirds of total energy needs to be imported, slightly more than in 1973.[11] Renewable sources cover about one quarter of Austria's energy needs. Next to hydroelectricity, wood is playing an increasingly important role. Since a large part of Austria is covered by forests, biomass in the form of wood chips would represent a viable fuel, at least for certain regions. In practice the expansion of natural gas into even those areas, usually pushed by the *Land* utilities, has constrained the development of biomass as a fuel. In the use of solar energy for water heating, Austria is (in Europe) second only to Greece, due to the activity of self-help groups supported by government subsidies. Still, the impact of solar energy is extremely limited so far.

When in 1986 oil prices (and to a lesser extent the prices for coal and natural gas) fell drastically, some countries increased their level of oil taxation. A proposal to this effect was also made by the Austrian minister of the environment at the time, but it met with stiff resistance from the two automobile associations and came to naught. The argument was renewed later on to protect the development of biomass systems but without effect. In 1988 in Toronto, Austria committed itself to reducing its carbon dioxide emissions to 20 percent below the level of that year within 17 years (by 2005); an energy tax would be an important instrument to achieve this goal. Subsequently many Austrian cities and several *Länder* joined the Climate Alliance, a coalition mostly of European cities and indigenous people of the rain forests, to support this commitment by action at the local and regional levels. But the associations of business, industry and labor, the SPÖ and parts of the ÖVP still opposed a tax. At best, they were prepared to introduce it simultaneously with other countries, replicating in this the stance of the European Community which postponed an energy/carbon dioxide tax as long as the United States and Japan did not take similar steps. Things seemed to change after the 1994 elections. Suddenly, all the parties favored an ecological tax reform, by which they meant a taxation of energy to increase regularly over the years, to be compensated by tax reductions in other areas, especially on labor. Also, there was a consensus this time that Austria could take such a step on its own. In fact, some Scandinavian countries have already introduced limited forms of energy taxation.[12] By mid-1995, however, the government seemed to have abandoned this idea; once more, budget consolidation displaced ecology from the government's agenda, even though this time there was no obvious conflict between the two goals (an ecological tax reform is expected to actually promote economic growth and employment).

As mentioned before, nuclear power is outlawed on Austrian territory. Since the late 1980s, the government developed a policy of active opposition to nuclear power in neighboring countries. At first this was directed against a nuclear reprocessing plant in Germany. In recent years, efforts concentrated on closing down old nuclear power reactors in such countries as the Czech Republic, Slovakia and Slovenia, or on preventing the construction of new ones. At the same time the Austrian government has offered help with alternative technologies or programs of energy efficiency.

Summary

The main feature of governmental policy in the environmental area is--or at least was--its reactive nature; impulses came from a new set of actors who had no obvious place in the Austrian political landscape. Their activism came rather suddenly, and the overwhelming successes of Zwentendorf and Hainburg represented a veritable shock to the established parties and interest associations, who at the time viewed the activists as outcasts trying to subvert the social and political order; some would have liked to exclude them from the political arena altogether.

In the second half of the 1980s, however, the two large parties came to accept the fact that the environmental issue held many votes, and proceeded accordingly. They loosened their ties to corporatist interest associations, who largely persisted in their antagonism to this new social movement. They began to compete for the environmentalist vote in positive terms, by domestic programs or activities abroad (against transit traffic or nuclear power). After a pause in the early 1990s, they seemed to awaken to new activity. In the meantime, organized labor had become more supportive of the environmental cause, and business partially sympathetic or at least less antagonistic. Recent reform proposals stressed market-based instruments such as the ecological tax reform discussed in 1995.

Today the situation of the environmental movement is not very clear. It is doubtful whether mass mobilizations as in the cases of Zwentendorf or Hainburg could still be achieved. But then those were highly spontaneous events, which are always hard to predict. The movement is much more organized by now. Traditional conservation groups have become somewhat politicized; in addition, activist groups such as Greenpeace, WWF or Global 2000 established themselves with a large circle of supporters, a campaign-oriented executive and a growing staff of experts. Further expertise comes from bodies such as the Austrian Ecology Institute (similar to its famous namesake in Freiburg in Germany, though more modest in dimension) and similar institutions. And, of course, there are the new political parties dedicated to the environmental cause (the Greens, whose future looks quite bright, and the Liberal Forum)[13] and the green wings in the other parties. Even if the inner circle of political decision-making still seems to be closed to the environmental movement, many governmental agencies are now entrusted with realizing goals that were once promoted only by environmental activists. It is true that some of these agencies lack enthusiasm in realizing their tasks; recent reports show that, as in earlier days, the authorities responsible for enforcing environmental standards in industry still usually side with industrialists, and there is no legal base for citizen suits to prod them into action. On the other hand, managers have become less reluctant, sometimes even quite active in looking for environmentally sound solutions. It is important for them that the state impose uniform standards in the name of competitiveness. Also, pollution control equipment and "sustainable" technology are becoming important articles for exports. As a result, there is definitely a different business culture regarding environmental questions in Austria today, compared to what it was only ten years ago.

During the discussions preceding the referendum on membership in the European Union, the Austrian Greens opposed joining on the ground that this would undercut existing Austrian standards and render impossible the realization of still more ambitious goals that were well within Austria's reach. It seems to be a fact that in the European context, Austrian environmental policy is quite impressive,[14] whereas the EU is lagging in many respects. For that very reason, many European green parties and environmental groups welcomed Austria as an ally in the battle for promoting higher standards in the EU. It is unlikely that Austria, had it decided to stay outside, would have become an enviromentalist's paradise; however, its role in shaping European regulations is also likely to be modest given the weight of the country. Still, it is widely expected that--along with Sweden and Finland--it will help initiate new advances in environmental policy. Whether this will be sufficient to meet today's major challenges (greenhouse effect, ozone layer) is, of course, an open question.

Notes and References

1. Christian Schaller, *Die österreichische Kernenergiekontroverse.* (Unpublished doctoral dissertation, University of Salzburg, 1987).
2. Franz Kok, *Politik der Elektrizitätswirtschaft in Österreich* (Baden-Baden: Nomos, 1991).
3. Volkmar Lauber, "Umweltpolitik," in Herbert Dachs et al., eds., *Handbuch des politischen Systems Österreichs* (Vienna: Manz, 1991). Pp. 558-567.
4. Armin Stolz, "Umwelt-, Natur- und Landschaftsschutz-Anwälte," in Maria Zenkl, ed., *Bürger initiativ* (Vienna: Böhlau, 1990). Pp. 148-183.
5. Erich Schäfer, *Umweltanwaltschaft und Umweltkontrolle* (Vienna: Umweltbundesamt-reports, 1993), pp. 9, 54-59 and 70.
6. Volkmar Lauber, "Umweltpolitik," op.cit.
7. Max Krott, and Franz Traxler, *Verbandsorganisation im Umweltschutz* (Vienna: research paper for the Bundesministerium für Umwelt, Jugend und Familie, 1993).
8. Volkmar Lauber, "The Political Infrastructure of Environmental Politics in Western and Eastern Europe," in Otmar Höll, ed., *Environmental Cooperation in Europe* (Boulder: Westview, 1994). Pp. 247-270.
9. Umweltbundesamt, *UBA-Info March 1995*, pp. 8-11.
10. *Salzburger Nachrichten*, June 2, 1995.
11. Bundesministerium für wirtschaftliche Angelegenheiten, *Energiebericht 1993* (Vienna, 1993), pp. 5-11 and 41.
12. OECD, *Climate Change. Designing a Practical Tax System* (Paris, 1992), pp. 25-54.
13. Volkmar Lauber, "The Austrian Greens," *Environmental Politics*, vol. 4, no. 2 (1995), pp. 313-319.
14. OECD, *Environmental Performance Review: Austria* (Paris 1995), p. 166.

8

Political Culture

Peter Gerlich

Patterns of Political Culture

Austrians, like nationals of other countries, are convinced that they are special. Among other beliefs there exists a widespread conviction that specific forms of political behavior characterize the political culture of the country. These patterns are not necessarily seen as positive but are still considered part of the nation's historical heritage. The patterns of behavior are consequences of specific historical experiences. The assumption both among general observers as well as political scientists is that aside from general patterns of behavior, there also exist specific patterns at different levels of society or more precisely in specific subsystems of the political system.

The German sociologist Niklas Luhmann proposed a threefold differentiation of the political system (Luhmann 1981, 42f). Accordingly the political system of the welfare state may be conceptualized as consisting of exchange processes between three subsystems. The subsystem of the politicians is confronted on one side by the general public of politically involved citizens, and on the other by the big and differentiated bureaucracy of the state. To treat the bureaucracy as a specific subsystem is something that comes easily to a German like Luhmann, and it can with even greater justification be applied to Austria, where the bureaucracy constitutes the oldest, most continuous and most influential element of politics. Here, the attempt will be made to describe which behavior patterns are typical for the three subsystems themselves, i.e. for their internal activity, as well as to describe which patterns of behavior characterize the mutual interactions between the three subsystems.

Figure 8.1 shows both internal as well as interactive behavioral patterns that may be assumed to be typical for Austria's political culture according to a number of descriptive analyses of the country's political system. Of course, this does not exlude the possibility that deviant behavior may also occur.

FIGURE 8.1 Cultural Patterns of the Political Subsystems

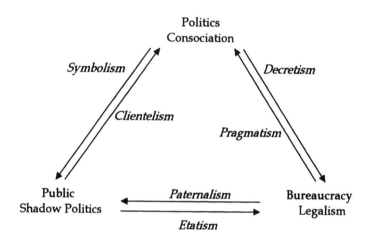

The dominant internal pattern of the subsystem of politics is that of consociation or, according to the term usually applied in German, of concordance (Lehmbruch 1967). This pattern has been frequently described as the typical behavioral pattern of Austrian political elites; in practical politics it is extolled again and again, or postulated as a norm for actual political action. Consociation does find its expression both in the cooperation of the big parties within the political regime of grand coalition government, in the tendency towards accommodation and unanimity in governmental advisory and representative bodies on different governmental levels (particularly also on the level of *Länder* and municipalities), and finally also within the framework of the many bodies of the so-called social partnership. Consociation implies that decisions can only be made after the essential political groupings have had the opportunity to express their point of view extensively in protracted negotiations. Therefore such decisions may as a rule be characterized as compromises. One precondition and quietly accepted assumption within Austrian political circles consists in the fact that nobody proposes serious initiatives without contacting all essential partners within the other parties or interest groups beforehand. This in turn makes it necessary for each of the partners to be open and receptive at any time for such discussions. Moreover, in order to be effective, consociation requires the loyalty of the subordinated organizations and individuals concerned. Their representatives negotiate amongst one another knowing beforehand that the results of their negotiations will be accepted by their organization. Consociation also implies avoiding open discussion and conflict. An often repeated saying states that in Austria one knows the compromise before even knowing the exact nature of the conflict.

In order to maintain the loyalty of party members and supporters, in spite of the close cooperation of their respective representatives in the system of politics, symbolism or symbolic politics have become quite important (Edelman 1964). The tendency to treat politics as showbusiness is certainly not limited to Austria but corresponds to a general development in a period in which the electronic media have become the most important way in which politics can be transmitted. However, it may not be by chance that the classical description of the phenomenon of symbolic politics originated with an American political scientist who had earlier devoted himself to empirically analyzing certain aspects of the Austrian system of consociation. Symbolic politics implies that the public should by means of rhetorical techniques such as appeals, promises, and emotional assurances be convinced that its respective interests are effectively represented (see Fabris 1989). Austrian politicians compromise backstage within the framework of consociation while at the same time on front stage they represent themselves as engaged in thunderous conflict. Towards the inside Austrian functionaries often practice harmony, while at the same time signalling differences of opinion and conflict towards the outside (Pelinka 1985).

With respect to the bureaucracy the political system in Austria often takes the attitude of decretism. This implies first of all the conviction that political problems may be considered solved when a--usually statutory--legislative order has been given to the administrative bureaucracy (Gerlich 1986). This view ignores the fact that many such apparent solutions meet with difficulties--or even failure--during implementation. A side aspect of decretism is the attitude of centralism, the notion that basically only the central state authority is able to solve social problems and therefore should also decide all connected political questions. The concept of true autonomy of lower governmental levels or social groupings cannot be considered realistic from such a viewpoint. The attitude of decretism has contributed to the fact that the public life in Austria is increasingly inundated by a "wave of legislation." The huge number of legal statutes, their almost unavoidable contradictoriness as well as the legal language, which is difficult to understand and which is the form of articulation of decretism, have reversed the concepts of rule of law in many areas of bureaucratic behavior.

The dominant internal attitude within the bureaucracy may be considered as that of legalism. Austrian bureaucracy is determined by legal forms of thinking and acting. Administrative behavior is traditionally programmed, guided and determined within legal forms. Law graduates have always dominated the government apparatus and almost all top positions have been reserved for them (Pelinka/Welan 1971). The deductive thinking of lawyers corresponds to the hierarchical and mutually segregated structures of bureaucracy and also to the tendency of administrative procedures to be oriented towards written documentation and record keeping. The subsystem of politics with its continuous (over)production of legislation satisfies the demand of the subsystem bureaucracy, for which it is a necessary medium.

For this reason it is interesting to note that concerning the behavior of the bureaucracy towards politics quite contrary patterns of behavior are typical. They could be described by the term pragmatism (Stiefbold 1975). When bureaucrats do not act as receivers of legal norms but as representatives of substantial demands vis-a-vis the subsystem of politics, the style of their behavior changes. Bureaucrats use different, essentially more political, but in any case non-legal forms of behavior to initiate, block or influence the production of political decisions. In this context it may be noted that the instrument of an administrative order, which should actually be the means of last resort ued by a hierarchical superior to force subordinated civil servants to act in certain way, usually serves the opposite purpose in administrative practice. Recalcitrant subordinates ask their superiors for a formal legal order when they do not want to behave in the way demanded, or will do so only under protest (Neisser 1974). Another pattern of behavior by which bureaucracy influences politics is that of "therapeutic nihilism" (Johnston 1962). Experienced Austrian officials are often convinced that political problems and conflicts may solve themselves automatically if one avoids conscious intervention. This orientation corresponds to the pattern of blocking disliked initiatives and is quite characteristic of bureaucratic hierarchies. As a rule the Austrian bureaucracy is more effective in hindering than in producing initiatives.

With respect to the public the bureaucracy traditionally exhibits the attitude of paternalism. Bureaucratic officials benevolently intervene into social or economic life to prevent negative developments, to promote positive tendencies, and to regulate conflicts. The figure of the district commissioner (*Bezirkshauptmann*) as a representative of central governmental authority on the lowest level of administration may in this context be seen as a typical institution. Characteristically, the plan of the federal constitution of 1920 to democratize the district administration, that is to cut down the paternal authority of its chief, has not so far been seriously discussed. Not only the general governmental administration, but also other areas of the Austrian bureaucracy are determined by this basic attitude. One might also enumerate the areas of school administration, the police, or the administration of welfare policies.

It is more difficult to describe the dominant form of internal patterns of behavior within the third subsystem, that of the general public. Possibly, one could in analogy to the term for the unofficial shadow economy use the term of shadow politics (Gerlich 1989). Shadow politics may be understood as a reaction to the dominant forms of influence of the two other political subsystems. Within the public a tendency can be observed to discuss, criticize, or even act against the various authorities in a half suppressed but nevertheless often consensual way. This does not usually take the form of open resistance or confrontation, but rather of latent dissent (Hanisch 1984). Shadow politics therefore includes both the traditional grouching about authorities (*"Raunzen"*) as well as the personal involvement in activities which are not primarily political. These patterns of behavior have become more and more obvious in recent periods. Thus surveys increasingly show a rising interest in political questions and at the same time growing detachment from the established institutions and groupings (Ulram 1990). This tendency is also increasingly obvious in electoral behavior (Haerpfer 1991).

As regards the relationship between the public and politics, the relevant behavioral pattern is that of clientelism. In this respect Austrians very often define themselves as members of big parties and interest groups or, even more often, are defined as such as a result of the obligatory membership within the chambers. Within the organizations an exchange between loyalty and the allocation of benefits is practiced (Müller 1988). In forms that are rather characteristic for pre-industrial societies, a system of dependencies and patronage is maintained, which constitutes the necessary counterpart to the effectiveness of consociational relationships between the elites of the different groupings (Fürstenberg 1985). Patronage in form of the so-called *"Proporz"* (distribution of spheres of influence in public life) also invades the two other subsystems and leads to self-blockade and inefficiency within some areas of the bureaucracy. A side aspect of clientelism is the so-called camp-mentality (*"Lagermentalität"*) between the clientele of the different parties and interest groups. It consists in an emotional rejection of members of "other" groups. This in turn serves to maintain social boundaries and promotes loyalty towards the leadership of the "own" group (Powell 1970).

The attitude of the public with respect to the state bureaucracy may be described as one of etatism (Ulram 1990). Different from the political culture of systems with stronger democratic traditions, the state in Austria in spite of some criticism is nearly always seen as a benevolent institution. Wherever social problems exist or arise, the demand for state action is rather quickly articulated. This pattern of expectations justifies and eases the attitudes of paternalism and decretism. Even groups that are in principle averse to authority, like the green movement, ultimately appeal to state authority in order to achieve solutions for problem areas, for example, within the field of environmental protection.

Origins of Political Culture

Patterns of attitudes and behavior within political culture are individually learned in processes of political socialization. In a larger context, they may be considered a consequences of a common historical experience. Three complexes of such experiences could have had particularly strong effects in Austria: The tradition of revolution from above, the problems and conflicts within the late Habsburg Monarchy and the traumatic insecurities created during the first decades after its dissolution (Hanisch 1984).

Unlike many other European countries Austria has never experienced a successful revolution. Popular movements for reforms have always been defeated ultimately by the traditional holders of power, who then often introduced reforms themselves. These "revolutions from above" were usually successful. In this context one should remember on the one hand the failure of the Reformation in the 16th and 17th centuries and of the revolution of 1848, and on the other, Josephinism (a period of enlightened reforms from above under Emperor Josef II, 1780-1790) and the founding period of neoabsolutism (1849-1860). Everything that stresses the weight and importance of government and bureaucracy within the political culture of Austria may be traced to this origin. Doubtlessly, behavioral patterns such as decretism, legalism, paternalism and etatism gained their relevance for behavior against the background of such historical experiences. The last decades of the Monarchy were determined by two circumstances: on the one hand by the conflicts between the different nationalities striving for independence, on the other hand by the, in comparison with Western states, relative economic underdevelopment. The difficulties of the national conflicts, which could not be overcome by traditional forms of politics, taught the political elites the styles of consociation and pragmatism. Economic backwardness reinforced already existing tendencies towards paternalism and etatism, since the government tried by massive state intervention to compensate for the barely existent culture of entrepreneurship and thus to initiate industrial development.

The increasing social and political conflicts of the decades after 1918, the repeated changes of regimes and the collective experiences of suffering and persecution led to strong socio- psychological insecurities and violations of the Austrian sense of self-understanding and identity. The experience of authoritarian and fascist regimes reinforced already existing tendencies of paternalism and etatism. During the reconstruction of Austria after the Second World War the remaining insecurities where eased by the adoption of political forms like consociation, clientelism, symbolism and shadow politics, which might in part also be understood as constituting forms of social therapy. During this period Austria concentrated very much upon itself and tried by a collective effort to heal the wounds that had been inflicted by the conflicts of the thirties and forties.

As this short look backwards makes clear, the political culture of the present may be seen as the result of different periods of preceding historical developments. Different traditions reinforce each other; others may, however, also contribute to a general recovery from the problematic heritage of collective historical experiences.

Implications of Political Culture

The patterns of political culture are not only curious reminiscences of a collective past, they are also directly and indirectly relevant for present day political behavior. Therefore they also are of eminent political relevance. On the one hand it may be correct to assume that actors as a rule act in order to maximize their interests. But just how these interests are defined or whether the violation of cultural norms leads to sanctions is partly determined by political culture. Politicians, for example, are confronted with certain accepted forms of behavior. It is difficult for them to break with such patterns because this would endanger their political success. For instance, decisions in Austria have to be sought in a consociational way. The public following the logic of the mass media has to be addressed in symbolic forms of politics. Decretism is the dominant mode of interaction with the bureaucracy. The role of cultural patterns is also very important with respect to the definition of problems or the determination of the political agenda. For example legalism, the tendency to transform all political questions into legal ones, dominates many areas of the definition of policies. In this way certain orientations and options are created but also new political problems appear, which are only due to the peculiarities of the legal mode. Nevertheless these forms of politics can be hardly avoided. One is reminded of the sigh of resignation of a *Land* politician, who when drafting a concept of land use planning for his province, would have liked at first to exclude his legal experts from the discussion and let them in only after the plan had been agreed upon in order to translate it into detailed legal language. The presence of the bureaucrat lawyers was bound to make an agreement more difficult.

Political culture ultimately determines what is allowed to be considered a political issue. One of the great disadvantages of the culture of consociation consists in the fact that because politicians must be considerate of one another, certain real problems, even when they are recognized, must not be brought up if this could upset the partner and therefore disturb the cooperation. Political culture may become, to use Niklas Luhmann's (1981) term, the self referential impediment of self reflective system learning and may thus prevent necessary innovations. That this is a real danger in Austria is not stressed often enough. At any rate the behavioral relevance of political culture does cause it to be a power factor that should not be underestimated. Ruling groups and structures profit from the maintenance and reinforcement of cultural patterns of behavior. Therefore, it is important to notice that political culture does not just happen in processes of political socialization but often serves to support manipulative politics. Political attitudes are not so much created by direct political experience but rather indirectly by role models within the family or at school, by the effects of the "underground curriculum" more often than by explicit civic education. This has the effect that the school as a bureaucratic institution determines attitudes and teaches behavioral patterns which perpetuate existing cultural norms (Steiner 1972). Not in the least because of these circumstances educational policy is of great political relevance in Austria. In only very few democratic states are details of the curriculum determined by central governmental decisions as much as in Austria. But, also, other institutions like the Church, the professions, cultural institutions, the health system, or even the world of sports assist in the maintenance and reinforcement of traditional behavioral patterns. These circumstances make it clear that a democracy with strong pre-democratic elements in its political culture really ought to practice something like a policy of political culture or, at least, should introduce democratic control in the areas these pre-democratic attitudes are reproduced.

Finally, it has to be pointed out that the political culture of Austria especially in recent times has been undergoing a process of change. The ambivalence of political behavioral patterns always allows for spontaneous reversals. For example, in the thirties in spite of the traditions of consociation, a civil war could not be avoided and the cooperation between political parties broke down completely. But that kind of change is not what is meant here. Under the pressure of social and international changes, as for example the increase of the average level of education or the system changes in Eastern Europe, the political culture changes gradually. However, one should not underestimate continuities within traditional institutions. In this context it may not be an accident that today's legal regulations for the state (i.e., secret) police date back to the period of the early nineteenth century (Pilz 1989). Still, many things change either by conscious reform (some changes are only proposed programmatically, others are also put into effect) or by simple changes in practice. Concretely, the following observations seem in order: The attitude of consociation has come increasingly under pressure, and the need to bring conflicts out into the open is being emphasized more and more. Symbolism and decretism are challenged by the demand for greater political openness and deregulation. Clientelism and shadow politics have been pushed into the background (and exposed to public view) by increasingly self-assured citizens and by new parties. Within the bureaucracy, planning and management considerations crowd out pragmatism and legalism. The relationship between the public and the bureaucracy is expected to come to resemble that prevailing between customers and their service institutions. It remains to be seen to what degree these tendencies will succeed in effectively changing attitudes with a strong base in psychology as well as in political structures. At any rate processes of modernization are on the way even in Austria.

Often, however, one gains the impression that in this context an increasing rift between political elites and the general population is developing. The public appears to be able to learn faster than the politicians. Survey research, which tends to see the masses through the eyes of the elites, cannot always convey which changes are on the way. This may lead to the result that political change does not take place gradually, but could at times also be convulsive and spontaneous. One should never forget that a number of such examples of sudden, unforeseen and momentous changes may be found in Austria's political history in the twentieth century.

References

Edelman, Murray. 1964. *The Symbolic Uses of Politics.* Urbana.
Fabris, Hans-Heinz. 1989. "Zwischen Politik und Politikinszenierung: Mediendiskurse der achtziger Jahre." *Österreichische Zeitschrift für Politikwissenschaft* 18: 119-128.

Fürstenberg, Friedrich. 1985. "Sozialkulturelle Aspekte der Sozialpartnerschaft," in Peter Gerlich, Edgard Grande, and Wolfgang C. Müller, eds., *Sozialpartnerschaft in der Krise*. Pp. 29-39. Vienna.

Gerlich, Peter. 1986. "Theories of Legislation: Some Austrian Evidence and General Conclusions." *European Journal of Political Research* 14: 357-368.

___. 1989. "Die Zukunft der Politik." *Internationales Jahrbuch für Rechtsphilosophie und Gesetzgebung 1989*. 171-185.

Haerpfer, Christian. 1991. "Wahlverhalten," in Herbert Dachs et al., eds., *Handbuch des politischen Systems Österreichs*. Pp. 475-492. Vienna.

Hanisch, Ernst. 1984. "Historische Übergänge in der österreichischen politischen Kultur." *Österreichische Zeitschrift für Politikwissenschaft* 13: 15-19.

Johnston, William M. 1972. *The Austrian Mind. An Intellectual and Social History*. Berkeley.

Lehmbruch, Gerhard. 1967. *Proporzdemokratie: Politisches System und politische Kultur in der Schweiz und in Österreich*. Tübingen.

Luhmann, Niklas. 1981. *Politische Theorie im Wohlfahrtsstaat*. Munich.

Müller, Wolfgang C. 1988. "Patronage im österreichischen Parteiensystem. Theoretische Überlegungen und empirische Befunde," in Anton Pelinka, and Fritz Plasser, eds., *Das österreichische Parteiensystem*. Pp. 457-487. Vienna.

Neisser, Heinrich. 1974. "Die Rolle der Bürokratie," in Heinz Fischer, ed., *Das politische System Österreichs*. Pp. 233-270. Vienna.

Pelinka, Anton. 1985. *Windstille. Klagen über Österreich*. Vienna.

___, and Manfred Welan. 1971. *Demokratie und Verfassung in Österreich*. Vienna.

Pilz, Peter. 1989. *Land über Bord. Kein Roman*. Vienna.

Powell, G. Bingham Jr. 1970. *Social Fragmentation and Political Hostility: An Austrian Case Study*. Stanford.

Steiner, Kurt. 1972. *Politics in Austria*. Boston.

Stiefbold, Rodney P. 1975. "Elites and Elections in a Fragmented Political System." *Sozialwissenschaftliches Jahrbuch für Politik* 4: 119-227.

Ulram, Peter A. 1990. *Hegemonie und Erosion, Politische Kultur und politischer Wandel in Österreich*. Vienna.

9
Agencies of Socialization
Franz Horner

Among the most important agencies of socialization for partisan politics were, and probably still are, the political parties and the web of organizations making up the *Lager* (dealt with in chapter 3). The present chapter deals with three other agencies of socialization: the mass media,[1] the educational system, and the Catholic Church.

Mass media

The Austrian media system changed fundamentally in the early 1990s. Technological innovation, complicated financial intertwining and the onset of massive foreign involvement changed the conditions for competition.

Particularly characteristic of the Austrian media system is a newspaper market with the highest concentration in Europe. The three largest newspapers (*Neue Kronen-Zeitung, Kurier,* and *täglich alles*) altogether have 65 percent of the total daily circulation. By comparison, in the late 1980s the three largest dailies in Germany had only 38 percent and in Switzerland only 27 percent of total circulation, even though Austria, with 2.77 million copies printed daily, is largely comparable to Switzerland with 2.68 million copies.

This unusually high degree of concentration is largely due to the dominant market position of the right wing tabloid *Neue Kronen-Zeitung*, with 39 percent of total printed copies. In the late 1980s, the *Neue Kronen-Zeitung* with 1,075,000 copies daily was the largest newspaper in Europe and the seventh largest newspaper world-wide. *Kurier*, with 443,000 copies printed daily, was the eighteenth largest paper world-wide.[2] In Germany, the largest publisher of a daily

(Springer Verlag) printed only 28.5 percent of total copies, while in Switzerland the largest publisher (Ringier Verlag) printed only 14 percent.[3]

TABLE 9.1 Austrian Newspapers Distribution

Newspaper title	Percentage (incl. regional editions)
I. Independent Newspapers	
Neue Kronen Zeitung (popular tabloid)	40.7
täglich alles (tabloid)	14.6
Kurier (tabloid)	12.6
Kleine Zeitung (Graz und Klagenfurt)	11.2
Oberösterreichische Nachrichten (Linz)	4.7
Der Standard (Vienna)	4.9
Tiroler Tageszeitung (Innsbruck)	4.1
Salzburger Nachrichten (Salzburg)	3.8
Die Presse (Vienna)	3.5
Vorarlberger Nachrichten (Bregenz)	3.1
Neue Zeit (Graz)	1.7
Neue Vorarlberger Tageszeitung (Bregenz)	1.0
Wiener Zeitung (Vienna, state owned)	1.0
II. Party Newspapers	
SPÖ Daily	
Kärtner Tageszeitung (Klagenfurt)	1.2
ÖVP Dailies	
Neues Volksblatt (Linz)	1.0
Salzburger Volkszeitung (Salzburg)	n.d.a.

Figures relate to 1994

Source: Verband Österreichischer Zeitungsherausgeber und Zeitungsverleger, *Pressehandbuch 1995* (Vienna, 1995), p.13.

The problem of press concentration has been complicated in recent years by extensive foreign involvement. All the newspapers were Austrian owned until 1987. Since then, German media conglomerates have attained decisive influence over about 70 percent of total circulation.[4] In addition to massive dependence on foreign capital, the "internationalization" of the Austrian press has also brought about an increase in the vertical concentration within the newspaper sector. Since the German publishing group *Westdeutsche Allgemeine Zeitung* (WAZ) acquired a 45 percent interest in each of the two largest newspapers (*Kronen-Zeitung* and *Kurier*), they both have access to the largest print and distribution company in Austria, Mediaprint.

The high degree of dependency on foreign capital, complex financial intertwining and dense commercial and logistic connections between the two largest dailies in the recent past caused financial and journalistic power structures to converge. As a result, competition within the Austrian press market has been distorted.

Corresponding to the dominant position of the largest dailies on the national level, regional newspapers in some provinces (*Länder*) have virtual monopolies of their markets, as in Tyrol and Upper Austria. However, these regional monopolies are being increasingly challenged by the two dominant national newspapers.

Until the late 1980s, newspapers affiliated to political parties were a significant factor in the Austrian media system. Forty years ago, party newspapers even accounted for more than 50 percent of the daily circulation in Austria. Most of these papers became serious financial liabilities for their respective parties and as a result were allowed to die out. When in 1990 the *Arbeiter-Zeitung* (Workers' Newspaper), a respected paper with a long history and published by the Socialist Party, was sold to a commercial publishing group, it had become clear that the party press had indeed lost its significance.

The consequences of the failing party papers for the political parties themselves were dramatic. Communication with their members and voters could now take place only indirectly through the commercial press or through television or radio. Inner-party communication dried up. Only occasional party pamphlets or issue papers appear, but they are rarely seen by more than party officials and activists.[5]

Another characteristic of the Austrian media system is the broadcasting monopoly of the state-owned ORF (Austrian Radio and Television Service). For about two decades after the Second World War, broadcasting was closely controlled by the two big political parties. In 1966 this gave rise to a strong protest movement which led to a reform introducing greater independence in reporting and program design. But even after this reform, the new statute of the ORF could not prevent the concentration of influence in the hands of the political parties and their related interest groups because the political parties have the right to choose the top management of the ORF through their representatives in the governing body, known as the *Kuratorium*. This, in turn, enables the influence of the parties to be felt in the leadership structure and other more sensitive positions within the ORF. Genuine autonomy is thereby restricted. While strategy in the daily newspaper market is influenced primarily by economic interests, the decisions at the ORF are shaped by the political situation.

During the 1990s, public discussion to abolish the monopoly in broadcasting reached its peak. In early 1993, the monopoly of the ORF was held to violate the European Human Rights Convention; as a result, the government announced that a reform would soon be submitted. Radio broadcasting was liberalized in July 1993 (but the corresponding law has been held unconstitutional since by the Constitutional Court); television has not been reformed yet. Of course, there are alternatives to the ORF, especially through satellite and cable TV (mostly from abroad), so that several dozen programs are actually available.

The Educational System

The Politics of Education

The Austrian Constitution of 1920 did not decide the question of jurisdiction, as far as education is concerned, between the Federal Government and the provinces (*Länder*). Ideological cleavages between the political parties prevented a definitive agreement during the First Republic and, indeed, at the beginning of the Second Austrian Republic as well. The most prominent issue in the area of education policy involved State-Church relations.[6] The major parties of the First Republic reflected, above all, a clerical-anticlerical cleavage. The Catholic Church's demands to have an influence on educational policy was supported by the Christian Social Party, whereas liberal demands for a separation of Church and State and, more specifically, of Church and schools were advocated by the Social Democrats, as well as by the German Nationalists.

By contrast, the Second Republic is marked by the rapprochement between the Catholic Church and the Socialist Party (SPÖ). The extensive school reform of 1962--which is closely connected to the treaty (*Konkordat*) between Austria and the Vatican of the same year--resulted in a guarantee of state subsidies to Catholic schools. Since 1971, the subsidy has amounted to 100 percent of their personnel costs. Today the Catholic Church also plays a significant role in preschool education and in the training of elementary school teachers (the Catholic Church maintains such academies in most of the Austrian dioceses, where they function side by side with the existing state schools).

The school reform of 1962 was the result of long and difficult negotiations within the Grand Coalition and led to a series of laws, in particular to the Constitutional Amendment of July 1962 which assigned education, in principle, to federal legislation passed with a two-thirds majority of the National Assembly (*Nationalrat*). The provincial parliaments (*Landtage*) legislate only on preschool education. The constitutional amendments of 1962 provide for education councils in the *Länder* (*Landesschulräte*) and their districts (*Bezirksschulräte*). These councils are--and this is typical of Austria--constituted in proportion to the strength of the political parties in their respective region, and they select school directors by the same criteria. In the 1990s, the role of these councils--which were originally designed to counter political polarization by promoting consensus among the different groups represented in them--was increasingly questioned, and their proposals sometimes ignored. This development reflects the general decline of party patronage but also the decline of ideological conflict in Austrian society, leading to personnel decisions based on a more open process.

The School System

As mentioned above, education is principally a matter of federal legislation. Thus the educational structures are somewhat uniform for the entire country, a tendency reinforced by the existence of the Federal Ministry of Education, which administers the whole system. Most of the elementary and secondary schools are run by federal or local agencies. Most private schools, accredited under the 1962 Law on Private Schools, are run by the Catholic Church in the areas of preschool education and the training of elementary school teachers.

The Austrian educational system used to be a strict "two-track system,"[7] as in other German speaking countries like Switzerland and Germany. This means that after four years of compulsory elementary or primary school (*Volksschule* or *Grundschule*), attended by all children from six to ten years of age, a decisive separation occurred. A large majority of the children (about 80 percent in 1960) went on to the normal secondary schools (*Hauptschulen*), while a minority attended the upper-track secondary schools (*Gymnasium*), which provided a liberal education and prepared them for higher, especially university, education. The decision regarding the educational track to be pursued had to be made already at the age of ten, with all the far-reaching consequences for the child's future social and economic status.

The school reform of 1962 led to substantial changes of the school system, which modified the "two-track system" somewhat, making the separation between the two tracks less absolute.

One type of secondary school, the *Hauptschule*, consists of four grades. For those students who do not intend to go to school beyond their compulsory education, one prevocational year has been instituted as a ninth year of schooling to prepare the student for work in business or industry. Apprenticeship is complemented by mandatory vocational schooling in the branch of business or industry chosen by the apprentice.

FIGURE 9.1 The Austrian Educational System

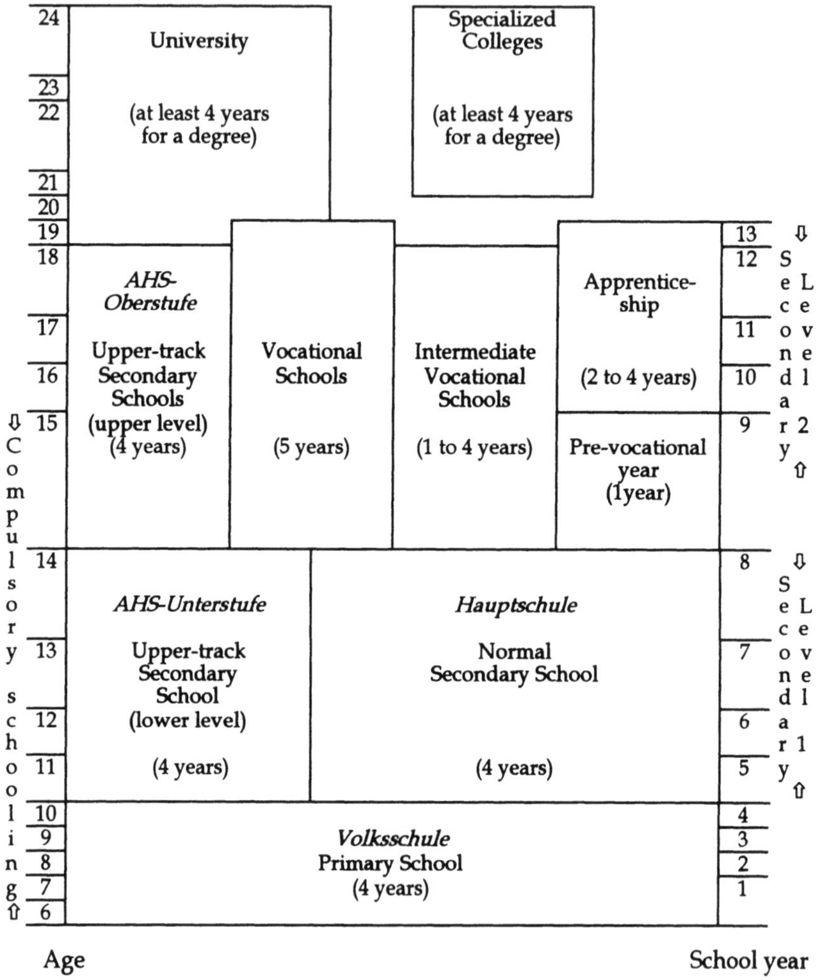

Age					School year
24	University		Specialized Colleges		
23					
22	(at least 4 years for a degree)		(at least 4 years for a degree)		
21					
20					
19					13
18	AHS-Oberstufe			Apprenticeship	12
17	Upper-track Secondary Schools (upper level) (4 years)	Vocational Schools (5 years)	Intermediate Vocational Schools (1 to 4 years)	(2 to 4 years)	11
16					10
15					9
				Pre-vocational year (1year)	
14	AHS-Unterstufe Upper-track Secondary School (lower level) (4 years)		Hauptschule Normal Secondary School (4 years)		8
13					7
12					6
11					5
10	Volksschule Primary School (4 years)				4
9					3
8					2
7					1
6					

Left margin: ⇓ Compulsory schooling ⇑

Right side labels: Second Level cycle 2 ⇑ / Second Level cycle 1 ⇑

Source: Norbert Kutalek, "Egalitäres oder elitäres Bildungssystem?," in Peter Bachmaier, (ed.), *Bildungspolitik in Osteuropa* (Vienna 1991), pp. 222-223.

The other type of secondary school, the *Allgemeinbildende Höhere Schule* (AHS), constitutes the "upper track."[8] In the past it was necessary to pass an admission test in order to enter the "upper track," but this test was abolished in 1971. Students may leave school after completing the four lower grades. Most students, however, continue for another four years in the upper level (*Oberstufe*) and then take a comprehensive written and oral examination (*Reifeprüfung* or *Matura*) which qualifies them for admission to a university or other institution of higher learning (*Hochschule*).

Besides these two types of schools, there are those that provide vocational training for occupations in trade, industry, agriculture, social work, the tourist industry, forestry, nursing and various crafts. Normally students enter such schools right after completing their compulsory schooling, but it is becoming more common to enter senior schools after a period of practical work. Attendance at those schools usually can substitute a certain period of apprenticeship. Only the senior vocational schools (normally five grades) can qualify students for entering a university.

Even though the reforms of 1962 facilitated the transfer from one school type to another, transfers remained difficult as long as the curricula of the tracks were quite different. Even so, the reforms of 1962 constitute a veritable landmark in the history of Austrian education and politics. Since then, the need for a better qualified workforce together with pressure for upward mobility led to an expansion of student numbers, especially at the secondary school level. Also, the number of female students attending upper-track schools increased significantly. Finally, regional disparities that had been typical in the past were partly corrected.

Higher Education

In 1990, about 20 percent of Austrian twenty year olds attended a university or school of art or music at university level, as compared to 6 percent in 1960. The universities are placed under federal jurisdiction (since 1971 under the newly created Ministry of Science and Research). They are much older than the state-run compulsory school system. The University of Vienna, founded in 1365, is the oldest university in German-speaking Europe. The University of Graz was established in 1585 and the one in Innsbruck in 1669. The University of Salzburg, originally founded in 1619, was reactivated in 1962. Technical universities were established in Graz (founded in 1811) and Vienna (founded 1815). The Economics University in Vienna originally dates back to 1873; a higher school for agriculture (*Hochschule für Bodenkultur*) was set up in 1872. In Leoben (Styria), there is a university specializing in mining that was founded in 1840. Two universities are completely new. (Linz, created in 1962; Klagenfurt, in 1970). In addition to these institutions, all of which are called "university," there exist, at a similar level, Schools of Art and Music (*Kunsthochschulen*), most of them founded in the 19th century.

All these institutions are, in effect, graduate schools preparing students for the rough equivalent of a master's degree. While such diplomas qualify the recipient for employment in various practical fields, a doctorate is the prerequisite for an academic career in science and research. There are no Austrian equivalents to the undergraduate curricula of American colleges; this is partly remedied by what is taught in the upper level of the "upper track" secondary schools, especially the AHS (*Allgemeinbildende Höhere Schule*). In comparative terms, the percentage of Austrians with a university education is still low. In recent decades there has been considerable discussion about reforming higher education to meet contemporary requirements. But political problems (especially the organization of the universities on the principle of equal representation of professors, assistants and students) make this process rather slow and intricate. Charging fees for university attendance was long considered too sensitive an issue to pursue, but it may be coming soon.

In addition to the university system, a 1994 law createdp specialized colleges (*Fachhochschulen*). They are meant to fill a gap in the educational system, as universities are not viewed as suffiently responsive to industrial and business needs. They provide vocational training at the level of higher education. As they are primarily intended for persons already working in a trade, the *Matura* is not a prerequisite for attendance. For at least four years, theory is combined with practice on a very high level. Students can obtain a special master's degree. Attendance at these colleges is free of charge for the time being.[9] The colleges are not necessarily operated by the state; municipalities or private organizations can do that as well.

The Catholic Church

Churches and religious communities are important agents of socialization for the political culture of a country. [10] In Austria about 80 percent of the population are at least nominally Catholic, 5 percent are Protestant, 1.5 percent are Muslims, 1 percent belong to the Orthodox Church, 0.3 percent are Jews. The rest belong to other denominations or are without any religious affiliation. As the largest religious group, the Catholic Church and its organizations play a significant role in the political process in Austria.[11]

Politics and the Catholic Church

The First World War led to a deep crisis of identity and legitimacy in Austrian society. The Republic had no integrating "civil theology" comparable to that of the Hapsburg mythology during the monarchy, when church and state ruled together. The formulation in the constitution of 1929, "Austria is a democratic republic, its law emanates from the people," pleased social democrats, but seriously alienated Catholics. In fact, most Catholic leaders found such a statement blasphemous.[12] In the ensuing struggle over political legitimacy the Church threw its political weight behind the Christian Social *Lager*. The conflict with the Social Democrats was sharpened by the Great Depression and came to a head in the civil war of 1934. The Catholic Church was to a large extent, whether consciously or not, responsible for initiating the political polarization during the First Republic. However, the experience of the civil war, and the problems which the Catholic Church encountered thereafter in its pastoral function among the working class, contributed to its depoliticization after World War II.

The biggest step in this direction was taken in 1952 with the Mariazell Manifesto, which proclaimed that the Church would henceforth stay out of party politics altogether. This step also led to a relaxation of tensions with the SPÖ. Unresolved constitutional problems between the Church and the state could finally be settled. In 1961 the Catholic Church also finally relinquished its opposition to the long overdue Protestant Law, which gave Protestant churches the status (already held by the Catholic Church) of organizations recognized by public law.

The Austrian people themselves clearly desire an unpolitical church. In 1990, 89 percent of those questioned believed the Church should be neutral towards the political parties, while 7 percent wanted the Church to support the ÖVP and 1 percent the SPÖ.[13] However, not even half the population believed that the Church avoids taking sides in controversies between the parties; 36 percent believed the Church favors the ÖVP on important issues. Even so, most Austrians believed the Church has little influence on social developments. In fact, its influence, though not insignificant, is more likely to be indirect and not necessarily effective on such issues as abortion or family and school policy.

Today, Church and state in Austria are not completely separated as in the United States; there is a system of cooperation. Churches and religions can be officially recognized under certain conditions (there are now fifteen such recognized religious communities) and are autonomous in their internal matters within the confines of Austrian law. Cooperation exists in the fields of religious instruction in public schools, subsidies for denominational private schools and theological departments at the public universities. Furthermore, the officially recognized religious communities must be taken into consideration in the programming of radio and television, but only the Catholic Church has a seat and voting rights in the supervisory body of the ORF. The Catholic Church itself controls a sizeable press system and has a wide network of high school and university student associations under its control which enable it to exert a considerable amount of influence.

In 1995, liberal catholics staged a petition campaign for renewal and democratization within the Catholic Church. Among the main demands were the access of women to the priesthood; the abolition of the celibacy requirement for priests; non-discrimination for those who remarry after divorce; a more positive view of sexuality and liberalization of birth control. The petition was signed by more than 500,000 Austrians; its effect on the Catholic hierarchy remains to be seen.[14]

Religiosity and Political Attitudes Today

Secondary analyses have revealed that there exists a deeper relationship between religion and political orientation than people themselves realize. It appears that political and religious orientations both stem from common underlying basic attitudes and beliefs. The key role of religion is that it helps many people in overcoming life's crisis. Religion is connected to consolation and hope. This may be called the "religion of the people,"[15] as opposed to religion in the sense intended by the churches themselves; it is a factor in the survival of the citizen in modern society and functions as some kind of holy shield or "sacred canopy"[16] that keeps out harm.

ÖVP supporters are considerably more religious and attend religious services much more frequently than supporters of other parties. In contrast, supporters of the FPÖ are the least religious, with the SPÖ and the Greens lying in between.

Statistical analysis shows, furthermore, that people who regularly participate in traditional church activities have a stronger need for stability, for a place to belong, and for security. They also have a markedly positive view of authoritarianism. This is particularly true of older and less educated Austrians. People thus inclined tend to vote for the ÖVP.

Notes and References

This chapter was updated and supplemented by Barbara Blümel.
1. Much of this section on the media is borrowed from Fritz Plasser, "Massenmedien," in Herbert Dachs et al., eds., *Handbuch des politischen Systems Österreichs* (Vienna, 1991). Pp. 419-432.

2. Peter Muzik, *Die Medienmultis* (Vienna, 1989), p. 238.
3. Gerhard Popp, "Zukunftsorientierte Alternativen in der österreichischen Medienpolitik," in Andreas Khol et al., eds., *Österreichisches Jahrbuch für Politik 1989* (Vienna 1990). Pp. 475-494.
4. Hans-Heinz Fabris, "Medienkolonie - na und?," in Margit Scherb, and Inge Morawetz, eds., *In deutscher Hand? Zu den Beziehungen Österreich-BRD* (Vienna, 1990), p. 116f.
5. Fritz Plasser, "Die populistische Arena: Massenmedien als Verstärker," in Anton Pelinka, ed., *Populismus in Österreich* (Vienna, 1987). Pp. 84-108.
6. Kurt Steiner, "Education and Educational Policy," in Kurt Steiner, ed., *Modern Austria* (Palo Alto, 1981), p. 327.
7. __, pp. 321-344.
8. __, p. 324.
9. Thomas Köhler, "Die neuen Fachhhochschulen. Wirksame Weltanschauung," in Andreas Khol et al., eds., *Österreichisches Jahrbuch für Politik 1994* (Vienna 1995). Pp. 681-684.
10. Based on Franz Horner, and Paul M. Zulehner, "Kirchen und Politik," in Herbert Dachs et al., eds., *Handbuch des politischen Systems Österreichs* (Vienna, 1991). Pp. 441-456.
11. Heinrich Schneider, "Katholische Kirche und österreichische Politik," in Andreas Khol et al., eds., *Österreichisches Jahrbuch für Politik 1978* (Vienna 1979). Pp. 153-224; Heinrich Schneider, "Kirche - Staat - Gesellschaft, ihre Beziehungen im Wandel," in Wolfgang Mantl, ed., *Politik in Österreich* (Vienna, 1992). Pp. 523-570.
12. Ernst Hanisch, *Die Ideologie des politischen Katholizismus in Österreich 1918-1938* (Vienna, 1977).
13. Paul Zulehner, *Religion im Leben der Österreicher* (Vienna, 1991).
14. *Der Standard*, July 5, 1995.
15. Paul Zulehner, *Leutereligion* (Vienna, 1982).
16. Peter Berger, *The Sacred Canopy* (New York, 1969).

10

The Politics of Regional Subdivisions

Herbert Dachs

Defining the Problem

Austria is, at least formally, a federal republic, even though the position of the central government is much stronger than that of the regional subdivisions, the member states or *Länder*.[1] Since the mid-1960s however, the *Länder* have been able to obtain a number of constitutional amendments that strengthen their position. For some decades, the considerable bargaining capacity of the *Länder* was on the rise. In political fields affecting more than one *Land* (e.g., transportation and energy policy), the federal government must take the positions of the *Länder* into consideration, whether it wants to or not. But when the *Länder*, faced with the perspective of a loss of authority after EU membership, demanded a new transfer of power from the federal government, they met with strong resistance.

Historical Developments

Austria is made up of nine member states or provinces (*Länder*) which differ substantially in size and population (see table 10.1). They are Burgenland, Carinthia, Lower Austria, Upper Austria, Salzburg, Styria, Tyrol, Voralberg and Vienna. The *Länder* in the east were at an economic disadvantage for decades, partly because of their vicinity to the Iron Curtain. This brought about population shifts to the west. Since 1989/1990 this structural disadvantage has become less important.

With the exceptions of Salzburg (formerly an archbishopric principality, Austrian since 1816) and Burgenland (established after the First World War, Austrian since 1922), the identity of the other *Länder* and their attachment to the Habsburg monarchy reaches back to the Middle Ages (e.g., Tyrol since 1363, Carinthia since 1335). Over the centuries this attachment led to the development of specific features that have partially survived in the twentieth century and which still influence the image the Austrians have of themselves and, thereby, also of their politics. The capital, Vienna, is at the same time a municipality and an independent *Land* (since its partition from Lower Austria in 1922).

TABLE 10.1 Austrian *Länder* (Provinces)

Land	Capital	Area in km²	Population 1991	Change since 1981 in percent
Burgenland	Eisenstadt	3,965	270,880	+0.4
Carinthia	Klagenfurt	9,533	547,798	+2.2
Lower Austria	St. Pölten	19,172	1,473,813	+3.2
Salzburg	Salzburg	7,155	482,365	+9.1
Styria	Graz	16,387	1,184,720	-0.2
Tyrol	Innsbruck	12,647	631,410	+7.6
Upper Austria	Linz	11,980	1,333,480	+5.0
Vienna	Vienna	415	1,539,848	+0.6
Vorarlberg	Bregenz	2,601	331,472	+8.6
Austria	Vienna	83,855	7,795,786	+3.2

The originally extensive power of the Austrian *Länder* or estates rooted in the Middle Ages, was continuously restrained by an increasingly dominant absolutism. The estates, robbed of all their relevant sovereign rights, sank to the status of provinces of a centralized unitary state. Only in the second half of the nineteenth century were there signs of a strengthening of the position of the *Länder*, at least with respect to administrative authority.

A completely new situation arose after the abolition of the monarchy in 1918. While the provisional National Assembly attempted to establish Austria as a centralized unitary state, the *Länder* displayed a revived desire for more power. They agreed that with the lapsing of the *Pragmatische Sanktion* (the Habsburg document on succession that until then had guaranteed the unity of the state) they had, at least in their own eyes, won back their freedom and sovereignty. As a result the *Länder*, parallel to the founding of the central government in Vienna, established their own provisional assemblies. These assemblies believed that, like the provisional National Assembly in Vienna, they had the right to self-determination and, in fact, executive power and immediately took over the execution of the law.

The Federal Constitution of 1920 represents a compromise between the two diverging views--between the (ÖVP) advocates of a federal state with strong subunits and those (SPÖ) of a decentralized unitary state. The tension between these two basic views still affects the constitutional and political discussion today.

When after the end of Nazi rule in 1945 the Second Republic was being established, it was once again the *Länder* that guaranteed the rule of law, founding the republic as it were from below. At the same time they made sure that unity in the divided and occupied country was guaranteed and that the provisional national government was recognized, thereby gaining authority over all of Austria.[2]

During the First, and even more so during the Second Republic, a striking dismantling of the federal aspect of the system took place as many powers were transferred to the federal government. The actors responsible for this movement towards stronger centralization during the inter-war period include the originally latent and, after 1933, open authoritarian forces; they were assisted by the state crisis as a whole. The federal government, formed by conservative parties, consistently tried to weaken the strong political position of the capital, Vienna, the only *Land* with a clear social democratic dominance. After parliament was closed down and political parties prohibited, the authoritarian government believed it had to meet the Nazi challenge with centrally influenced means of action. On the whole, one can say that during the years between the wars there was a large gap between the rhetoric of the Christian Social Party, based on subsidiarity[3] and federalism, and the actual policies it pursued.

After 1945 the following elements had a unifying and centralizing effect: the domination of politics by party headquarters during the phase of the Grand Coalition (1947-1966), oversized bureaucracies in the ministries, the consequences of the war and occupation, the continuation of legal and administrative structures of a highly centralized "Greater Germany," the decisive influence of chambers and interest groups and, finally, the domination of an anti-federalistic theory of law and constitutional interpretations. All these developments and the constitutional changes further undermined an already weak federalism, so that one can rightly speak critically of Austria as a "quasi-federal state."

The autonomy and self-administration of the municipalities, the *Gemeinden*, fell victims to absolutism in Austria even earlier than the

Länder had.[4] But in the middle of the nineteenth century, as a result of the middle-class revolution of 1848/49, the Provisional Municipality Law of 1849 established the self-administration of the municipalities and set up the basis that essentially still exists today. After a brief neo-absolutist period, the *Reichsgemeindegesetz* (the Imperial Municipality Law) was passed in 1862. Since then there has been real municipal self-administration with a relatively large autonomy and a democratic constitution. The municipalities would at the same time become the basis for all later forms of democratic practice. Programmatic for that is Article I of the Provisional Municipality Law of 1849: "The foundations of the free state are the free municipalities." A constitutional amendment on the *Gemeinden* in 1962 brought about a reform of municipal self-administration, which on the whole increased its importance.

The Role of the Provincial *(Land)* Governments

The Federal Constitution defines Austria as a federal state with centralistic features. Public business is divided into four categories. First, there are matters for which legislative and executive authority rests solely with the federal government; second, matters on which the *Länder* legislate and execute; third, matters on which the federal government legislates and for which execution rests with the *Länder*; and fourth, matters on which the federal government legislates the basic framework, with the *Länder* in charge of implementation, legislation and execution.[5]

A closer look at the scope and meaning of the assigned powers and rights reveals a striking preponderance in favor of the federal government, which has sole legislative and executive power over most of the important matters of state. The most important governmental powers (maintenance of law and order, finances, most economic and social welfare matters, education and all powers of jurisdiction) belong to the federal government. In comparison, the powers of the *Länder* carry little weight, are fewer and unconnected. They are related to areas like public events, local security, conservation, hunting and fishing regulations, sports, municipal regulations, agricultural ordinances, tourism, government-supported housing, rent laws, zoning (development plans), etc. Until 1985, this division of power could only be changed by the federal government. Parliament's second chamber, the *Bundesrat*, in which the *Länder* are represented, only had the right to exercise a delaying (suspensive) veto; this led to massive centralization after 1945. After the constitution was amended in 1984, the position of the *Länder* improved somewhat in this regard. Constitutional laws (and laws that include constitutional provisions) that reduce the legislative and/or executive power of the *Länder* now need to be approved by the *Bundesrat*.

In every federal system, adequate participation in the legislative process by the constituent units of the federation is viewed as essential. In Austria the *Bundesrat* should ensure that. The *Länder* are represented in it according to the size of their population (at the present there are a total of sixty-three deputies; Lower Austria and Vienna each have twelve deputies, while Burgenland has only three). The deputies to the *Bundesrat* are elected by the legislatures of the *Länder*, the *Landtage*, proportionally to party strength.

The *Bundesrat's* powers are in all respects subordinate to the first chamber, the *Nationalrat*. In principle, it can propose laws and use its delaying veto on bills passed by the *Nationalrat*. This rarely happens, and if there are objections on the part of the *Bundesrat*, they are usually motivated by party politics and are seldom the result of the unified representation of the interests of the *Länder*. The deputies in the *Bundesrat* usually act along party lines, thereby duplicating the conflicts and positions of the *Nationalrat*. As a result, the overpowering influence of the political parties is responsible for the relative lack of importance and the political ineffectiveness of the *Bundesrat*, compounding the constitutional provisions which limit its influence.

Another important indicator of the importance of the subdivisions (*Länder*) in a federal system is tax legislation. In keeping with the overall picture, the *Länder* are only allowed to impose taxes in areas not taxed by the federal government. But the federal government has already used every conceivable possibility to impose taxes. Taxes are collected only by a federal agency; the money is divided between federal, *Land*, and local government by means of a complicated, and over the years often modified, formula incorporated into the *Finanzverfassungsgesetz*, the Finance Constitution Act, which is valid for a number of years. It helps poorer regions with subsidies, but the particularly dynamic regions that yield high taxes are also taken into account. Basically, the negotiations for this distribution of public revenue (*Finanzausgleich*), which take place every four or five years, are dominated by the federal government. The *Länder* and municipalities find themselves in a more or less subordinate and dependent position, which is unusual for a federal system.

As to the execution of the law, the so-called "indirect federal administration" (*mittelbare Bundesverwaltung*) is the most important element in the relationship between the federal government and the *Länder*. Partly to balance out the strongly centralized division of power, partly for reasons of economy and efficiency, the federal government's administrative tasks are handled by the provincial governor (the

Landeshauptmann) and the agencies of the *Land* under his authority, unless the constitution explicitly assigns the federal government its own agency, as, for example, in the case of the police. The most important position falls to the governors of the *Länder*. They are bound to the directives of the federal government or the ministers, but they in turn can give directives to *Land* agencies. Usually, final appeals in administrative cases are made to the governors.

With the exception of Vienna, the *Länder* are divided into municipalities (*Gemeinden*). Including Vienna, which is both a city and a *Land*, there are 2,304 *Gemeinden* in Austria at present. With the exception of a few cities and metropolitan areas, small and middle-sized municipalities predominate. More than 50 percent have less than 2,500 inhabitants.

The municipalities carry out two different kinds of tasks: On the one side, they act as administrative districts for the federal government and the *Länder*, bound to their directives in a variety of areas (e.g., local development plans, construction, rescue services); on the other side, they are self-governing bodies in areas where they are free to make their own decisions. The emphasis in the latter case is on services rendered to their citizens, such as kindergartens and nursery schools, elementary and general secondary schools, hospitals, nursing homes, water supply, sewage, garbage collection, the construction and maintenance of sports facilities, swimming pools, community centers, and so on.

The municipalities are also independent economic bodies with the right, within the framework of the law, to plan budgets and raise their own taxes. The largest part of their money comes from the *Finanzausgleich* mentioned above. Most of the towns are heavily in debt as a result of their cost-intensive responsibilities.

The organization of the municipalities is based on democratic elections and is made up of a general representative assembly (*Gemeinderat*), a town council (*Gemeindevorstand, Stadtsenat* and/or *Stadtrat*), the mayor (*Bürgermeister*), and the local government bureaucracy.

The Constitutional System of the *Länder*

All the *Länder* are organized basically on a parliamentary system. The provincial legislatures (the *Landtage*) enact laws and elect the members of the *Land* government and the delegates to the *Bundesrat*. They also supervise the administration of the *Land*.[6]

Most *Landtage* have thirty-six members. Those of Lower Austria, Upper Austria, and Styria have fifty-six delegates, that of Vienna one hundred. For a long time it was only possible to vote for a rigid party list. Lately, there has been an increasing trend towards the personalization of the elections. The share of the votes each party received in the elections is reflected in the composition of the *Land* government and other institutions. School inspectors who have extensive power in educational matters, especially regarding personnel decisions, are also chosen according to the strength of the parties in the legislature. This system of *Proporz* is an essential element of concordance democracy in the *Länder*.

Although bills may be initiated in the *Landtage*, most bills in fact originate with the government. This is in part due to the lack of professional qualifications of the *Landtag* members. The federal government is also involved in the legislative process since all laws that are passed must be communicated to the Federal Chancellor before they are promulgated. If he raises an objection, the *Landtag* may insist on its position; in cases of continued dissent, the issue can be brought before the Constitutional Court.

Next to legislation, the control function of the *Landtage* is an important part of the parliamentary system. The use of this function is hampered by insufficient legal provisions (minorities can rarely exert the rights of control) and by the *Proporz* system (with its bias against open conflict).

The *Landtag* also elects the government of the *Land*.[7] In most cases this is done by a system of proportional representation. That means that the political parties must be represented in the government in proportion to their their strength in the *Landtag*. Only two *Länder* make exceptions in this regard. In Vorarlberg, the government is elected by majority rule. In Vienna, the members of the *Land* government are elected on the basis of proportional representation, but the *Landtag* majority can prevent the members of the minority from assuming any real governmental functions.

At the head of the *Land* government (with six to eight other members) is the *Landeshauptmann*, the governor. The executive power is exercised by the *Land* government. In fact, this government represents the most important political institution of the *Land* and has a great variety of functions to carry out. This is not limited to the execution of the laws, but also includes creative and planning functions. The individual functions are either fulfilled by the government collectively or by one of its members on the basis of the portfolio principle.

The governor has a special position. His specific duties show some features of a head of state. He is active in legislating; he represents the *Land* in dealing with the federal government and other countries; he has wide powers with regard to government organization and personnel and important emergency powers. Finally, he is responsible for the indirect federal administration; in this function, he stands above the other members of the government and can issue directives to them. In addition, the governor is usually the leader of the strongest party in the *Landtag* and, due to his prominent position, receives extensive media exposure.

The Transition to a "Cooperative Federal State"

The essential elements that brought about the weakening of the federalistic principle in Austria have been identified in the previous sections. Concerned critics used to speak of "creeping constitutional change" towards a decentralized unitary state. But since the 1960s, a modest reversal has developed. The interesting combination of small constitutional changes and the build up of "bargaining capacities" in informal political areas will be sketched below.[8]

Because of its serious financial problems, the federal government in the 1960s pressured the *Länder* and the municipalities to make an emergency financial contribution. The *Länder* agreed under the condition that the federal government enter into negotiations about increasing *Länder* authority. A catalogue of demands (a mixture of some basic, detailed, and practical proposals) was formulated and guided the negotiations and reform attempts for two decades.[9] During the negotiations, several cooperative administrative and organizational forms were established. Federalism reform in the style of the "grand cooperation" was also important to the federal government under Kreisky because it fit in with the Austrian political idea of a "big bargain" in a "cooperative society." The results became tangible with the amendments to the Federal Constitution in 1974, which anchored cooperative federalism in the constitution and brought about a number of other more or less important changes favoring the *Länder*. Altogether, an important change in the "constitutional atmosphere" was achieved inasmuch as now the federal government and the *Länder* met each other in essential areas as partners in a cooperative constitutional and political system, and the traditional dominating form of a central bureaucracy was somewhat weakened.

Since a grand coalition (SPÖ/ÖVP) was established again in 1987, the reform process has stagnated, thwarted by recent significant centralizing steps of the new government alliance. Obligations towards the political plans of the coalition, as well as disparate positions, weakened the potential of the representatives of the *Länder* to block these developments.

A completely new turn in the relationship between the federal government and the *Länder* occurred in view of the imminent membership in the European Economic Area and the European Union. The *Länder* were early and emphatic supporters of membership, thereby welcome partners to the federal government. Moreover, it was clear that they would be able to influence the outcome of the necessary referendum. On the other hand they were aware from the beginning that joining the EU would mean clear negative consequences for their already modest powers and that direct participation in the consensus-building process in the EU would be impossible.

There were two reactions to this initial political situation: First, a complicated procedure was to guarantee that the representatives of the *Länder* were not only informed of the progress of the negotiations, but could also, when they were of one opinion, make "binding statements." Second, in compensation for expected losses of functions, the *Länder* demanded a basic structural reform of the distribution of powers between the federal and the *Land* level. The corresponding negotiations ran parallel to Austria's EU negotiations and were supposed to lead to new legislation by the time of the EU referendum. The basic outline of that reform was laid down in a political agreement on the reorganization of the federal state signed by the federal government and the *Länder* in 1992. But no reform has been implemented so far, much to the latter's dismay.[10]

Cooperation Among the *Länder*

Länder are not only a part of a constitutional structure, but also a conglomerate of political, economic, socio-cultural, and bureaucratic interests. There are ways outside the legal structures to articulate their interests and to influence the relationship between the federal and the *Land* levels. Particularly after 1945, informal cooperative federalist networks were set up in Austria, which are still politically important today.[11]

Among the most important forms of this informal kind of collaboration are several so-called "conferences" in varying configurations (e.g. provincial governors, department directors, cultural or financial advisors of the different *Länder*).

> Since entering into a new period of dynamism, these conferences have received more media coverage. The politically important steps that coordinate all areas that are touched by the competences of the *Länder* or where the *Länder* are indirectly involved in the administration of federal laws, are made at these conferences.[12]

These conferences have their roots in the historically significant Conferences of the *Länder* in 1945 that were, to a large extent, responsible for the legal and orderly reconstruction of the new nation.[13] This model of cooperation proved to have an enormous potential in resolving conflicts and was continued intermittently. As a minimal amount of institutionalization, in 1951 a so-called "Liaison Office of the Austrian Federal *Länder*" was established, which--without reducing the rights of the individual *Länder*--coordinated the ever-expanding informal contacts. These conferences exist without any legal foundation; decisions are based on unanimity; no transcript of the consultations is published, but when agreement is reached, the consensual position is announced. This mechanism of cooperation is therefore flexible and dynamic, but not transparent or legally established. Party politics, otherwise a dominating factor in Austria, is at least in this case relatively unimportant.

Of these various conferences, the Conference of the Governors is considered the most important by far. These consultations take place twice a year and in some cases, depending on the need and the topic, high government officials and ministers are invited. Among the most important themes handled at the governors' conferences are basic problems of financial policy and federalism, while other conferences deal with translating the governors' decisions into practice and other specialized political fields.

In the past, these conferences have vigorously promoted *Länder* demands. Time and again they pushed their issues before the matter was formally put to parliamentary decisions-making. Their involvement in the preparations for Austria's membership in the EC was particularly important. Unanimous resolutions reflect the lowest common denominator, but they also--despite their informal character--carry substantial authority. The *Länder* are not interested--and this comes as no surprise--in having the conferences firmly established in the constitution.

Parties and Politics in the *Länder*

Depoliticization

Each *Land* has a fully developed political system.[14] *Länder* politics carries some very specific traits:

- In seven of the nine *Länder* government by *Proporz* is required by the constitution. That means all groups running for election that obtain the minimum number of mandates in the *Landtag* must be included in the government. Only Vienna and Vorarlberg are exceptions, as mentioned above. The consequences of these kinds of proportional, or *Proporz*, governments (in most cases all the parties in the *Landtag* are represented in the government) are of utmost importance for explaining the political patterns of the *Länder* and are also not clearly democratic. Governments by *Proporz* further the early integration of all relevant political interests and groups in the decision-making process. These circumstances keep the conflict level low and encourage the development of basic pragmatic consensus. The limited freedom resulting from decisions at the federal level and the inclusion of many different interests usually lead to a succession of compromises that show no coherent ideology so that voters find it difficult to identify them as comprehensive, well-planned programs. Each of the parties with a majority has a wide variety of opportunities open to it in order to include its political competitors and still implement a large part of its own goals and ideas. While participation in power means assuming responsibility, it also makes opposition and control more difficult. Because sensitive departments are interlinked, even partial control and competition are difficult and have clearly been weakened in most *Länder* as a result of the *Proporz* system that has predominated for decades.

- The office of the *Landeshauptmann*, the governor, has a stabilizing and, for the existing hierarchy of power, solidifying effect. The position was strong from the start on the basis of the constitutions of the *Länder*, and it has expanded as a result of the indirect federal administration. Supported by the proverbial *Landeshauptmann* bonus, the office holder attempts to lift himself above the seamy side of party and interest politics as a father figure with a statesmanlike interest in the good of the whole *Land* and all its citizens. Ideally, the person, the party and the *Land* become synonymous for one another. This was true particularly for governors who remained in office for a long period of time (sometimes for decades).

- The easy manageability of the individual territories must also be kept under consideration. Information and feedback paths are short; prompt reactions to problems are at least theoretically possible. Joint problem-solving brings the political elite closer together; they are easily identifiable as a group and in close contact to one another.

- From a qualitative point of view, the democracies in the *Länder* have shown a strongly depoliticized character in every respect. That means that politics in the *Länder*, as a rule, was viewed--and indeed presented--as a series of concrete problems the solutions of which gave only occasional advantages to one or the other clientele. Consensus, integration, and pragmatism are preferred to conflict and ideology; hence, convincing personalities seem more important than ideologically-based programs. For the lack of relevant conflicts on the regional level, election campaigns in the *Länder* often use national issues.

A Long Phase of Political Stability

The *Landtag* elections until the mid-1980s--the most recent developments will be handled separately--show a very high amount of continuity and stability:

- In no less than eight *Länder* there were absolute majorities over long periods of time (the exception was Salzburg, where relative majorities predominated).
- In contrast to the First Republic--at that time only Vienna had a stable socialist majority--after 1945 there were two (Vienna and Carinthia) and since 1964 three (after a shift in the majority in Burgenland) *Länder* with socialist majorities in the *Landtag* and in their governments. The other six *Länder* were dominated by the ÖVP.
- Until the mid-1980s, third or fourth political parties had very little influence on the *Land* level. By the end of the 1950s the Communist Party had lost most of its few mandates, while the Freedom Party could regularly hold on to mandates in seven *Landtage* and even managed to be included in some governments.

In order to further characterize the competition between the parties in the *Länder*, it would be useful to look briefly at the combined share of the vote achieved by the largest and second largest party and at the difference between them. For a long time there was such a high degree of concentration (the two largest parties obtained together more than 90 percent of the vote) in six *Länder* that one could have spoken of a two-party system (Burgenland, Lower Austria, Upper Austria, Styria, Tyrol and Vienna). In most provinces, the majority of one party was so well established that until the mid-1980s, one could speak of predominant party systems in Sartori's sense.[15] For these four decades, there were six provinces in which the strongest ("dominant") party had an absolute majority of votes in the *Landtag* (Carinthia, Lower Austria, Tyrol, Vienna, Vorarlberg); in five of these (same as above but without

Carinthia) the dominant party had a 10 percent edge on its nearest competitor.

There are two basic reasons why this kind of ultra-stability was possible. On the one hand, this is due to the pragmatic yet effective modernization policies of the political leadership. On the other hand, *Proporz* had a status-quo maintaining and power-securing effect. The majority party, which in most cases provides the *Landeshauptmann*, has most of the trump cards. Challengers have a difficult time developing convincing alternative positions.

The relatively limited room for shaping policy and making decisions, as well as a political style characterized largely by personalities, are responsible for the fact that the political discourse in the *Länder* was limited on the whole to pragmatic problems and questions of interest groups politics, while fundamental ideological debates played a very small role. Since the early 1970s, there has been a shift in accent in several of the *Länder*. If the political business of the *Länder* was carried out in the past almost exclusively under narrow interest viewpoints, a new understanding was added that sees politics more as a public discourse on problems of planning and managing the community as a whole.

Clearly Increased Political Mobility

For many decades, parties and political systems at the *Land* level meant limited electoral mobility and high stability. Only in Burgenland was there a lasting change in the majority relationships in 1964 (the SPÖ profited here from the belated start in structural changes from the primary to the secondary sectors). A considerable amount of movement has been taking place in the *Länder* since the mid-1980s.[16]

- The percentage of eligible voters that actually vote in the *Landtag* elections, for years over 90 percent, has sunk clearly under this mark. Vienna (61.7 percent), Salzburg (74.8 percent), and Lower Austria (74.7 percent) are particularly drastic examples in recent years. Absolute majorities of one party tend to disappear at the *Land* level. As for the hegemonial parties of the 1950s (SPÖ in Vienna, Carinthia and Burgenland; ÖVP in the other *Länder*), they experienced drastic losses in recent elections (especially in Tyrol: ÖVP from 64.6 percent to 48.7 percent; in Vienna: SPÖ from 55.0 percent to 47.7 percent; in Styria: ÖVP from 51.7 percent to 44.2 percent).
- The joint electoral dominance of the two major parties is also decreasing. Particularly impressive are the examples of Tyrol (where the combined share of the vote in a recent election fell from

89.7 percent to 71.5 percent), Vienna (from 90.3 percent to 83.4 percent), Salzburg (from 85.3 percent to 75.1 percent) and Carinthia (from 79.9 percent to 67.0 percent). If this trend continues, a multi-party system will emerge.
- The nation-wide process of increasingly critical voting behavior, as well as protest against the major parties and *Proporz* governments, has also been observed in the *Länder*. The reinvigorated FPÖ and the partly successful Green parties have both profited from this process. Today there are Green representatives in four *Land* parliaments, i.e. in Vorarlberg (since 1984), Styria, Salzburg and Tyrol; in Tyrol there is even a Green member of the provincial government. The Liberal Forum has obtained seats so far in one *Land* parliament (after running in several electoral contests).

Changing Trends

In summing up the findings, the following trends seem to emerge:

- A broad deconcentration process can be observed, despite the existing stabilizing structures, which is likely to continue for some time. The shift from relative contentedness and apathy to more competition and protest observed in the last three nation-wide parliamentary elections, is spreading to *Land* politics. The portion of voters ready for change and protest (mostly consisting of non-voters, voters invalidating their ballots, parts of the SPÖ voters, and Green and Liberal Forum voters) should become even more dynamic, especially in *Länder* with strong service sectors or with large urban and suburban segments like Vienna, Styria, Salzburg, Tyrol and Vorarlberg. In the cities, this process is much more advanced. The scene there is partly more colorful than in the *Landtage* (in the Salzburg city council no less than seven parties were represented since 1991).
- National political trends and problems have always--and even more so with the growth in mass media reporting since the radio and TV broadcasting reform in 1967--played an important role for politics in the *Länder*. Still, *Land* protagonists have always been able to draw a clear line between the national and local milieu, often by drawing on anti-Vienna sentiment. In the future, it will become more difficult to maintain this dividing line and to isolate the political climate in the *Länder* from unwanted national influences. In fact, the national political climate (characterized by the readiness for political change, extensive weariness towards

politics and the parties, scandals etc.) has increasingly affected the milieu in the *Länder.*
- The dominating model of *Land* politics, characterized by seemingly depoliticized issues and strong personalization, tends to disappear; there is now a strong trend towards re-politicization. Changing thematic priorities and new problems that do not stop at the borders of the *Länder* (e.g. ecological, traffic, integration, and waste problems) strain the capacities of the *Länder* to solve them. In the past, problems often ended in obscure compromises, but now conflicting interests develop sharply and are discussed more clearly. The political compromises in the *Länder* that until now were so popular, have been somewhat discredited in view of the demands of citizens' groups for fast and decisive (re)action. Futhermore, they have lost some of their comforting aura. At any rate, the need of the majority for explanations has increased.
- A number of home-made shortcomings and scandals in several of the *Länder* has strengthened this trend. To name a few examples: unlawful practices and large-scale fraud in the area of subsidized housing have revealed insufficient mechanisms for controlling corruption; the same could be said of the diverse affairs in highway construction. The turbulent events around the transport policies in Tyrol have been spectacular: wide-spread protest from grass roots groups against a policy of allowing the steady increase of truck transit traffic had long been ignored by the government of the *Land*, that is, by the ÖVP ruling with its comfortable absolute majority until the unexpected and drastic reaction of the voters in 1988 (the ÖVP fell from 64,6 percent to 48,7 percent, the Greens entered the *Landtag* for the first time with 8,3 percent of the vote).[17]
- Competition has increased in several *Länder.* This is partly due to new opposition parties who are unencumbered by the responsibility of governing. But there is also the new, right-wing, populist *FPÖ* which holds governmental posts in several *Länder,* yet simultaneously asserts itself as opposition. The consensus principle has been challenged, decision-making in the *Landtag* is more complicated and the importance of opposition and control has increased.
- The political elite in the *Länder* has also lost its monopoly on politics. As a result it feels insecure and in some respects on the defensive. Because of its weak position, which until now could be papered over with symbolic political acts and the pretence of universal competence, it often finds itself in situations in which it is powerless, but still pressured from several sides. These pressures come, first, from a federal policy that is seldom, and at best

cautiously, willing and able to react to the wishes of the *Länder* (in environmental questions and other areas it vehemently and successfully reclaims power); second, from the representatives and lobbies of important occupational groups and branches of the economy (e.g., farmers, transportation and tourist industries); and, third, from active, unsatisfied, and increasingly self-confident voters and the initiatives and protest groups that stem from them, which are often highly effective.

These and other factors force the political actors and institutions in Austria's *Länder* to be more sensitive and responsive. This will require a substantial willingness to change and to learn.

Notes and References

1. This chapter is based on: Joseph Marko, "Verfassungssysteme der Bundesländer;" Heinz Schäffer, "Gesetzgebung und Kontrolle;" Peter Pernthaler, and Karl Weber, "Landesregierung;" Gerhard Wielinger, "Verwaltung;" Hans Neuhofer, "Gemeinden;" Herbert Dachs, "Parteiensysteme in den Bundesländern;" Christian Schaller, "Verbände und Sozialpartnerschaft;" Kurt Richard Luther, "Bund-Land Beziehungen: Formal- und Realverfassung;" all in: Herbert Dachs, Peter Gerlich, Herbert Gottweis, Franz Horner, Helmut Kramer, Volkmar Lauber, Wolfgang C. Müller, and Emmerich Tálos, eds., *Handbuch des politischen Systems Österreichs* (Vienna 1991), ch. VIII. Pp.729-833.

2. Peter Pernthaler, *Die Staatsgründungsakte der österreichischen Bundesländer. Eine staatsrechtliche Untersuchung über die Entstehung des Bundesrates* (Vienna 1991).

3. The principle according to which problems are to be dealt with at the level most competent to address them.

4. Neuhofer, op. cit., pp. 774-777.

5. Peter Pernthaler, "Österreichs Länder und Gemeinden," in H.G. Wehling, ed., *Österreich* (Stuttgart-Berlin 1988), pp. 98-100. See also Luther, op.cit., pp. 816-821.

6. Marko, op.cit. Pp. 729-743. Schäffer, op. cit. Pp. 744-754.

7. Pernthaler and Weber, "Landesregierung," op.cit. Pp. 755-764.

8. Felix Ermacora, *Österreichischer Föderalismus. Vom patrimonialen zum kooperativen Bundesstaat* (Vienna 1976).

9. Peter Pernthaler, *Das Förderungsprogramm der österreichischen Bundesländer* (Vienna 1980).

10. Peter Pernthaler, "Föderalistische Verfassungsreform: Ihre Voraussetzungen und Wirkungsbedingungen in Österreich," in *Österreichische Zeitschrift für Politikwissenschaft*, Vol. 21, No. 4, 1992, pp. 370-373, 384-387.

11. Luther, op.cit., pp. 821-825.

12. Karl Weber, "Macht im Schatten? (Landeshauptmänner-, Landesamtsdirektoren- und andere Landesreferentenkonferenzen)," in *Österreichische Zeitschrift für Politikwissenschaft*, Vol. 21, No. 4, 1992, p. 406.

13. Pernthaler, *Die Staatsgründungsakte der österreichischen Bundesländer*, pp. 35-48.

14. Herbert Dachs, op. cit. Pp. 785-803. Herbert Dachs, ed., *Parteien und Wahlen in Österreichs Bundesländern 1945-1991* (Vienna-Munich 1992).

15. Giovanni Sartori, *Parties and Party Systems* (Cambridge 1976), pp. 192-201.

16. Herbert Dachs, *Parteien und Wahlen*, pp. 624-635.

17. Christian Laireiter, "LKW Transitverkehrsdiskussion im Bundesland Tirol--ein Beispiel für den neuen Föderalismus in Österreich," in *Österreichische Zeitschrift für Politikwissenschaft*, Vol. 21, No. 4, 1992. Pp. 419-431.

11

Conclusion and Outlook

Volkmar Lauber

This chapter will raise questions that cut across the individual contributions to this volume and which relate to the present state (and the discernible future) of Austrian politics: How are the two grand coalition parties likely to develop? What kind of politics will come in their wake? What alignments and coalitions are likely in the near future? And what change is occurring at the level of society as the two large parties are progressively losing their hold?

Rise and Decline of the SPÖ-ÖVP Duopoly

The pervasive influence that these two parties came to exert for decades over Austrian society was quite unusual by Western standards. At the high point of their influence, they were at the top of a network which not only dominated parliament and the government, but also controlled the civil service, the judiciary, a public sector of the economy which was the largest of any Western country, the schools and universities, and radio and TV broadcasting. In addition, they owned about half of the print media in terms of circulation. In the economic area, they had parallel organizations in the top interest associations. All this made for important possibilities of patronage, particularly by facilitating access to employment, careers, and housing. In terms of absolute membership numbers, they had about as many members as political parties in West Germany (with a population ten times as large).

How did such a situation come about? This degree of party control was in part a response to the difficult post-war situation (the need to cooperate during reconstruction and occupation). But even more so, it was a reaction to the political disasters which befell the First Republic.

These had their origin in the extreme political polarization of rank-and-file militants; eventually they led to civil war and authoritarianism. After the Second World War, the political leaders of the two large parties agreed that such a situation must not occur again. Even if activists might be prone to radicalism, the party leaders should look for solutions acceptable to both sides. Experience dictated that this should not rely solely on good intentions or legal rules. Political guarantees were designed to make it difficult for one party to try to oppress the other; this was the reason for carving up the state into zones of party influence. The grand coalition was merely the supreme expression of the new principle of consociationalism. This approach was not questioned by the population. While it minimized political conflict and promoted cooperation, there were very few checks on the power of the two parties.

There was a first chafing at party control in 1966. The independent media (with the sympathy of the ÖVP, but against the will of the SPÖ) started a popular initiative to limit party control over radio and TV. The initiative was successful and led to a more liberal broadcast regime. Along with the decline of party newspapers (which continued for another two decades) and the rise of independent print media, this contributed to the emancipation of thinking about politics. It also reinforced the general decline of ideology among the population. In the same year, Austria experienced its first one party government (with the ÖVP). But consociationalism and joint party influence were still strong and continued in practically all areas except in the composition of the federal government. Most laws by far were still passed with the support of both parties, and social partnership was at that time expressly insulated from the effects of changing governmental majorities to guarantee future cooperation.

By this time public attitudes about party membership were already beginning to change. From a family tradition based on deeply ingrained loyalties, membership was increasingly becoming a matter of opportunism inspired by the pervasive influence of patronage. The memory of the historical breaking points of 1918, 1934, 1938 and 1945 operated in the same direction. On these occasions, civil servants in particular had to make a show of loyalty to the new regime, even if this was not to their liking. Due to economic and structural change, the "natural constituencies" of the two parties, i.e., farmers and blue collar workers, were shrinking fast.

Despite these developments, neither the SPÖ nor the ÖVP had much of an incentive to attack party influence over the public sphere while in opposition (the SPÖ from 1966-1970, the ÖVP from 1970-1986); rather, they were hoping to catch that prize for themselves. The FPÖ, after 1970,

Conclusion

neglected such a role in exchange of favors from the SPÖ. Eventually, this led to a small coalition between the two parties from 1983-1986. Market forces, however, reduced the scope of party influence. Party newspapers increasingly lost their readers. And when public sector industry found itself in trouble, the SPÖ (under heavy attack from the ÖVP) developed a new pragmatism. Under the influence of neo-conservative ideas, it stated that there was no reason of principle to keep an industry in the public sector. When the nationalized steel industry (a traditional SPÖ fief) made a catastrophic loss in 1985, the SPÖ-FPÖ government fired the whole management and set up a new structure designed to promote commercial efficiency rather than party patronage. Since that time, commercial criteria have become increasingly important and frequently a prelude to privatization, even though both major parties were often hesitant to privatize their own fiefs.

Beginning with the elections of 1986 and the grand coalition which took office in 1987, there was again a very lively opposition which seriously questioned the pervasive influence of the two large parties. The Greens and the Freedom Party, and after 1993 also the Liberal Forum, delighted in exposing the latent, and sometimes open, corruption that often resulted from the cozy relationship between Social Democrats and Conservatives. The main rationale for this coalition was no longer the danger of a rank and file polarization that might get out of hand; this danger had long passed. Now the concern was about populism and the way it could undermine a government set on a consolidation course. Both parties agreed that public finances needed a cure of austerity, but neither wanted to face the electoral cost of such a course without the active involvement of the other.

It is remarkable that, despite the continued existence of a grand coalition government since 1987, the influence of the two large parties has declined greatly. This influence was increasingly difficult to justify in the face of public opinion. Thus, the portfolio of the Minister of Justice has since that year been given to a person who belongs to neither coalition party. Ties with the top interest associations of the social partners were loosened when they turned out to be a liability (as when interest associations took up positions which were viewed as decidedly anti-environmental, as they did in the cases of the Zwentendorf and Hainburg power plants). In a development similar to what happened in Italy in the 1990s, practices which had long been considered normal were suddenly viewed as shocking as e.g., the appointment of school principals along party criteria, or the collusion between political parties and large construction firms (exchange of contracts against contributions to party finance). Judges and civil servants became more self-confident and showed more real independence. As the pervasive old boy network of the two major parties began to recede, the formal institutions became more important.

Also since 1986, the electoral basis of the two large parties began to shrink. High levels of economic security, rising educational levels and greater mobility led to a diminished reliance on political parties in the search for life chances. The process had been going on for some time, but it was in 1986 that the voters began to defect most clearly. In 1994, the SPÖ and ÖVP together no longer managed to secure even the two-thirds majority necessary to pass constitutional laws in parliament, a major setback in the Austrian context. Given the age structure of the parties' electorates (the opposition parties attract a disproportionately large share of young voters), this process of erosion is likely to persist for some time.

In the mid 1990s even social partnership faces an uncertain future. Over the last ten years and particularly with EU accession, the role of the market has consistently increased. This means a reduced scope of activity for government and the social partners. Also, the legitimacy of this institution has been considerably eroded over the last decade. In addition, the Trade Union Federation--one of the key members of social partnership--is confronted with a steady decline of its membership. The basic industrial sectors especially are highly unionized, and the diminution of their work force (partly a result of increasing productivity) will be accelerated by the opening of the borders with Eastern Europe (cheap imports, shift of production abroad). In the small firms of the tertiary sector which are expected to provide new employment, unionization seems to be more difficult.

The Changing Stage of Politics

Despite their decline, the two main actors, the SPÖ and ÖVP, still dominate the political stage today, and they may do so for some time yet. However, we can see them diminish as we look ahead; the elections of December 1995 may yield a new constellation. New actors (in the order of their appearance: the Greens, the new Freedomites, and the Liberal Forum) have entered the scene, with their role growing in importance. What will this mean for politics and society in the years to come?

The recent grand coalition was concluded for the legislative period lasting from 1994 to 1998. It broke down after less than one year, and though it might possibly be renewed once more, both parties are looking out for other allies. Three possibilities are under discussion today: a renewal of the grand coalition; a coalition of the right (ÖVP and FPÖ);

Conclusion 257

and finally, a government formed by the SPÖ, the Greens and the Liberal Forum.

Renewal of the Grand Coalition

When ÖVP leader and vice-chancellor Wolfgang Schüssel broke off budget talks with the SPÖ in October 1995 and called for new elections, he argued that it was up to the electorate to decide between the "spending" policies of the SPÖ and the "serious" consolidation course embodied by the ÖVP. At the same time he indicated that he was prepared to again work with the SPÖ after the elections; presumably this is dependent on the ÖVP becoming the strongest party, with a claim to the offices both of the chancellor and the finance minister (Vranitzky has announced that in this case he would withdraw from the government). But such a coalition would entail a high political cost for the SPÖ (if it had to yield on key issues) or for the ÖVP (if it had to abandon some of its central tenets during coalition negotiations). The electoral campaign will deepen the rift between the parties. If it were to come about anyhow, such a government would presumably adopt a stricter course on consolidation, but change few other policy fundamentals.

Coalition of the Right?

One of the more important new actors is, of course, Jörg Haider, the leader of the right-wing, populist Freedom Movement/Party. He achieved this position in 1986 and led the party from one electoral success to the other. But with his views he is still something of an outcast; most parties reject cooperation with him, only the ÖVP is ready to envision a coalition with the new Freedomites. Haider hopes to become chancellor with the help of the ÖVP and has taken many steps to pry this party loose from its SPÖ coalition partner.

It is difficult to establish a clear profile of Haider since his views change very rapidly on a broad range of issues. He openly admits to being a populist. Still there are some elements of continuity in the way he appeals to the electorate. These include a preference for strong government, a "sound" nationalism and attacks on SPÖ-ÖVP collusion.

Haider talks of a "Third Republic" to replace existing institutions. The content of this formula is not quite clear. Presumably, it is a question of strengthening the executive, perhaps by a direct election of the chancellor, at the expense of the political parties and parliamentary institutions. Something similar was advocated in Italy by Berlusconi. In any case, the importance of parties and their patronage is viewed as excessive.

The second feature of Haider's politics is his appeal to what might be termed a "sound" nationalism, resembling that of Le Pen. For nearly a decade, he stressed the importance of a relatively homogeneous German culture. This nationalism was directed at minorities and Jews (of whom only a few are left), and more recently against immigrants, especially from Eastern Europe and beyond. His xenophobic rhetoric led to the splitting off of the Liberal Forum deputies in 1993. But Haider continued in the same vein: in the fall of 1995, he argued that Austria should unilaterally suspend certain articles of the European Convention on Human Rights regarding refugees, because their rights could not be guaranteed anyhow, and proposed a repatriation program for immigrants. A few months earlier, he had surprisingly disassociated himself from German nationalism, in an effort to widen his electoral appeal. In the Austrian context German nationalism ususally includes sympathies for the Third Reich. Here Haider benefits from an important omission in Austrian politics after World War Two. Austria then emphasized that it was the first victim of Nazi aggression to enhance its position vis-à-vis the occupying powers. But it passed over Austrian support for the Nazi regime and the role of many Austrians in the Third Reich's machinery, and this neglect and the resulting ambiguity proved a boon for Haider. Only in the Waldheim presidential campaign in 1986 was the taboo about the role of Austrians in the Third Reich finally lifted.

Similarly to Le Pen, Haider recruits disappointed voters from several directions. It is hard to sort out the protest voters from genuine supporters of a Haider government; recent estimates held that his sympathizers were about evenly divided on this point. His electorate includes disaffected blue collar workers from declining industrial regions (who used to vote for the Social Democrats) as well as former Conservatives and non-voters.

The ÖVP itself is divided on the issue of whether to join into a coalition with the FPÖ. There is a risk that with similar levels of electoral support, the FPÖ will become the dominant partner in such a coalition since Haider is a very autocratic and effective leader, while the ÖVP is forever divided internally. For some time, the ÖVP seemed to be torn by this prospect; recently Schüssel has decided to take a chance. A government formed by these two parties would probably upset the current distribution of income, privileging the more affluent, and initiate a strong polarization. It would also be likely to restrict immigration laws (and to some extent civil liberties) in the name of law and order. Whether it would really consolidate public finances is less clear as the ÖVP will be reluctant to alienate the ÖAAB, the group that organizes the wage-earners in that party.

Haider's recent success stems, at least in part, from the fact that he is riding a wave of dissatisfaction with the established parties. This dissatisfaction is a wider phenomenon that can be found in many Western countries; in Austria it gained particular significance due to the two large parties' overextended realm of influence. By their own practices, the SPÖ and ÖVP often furnished the best ammunition for Haider's criticism. But despite his rhetoric of clean government, it seems that Haider wants to get into this game as much as he wants the others to get out. Unlike the Greens and the Liberal Forum, Haider and his supporters have shown a very strong appetite for positions of power.

A Red-Green-Liberal Coalition?

Even though the SPÖ is likely to remain the strongest party in the near future, it may never again be able to achieve a parliamentary majority under the Austrian electoral system based on proportional representation. After the collapse of the grand coalition, a government consisting of the SPÖ, Greens and the Liberal Forum is one of the possible combinations. At the last elections, these three parties gathered about 50 percent of the vote (the other half being held by the ÖVP and FPÖ). After their recent transformation in the course of the 1994 electoral campaign, the Greens stressed their desire to participate in government at the federal level (hoping that they will be asked by the Vienna Social Democrats to join them in a coalition in 1996, after elections to the Vienna city council). On the national level, such a coalition would probably be committed to maintaining the welfare state (with greater selectivity), stress environmental reform, take a more secular approach to matters of religion, sex and morality and reduce party influence outside the immediate area of politics. But it is doubtful whether an agreement could be worked out: the Greens are unlikely to support budget consolidation, the Liberals on the other hand demand a stiff approach. The Social Democrats in turn may be reluctant to make concessions in the environmental area, which is definitely not their strong suit.

More Liberalism in Society and Economy

It has often been observed that Austria has no great liberal tradition. Catholicism prevailed over Protestantism in the counter-reformation of the seventeenth century. Imperial absolutism existed as late as the middle of the nineteenth century. There was no strong, self-confident bourgeoisie at the turn of the century, and conditions were not favorable for its development in the first half of this century. Of the three *Lager*, only the third--the German-National one--held liberal ideas (restricting the power of state and church) early on, but its chief characteristic was nationalism rather than liberalism. During the First Republic, the Catholic-Conservatives (and part of the Socialists) presented their ideas as truths which were not really up for discussion. This attitude contributed to the breakdown of democracy in the First Republic and impeded liberal principles even in the Second Republic. To be sure, such principles were increasingly accepted by that time. But they went against the grain of tradition and established practice, and their implementation met with many difficulties.

The current change brings a correction in this area as well. Social Democrats and Conservatives have agreed to pull back the borders of state and party influence. This process of gradual withdrawal is powerfully assisted by the three current opposition parties, all of whom take various parts of their inspiration from liberalism. In the FPÖ, there is a criticism of overextended state and party influence. The Liberal Forum is more universalist and shows particular concern for civil and human rights: it also emphasizes the free market. The Greens are suspicious of the party state and in favor of increased participation and the human rights of the underprivileged.

This change in political thinking and practice is paralleled in other areas. The large hierarchical organisations are also declining. At the institutional and governmental level, the gradual withdrawal by the two parties led to the emancipation of civil servants, teachers, judges, etc. A more liberal economy is developing, with public sector firms subjected to commercial criteria, if not privatized alltogether. This in turn weakens some of the most important strongholds of the labor movement, who were particularly strong in the public sector (this served to strengthen their power at the national level). Market mechanisms further restrict state and social partnership influence. Not all firms welcome this process, as some sectors were quite successful in limiting competition with the help of interest associations, party influence, and the state. But there is also the rise of a new kind of entrepreneurs in Austria, who are more self-confident than their predecessors. Finally, at a different level, the hierarchy of the Catholic Church also seems to lose influence as secularization and rejection of authoritarianism proceed.

Outlook

Until recently, the politics of Austria's Second Republic was characterized by a very small number of actors and a high degree of coordination among them. The central actors held together a great number of groups, refraining them from the strong particularistic pursuit of their interests. The last decade has seen this pattern fall apart with increasing rapidity.

The new politics is characterized by a multitude of actors. The number of viable political parties has increased. The two government parties are losing (and sometimes abandoning) control over many sectors of public life. The new actors are becoming more independent, relying more on their own strength in pursuing their self-interest than on their integration into a larger group.

The new politics is clearly less predictable. But it does not seem to portend a crisis of governability or democracy, at least not in the usual sense. As in other Western European countries, it seems extremely difficult in Austria to really consolidate public finances or to make economic actors pay for the environmental damage they cause (which means that the problem is shifted onto future generations).

The progressive shrivelling of the social democratic and conservative networks, of their reach into Austrian society, does not amount to a crisis of the country's democratic institutions. In fact, these institutions (as laid down in the constitution of 1920/1929) used to play a somewhat secondary role, in Austria more so than in most Western countries. The recent change opens the possibility that these formal institutions of liberal democracy become more important than hitherto.

Some hope that these changes will bring more active participation, a more active and more professional parliament, more transparency and a greater reliance on criteria of qualification or competitiveness rather than on patronage. However, it is also conceivable that they will bring more conflict if the basic consensus on distribution is upset, or that the influence of money and simplistic slogans will grow as PACs and media image politics come to play a greater role. Finally, national political life may lose some of its substance as part of it is transferred to the European level. In fact, all these three elements may come to play a role.

The future is always veiled. But the days of pervasive party influence throughout society, of corporatist shadow government, of predictability and ultra-stability, are undoubtedly a thing of the past.

Basic Statistics

Population	7.99 million (1993)
Surface	83, 859 square kilometers
Capital	Vienna 1.54 million (1991)
National Currency	Austrian Schilling
GDP	Sch2.12 billion (1993)

Source: OECD, *Economic Surveys: Austria* (Paris, 1995)

Chronology

Basic Historical Dates

Nov. 11, 1918	End of the Habsburg Monarchy; Proclamation of the First Republic (1918-1938)
Sept. 29, 1920	Federal constitution (*Bundes-Verfassungsgesetz*) enacted
March 4, 1933	End of parliamentary government in the First Republic
Feb.12-15,1934	Brief civil war; governmental suppression of the Social-Democratic Party and its organizations
July 25, 1934	Attempted putsch by Austrian National Socialists, in the course of which Chancellor Dolfuss is assassinated
March 12/13, 1938	German troops enter Austria; *Anschluss*: Austria becomes part of the Third Reich
Oct. 30, 1943	Moscow Declaration of the Allies on re-establishing a free and independent Austria

April 27, 1945	Proclamation of a provisional Austrian government (beginning of the Second Republic)
July 9, 1945	The Four Power Declaration on Austria on the occupation by the allies and the preparation of Austrian independence
May 15, 1955	Signing of the Austrian State Treaty reestablishing full sovereignty
Oct. 26, 1955	Law on Permanent Neutrality passed in parliament
Dec. 15, 1955	Austria admitted to the United Nations
Jan. 1, 1960	Austria joins the European Free Trade Association (EFTA) as a founding member
July 22, 1972	Free Trade Agreement with the European Community
Fall 1989	Dissolution of the Soviet bloc and fall of the iron curtain
Jan. 1, 1994	Austria joins the European Economic Area
Jan. 1, 1995	Austria becomes a member of the European Union (formerly the European Community)

List of Acronyms

AHS	Upper-track Secondary School	Allgemeinbildende Höhere Schule
AK	Chamber of Labor	Kammer für Arbeiter und Angestellte/Arbeitskammer
AMAG	Nationalized aluminum corporation	Austria Metall Aktiengesellschaft
BWK	Chamber of Business	Bundeswirtschaftskammer (now Wirtschaftskammer Österreich)
CEI	Central European Initiative	
CSFR	Czecho-Slovak Federal Republic	
CSP	Christian Social Party	Christlichsoziale Partei
CV	Catholic Student Fraternity	Kartellverband der österreichischen Studentenverbindungen
EC	European Community	
ECA	Economic Cooperation Agency	
EEA	European Economic Area	
EEC	European Economic Community	
EFTA	European Free Trade Association	
EPC	European Political Cooperation	
ERP	European Recovery Program	
EU	European Union (since 1994; formerly EC)	

FAO	Food and Agricultural Organization	
FCG	Christian Trade Unionists	Fraktion christlicher Gewerkschafter
FPÖ	Freedom Party of Austria	Freiheitliche Partei Österreichs
FRG	Federal Republic of Germany	
FSG	Socialist Trade Unionists	Fraktion sozialistischer Gewerkschafter
FWV	Free Business Association (Social Democratic)	Freier Wirtschaftsverband
GA	Green Alternative	Grüne Alternative
GATT	General Agreement on Tariffs and Trade	
GDP	Gross Domestic Product	
GDVP	Greater German People's Party	Großdeutsche Volkspartei
GNP	Gross National Product	
IAEA	International Atomic Energy Agency	
ILO	International Labour Organization	
IMF	International Monetary Fund	
KPÖ	Communist Party of Austria	Kommunistische Partei Österreichs
LB	Agrarian League	Landbund
LF	Liberal Forum	Liberales Forum
LWK	Chamber of Agriculture	Landwirtschaftskammer
MP	Member of Parliament	
N+N	Neutral and Non-aligned	
NATO	North Atlantic Treaty Organization	
ÖAAB	Austrian Workers' and Employees' League	Österreichischer Arbeiter- und Angestelltenbund
ÖAKT		Österreichischer Arbeiterkammertag
ÖBB	Austrian Farmers' League	Österreichischer Bauernbund
OECD	Organization for Economic Cooperation and	

	Development	
OEEC	Organization for European Economic Cooperation	
ÖGB	Austrian Trade Union Federation	Österreichischer Gewerkschaftsbund
ÖIAG	Austrian Industrial Holding Corporation	Österreichische Industrieholding AG
OMV	Austrian Oil Corporation	Österreichische Mineralöl-Verwaltung
OPEC	Organization of the Petroleum Exporting Countries	
ORF	Austrian Radio and Television	Österreichischer Rundfunk und Fernsehen
ÖSTAT	Austrian Statistics	Österreichische Statistik
ÖVP	Austrian People's Party	Österreichische Volkspartei
ÖWB	Austrian Business League	Österreichischer Wirtschaftsbund
PAC	Political Action Committee	
PLO	Palestine Liberation Organization	
RS	Revolutionary Socialists	Revolutionäre Sozialisten
Sch	Austrian Schilling	
SDAP	Social Democratic Workers' Party	Sozialdemokratische Arbeiterpartei
SPÖ	Socialist (since 1991 Social-Democratic) Party of Austria	Sozialistische (Sozialdemokratische) Partei Österreichs
UBA	Federal Office of the Environment	Umweltbundesamt
UN	United Nations	
UNESCO	United Nations Educational, Scientific and Cultural Organization	
UNHCR	United Nations High Commissioner for Refugees	
UNIDO	United Nations Industrial Development Organization	
UNRWA	United Nation Relief and Works Agency for Palestinian Refugees in the Near East	
USA	United States of America	

VdU	League of Independents	Verband der Unabhängigen
VGÖ	United Greens of Austria	Vereinigte Grüne Österreichs
VOEST	Nationalized steel corporation	Vereinigte österreichische Stahl- und Eisenwerke
WEU	Western European Union	
WHO	World Health Organization	
WIFO	Austrian Institute of Economic Research	Österreichisches Institut für Wirtschaftsforschung
WWF	Worldwide Fund of Nature	

Selected Bibliography

Alcock, Antony E. 1970. *The History of the South Tyrol Question*. London.
Anton Pelinka, and Fritz Plasser, eds., *The Austrian Party System*. Pp. 173-196. Boulder.
Arndt, Sven W., ed., 1982. *The Political Economy of Austria*. Washington.
Austrian Foreign Policy Yearbook, condensed version of the Jahrbuch der österreichischen Außenpolitik, Foreign Ministry, Vienna, annual publication (since 1988).
Austrian History Yearbook, Center for Austrian Studies, University of Minnesota, annual publication (since 1970).
Burgess, Michael, ed., 1986. *Federalism and Federation in Western Europe*. London.
Chaloupek, Günter. 1985. "The Austrian Parties and the Economic Crisis." *West European Politics* 8: 71-81.
Contemporary Austrian Studies, New Brunswick, annual publication (since 1993).
Cronin, Andrey K. 1986. *Great Power Politics and the Struggle over Austria. 1945-1955*. Ithaca.
Dachs, Herbert, ed., 1992. *Parteien und Wahlen in Österreichs Bundesländern 1945-1991*. Vienna.
___ , Peter Gerlich, Herbert Gottweis, Franz Horner, Helmut Kramer, Volkmar Lauber, Wolfgang C. Müller, and Emmerich Tálos, eds., 1991. *Handbuch des politischen Systems Österreichs*. Vienna.
Dreijmanis, John. 1982. "Austria - the 'Black' - 'Red' Coalitions," in Eric C. Browne, and John Dreijmanis, eds., *Government Coalitions in Western Democracies*. Pp. 237-259. New York.
Elazar, Daniel. *Federal System of the World: A Handbook of Federal, Confederal and Autonomy Arrangements*. Comp. and ed. by Daniel J. Elazar, and the Staff of the Jerusalem Center for Public Affairs, Harlow/Essex.
Engelmann, Frederick C. 1966. "Austria: the Pooling of Opposition", in Robert Dahl, ed., *Political Opposition in Western Democracies*. Pp. 260-283. New Haven.

___, and Mildred A. Schwartz. 1974. "Partisan Stability and the Continuity of a Segmented Society: The Case of Austria." *American Journal of Sociology* 79: 948-966.

Gerlich, Peter. 1986. "Theories of Legislation: Some Austrian Evidence and General Conclusions." *European Journal of Political Research* 14: 357-368.

___. 1987. "Consociationalism to Competition: The Austrian Party System since 1945," in Hans Daalder, ed., *Party Systems in Denmark, Austria, Switzerland, the Netherlands and Belgium*. Pp. 61-106. London.

___ et al. 1985. *Sozialpartnerschaft in der Krise*. Vienna.

___. 1992. "A Farewell to Corporatism," in: Kurt R. Luther, and Wolfgang C. Müller, eds., *Politics in Austria*, Pp. 132-146. London.

___, and Wolfgang C. Müller. 1988. "Austria: Routine and Ritual," in Jean Blondel, and Ferdinand Müller-Rommel, eds., *Cabinets in Western Europe*. Pp. 138-150. London.

___, Wolfgang C. Müller, and Wilfried Philipp. 1988. "Potentials and Limitations of Executive Leadership: The Austrian Cabinet since 1945." *European Journal of Political Research* 16: 191-205.

Haerpfer, Christian. 1985. "Austria," in Ivor Crewe, and David Denver, eds., *Electoral Change in Western Democracies*. Pp. 264-286. London.

Hakovirta, Harto. 1988. *East-West Conflict and European Neutrality*. Oxford.

Hankel, Wilhelm. 1981. *Prosperity Amidst Crisis*. Boulder.

Höll, Otmar, ed., 1993. *Small States and Dependence in Europe*. Boulder.

Horner, Franz. 1987. "Austria 1949-1979," in Ian Budge, David Robertson, and Derek Hearl, eds., *Ideology, Strategy and Party Change. Spatial Analyses of Post-War Election Programmes in 19 Democracies*. Pp. 270-293. Cambridge.

Houska, Joseph J. 1985. *Influencing Mass Political Behavior. Elites and Political Subcultures in the Netherlands and Austria*. Berkeley.

Institut für Föderalismusforschung, ed., 1977-1995. *Bericht über die Lage des Föderalismus in Österreich*. Vienna.

Janik, Allan, and Stephan Toulmin. 1973. *Wittgenstein's Vienna*. New York.

Johnston, William M. 1972. *The Austrian Mind. An Intellectual and Social History*. Berkeley.

Katzenstein, Peter J. 1984. *Corporatism and Change: Austria, Switzerland, and the Politics of Industry*. Ithaca.

Kausel, Anton. 1993. *Four Decades of Success. Austria's Economic Rise Within the OECD from 1950 to 1992*. Vienna.

Kneucker, Raoul. 1981. "Public Administration: The Business of Government," in Kurt Steiner, ed., *Modern Austria*. Pp. 261-278. Palo Alto.

Koren, Stefan. 1981. "Monetary and Budget Policy," in Kurt Steiner, ed., *Modern Austria*. Pp. 173-189. Palo Alto.

Lauber, Volkmar. 1992. "Changing Priorities in Austrian Economic Policy." *West European Politics* 15: 147-172.

Lehmbruch, Gerhard. 1982. "New Corporatism in Comparative Perspective," in Gerhard Lehmbruch, and Philippe C. Schmitter, eds., *Pattern of Corporatist Policy Making*. Pp. 1-28. London.

___. 1991. "The Organization of Society, Administrative Strategies and Policy Networks," in Roland M. Czada, and Adrienne Windhoff-Heritier, eds., *Political Choice*. Pp. 121-158. Frankfurt.

Lehne, Stefan. 1991. *The Vienna Meeting of the Conference on Security and Cooperation in Europe*. Boulder.

Luif, Paul. 1995. *On the Road to Brussels. The Political Dimension of Austria's, Finland's, and Sweden's Accession to the European Union*. Vienna.

___. 1986. "The Revitalization of Austrian Federalism," in Michael Burgess, ed., *Federalism and Federation in Western Europe*. Pp. 154-186. London.

Luther, Kurt Richard. 1988. "The Freiheitliche Partei Österreichs: Protest Party or Governing Party?," in Emil Kirchner, ed., *Liberal Parties in Western Europe*. Pp. 213-251. Cambridge.

___. 1989. "Dimensions of Party System Change: The Case of Austria." *West European Politics* 12: 3-27.

___. 1992. "Consociationalism, Parties and the Party System in Austria," in Kurt Richard Luther, and Wolfgang C. Müller, eds., *Politics in Austria. Still a Case of Consociationalism?* Pp. 45-98. London.

Müller, Wolfgang C. 1988. "Conservatism and the Transformation of the Austrian People's Party," in Brian Girvin, ed., *The Transformation of Contemporary Conservatism*. Pp. 98-119. London.

___. 1988. "Privatising in a Corporatist Economy: The Politics of Privatisation in Austria." *West European Politics* 11: 101-106.

___. 1992. "Austria (1945-1990)," in Richard S. Katz, and Peter Mair, eds., *Party Organizations*. Pp. 21-120. London.

___. 1992. "Austrian Governmental Institutions: Do They Matter." *West European Politics* 15: 99-131.

___. 1992. "The Catch-All Party Thesis and the Austrian Social Democrats." *German Politics* 1: 181-199.

___. 1993. "Executive-Legislative Relations in Austria." *Legislative Studies Quarterly* 18: 467-494.

___. 1993. "After the 'Golden Age': Research into Austrian Political Parties since the 1980s." *European Journal of Political Research* 23: 439-463.

___. 1994. "Models of Government and the Austrian Cabinet," in Michael Laver, and Kenneth A. Shepsle, eds., *Cabinet Ministers and Parliamentary Government*. Pp. 15-34. Cambridge.

___. 1994. "The Development of Austrian Party Organizations in the Post-War Period," in Richard S. Katz, and Peter Mair, eds., *How Parties Organize: Adaptation and Change in Party Organizations in Western Democracies*. Pp. 51-79. London.

___, and Delia Meth-Cohn. 1991. "The Selection of Party Chairmen in Austria: A Study of Intra-Party Decision Making." *European Journal of Political Research* 20: 39-61.

___, and Fritz Plasser. 1992. "Austria: The 1990 Campaign," in Shoun Bowler, and David Farell, eds., *The Campaign: Electoral Strategies and Political Marketing in Contemporary Elections*. Pp. 24-42. London.

___, and Barbara Steininger. 1994. "Christian Democracy in Austria: The Austrian People's Party," in David Hanley, ed., *Christian Democracy in Europe*. Pp. 87-100. London.

___, and Barbara Steininger. 1994. "Party Organisation and Party Competitiveness: The Case of the Austrian People's Party." *European Journal of Political Research* 26: 1-29.

Neuhold, Hanspeter, ed., 1992. *The European Neutrals in the 1990s. New Challenges and Priorities*. Boulder-San Francisco-Oxford.

___, and Hans Thalberg, eds., 1984. *The European Neutrals in International Affairs*. Boulder.

OECD. 1993. *Economic Surveys 1992-93: Austria*. Paris.

___. 1995. *Economic Surveys 1995: Austria*. Paris.

Pernthaler, Peter. 1992. *Der differenzierte Bundesstaat. Theoretische Grundlagen, praktische Konsequenzen und Anwendungsbereiche in der Reform des österreichischen Bundesstaates*. Vienna.

Plasser, Fritz. 1987. *Parteien unter Stress*. Vienna: Böhlau.

___, Peter A. Ulram, and Alfred Grausgruber. 1992. "The Decline of 'Lager Mentality' and the New Model of Electoral Competition in Austria." *West European Politics* 15: 16-44.

Powell, Bingham G. 1970. *Social Fragmentation and Political Hostility. An Austrian Case Study*. Stanford.

Pulzer, Peter. 1969. "Austria," in Stanley Henig, ed., *European Political Parties*. Pp. 282-319. New Yorker.

Riedelsperger, Max. 1978. *The Lingering Shadow of Nazism: The Austrian Independent Party Movement since 1945*. Boulder.

Riekhoff, Harald, and Hanspeter Neuhold, eds., 1993. *Unequal Partners. A Comparative Analysis of Relations Between Austria and the Federal Republic of Germany and Between Canada and the United States* . Boulder.
Schäffer, Heinz. 1993. *Der österreichische Föderalismus, Rechtskonzept und politische Realität* Vienna.
Schambeck, Herbert, ed., 1992. *Föderalismus und Parlamentarismus in Österreich.* Vienna.
Schmitter, Philippe C. 1979. "Still the Century of Corporatism?" in Philippe C. Schmitter, and Gerhard Lehmbruch, eds., *Trends Towards Corporatist Intermediation.* Pp. 7-52. London-Beverly Hills.
Secher, Herbert P. 1958. "Coalition Government: The Case of the Second Austrian Republic." *American Political Science Review* 52: 791-809.
Shell, Kurt L. 1962. *The Transformation of Austrian Socialism.* New York.
Steiner, Kurt. 1972. *Politics in Austria.* Boston.
Sully, Melanie A. 1982. *Continuity and Change in Austrian Socialism.* Boulder: East European Monographs.
Sundelius, Bengt, ed., 1987. *The Neutral Democracies and the New Cold War.* Boulder.
Tálos, Emmerich, ed., 1993. *Sozialpartnerschaft, Kontinuität und Wandel eines Modells.* Vienna.
___ , and Bernhard Kittel. 1995. "Roots of Austrocorporatism: Institutional Preconditions and Cooperation Before and After 1945." *Contemporary Austrian Studies* 4: 21-51.
___ , Kai Leichsenring, and Ernst Zeiner. 1993. "Verbände und politischer Entscheidungsprozeß," in Emmerich Tálos, ed., *Sozialpartnerschaft* Pp. 147-185. Vienna.
Traxler, Franz. 1992. "Interests, Politics, and European Integration." *European Journal of Political Research* 22: 193-217.
___ . 1995. "From Demand-Side to Supply-Side Corporatism?," in Colin Crouch, and Franz Traxler, eds., *Organized Industrial Relations in Europe.* Pp. 271-286. Avebury.
Verdross, Alfred. 1978. *The Permanent Neutrality of Austria.* Vienna.
Waarden, Frans v. 1992. "Dimensions and Types of Political Networks." *European Journal of Political Research* 21: 29-52.
Welan, Manfried. 1988. "Constitutional Review and Legislation in Austria," in Christine Landfried, ed., *Constitutional Review and Legislation.* Pp. 63-80. Baden-Baden.

Postscript

(added after completion of the manuscript)

The Parliamentary Elections of December 17, 1995

	SPÖ	ÖVP	FPÖ	Liberal Forum	Greens	Others
Votes (percent)	38.32	28.30	22.08	5.28	4.57	1.53
Gains/ Losses	+ 3.4	+ 1.6	- 0.4	- 0.7	- 2.7	+ 0.1
Seats in Parliament	72	53	41	9	8	-

Source: *Der Standard* December 18, 1995.
These results will be slightly modified by the votes of Austrians residing abroad (tabulated later on).

Election results from 1945 to 1994 are listed on p. 74 above. The 1995 elections were called when the coalition between the Social Democrats and the People's Party broke down in October 1995 (see p. 256 above).

About the Contributors

Herbert Dachs is professor of political science at the University of Salzburg.

Peter Gerlich is professor of political science at the University of Vienna.

Franz Horner is professor of political science at University of Salzburg.

Helmut Kramer is professor of political science at the University of Vienna.

Volkmar Lauber is professor of political science at the University of Salzburg.

Wolfgang C. Müller is associate professor of political science at the University of Vienna.

Emmerich Tálos is professor of political science at the University of Vienna.

About the Book

Long characterized by stability--even rigidity--Austrian politics is becoming more dynamic and combative. Tracing the disruption of the "postwar pattern" in Austria, this book explores the recent dramatic evolution in Austria's political system.

The contributors examine the decline of the established Social Democratic and Conservative parties and corporatist associations, and the concomitant rise of the "reformed" right-wing Freedom Party and the newly emerged Green and Liberal parties which relish a more conflictual political style that challenges traditional taboos. These internal changes have been accompanied by Austria's abandonment of its long-held neutrality and by its recent entry into the European Union. Reflecting on the end of a long era of tranquility that brought unprecedented prosperity, as well as a sometimes uncomfortable two-party hegemony, the contributors assess the implications of sweeping changes on the country's polity, economy, and society.

Index

Acid rain, 206
Administration, 36-39
   indirect federal, 48-50
Agrarian League, 61
Agriculture
   organic-biological, 207
Anschluss, 16
Armed forces, 161
Audit office, 43-45
Austerity program, 145
Austrian People's Party, 61
Austro-Keynesianism, 116, 127, 131, 143
Atomic energy, 201, 202, 209
Avis, 177

Balkans, 7, 9
Banks, 9
Beirat für Wirtschafts- und Sozialfragen, 130
Big bargain, 131
Bosnia-Hercegovina, 189
Broadcasting, *See* Radio, TV
Budget
   consolidation, 136, 137, 138, 144, 146
   deficit, 134, 145
Bundesrat, 47-48, 238, 289
Bureaucracy, 36-39, 213, 216

Cabinet, 32-36
   decision-making, 33-36
Capital
   foreign, 3, 9

Catalytic converters, 202
Catholic
   Church, 61, 79, 230
   Family Association, 79
   Student Fraternity, 79
Centralization, 106
Chamber
   compulsory membership, 118
   of Business, 77 (fig.), 105
   of Labor, 77 (fig.), 78, 105
   -s, 78, 105
   -s of Agriculture, 77 (fig.9), 105
   second, 47-48, 238, 289
Chancellor
   federal, 33-36
Change, 220
Chernobyl, 202
Christian
   Social Party, 61
   Trade Unionists, 78
Church, *See* Catholic, Church
Citizen
   initiatives, 63
   participation, 204, 205
Civil servants, 36-39
Clientelism, 217
Climate Alliance, 208
Coalition
   committee, 27, 34
   grand, 253
Colleges,
   specialized, 230
Colonial territories, 8

Colonialism, 9
Communist
  Party, 60-61, 82. *See* KPÖ
Compromise, 215
Concentration, 106
Concertation, 104
Conference on Security and
  Cooperation in Europe, 164
Consensus, 107
Consociation, 214, 221
Consociationalism, 254
Constitution, 23, 47
  Federal of 1920, 237
Constitutional Court, 39-42, 49, 64
Corporatism, 104, 128
  continuity, 118, 119
  decision-making, 113
  demand-side, 120
  development, 109
  extent, 114
  fields, 114
  future, 120
  parties and -, 108
  political role, 113
  preconditions, 104, 108
  recent changes, 117
  structure, 109, 111
  supply-side, 120
Corruption, 76 (fig.), 255
Council
  of Europe, 156, 157, 164
  -s, advisory, 111
Croatia, 188
CSCE, *See* Conference on
  Security and Cooperation in
  Europe
Culture
  political, 213
Curricula
  undergraduate, 230
Czechoslovak Crisis, 161

Decretism, 215
Defence budget, 191
Deficit spending, 131, 134
Deflation, 126
De-industrialization, 126
Democracy, 220
  direct, 25-26
  intra-party, 76, 85-87
Dependence, 2
  on Germany, 3
Depoliticization, 130, 144, 244
Development
  economic, 5
Diplomatic
  missions, 155 (fig.)
  relations, 159
  service, 154

East-West Conflict, 175
Eastern Europe, 141, 160, 175
  aid, 185
  trade, 185
EC, *See* European Community
Economic
  - and Monetary Union, 143, 144
  instruments, 203
  policy, 114, 115
Education
  -al system, 228
  higher, 229
  policy, 226
EFTA, *See* European Free Trade
  Association
Elections
  Land, 246
  presidential, 31
  parliamentary, 74, 91 (fig.)
  turnout, 75 (fig.)
Electoral
  behavior, 72-73
  system, 29, 68-71
Emissions

carbon dioxide, 208
Energy, 207
Environmental
 advocate, 204
 movement, 210
Etatism, 218
European
 Common Foreign and
  Security Policy, 179
 Economic and Monetary
  Union, 144
 Economic Area, 142, 181
 Free Trade Association, 129,
  160, 173, 181
 Human Rights Convention,
  226
 integration, 142
 Political Cooperation, 179
 Union, 29, 36, 120, 142, 206,
  207, 210
  referendum, 184
European Community, 129, 132,
 160, 163, 171, 173
 membership
  application for -, 171
  avis, 177
  negotiations, 183
  opinions on -, 174
  Soviet opposition to
   Austrian -, 177
Exports
 arms, 169

Factions, 76-79
Federal
 chancellor, 33-36
 Constitution of 1920, 237
 president, 25, 29-33
Federalism, 45-50, 237
Finance capital
 western, 14
Finanzausgleich, 239
Finanzverfassungsgesetz, 239

Fin-de-siècle Vienna, 10
Finland, 177
Foreign
 aid, 168 (fig.)
 influence, 15
 ministry, 156, 159, 191
 trade, 185
Foreign policy, 2, 7, 15, 16,
 bipartisan, 154, 161
 interest in, 174, 175 (fig.)
 "realistic", 170
FPÖ, 62, 80
 party ideology, 88-90
Fractionalization, 91
Fraktion
 parliamentary, 65-66, 67-69
Free Business Association, 78
Free Trade Agreement, 163
Freedom Party of Austria, *See*
 FPÖ

Gemeinden, See municipalities
Germany, 4, 7
 dependence on, 3
Government
 formation of, 32-33
 Land, 238
Governor, 48-50
 Land, 239, 241, 245
Great Depression, 13
Greater German People's Party,
 62
Greens, 62-63, 80-81
 Green Alternative, 62
 United G. of Austria, 62

Haider, Jörg, 75, 257
Hainburg, 202, 205, 209, 255
Hard currency policy, 129, 132,
 134
Hitler, Adolf, 16
Human Rights, 190
Hungarian uprising, 157

Identity, 218
Ideology, 87-90
   catch-all -ies, 89-90
Incomes policy, 114, 115
Industrializiation, 5, 126
Industry, 11
   nationalized, 136, 139
Initiative
   citizen -s, 63
   people's, 25
Institutions
   governmental, 23, 50-51
Instruction,
   religious, 231
Interest
   associations, 105
      characteristics, 105
      corporatist, 209
      influence, 119
      top, 255
   group politics, 105
   groups, 77 (fig.)
Internationalism, 4
Internationalization, 18
   dependent, 4
   economic, 1
   profile, 2
Investment
   foreign, 3, 9, 12
Iron Curtain, 127
Israel, 165

Joint Commission for Wages
   and Prices, 110, 111, 112 (fig.),
   119, 130, 132
Judicial self restraint, 41
Judiciary, 42-43
   review, 39-42

Katholische Aktion, 79
KPÖ, 60-61, 82
Kreisky, Bruno, 32, 33 (fig.), 134,
   158-170

Labor movement, 10
   conflict, 115
Lager, 60-63
   ties, 71
Land
   conferences, 244
   constitutional system, 240
   elections, 246
   European Union, 242,
   government, 238, 241,
   governor, 48-50, 239, 241, 245
   legislatures, 240
   parties, 244
   politics, 244
   taxation, 239
Länder
   cooperation among -, 243
   historical development, 235
   Liaison Office of the
      Austrian Federal -, 244
Landeshauptmann, See Land
   governor
Landtag, See Land legislatures
League
   Agrarian, 61
   Business, 77 (fig.)
   Farmer's, 77 (fig.)
   of Independents, 62. *See* VdU
   -s, 76-78 (fig.). *See* ÖVP
   Workers' and Employees', 77
      (fig.)
Legalism, 216, 219, 221
Legislation, 28, 47
Liaison Office of the Austrian
   Federal *Länder,* 244
Liberalism, 259, 260
Like-mindedness, 152

Maastricht, 143, 145, 146, 179
Mariazell Manifesto, 231
Marshall Plan, 127, 153
Media, 223, 254
   mass, 63, 223

Index

system, 223
Middle East, 166
Military
    defeats, 6
Ministry
    -of the Environment, 203, 204
    -of Environmental Protection, 204
Minority,
    Slovenian, 164
Mobility,
    political, 247
Mock, Alois, 170-171, 179-182, 188, 194
Movement
    social -s, 63
Municipalities, 237, 240

N+N, *See* Neutral and Non-aligned Group
Nationalities, 8
Nationalization, 128
NATO, *See* North Atlantic Treaty Organization
Neo-conservative, 255
Neo-corporatism, 104
Neutral and Non-aligned Group, 164
Neutral countries, 176
Neutrality, 151, 158, 178, 180, 182
    Declaration of Permanent -, 156
    "realistic"-policy, 171
Newspapers, 223. *See* press
North Atlantic Treaty Organization, 180
North-South conflict, 165
Nuclear power, 201, 202, 209

Occupation,
    allied, 153
Oil crises, 133, 201

Opposition, 27, 28
Organization
    forefield -s of parties, 77-79
    international, 155, 159
ÖVP, 61
    leagues, 76-78
    party ideology, 88

Palestinians, 165
Parliament, 26-29, 44-45, 47-48, 74, 108
Party
    Austrian People's, 61
    Christian Social, 61
    Communist, *See* KPÖ
    competition, 92, 118
    finance, 66-68
    forefield organizations of -ies, 77-79
    Freedom P. of Austria, *See* FPÖ
    Greater German People's, 62
    identification, 72, 73 (fig.)
    ideology, 87-90
    influence, 253-256
    intra-p. groupings, 76-79
    law, 64-65
    loyalty, 74
    members, 81 (fig.), 81-85
    membership, 76-77, 254
    newspapers, 225, 255
    organizations, 76-87
    supporters, 71, 72 (fig.)
    system, 90-95, 107
        bipolar, 108
"Party state", 59
Paternalism, 216
Patronage, 37-38, 80, 83 (fig.), 217
Peak associations, 106
Pedersen index, 72, 73 (fig.)
People's initiative, 25
Polarization

political, 254
Policy
  foreign, 2, 7, 15, 16, 151-200
Politics
  shadow -, 217, 221
  subsystem of -, 214
Position
  international, 5
Powers
  distribution of, 46
Pragmatische Sanktion, 236
Pragmatism, 216
President
  federal, 25, 29-33
Press, 223. *See* newspapers.
  concentration, 224
  regional monopolies, 225
Pressure group strategies, 105
Primaries, 71
Privatization, 136, 138, 139, 143
Proporz, 37-38, 40, 244-245
Protectionism, 11
Provincial government, *See*
  Land government
Public
  debt, 132, 133 (fig.), 134
  sector, 128

Radio, 225
  monopoly, 225. *See* TV.
Rank-and-file militancy, 254
Recycling, 206
Referendum, 25
  consultative, 26
Refugees, 186, 187 (fig.), 258
Religiosity, 232
Religious communities, 230
Repoliticization, 249
Republic
  First, 10-16, 126
  Second, 16-18
Revolution, 218

School
  compulsory elementary -s, 227
  elementary -s, 227
  graduate -s, 230
  primary, 227
  reform of 1962, 226
  secondary -s, 227
  system, 227
Schüssel, Wolfgang, 146, 257
Second rate power, 9
Second Republic, 17
Security,
  policy, 170
  national, 179
Serbia, 187, 189
Sheltered sector, 140
Slovenia, 188
Small state, 1
  strategies, 152
Social
  Democrats, *See* SPÖ
  Movements, 63
  Partnership, 103, 119, 131, 144, 254, 256
  Welfare Policy, 114, 116
Socialist
  -s, 60-61. *See* SPÖ
  Trade Unionists, 78
South Tyrol, 154, 156, 160, 163
Soviet Union, 158
SPÖ, 60-61, 78, 79,
  farmers, 78
  party ideology, 87
Stability
  political, 246
Stabilization, 129
Stabilizers
  automatic, 132
State Treaty,
  Austrian, 153, 156
Strikes, 115

Index

Structural
    reform, 138
    weaknesses, 10
Supply-side, 130
Sweden, 177
Symbolism, 215
System
    electoral, 29, 68-71

Tax reform, 139, 145
    ecological, 208
Third Reich, 14, 258
Third Republic, 257
Third World, 162, 167
Trade, 13
    foreign, 12, 77 (fig.)
    Union Federation, 77 (fig.), 78, 105
    Unionists, Christian, 78
Traditions, 219
Training
    vocational, 229
Transit traffic, 203, 207
Turn- und Sportunion, 79
TV, 225
    monopoly, 225. *See* radio

UN, *See* United Nations
Unemployment, 13, 126, 129, 135 (fig.), 141, 142

Union
    European, 29, 36, 120, 206, 207
United Greens of Austria, 62
United Nations, 155, 157, 164, 170, 176, 190
    Security Council, 178
    Vienna International Center, 165, 167
United States, 158

VdU, 62
Voting
    intra-party preference, 70-71
Vranitzky, Franz, 33 (fig.), 36, 136-137, 173-174, 180, 182

Wage
    differentials, 115
    policy, 115
Wage-price agreements, 109
Waldheim affair, 172
War, 6
Washington, 166
West European Union, 180

Xenophobia, 258

Yugoslavia, 156, 186, 187, 189

Zwentendorf, 202, 209, 255